ca. 27–30 CE	The ministry of Jesus of Nazareth. The beginning of worship in synagogues
1st–2nd centuries CE	Diaspora communities established in Asia Minor, Parthia, Cyrenaica, Numidia, Mauretania
66	Outbreak of the revolt against Rome
70	Titus destroys Jerusalem and the Second Temple. Traditional date of the beginning of the second exile
ca. 37–103	Josephus Flavius, Hellenistic Jewish historian
132–135	The revolt of Bar Kokhba
ca. 200	Rabbi Judah HaNasi compiles the Mishna
ca. 425	The Palestinian ("Jerusalem") Talmud completed
ca. 500	The Babylonian Talmud completed
5th–6th centuries	Jewish kingdom in Himyar, Southern Arabia
589–1038	The Babylonian Gaonate and the Talmudic academies of Sura and Pumbedita
635	The eastern Diaspora comes under Muslim Arab rule
ca. 740–965	The Jewish Khazar kingdom
ca. 760	The Karaite schism
8th century	Earliest mention of Jews in the Caucasus
	Possible arrival of Jews in India
892–942	Saadia Gaon, philosopher, translator of the Bible into Arabic
ca. 900–1200	The Golden Age in Muslim Spain
ca. 1000	Rabbenu Gershom's synod in Mayence outlaws polygyny
1013–1103	Rabbi Isaac Alfasi, first codifier of Jewish law
1040–1105	Rashi of Troyes, greatest commentator of the Bible and the Talmud
1096–1189	The Crusaders massacre Jews
1135–1204	Maimonides, greatest of medieval Jewish philosophers, second codifier of Jewish law

TENTS
OF
JACOB

THE DIASPORA—
YESTERDAY AND
————TODAY

By Raphael Patai

The Poems of Israel B. Fontanella (in Hebrew), 1933
Water: A Study in Palestinian Folklore (in Hebrew), 1936
Jewish Seafaring in Ancient Times (in Hebrew), 1938
Man and Earth in Hebrew Custom, Belief and Legend (in Hebrew), 2 vols.,
    1942–1943
Historical Traditions and Mortuary Customs of the Jews of Meshhed (in
    Hebrew), 1945
The Science of Man: An Introduction to Anthropology (in Hebrew), 2 vols.,
    1947–1948
Man and Temple in Ancient Jewish Myth and Ritual, 1947, 1967
On Culture Contact and Its Working in Modern Palestine, 1947
Israel Between East and West, 1953, 1970
Jordan, Lebanon and Syria: An Annotated Bibliography, 1957
The Kingdom of Jordan, 1958
Cultures in Conflict, 1958, 1961
Sex and Family in the Bible and the Middle East, 1959
Golden River to Golden Road: Society, Culture and Change in the Middle
    East, 1962, 1967, 1969
Hebrew Myths: The Book of Genesis (with Robert Graves), 1964
The Hebrew Goddess, 1967
Tents of Jacob: The Diaspora—Yesterday and Today, 1971

Edited by Raphael Patai

Anthology of Palestinian Short Stories (with Zvi Wohlmut; in Hebrew), 2
    vols., 1938, 1944
Edoth (Communities): A Quarterly for Folklore and Ethnology (with Joseph J.
    Rivlin; in Hebrew and English), 3 vols., 1945–1948
Studies in Folklore and Ethnology (in Hebrew), 5 vols., 1946-1948
Social Studies (with Roberto Bachi; in Hebrew and English), 2 vols., 1947-
    1948
The Hashemite Kingdom of Jordan, 1956
The Republic of Lebanon, 2 vols., 1956
The Republic of Syria, 2 vols., 1956
Jordan (Country Survey Series), 1957
Current Jewish Social Research, 1958
Herzl Year Book, 7 vols., 1958–1971
The Complete Diaries of Theodor Herzl, 5 vols., 1960
Studies in Biblical and Jewish Folklore (with Francis L. Utley and Dov Noy),
    1960
Women in the Modern World, 1967
Encyclopedia of Zionism and Israel, 2 vols., 1971

TENTS OF
OF
JACOB

THE DIASPORA—
YESTERDAY AND
TODAY

BY

RAPHAEL
PATAI

PRENTICE-HALL, INC.
ENGLEWOOD CLIFFS, N.J.

Some three years ago, in connection with a discussion of cultural variability in one of my anthropology classes at Fairleigh Dickinson University, I was asked what I consider the most essential difference between the Jews and other peoples. When I answered, "the Diaspora," the student who asked the question wanted to know whether I could recommend a book in which he might read about the Diaspora. This time it took me longer to reply, and when I did, the answer had to be, "No; I don't know of such a book." A short time later, by one of those strange coincidences which are designated, but by no means explained, by the term "clustering phenomena," I was asked by Prentice-Hall to write a book on the Jewish Diaspora. That is the genesis of the present book.

At an early stage of my work on the book I recognized that I would have to treat the Diaspora primarily as the basic historical circumstance that determined, more than any other factor, the unique cultural physiognomy of the Jewish people. It was only in order to round out the picture of the effects of life in the Diaspora on the Jews that I included a chapter on the Jewish "race," which shows that the variegating influence of the dispersion affected not only the culture but also the bodily form of the Jewish communities. Apart from that one chapter, the central question around which the discussion in the entire book revolves is: how did the fact of dispersion influence Jewish cultural variety?

In trying to clarify this focal issue, I found I had to touch upon a number of ancillary points, such as the relationship between the various factors that went into the making of the Jewish cultural specificity (or ethnicity) in the various Diasporas; between language and culture; between the officially pursued endeavor of religio-cultural separatism and the popularly followed mores, and the like.

v

After discussing in Part I several of the major overall issues touching upon the nature and phenomenology of the Diaspora, I would have liked to present a profile, even if only a sketchy one, of the Jewish community in each country of the world. For purely technical reasons (primarily considerations of space) this proved impracticable. Since there are Jewish communities in no less than eighty-six countries, selectivity was obviously unavoidable.

The decision as to which countries to include and which to omit was not an easy one. Having settled on grouping the Diasporas according to the three great historical divisions of the Jewish people, I decided to discuss all the Oriental Jewish communities, because they are largely unknown, not only to the English reading public but even to their next door neighbors, and because they exhibit a fascinating cultural variability. The Sephardi division presented no problem of choice, because it remained throughout its history confined to a few countries, all of which could be discussed within the confines of one chapter.

It was the Ashkenazi division that presented the most difficult problem. It is by far the largest of the three, and its Diasporas are dispersed over a very large number of countries (about sixty). Even the briefest discussion of each would have filled an additional volume. Therefore the difficult decision was made to have no separate chapters on those Diasporas that bore the brunt of the Nazi genocide and of which only small remnants have survived. This does not mean, of course, that no trace at all of them is found in the book. In fact, reference is made to them repeatedly: to Polish Jewry throughout the chapter on the Ashkenazi Jews (Chapter XV), to German Jewry in Chapters III, V, VII, VIII, and XV; to Hungarian Jewry on several occasions in connection with personal reminiscences. But since the main emphasis of the book is on the relationship between the past and the present in the life of the Diasporas, I felt justified in not devoting separate chapters to these martyred communities, however great their historical significance.

Having made this decision, I selected of the remaining Ashkenazi Diasporas the five largest ones, those of the United States, Russia, France, Argentina, and England (in descending numerical order), which, among them, account for more than 90 percent of all Ashkenazi Jews living outside the State of Israel.

The division of the Jewish people into three major groups (Oriental Jews, Sephardim, and Ashkenazim) leaves several Jewish Diasporas which do not fit into this scheme. The most important and most interesting of these, the Italian, Greek, Caucasian, Indian, and Ethiopian Jews, are discussed in Chapter XXI, "Five Exceptional Communities."

Finally a picture of Diaspora Jewry would not be complete without a discussion of the relationship between it and the old-new homeland of the Jewish people—the land, and since 1948 the State, of Israel. Accordingly, a brief chapter devoted to this subject brings the volume to a close.

It is my pleasant duty to express my thanks to those who, in various ways, rendered me important help in writing this book. A number of scholars and experts either read and commented upon individual chapters in the book, or discussed them with me orally. They are listed here in the order of the chapters they reviewed, with the names of the chapters added in parentheses: my daughter Dr. Ofra Jennifer Patai Wing (Chapter IV, The Jewish Race); Professor Meir M. Bravmann and Dr. Judel Mark (Chapter VII, The Languages of the Jews); M. Armand Kaplan, Dr. Arnold Mandel, and Dr. Zachariah Shuster (Chapter XVI, France); Mr. Chaim Bermant, Dr. Elizabeth Eppler, Mr. Josef Fraenkel, Dr. Lionel Kochan, and Dr. Shneier Levenberg (Chapter XVII, England), Mr. Leon Shapiro (Chapter XVIII, Soviet Russia); Mrs. Naomi F. Meyer and Miss Flora Toff (Chapter XX, Argentina); Dr. Giulio Anau and Sre Napoleone Sadun (Chapter XXI, Five Exceptional Communities, section The Jews of Italy); Professor Simon D. Messing (same chapter, section The Falashas of Ethiopia). While the responsibility for the final formulation of each chapter rests with me alone, I am deeply grateful to all of them for their help. I also wish to thank Mrs. Sylvia Landress, Director of the Zionist Archives and Library and its staff; Miss Dora Steinglass, chief of the Jewish Division of the New York Public Library and its staff; and Mr. Francis Paar of the Oriental Division of the New York Public

Library, without whose help this book could not have been written. My thanks are due also to Miss Gertrude Hirschler, Associate Editor of the Herzl Press, and to my secretary Mrs. Betty Gross. Finally, I gratefully acknowledge the grant given by the Memorial Foundation for Jewish Culture to help in the preparation of the manuscript.

R.P.

Forest Hills, N.Y.

How goodly are thy tents, O Jacob,
Thy dwellings, O Israel!

(Numbers 24:5)

There is a people scattered abroad
And dispersed among the nations.

(Esther 3:8)

_____

ONE

1

THE EMERGENCE OF THE DIASPORA

The Primacy of the Diaspora ————————————————

The many unique features that characterize the history of the Jews have so often been enumerated, described, discussed, and analyzed that in the present context the merest reference to some of them will suffice. There is, to begin with, the unparalleled attachment of the Jews to their ancient homeland, retained by them despite the fact that for almost nineteen centuries they had no dominion over it and few of them had lived there. There is, too, their demanding religion, which attained its full development in important Jewish centers outside Palestine but which nevertheless remained essentially Zion-centered. There is the Hebrew language which, though not used colloquially for two thousand years, remained a living and vital medium, never losing the attribute of holiness it shares with the Tora, the fountainhead of Jewish religion, and the Land, the source of Jewish tradition and the goal of Jewish dreams. There is the apparent paradox of the stubborn survival of the Jews in the face of adversity and the danger of their succumbing to assimilation in friendly environments. There is the even more puzzling contradiction between the dissent, strife, and even contumely often characterizing the relationship among various Jewish communities, and of the unbreakable ties that bind them together and make all of them suffer—either actually or psychologically—the consequences of events overtaking, or acts committed by, any one of them. There is the peculiar, almost uncanny Jewish ability to open up new horizons, whether in the realm of religion, in the area of social interrelationships, at the depths of the psyche, or on the frontiers of the physical universe. There is the tragic Jewish history of discrimination, persecution, and pogroms, culminating in the most horrible holocaust that

3

mankind has ever known. And there is, of course, that other unparalleled event in the annals of man—a people reestablishing its sovereignty in its own land after nearly nineteen centuries of dispersion.

All these and many more features that set Jewish history apart are well known. There is, however, a special set of circumstances that requires mention, especially as it has a direct bearing on the concept of the Diaspora and its role in Jewish history: the Jewish people originally came into being outside the Land of Israel. As early as the Biblical era of the First Hebrew Commonwealth, two other countries, Mesopotamia and Egypt, began to figure in the historic consciousness of the Jews as the locales of their earliest genetic origin and ethnic development.

This in itself, while unusual, is not unique. Other nations, too, can look back to an early period in their history when they lived in territories other than their own historic lands. The Arabs, the Hungarians, the Turks in the Old World come readily to mind, as do the Spanish, Portuguese, and English speaking nations in the New. But all of these peoples merely *changed* countries: they had "old countries" of their own from which at some juncture they moved to new ones as a result of various historical circumstances. In most cases only part of the population that lived in the "old countries" made the move. Moreover, prior to settling in it, the migrants knew little if anything of the new country. They went, conquered the new land, and before long the ties that had bound them to the old country grew slack and were severed. The process was one of historical fission: instead of one people, there emerged two (or more) separate nations. Today only a few scholars among them care that, once upon a time, they formed a single entity. The majority, if not ignorant of its ancient history, is indifferent to it. To the average Turk it means nothing that his nation came from and has historic kinfolk in Turkestan in Central Asia. Nor is it a matter of concern or significance for most Argentinians or Chileans that their language, culture, and social order have their roots in Spain. Although discussed in school, such historical connections have little or no role in popular consciousness.

The forces that molded the Jewish people at the dawn of their history were very different. While precise historical data are not available, enough is known of the emergence of the Hebrew tribes to indicate the uniqueness of their genesis. Thus there can be no doubt as to the historicity of the Egyptian slavery, the period in which a small band of semi-nomadic shepherds grew into a relatively large confederation of tribes—in fact, into one people. Again, we do not know whether or not it is a *historical* fact that the leaders of this people were motivated by a concrete desire to bring the Hebrews not only out of the "house of bondage" but into the Promised Land. It is, however, a historical fact that very soon after the conquest of Canaan by the Hebrew tribes, which had come up from Egypt and the Sinai Peninsula, probably in several successive waves, there existed a tradition to the effect that the purpose of the miraculous Exodus had been not only the liberation of the Children of Israel from Egyptian slavery but, equally, their settlement in the Promised Land. This tradition, which, we may add, was also a historical conviction, is expressed in the moving and powerfully motivating myth which tells how God heard "the groaning of the Children of Israel," remembered His covenant with Abraham, Isaac, and Jacob, and spoke to Moses from the midst of the burning bush: "I am come down to deliver them out of the hand of the Egyptians, and to bring them up out of that land unto a good land flowing with milk and honey . . . ."[1]

Thus, in the retrospect of popular tradition, which as early as the days of their first monarchy informed the Hebrew people, the years their ancestors had spent in Egyptian slavery were the period during which the extended family of Jacob (seventy persons) grew into twelve large tribes, aware that they dwelled in a strange land and desirous of leaving it for the land God had promised to their tribal forefathers.

It is this unique historical-mythological background—whose importance, I repeat, lies in the psychological effect it had on the Hebrews following their settlement in Canaan—that set them apart from the other peoples of the contemporary world and that continued to exert its influence in all subsequent periods of Jewish history.

If we take the liberty, for the moment, of reinterpreting the term Diaspora (which, of course, literally means "dispersion") so as to refer to the Hebrews living outside of the Land of Israel, as distinct from the Hebrews living in it, then we can say that the Hebrew people came into being in the Egyptian Diaspora, that in the history of the Hebrews Diaspora came first, and nationhood, country, and sovereignty second.

Abraham the Chaldean

This argument for the historical primacy of the Diaspora (in the above sense) is further strengthened by another myth cycle surrounding the very earliest familial origins of the Hebrews. Hebrew historical tradition traces the provenance of the twelve tribes, beyond the Egyptian slavery, to one single man named Abraham (originally Abram, meaning "exalted father"), who was born neither in Egypt nor in Canaan, but in yet another country, Mesopotamia (the modern Iraq), in the city of Ur of the Chaldees. Abram's father, Terah, decided to leave his native land and go to the land of Canaan.[2] However, Terah managed to get only as far as Haran, in the far northwest of Mesopotamia, where he died. It was in Haran that God first spoke to Abram and commanded him to go "unto the land that I will show thee."[3] The Biblical text does not specify the place to which God commanded Abram to go, but evidently Abram took God's word as referring to the same land for which his father Terah had set out without a divine command; consequently he proceeded to Canaan. From Canaan Abram, renamed by God Abraham, went on to Egypt. After a sojourn there of unknown duration, he returned to Canaan, where he led the life of a semi-nomadic chieftain.

Thus, the early history of the Hebrews had as its locale not one but two Diaspora countries, first Mesopotamia and then Egypt—incidentally, the same two countries into which the earliest *historic* exile was to lead the people of Israel and Judah in the eighth and sixth centuries BCE (Before the Common Era). Let me emphasize again: the question of the historicity of Abraham, and even of that of the Egyptian slavery, is irrelevant to the point I wish to make here, which is that in the earliest national-traditional Hebrew consciousness (i.e., in the days of

6

the monarchy) the Diaspora had primacy over the Land of Israel, in the sense that the commonly held view was that the Hebrews had originated from the Mesopotamian Abraham and had developed into a nation known as the "Children of Israel" in Egypt. In this sense the early history of the Hebrews is unique.

Moreover, again as seen in the retrospect of mythical-historical tradition, the very concept of the Diaspora, of living in an alien land which one is not entitled to possess because one does not have a divine charter granting rights of ownership, is firmly embedded in the stories of both Abraham and the Egyptian bondage. The very first words that God addressed to Abraham, who at the time did not even know that He existed, were not, as one would have expected, words of self-identification. God did not say, "I am God, creator of the world," as He did later when He first spoke to Moses, saying: "I am the God of thy father . . . ."[4] Instead, He addressed Abraham with an abrupt command: "Get thee out of thy country, and from thy kindred, and from thy father's house, unto the land that I will show thee."[5] The effect of this command was to make Abraham aware that until he reached the Promised Land, which for the time being was unknown and unidentified, he was in the Diaspora, not in the sense of "dispersion," but in the sense that he dwelled in alien lands.

The Biblical tradition conceives of Abraham's move from Haran to Canaan as having taken place over a period of several years. Throughout those years the state of being in the Diaspora, of alienhood in alien lands in which he was but a temporary sojourner, was a reality; the Promised Land only a goal, a distant dream.

From the days of Abraham to the time of Moses six generations later (Abraham-Isaac-Jacob-Levi-Kohath-Amram-Moses),[6] the Land of Promise increasingly became the center of gravity of early Hebrew history, despite the fact that many of the fateful developments in the life of the growing clan took place in the two countries of the Diaspora, Mesopotamia and Egypt. In fact, there was only one among those early patriarchs whose entire life—a rather passive though not uneventful one—took place in Canaan. This was Isaac, who was born in Canaan, lived there all his life, and died there. All the others either were born "abroad"

7

or had spent considerable periods of their lives in either Mesopotamia or Egypt or both. Moses himself was born in Egypt and
in fact never set food on Canaan, although he saw the Promised
Land from a lofty Transjordanian peak.[7]

The powerful Biblical myths recounting the stories of these
early patriarchs, whose lives epitomized and symbolized the life
of the Hebrew nation as a whole, served two basic functions.
One was to validate and repeatedly revalidate the chartered right
of the Hebrew people to possess the Land of Israel: the divine
promise "unto thy seed will I give this land" is repeated again
and again to Abraham, Isaac, and Jacob,[8] and then to Moses.[9]
The other function was to show that whenever circumstances,
such as a famine, a quarrel between brothers, or involuntary
servitude, forced the great ancestral figures to leave the Land of
Canaan and to dwell in a land of "dispersion" (Mesopotamia or
Egypt), they invariably longed to return to the Promised Land
and ultimately succeeded in doing so. Each time that an
ancestor repeated the original feat of Abraham and returned to
Canaan from a strange land, this act served to strengthen the
mythical validation, and therewith the psychological and historical imperative to go back to the Promised Land. Thus the
reenactment of this first ancestral move became an increasingly
stringent obligation, paralleled by a firmer and firmer conviction
that it was entirely impossible for the Jewish people to live a full
and happy life in the lands of the Diaspora, outside of Canaan.

According to the Biblical tradition, the first to reenact Abraham's feat was his grandson Jacob, who returned to Canaan after
spending twenty years in Paddan Aram, and who, on his
deathbed in Egypt, commanded his sons to take his bones back
to the Land of Promise for burial; here, incidentally, is the early
mythical validation of the Jewish custom, practiced in all
generations, of interment in the Holy Land, or, failing that, of
placing a little sack filled with soil from the Promised Land
beneath the head of the dead inside the coffin.

The Egyptian Slavery

In the course of the five centuries that elapsed between the
conquest of Canaan by the Hebrew tribes and the conquest of

Gilead, Galilee, and all the land of Naphtali by Tiglath-pileser, King of Assyria (732 BCE: see 2 Kings 15:29), there was no Diaspora, but only a Hebrew people living in the Land of Israel—at first grouped into independent tribes or into a tribal amphictyony led by "Judges," then as one nation under Saul, David, and Solomon, and finally as two sister-states, the Kingdom of Judah in the south, with Jerusalem as its capital and the descendants of David as the ruling dynasty, and the Kingdom of Israel to the north, with Samaria as its capital and a succession of ruling houses. Yet even in this period, the only era in Jewish history without a dispersion, the memory of the Diaspora was not allowed to fade from the consciousness of the people. On the contrary, the Egyptian bondage, that prototype of all the subsequent sufferings and miseries through one exile after the other, was made by tradition into a veritable cornerstone of Biblical Hebrew religion.

In the great myth of the origin and the chosenness of the Children of Israel, telling of the awesome nocturnal drama known as the "Covenant between the Pieces" *(B'rit Ben haB'tarim),* God reminds Abraham that He brought him out of Ur of the Chaldees, and then tells him that before his seed will inherit the Land of Canaan it "shall be a stranger in a land that is not theirs and shall serve them."[10] Since there can be no doubt that this myth was part and parcel of the Hebrew popular lore in the days of the first monarchy—incidentally, as already indicated, it also had the character of a charter validating the historic claim of the Hebrews for the possession of Canaan—it follows that the tradition of the growth of the original Hebrew extended family of Jacob into a group of tribes in a "strange land that was not theirs" was also present and active in popular consciousness.

In this old tradition the motif of slavery was inseparably interwoven with that of sojourn in "a strange land," a condition that later came to be termed "exile." This myth taught the Hebrews of the monarchic period that their ancestors, prior to conquering Canaan, had to live in another land, enduring an exile in which they suffered slavery. The memory of both slavery and exile became in popular Hebrew consciousness a mainspring for humane attitudes as well as for ritual duties toward

9

God. Thus, for instance, the repeated commandments to be kind to slaves and strangers are accompanied by the reminder "for thou wast a slave in the land of Egypt."[11] The motivation for a similar though differently worded commandment, not to oppress the stranger, is explained by "for ye were strangers in the land of Egypt."[12] The same reason is given for the commandment "Love ye therefore the stranger."[13] The sojourn of the Children of Israel as strangers in Egypt was considered as having endowed all their succeeding generations with an understanding of the psychology of foreigners in a strange land: "And a stranger shalt thou not oppress, for ye know the soul of the stranger, for ye were strangers in the land of Egypt."[14]

At the same time, and all the suffering in Egypt notwithstanding, the Egyptian sojourn created something of a bond akin to ethnic blood relationship between Israel and the Egyptians. Biblical law accords special consideration to members of two nations: the Edomite "for he is thy brother" (i.e., a descendant of Edom or Esau, twin brother of Jacob), and the Egyptian "because thou wast a stranger in his land."[15] For these two reasons, the children of the third generation born to Edomites and Egyptians were allowed to "enter into the assembly of the Lord," while even the tenth generation of Ammonites or Moabites were not given this privilege.[16]

These frequent references to Israel's sojourn as strangers in Egypt and the humane social laws based on it kept that ancient historical experience alive and in the forefront of popular consciousness. In addition, it was the Egyptian sojourn that made the miraculous redemption from the house of bondage both possible and necessary, a redemption which, in turn, became for the Biblical Hebrew the basis of many of his holy days and much of his ritual. Whatever other Canaanite sources or antecedents they may have had, the three great annual pilgrimage festivals—Passover *(Pesah)*, Pentecost ("Weeks," *Shavu'ot*) and Tabernacles ("Booths," *Sukkot*)—became closely associated with the Exodus which was their mythical validation. The immediate purpose of the Exodus, repeated with insistent monotony more than ten times in the myth of the Ten Plagues, was to enable the Children of Israel to serve God. God com-

10

manded Moses again and again to say to Pharaoh: "Let my people go that they may serve me in the wilderness."[17] On the very day of the Exodus it became manifest that this service of the Lord was, to begin with, the observance of the Passover ritual. The Revelation of the Law on Mount Sinai seven weeks later became the traditional foundation of Feast of Weeks, and the autumnal Feast of Booths became associated with the very circumstance of the journey through the wilderness where the Israelites dwelt in tents.

In this manner, in traditional retrospect the Egyptian slavery and sojourn became the foundation of both ritual and moral law in the days of the Hebrew monarchy. Thus there can be no doubt that while the Diaspora in the monarchic period was not an actual reality, it certainly had a strong psychological imminence in the life of the Hebrews.

The First Exile

The centuries following the conquest of Canaan comprised the period during which the Hebrew tribes were welded together into a nation. In many respects their history during this epoch resembled that of other nations of the area: they fought first to conquer, then to quell internal resistance, to secure and expand their boundaries, or to repel aggressors. They were victorious at times, and sustained defeats at others. They interbred with the peoples who remained within the territory controlled by them. Their condition differed from that of their neighbors primarily as a result of the bitter denunciations of prophets who arose from their midst to reproach them with idolatry and moral failings.

As the centuries wore on, increasing emphasis was put, in the religious realm, on monotheistic worship centralized in Jerusalem, and on the moralistic and ethical components of religion. The initial tribal monotheism of the conquerors of Canaan, which for a time ran the danger of being submerged into a Canaanite-type religion replete with such nature gods as El, Ba'al, Haddad, and Tammuz, and such fertility goddesses as Asherah, Anath, and Astarte, emerged victorious, although in a

11

greatly altered form. When Nebuchadnezzar, king of Babylon, destroyed Jerusalem in 586 BCE, the religion which the Jews took along with them to their Babylonian captivity was still Yahwism, but no longer of the narrowly ethnocentric tribal variety of the early period. Under the influence of the great Hebrew prophets it had become a universal, ethical monotheism proclaiming the belief that the God whom the Judeans worshiped was the only God existing.

The northern kingdom of Israel had first experienced exile 146 years earlier, when Tiglath-pileser, king of Assyria, captured its northern and eastern provinces (2 Kings 15:29). Eleven years later, in 721 BCE, "in the ninth year of Hoshea [king of Israel], the king of Assyria [Shalmaneser] took Samaria, and carried Israel away unto Assyria, and placed them in Halah and in Habor on the river of Gozan and in the cities of the Medes."[18] This single sentence is the entire Biblical record of the tragic event of the fall of Israel. From 732 BCE until the present there has never been a time when all the Jews were concentrated in the land of their fathers; Israel and the Diaspora have remained the two stages of Jewish history.

Like her northern sister-state, the southern kingdom of Judah also experienced two exiles eleven years apart. The first occurred in 597 BCE, when Nebuchadnezzar, king of Babylon, took Jerusalem and exiled its king, its nobles, and thousands of people to Babylon. The second came in 586 BCE, when Jerusalem, including the Temple, was destroyed and large numbers of Judeans were exiled to Babylon. From that time on the role of the Diaspora became predominant in the life and history of the Jewish people. Babylonia now was the center of Jewish life, although small and insignificant contingents of Judeans managed to flee to Egypt (taking with them Jeremiah, the great prophet of a tragic age); only some "of the poorest of the land" were left behind in Judah.[19]

From 586 BCE down to our present day only a minor part of the Jewish people has lived in the Land of Israel; the majority lived in the lands of their dispersion, whose number grew continuously until, more than twenty-five centuries later, the trend was reversed with the reestablishment of the State of Israel.

However, while the destruction of the First Temple (as the conquest of Judah by the Babylonians is usually referred to in Jewish tradition and history) denotes the origin of the Babylonian and Egyptian exiles, it did not signify the end of Jewish sovereignty in Palestine, but merely interrupted it for a short period. Only forty-seven years after the Babylonian Exile Babylon herself was conquered by Cyrus the Great, king of Persia, who gave permission to the Jews to return to Judah and rebuild their country, its capital Jerusalem, and its religious center, the Temple. A group of about forty-two thousand, led by Zerubabel, returned, accompanied by more than seven thousand male and female servants.

The rebuilding of Jerusalem took many years, and it was not until 516 BCE that the Temple was completed and rededicated. For at least another two centuries, although they enjoyed semi-independence, the Jews of Judah remained a poor and small people. In 333 BCE Alexander the Great brought Palestine under Greek rule, which was not overthrown until 166–164 BCE by the Maccabean revolt. Thereafter the country remained an independent Jewish state for about a century, until its conquest by the Romans in 63 BCE. After 130 years of semi-independence under Roman rule the Jews staged a countrywide rebellion, but were eventually overwhelmed by the Romans who took Jerusalem in 70 CE.

The Babylonian and Egyptian Diasporas

While the Judeans suffered their vicissitudes, the Babylonian Diaspora prospered. This is evident from the fact that even after the Cyrus Declaration many Judeans preferred to stay on in Babylonia, and also from the scattered reports about the widening spectrum of occupations followed by these expatriates. Their numbers were augmented by groups who preferred Persian to Roman rule, and especially by Judeans who escaped to Babylonia during and after the Jewish-Roman War of 66–70 CE. The Jews of Babylonia became active in agriculture as well as in artisanship and a variety of trades; they supervised the digging and maintenance of the canals—water for irrigation was as vital in Babylonia as it was in Egypt—and sailed their own ships on them as well as on the great rivers of Babylon. And since Babylonia was a much richer country than Judea, the economic position of the Babylonian Jews before long was better than it had been in the "old country," especially in the strife-filled days immediately prior to the destruction of the Second Temple in Jerusalem.

Once the Persians had established their rule over Babylonia, they granted the Jews a consideraxle degree of internal autonomy. The community was headed by a scion of the House of David with the title of *Resh Gelutha,* or Exilarch, who wielded wide powers and functioned as a dignitary of the empire. This office continued for no less than fifteen centuries (until 1038 CE)—that is, longer than the periods of the First and Second Commonwealths together. At the same time, however, the Jews of Babylonia had to pay not only a land tax but also a head or poll tax. Thus the main outlines of the pattern that was to characterize the life of the Jewish communities in all the lands of the Near and Middle East almost until the present time had been drawn as early as the days of the Babylonian Exile: internal autonomy, coupled with legal inabilities and subservience to despotic, though not always inimical, rulers.

Even as Jerusalem fell in 586 BCE, a Jewish community was being established in Egypt, the land of Israel's slavery, to which the Bible had enjoined the Jews not to return.[20] Jeremiah inveighed powerfully against the plan of Johanan the son of Kareah to lead the Judean remnants to Egypt, but in vain. They not only went to Egypt, but forced Jeremiah to go with them.[21] Once in Egypt, where they settled in Migdol, Tahpanhes, Noph (Memphis), and Patros, the Judeans reverted to the service of the Queen of Heaven as their fathers had done in Judah, provoking Jeremiah to prophesy the utter destruction of the remnant of Judah in Egypt.[22]

However, for once the predictions of the great prophet of Judah's doom did not come true. The Jews continued to live, multiply, and prosper in Egypt until, some twenty-five centuries later, their present-day progeny returned to the land of their fathers where Jeremiah had wanted them to stay after the destruction of Jerusalem.[23]

14

Not long after this second "descent" of Israel into Egypt (the first, led by Jacob, had taken place around 1600 BCE; the second, led by Johanan ben Kareah, about a thousand years later), the Egyptian kings settled some Jews on the island of Yeb (Elephantine) and in Aswan in Upper Egypt to form military frontier colonies. These Jews spoke Aramaic and their religion was a mixture of Yahwism, Ba'alism, and the worship of Canaanite goddesses. Other Jewish communities developed in the larger cities of Egypt, especially Thebes and Memphis, and engaged in agriculture, trade, and commerce.

When Alexander the Great founded the city of Alexandria (in 332 BCE), the Jews were there, and soon they settled in the new Hellenistic city in large numbers. They occupied two of the five districts of the city, had numerous synagogues, and constituted an independent political community, while enjoying full civil rights. By the middle of the third century BCE, after only two generations of Hellenization, Greek had become the principal language of the Jews of Egypt, and the Bible had to be translated into that tongue in order to make it intelligible to them. Greek was the principal language of synagogue worship as well.

Hellenized Egyptian Jewry showed greater independence from the religious center of Judaism in Jerusalem than did the Aramaic-speaking Babylonian Diaspora. This was demonstrated most strikingly by the erection in 154 BCE of a splendid Jewish temple in Leontopolis, in Lower Egypt, by a priest, Onias IV, son of a high priest at the Jerusalem Temple. This was the only time that such a place of worship and sacrifice was erected outside Jerusalem since the rebuilding of the Jerusalem Temple in the sixth century BCE. Incidentally, the Egyptian Temple of Onias survived the Temple of Jerusalem by three years: it was destroyed after having functioned for 227 years, in 73 CE, the same year in which the fortress of Massada near the Dead Sea fell to the Romans.

The Hellenistic period saw also the earliest dispersion of Jews into Europe, first into the Greek islands and mainland, and later into Rome as well. When Rome became the mistress of the antique world, Jews settled in several countries bordering the Mediterranean to both south and north, and, by the second

15

century CE, they were found in all parts of Roman-dominated Europe.

The Three Major Divisions ————————————————

Jewish ethnic diversity has its origins, like much else Jewish, in Biblical times. In the early period after the conquest of Canaan by the Hebrews, ethnic differences among their tribes were expressed in such features as descent traditions (i.e., tribal affiliations), group loyalties, dialectal variations in language, religious customs, and popular mores. After the establishment of the Hebrew monarchy, some of these differences persisted, and, following the death of Solomon and the emergence of two separate Hebrew kingdoms, they jelled into a northern, or Israelite, and a southern, or Judean, ethnicity.

Not much is known as to what transpired in this respect during the period of the Second Commonwealth, but when we reach Talmudic times we find at least two clearly distinguished Jewish ethnic groups in Palestine: the Judean and the Galilean. In the same period, the Jewish communities outside Palestine became more and more widely scattered, with the process of absorbing outside influences getting under way as soon as a group settled in a new non-Jewish environment. In this manner the historic development of new Diasporas led to the emergence of an increasing number of new Jewish ethnic groups.

At the time the Romans put an end to the Second Jewish Commonwealth, Diasporas existed in the three continents of the Old World, centering around, but not limited to, the circum-Mediterranean area. This was the time when the separation of the Jewish people into three major components began. However, it was not until the early Middle Ages that there emerged a clearcut differentiation into three main groups—which we shall term *divisions* so as to distinguish between them and the communities or Diasporas comprised in each of the three—the Oriental, Sephardi, and Ashkenazi Jews.

THE ORIENTAL DIVISION   The Oriental Jewish division comprises those Jewish communities whose course of history never took them outside Asia and Africa, and which, moreover, have lived ever since the rise of Islam in Muslim lands. Since these communities inhabited the world area known as the Middle East, they could also be called Middle Eastern Jews. If we prefer the term Oriental Jews, we do so for two reasons: firstly, because the term Oriental Jews, in its Hebrew form, *Y'hude haMizrah* (or *'Edot haMizrah,* meaning "Oriental communities") is the one used exclusively in Israel to denote this division of the Jewish people, which since about 1967 has constituted more than half of the Jewish population of Israel; secondly, because the term "Middle East" itself came into vogue only in the days of World War II, and when using it one always feels that one should add "and North Africa" for the sake of readers not familiar with the anthropological meaning of the designation "Middle East."

Even if we disregard the earliest historic origins of the Hebrews, the Oriental Jewish division is by far the oldest of the three. Jews have lived in Babylonia from the eighth century BCE, in Egypt from the sixth century BCE, and one or two hundred years later they were found in many more countries surrounding these two. They were old-established indigenous populations of these countries when, in the late fourth century BCE, they became exposed to Hellenistic influence. Some three centuries later, several of them, especially those in Syria, Anatolia, Egypt, and North Africa, came under Roman rule, followed in about the fourth century CE by the Byzantine Christian influence in the east and then the Vandal rule in North Africa (430). However, all these and other more transitory early influences were largely obliterated when they were overlaid, from the seventh century on, by the lasting influence of Islam, which became and remained down to the twentieth century the dominating external factor in the life of the entire Oriental Jewish division. For close to thirteen centuries the cultural ups and downs of the Oriental Jewish communities were largely determined by the rise and decline of the Muslim culture of their host peoples. This cultural dependence on Islam is the most basic and most characteristic feature of the Oriental division of the Jewish people, and it is thrown into relief by the absence of all contact between it and Western Christianity until the nineteenth century.

17

THE SEPHARDI DIVISION   The second division, that of the
Sephardi Jews, called thus from the Medieval Hebrew name of
Spain, *S'farad,* comprises a smaller variety of communities than
the Oriental one, but was formed by a more varied series of
historical circumstances and processes. The place in which it
acquired its language and developed its ethnic character was the
Iberian Peninsula; the time, the Middle Ages. But the ethnic
strands that went into its making were many, and each represented a specific set of historical experiences. Jews first settled in
Spain after its conquest by the Romans (133 BCE); were there
when the Vandals irrupted (406 CE); remained under the Visigoths (415); and, after the latter converted from Arianism to
Catholicism (589), were cruelly persecuted, forced to be bap-
tized, and subjected to expulsions. Their numbers increased
considerably after the Arab conquest of Spain (711), and they
became in the subsequent centuries an important part of the
splendid Arab culture that flourished in the peninsula. Thus far
the historical experience of the Sephardi Jews did not differ
significantly from that of many Oriental Jewish communities.
But then came the gradual ouster of the Moors from Spain by the
Christians, as a result of which more and more Iberian Jews
came under Spanish and Portuguese rule and influence. While
the Christian advance signified the end of the Jewish Golden
Age in Spain, it was precisely during these centuries that the
Sephardi division crystallized with regard to its language, folk
culture, popular character, and ethos. Its vernacular became
Ladino, that is medieval Spanish (with an admixture of a
Hebrew vocabulary); its culture was molded by a superimposition of Spanish (and, to a lesser extent, Portuguese) influence on
top of the older Muslim Arab one; and the same process could be
observed also with reference to character, ethos, and values. The
resultant divergence between the Sephardim and the Oriental
Jews was so great that when, after the wave of persecutions in
1391, and again after the expulsion of 1492, Sephardi Jews
settled among their Oriental brethren in North Africa and the
Asian lands of the Ottoman Empire, the two divisions faced
each other like strangers from two different worlds.
    While they lived in Spain, the Sephardi Jews constituted one

18

single cultural aggregate; but after their dispersion they broke up into several different communities, each of which absorbed cultural influences from its new environment. Some of them— e.g., in certain places in North Africa—completely merged into the Oriental Jewish majority. Others—e.g., in Turkey— assimilated the indigenous Oriental Jews to themselves, while absorbing some of their cultural characteristics and values and being exposed also to external Muslim influences. As far as the sequence of cultural influences was concerned, these Sephardim, who fled from Christian Spain into Muslim Turkish domains, thus had a new Muslim layer superimposed upon their already numerous and varied phases of acculturation. Still others, who went to Italy, maintained themselves for many generations as separate Sephardi communities in several cities, but ultimately became Italianized. Those who moved up north to find a haven in the Netherlands and in England kept themselves aloof from the Ashkenazim they encountered there, but absorbed many Dutch and British influences respectively, so that they soon developed into a Sephardi type that was almost as different from, say, that of the Sephardim of Greece, as were the Dutch or British from the Greeks.

These divergencies notwithstanding, the Sephardim everywhere retained a great pride in their Sephardi descent, and, together with it, a strong feeling of Sephardi unity. As long as Ladino remained their vernacular, it constituted a powerful bond among all Sephardim. With its replacement by Dutch, English, and French in western Europe, the Sephardi consciousness inevitably weakened and its place was taken by an increasing rapprochement with the Ashkenazi Jews in those countries. As to the Mediterranean Sephardim, most of those who survived the Nazi holocaust found their way to Israel, where they increasingly intermarried with both the Ashkenazim and the Oriental Jews.

THE ASHKENAZI DIVISION The third division, that of the Ashkenazim, emerged as a historically significant component of the Jewish people later than the other two, but for the last three or four centuries it not only has been numerically the largest of

19

the three but also took the unquestionable lead culturally and in historic importance.

As is often the case with historical origins, those of Ashkenazi Jewry, too, cannot be pinpointed with any accuracy. Some Jews, in all probability, moved up from Anatolia to the north shore of the Black Sea even prior to the end of the Second Jewish Commonwealth. Others, who in the same period settled in Rome, and whose numbers were augmented by the Judean captives brought back by the victorious Romans after the conclusion of Jewish-Roman war (70 CE), proceeded into Roman-occupied Europe in the second and third centuries. In this manner Jewish communities were founded not only in Hispania (Spain) and Gallia (Gaul, i.e. France) in the west, but also in Germania and Pannonia (Hungary) in Central, and in Dacia (Rumania) in Eastern Europe.

These early beginnings of a Jewish Diaspora in Central and Eastern Europe were followed by a long period of quiescence in which practically nothing is known about the fate and circumstances of the Jews who were the forerunners of the Ashkenazim. The name "Ashkenazi" itself points to the Middle Ages, for it was only in medieval days that the German lands came to be called *Ashk'naz* in Hebrew. Those Ashkenazi Jews who first appeared on the world Jewish scene when they lived in the Rhine provinces did not use German but French as their vernacular.[24]

One of the greatest and earliest Jewish scholars who arose among Ashkenazi Jews was Rashi (Solomon ben Isaac, 1040–1106), who lived in the French town of Troyes, some eighty miles southeast of Paris, and used the French vernacular. From about the eleventh or twelfth century the Jews of the Rhine provinces spoke German. In the thirteenth and fourteenth centuries, when the Jews were expelled from Germany, they took their Yiddish language along to Poland and other countries of Eastern Europe, and made it the dominant Jewish language there.

As Ashkenazi Jewry spread into all parts of Eastern Europe, the familiar process of differentiation set in. Local dialects emerged within Yiddish, local varieties of Jewish custom and costume developed, and so did varying food habits, trends within Jewish learning, occupations, intellectual bents, values, and personality types. Before long, the Eastern European Ashkenazi Diaspora comprised a number of clearly distinguished separate ethnic groups, whose common cultural basis becomes apparent only when compared with the Western half of the Ashkenazi division.

As to the latter, the same process of differentiation took place within it as well. Although Yiddish, which was introduced into all countries of Western Europe by refugees and migrants from Eastern Europe, created a common element and a cultural bond among the Jewish communities of the continent, this could not counteract the emergence of disparate Jewish ethnic groups under the influence of the national character of their host countries. Here too, as in Eastern Europe, the common religio-cultural substratum remained, as did the feeling of a community of fate, but the cultural differences between British, French, German, etc., Jewries became increasingly pronounced with each successive generation. In the nineteenth century, enlightenment, assimilation, and emancipation in rapid succession considerably reduced the remaining common element among the Western European Diasporas while at the same time greatly increasing the cultural similarities between each Diaspora and its host country and with it the ethnic differences between one Diaspora and the other. By the mid twentieth century these acculturative processes had reached such a stage that the remaining common Jewish cultural elements among the Western European and American Diasporas ran the risk of being completely buried under the mass and weight of the national cultures of each country, of which the Jews as much as the Gentiles had become carriers.

An Exercise in Semantics—————————————————

Two terms are used by historians, sociologists, statesmen, and politicians in reference to the dispersed state of the Jewish people in all parts of the world. One is Exile, the other Diaspora. Often one finds that the two terms are used interchangeably, as if they were synonymous. Is this justified, or is there a semantic difference between the two which renders their undifferentiated use incorrect and improper? Let us have a closer look at the origins of the two words and the meanings attributed to them in historic times.

Exile (from the Latin *exilium* or *exsilium*) is defined in Webster's *New World Dictionary* as "1. a prolonged living away from one's country, community, etc., usually enforced; banishment, sometimes self-imposed. 2. a person in exile." In Jewish context, the word exile is the English rendering of the Biblical Hebrew noun *galut* or *gola,* and has the connotation of "captivity" (Hebrew *sh'vi* or *shevi;* also *shivya, sh'vut, sh'vit*). The primary meaning of the latter noun is people captured and taken prisoner in a battle. In this sense it first appears in the old paean of victory known as the Song of Deborah.[1] In it we read: "Arise, Barak, and capture your captivity, O son of Avinoam." Occasionally the two nouns *shevi* and *galut* appear as parallels, e.g. in Isaiah 20:4: "So shall the King of Assyria lead away the captivity [*sh'vi*] of Egypt and the exile [*galut*] of Ethiopia . . ."; or in Nahum 3:10: "She, too, into exile [*gola*] she went, into captivity [*shevi*] . . ."; or in Ezra 8:35: "They who come from the captivity [*sh'vi*], the children of the exile [*gola*]. . . ." At other times, as if for good measure, Biblical authors use the phrase "the captivity of the exile [*sh'vi hagola*]."[2]

All this makes it clear that the term *gola* or *galut*, exile, refers to a condition closely resembling that of prisoners of war. While not confined to a prison camp, exiles are constrained from leaving the town or province or country to which they were brought by their victorious captors. It is in this sense only that the word exile (*gola* or *galut*) is used in the Bible. It appears several dozens of times, most frequently in the books of Jeremiah, Ezekiel, and Ezra, and almost invariably it refers to the Babylonian exile which, up to the return under King Cyrus of Persia, was a veritable captivity.

It follows that the only proper sense in which the term "exile" can be used in the context of Jewish history is to denote the condition of a Jewish community in a country in which its sojourn is involuntary. A community in exile is prevented from emigrating by government regulations, or by force of arms, and under penalty of imprisonment or even death. Present-day Jews in Soviet Russia and certain Arab countries are typical examples of such a condition of exile.

Diaspora (from the Greek *diaspora*), again according to Webster's, is "1. the dispersion of the Jews after the Babylonian exile. 2. the Jews thus dispersed. 3. in the time of the apostles, Jewish Christians who lived outside of Palestine." In the entire Bible there are only two passages in which a Hebrew noun form corresponding in meaning to Diaspora appears, and even of these one is doubtful. In Isaiah 11:12 we read: "And He will set up an ensign for the nations, and will assemble the expelled of Israel (*nidhe Yisrael*), and gather together the scattered of Judah (*n'futzot Y'huda*) from the four corners of the earth." Here *n'futzot* clearly corresponds to Diaspora. The doubtful passage is found in Jeremiah 25:34 where a word can be read as "your dispersion" (*t'futzotekhem*).

Both noun forms, *n'futzot* and *t'futzot,* are derived from a Hebrew verb occurring frequently enough in the Bible and having the meaning "to disperse" or "to scatter." It is the verb the builders of the Tower of Babel are said to have used when they proposed to build a city and a tower "lest we be scattered abroad upon the face of the whole earth."[3] Or, with reference to the hoped-for return to the Land of Israel, Ezekiel says: "Thus saith the Lord God: When I shall have gathered the house of

24

Israel from the peoples among whom they are scattered. . . ."[4]
When Moses threatens the Children of Israel with divine
punishment should they become guilty of idolatry, he says: "The
Lord shall scatter you among the peoples, and ye shall be left
few in number among the nations whither the Lord shall lead
you away."[5] However, repentance will be rewarded by redemption: "If thou shalt return unto the Lord thy God . . .
then the Lord thy God will return thy captivity [sh'vut], and
have compassion upon thee, and will return and gather thee
from all the peoples whither the Lord thy God hath scattered
[hefitz] thee."[6]

It is thus apparent that the dictionary distinction between the
English words *exile* and *Diaspora* corresponds to the difference
in the Biblical usage between the noun *galut* or *gola* (exile), and
the verb *l'hafitz* (to scatter), from which a noun meaning
"scattering" or "Diaspora" (*n'futzot* or *t'futzot)* was derived.
Exile brought the Hebrews or Judeans to one particular place of
banishment or captivity, Diaspora resulted from a scattering of
Israel among many peoples.

One more rather significant difference between *exile* and
Diaspora can be found in Biblical usage. When Biblical authors
speak of *galut* or *gola* (exile), they attribute it to the defeat of
Israel (or Judah) by the army of another nation. It is the king of
Assyria or Babylonia, or a commander of his forces, who
"exiles" Israel, who carries them away into captivity.[7] Only very
rarely, in fact in no more than five passages, do Biblical authors
state explicitly that it was God who exiled the people of Israel,
and in each of these passages there was a special theological-
didactic reason for doing so.[8]

The Diaspora, on the other hand—that is, the scattering of
Israel among the nations—is in most Biblical passages attributed directly to God. It is He, and He alone, without any
reference to the human agents employed by Him to carry out His
will, who scattered, or will scatter, His people as a punishment
for their sins, and it is He who will gather them together from
their dispersion.[9]

It appears, then, that in common Biblical usage exile is,
generally speaking, a historical condition brought about by a

military defeat of Israel; Diaspora, on the other hand, is a divinely meted out punishment, the result of a fall from grace.

This distinction bore importantly on the Jewish national self-image in the long exile that began with the destruction of Jerusalem by the Romans. As the centuries wore on, the Diaspora aspect of the scattered condition of the Jewish people—that is, the consciousness of this condition as a God-ordained punishment—receded into the background, and the dwelling of the Jews among the nations of the world was felt to be, more and more emphatically, due to the wickedness of the gentiles.

This does not mean, of course, that the dispersion was never referred to. The two Biblical noun forms equivalent to "Diaspora," *n'futzot* and *t'futzot*, are mentioned occasionally in Talmudic and later Hebrew literature, as is their post-Biblical synonym *pizzur* or, in plural, *pizzurim*.[10] But in common usage it was the word *galut*, exile, that referred to the condition of the Jews among the nations of the world ever since the Roman exile, the *galut Edom*.

This term was used even when the intention was to juxtapose or contrast the Jewish community of Palestine with the Jewish communities dispersed in the Diaspora. Thus already in Talmudic usage we find references not only to the "children of the Babylonian exile" *(b'ne galuta diBavel)*,[11] but also to "the two holy days of the exiles,"[12] or "your brethren who are in the exile,"[13] or "the sons of the exile."[14] Similarly in the Midrash we find references to "four exiles": the Babylonian,[15] the Median, the Greek (i.e., Syrian), and the Edomite (i.e., Roman).[16] The expression which was to become a stock phrase in Jewish prayer, "ingathering of the exiles" *(kibbutz galuyot)*, is of Talmudic origin.[17] When Rabban Gamaliel sent an epistle to the Jewish communities outside of Palestine, he addressed it "To our brethren, the sons of the exiles in Babylon, and to our brethren in Media, and to the rest of the exiles of Israel, be your peace always great."[18]

In the post-Talmudic literature, as in the Talmudic, the Diaspora is consistently referred to, not by one of the several Biblical or post-Biblical Hebrew words that mean dispersion, but by the word "exile," or, frequently, in plural, "exiles," *galuyot* or *galiyot*.[19]

The Historical-Theological View

To return to the point already touched upon, exile, even if it was originally ordained by God as a punishment for Israel's sins, was imposed in all its severity by the nations who hated Israel and wished to cause it sufferings, without being ordered by God to do so, or even against His will. In fact, several Talmudic pronouncements about the exile can only be understood as predicated on the view that after God brought about the exile, He lost control over it. The idea is reminiscent of the Greek myth of Pandora's box: it was she who had opened the box, but once she had done so, the calamities that escaped from it and befell mankind were beyond her control. In a like manner some Talmudic sages held that after God had caused Israel to be exiled, it was no longer possible for Him to stem the floodtide of man-made evil that the nations of the world let loose upon Israel. Some express this idea with unmistakable clarity, others in veiled hints.

To the latter category belongs the saying of Rabbi Yohanan, the early third-century Palestinian Amora teacher: "If you see an age upon which many sufferings come like a stream, hope for him [the Messiah]."[20] More explicit is the saying of Rabbi Sh'muel bar Nahman, another Palestinian Amora of the same period: "God longs for the end of the exile just as much as does Israel."[21] Still clearer are the pronouncements of two later masters, Rabbi Hana bar Aha and Rabbi Tanhum bar Hanilai. The former, an Amora of the late third century, said in the name of the "house [i.e., school] of Rab," that one of the things that God regretted having created was the exile.[22] And according to Tanhum bar Hanilai, who was a Palestinian Amora of the middle of the third century, God said: "Behold, what that Babylonian dwarf [i.e., Nebuchadnezzar] has done to Me: he exiled My children and destroyed My house and burned My Temple."[23] These last three statements are incompatible with

27

the idea expressed by other Talmudic masters that God Himself brought about the destruction of Jerusalem and the Temple and the exile of Israel.

The idea that God is not able to exercise control over the nations who keep Israel in exile is expressed even more emphatically by Rabbi Yose b'Rabbi Hanina: "The Holy One, blessed be He, beseeched the nations of the world that they should not oppress Israel too severely. . . ."[24]

In medieval Hebrew literature it is repeatedly stated that God's primary purpose in exiling Israel was not to punish the Jews but to have them proselytize, that the gentiles oppress and torture Israel against the will of God, and that the duration of the exile is extended by the nations against God's will. As to the first point, we read, for instance, in the *Sepher Mitzvot Gadol* (The Great Book of Commandments) of Moses ben Jacob of Coucy, a French rabbi and codifier who lived in Paris in the early thirteenth century: "Does a man sow [*zore'a*] one measure [*kor*], except in order to obtain several measures? Likewise, God scatters *(zore'a)* Israel in the countries in order to have proselytes join them."[25]

Isaac Aboab, the thirteenth-century Spanish rabbi, repeatedly indicates that God's desire to succor Israel is opposed by the gentiles who wish to hurt Israel: "Although exiles and sufferings have come over Israel, the merciful God always has compassion with them. . . . And if the nations of the world rejoice over the downfall of Israel, . . . the Lord, the God of vengeance, will avenge on them the vengeance of Israel. . . ." Referring to the Talmudic saying of Rabbi Sh'muel bar Nahman quoted above, he says: "When Israel suffers persecution in exile, let them not despair of redemption but let them long for it always, because God longs for it even more. . . ."[26]

With regard to the duration of the exile beyond the period decreed by God, Eleazar Azkari who lived in Safed, Palestine, in the sixteenth century, has the following to say in his *Sepher Haredim* (Book of the Devout, written in 1585): "Our King [God] decreed for us an exile of one thousand years which is one day for God . . . and since we were not aroused to repentance, the time of our exile became lengthened by another half-day [i.e., five hundred years] and more."[27]

Many more quotations could easily be gathered to show that Jewish thinkers and teachers, from Talmudic times down to modern days, have attributed the sufferings and persecutions of Israel in exile, to "the hand of the nations that weighs on us" and not to the will of God. And since this was the case, the exile of Israel was not termed "Diaspora," because that would have implied that it was still God's will that the dispersion continue, which, in turn, would have meant that the Jewish people was still caught up in the same web of sins that had brought down upon them the divine punishment of dispersion in the first place. But those old Biblical sins were primarily idolatry and the immorality accompanying it—sins which, after the destruction of the Temple by the Romans, not even Israel's most severe critics could accuse it of committing. Therefore, the continuation of the dispersed state of the Jewish people was no longer due to the direct effect of the metaphysical sin-and-punishment syndrome, and thus was not "Diaspora." It was "exile," *galut,* in the old Biblical sense, brought about and perpetuated by human agents inimical to Israel, by Edom-Rome and its successors the Christian countries, on the one hand, and by Ishmael—i.e., the Arab and, by extension, Muslim countries—on the other.

The distinction between Diaspora and exile was thus an important one from the traditional Jewish theocentric point of view. To consider the Jewish people as being in Diaspora would have meant to acknowledge that the Jews continued to perpetrate the ancient mortal sins for which the Diaspora was originally the divine punishment. To regard the Jewish dispersion as *exile,* on the other hand, meant to attribute and ascribe the sufferings of the Jewish people to the nations of the world and to believe that the exile continued, not because the people of Israel was sinful, but because it had not yet achieved a sufficiently high degree of virtue, nor the nations a sufficiently high degree of wickedness, to warrant the divine intervention of catastrophic dimensions and consequences which alone could put an end to the exile.

It may be difficult to establish to what extent this distinction was consciously present in the Jewish psyche in the long centuries of Israel's exile. But the fact remains that the Jews throughout felt that they were in exile, spoke of their condition as "exile," *galut,* and, whenever they used the term, they consciously or subconsciously evoked the memory of the many Biblical passages that speak about the exile and the cruel enemy who brought it about.

The preponderance of the human (as against the divine) factor in the persistence of the exile was correlated, in a sense, with the acute feeling of unhappiness in the exiles of many lands and in many times. The term "exile," especially in its popular Yiddish form, *goles,* had the connotation of a state of misery, of persecution, of homelessness, of sojourning as a stranger among strangers. All the misfortunes, the innumerable degradations and indignities the Jews frequently had to suffer in the lands of their exile could not be attributed directly to the will of God. They were the manifestations of the evil that was part of the nature of gentiles, they were expressions of human ill will directed against the Chosen People of God.

By the same token, when Jews throughout the centuries entreated God to put an end to their exile and gather them together in the land of their fathers, this prayerful request implied the man-made character of the exile itself. One simply could not, if one was deeply and truly religious, direct a prayer to God and ask Him to cease willing what He did and instead will its opposite. If it were God's will, that is, His active, ongoing decision, to keep Israel in exile, how could a pious Jew presume and try to make his own will prevail against that of God? How could he ask God to abandon a course that God in His infinite wisdom decided to follow, and adopt an opposite course found more desirable in the eyes of man, who is notoriously (in the religious view) lacking in understanding? If, however, Israel was kept in exile by the malice of the inimical gentiles, and even God yearned for the exile's end, then, of course, it was perfectly proper to implore God for help against the godless oppressors, and ask Him to bestir Himself to action to end the exile. Only in this manner can we understand that ever since the destruction of the Temple by the Romans the Jews were not only able, but considered it a religious duty, to pray three times a day: "Sound a great trumpet for our freedom, and raise up an ensign to gather our exiles, and gather us together

30

from the four corners of the earth. Blessed art Thou, O Lord, who gatherest together the expelled of Thy people Israel." Every phrase in this nineteen-centuries-old benediction is a quotation from the Bible, so that actually it epitomizes the Biblical belief in the future ingathering of the exiles.

In the same prayer, in several subsequent benedictions, God is entreated to restore the ancient judges of Israel, to return to, dwell in, and build up Jerusalem, reestablish the throne of David, bring the Messiah (called "the sprout of David"), restore the Temple service, and cause His Shekhina ("presence") to return to Zion. This most important and most frequently repeated prayer of Juadism expresses the central quest of the Jewish people ever since 70 CE. Wherever Jews lived they were in exile, which they were able to endure only because they never ceased hoping for the coming of the Messiah, and because in every ghetto they could erect their impregnable spiritual fortress: a life devoted to the study and the fulfillment of God's Law, the Tora.

The Four Pillars of Judaism in Exile

What were the foundations on which this traditional Jewish life in exile rested? Characteristically, they were books, nothing more and nothing less. The oldest, holiest, and therefore most important of these books was the Bible, whose writing was begun by the Hebrews at a very early period of their history and which was completed by the Jews about the second century BCE. The Bible is almost entirely a Palestinian product, although some of its late books originated in Babylonia during the captivity.

Throughout the six centuries that elapsed between the return from the Babylonian captivity and the end of the Second Jewish Commonwealth, the Jews of Palestine retained the intellectual and religious leadership of the Jewish people. That this was due not merely to the existence of the Jerusalem Temple, which, of course, was the religious center for the Diaspora as well, is attested by the fact that even after the destruction of the Temple the spiritual leadership remained in the hands of Palestinian

31

Jewry for another four or five generations. Practically all the literary documents which survive from the epoch that came to a close in 200 CE were authored in Palestine. It was this age that saw in its early part the composition in Palestine of the last books of the Bible, and later the collection and canonization of the twenty-four books making up the Hebrew Bible in its totality. The Apocrypha and other religious literary works not admitted to the canon were also, for the most part, written in Palestine. Palestinian Jews were the authors of most of the writings included in the New Testament, the earliest versions of some of which may have been formulated just prior to the destruction of the Temple. The scribes and first sages and teachers, whose religious and ethical ideas were subsequently incorporated into the Mishna, the first post-Biblical Jewish code of laws, lived toward the end of this period in Palestine, where the Mishna itself received its final form about 200 CE. The first Jewish historian to write in Greek, who witnessed and described the Roman siege of Jerusalem and the destruction of the Temple by Titus, was a Palestinian Jewish priest from the Hasmonean family, Josephus Flavius.

For about two centuries following the destruction of the Second Temple the Jews were able to hold on to Palestine even though they had no sovereignty over it. In this period they laid the foundations for all subsequent Jewish religious development by gathering, organizing, and putting into final shape the Mishna. Rabbi Judah the Patriarch who accomplished this feat about the year 200 CE in a country ruled by a foreign, pagan, polytheistic power, Rome, which saw in a refusal to pay homage to its gods something akin to treason, is rightly considered as one of the greatest contributors to the development of that value system which enabled the Jews to maintain their traditions and thus their identity through many centuries of exile and dispersion, down to the onset of enlightenment, emancipation, and assimilation.

In the third and subsequent centuries the significance of Palestinian Jewry in relation to the Diaspora declined. True, it still produced several Midrashim as well as the Jerusalem (or Palestinian) Talmud, which was completed about 425 CE but was overshadowed by the Babylonian Talmud (completed ca. 500 CE), but its spiritual leadership of the Jewish world became a thing of the past and its numbers gradually dwindled into insignificance.

The decline of Palestinian Jewry was paralleled (or counter-balanced) by the rise of the Babylonian Jewish community. In fact, Babylonia herself acquired something of a secondary sanctity in the eyes of the Jews after they had lived in the country for several centuries. Some of the sages whose opinions and pronouncements are recorded in the Babylonian Talmud even went so far as to say that "all those who live in Babylonia are as if they lived in the Land of Israel," and that "he who moves ["goes up"] from Babylonia to the land of Israel transgresses a commandment."[28] They also warned that "just as it is forbidden to move from the Land of Israel to Babylonia, so it is forbidden to move from Babylonia to other countries."[29]

Babylonia's intellectual preeminence enabled its Jewry to supply the first post-Talmudic codifiers of Jewish law in the persons of the *geonim,* heads of the Talmudic academies that flourished in Sura and Pumbedita until the eleventh century.

Other Diasporas were slow to challenge Babylonia's intellectual and spiritual primacy. It was not until the eleventh century that a Jewish scholar who lived in the far west, in Morocco and Spain, compiled a law code that was accepted as authoritative by the entire Diaspora. He was Rabbi Yitzhak al-Fasi (Isaac of Fez, 1013–1103), whose *Halakhot* (usually referred to as *The Rif*) contains the essence of all legal decisions found in the Talmud and applicable to Jewish life in the Diaspora. His code was supplanted by the *Mishne Tora* ("Second Law"), also known as *Yad HaHazaka* ("The Strong Hand"), written by Moses Maimonides (1135–1204), a Spanish Jew who spent the second half of his life in Egypt and who was also the greatest medieval Jewish philosopher and an outstanding physician and astronomist. Maimonides gives a brief final decision in the case of each law and it was his purpose thereby to make it possible for all Jews, even those who were unable to delve into a study of the Talmud, to know and obey all the commandments.

A century and a half later the Maimonidean code was superseded by a new one, the *Arba' Turim* ("Four Orders"), written by Jacob ben Asher (ca. 1270–ca. 1340), who lived first in Germany and then in Spain. This compendium remained the standard code of both Sephardim and Ashkenazim until it in turn was superseded by the *Shulhan 'Arukh* ("Set Table"). Written by the Sephardi Joseph Caro (1499–1575) in Safed, Palestine, the *Shulhan 'Arukh* is the last authoritative codification of Jewish law, followed to this day by observant Jews in all parts of the world.

Another authority without whose work the traditional Jewish "Talmud Tora" (i.e., study of the Law) could not be imagined is Rabbi Sh'lomo ben Yitzhak, better known by his initials, Rashi (1040–1105), who lived in Troyes, France. Unlike other Jewish religious authorities, Rashi never wrote an independent or separate book, but authored only commentaries which became the key to an understanding of the Bible and the Talmud. From the sixteenth century on, Rashi's commentaries were printed as inseparable marginal glosses with the standard editions of the Bible and the Talmud.

Thus, until the enlightenment and assimilation, the spiritual world of the Jewish people in all the lands of its Diaspora rested on these four pillars: the Bible, written by many authors in Palestine from ca. 1200 to 200 BCE; the Talmud, consisting of the Mishna written in Palestine, ca. 200 CE, and the Gemara, compiled in Babylonia, ca. 500 CE; the Biblical and Talmudic commentaries of Rashi, written in France in the eleventh century; and the *Shulhan 'Arukh,* written in the sixteenth century in Palestine by a Spanish Jew, and supplied with interlined comments by Moshe Isserles (1520–1572), a Polish Talmudic scholar. Palestine, Babylonia, France, and Poland were thus the four countries in which were written the religious sourcebooks that had the greatest significance for the perpetuation of the Jewish people. In time, these four works span almost three millennia. Their authors represent the three major divisions of the Jewish people that developed in the Diaspora. Yet whether it was Oriental Jewish (Babylonian) Talmudic argumentation, Ashkenazi commentary and exegesis, or Sephardi religio-legal codification, all the intellectual effort put forward by the best Jewish minds of three continents, while formally centering on the Book of Books, the Holy Writ, its explanation, amplification, and actualization, subserved, in effect, not a theocentric but an ethnocentric purpose: the insurance of the survival of the Jewish people in its Diaspora, by protecting it with a canopy of faith supported on four mighty pillars: the Bible, the Talmud, the *Shulhan 'Arukh* and Rashi.

DIASPORA IN MODERN JEWISH THOUGHT

The Denial of Exile

While Orthodox Jewry, especially in Eastern Europe, continued to consider itself living in exile and to pray fervently for a miraculous return to Zion, assimilated or modernized Jews in the Western world—that is, in Central and Western Europe and, most recently, also in America—emphatically denied that they were in exile and, at least as far as their own communities were concerned, discarded the very concept.

It is not difficult to understand how this attitude emerged. First of all, the old term "exile" (galut, goles), as we have seen, was loaded down with connotations of misery, persecution, and suffering to such an extent that it was considered inapplicable to the new situation that developed in the West in the wake of enlightenment, emancipation, and assimilation. The assimilationist German, French, or British Jews, enjoying full civil rights and rapidly advancing their political, economic, social, and cultural status as Germans, Frenchmen, or Englishmen, found it objectively improper and emotionally repugnant to refer to their community as the German, French, or British "exile." It so happened that in each of those countries there lived other groups as well who did not share the religion of the majority, and this circumstance made it easier for the Jews to consider themselves as but another of those religiously differentiated groups which were integral elements in the national body politic.

To to do so, and to have the gentiles accept them as German, French, or British citizens of the "Israelite" or "Mosaic" faith, the assimilationist Jews were willing to throw overboard almost everything that in the past had given substance and sustenance, content and contentment to Jewish life. The special Jewish

37

languages were abandoned, Jewish mannerisms were carefully brought under control, the Jewish apparel was discarded, the traditional Jewish fashion of wearing one's beard and hair was given up, the ghetto was evacuated, and the study of the Law was discontinued. For all this, gentile equivalents were substituted, in addition to which gentile occupations, formerly closed to Jews, were eagerly adopted.

The result was that from the early nineteenth century on, an increasing number of Jews in the West were convinced that they had, in fact, become full Germans, Frenchmen, Englishmen, or Americans, with the Jewish faith remaining the only differentiating factor between them and other segments of the population. Religion itself was something that they were not (or were not yet, as the case may be) ready to give up, although they were willing, even in the religious field, to introduce reforms calculated to bring their own Judaism in line with the various Christian religions. Their fond belief was that after the introduction of these reforms their religion, while retaining what they considered the "essence" of Judaism, would, as to outward appearances, differ from any Christian church to no greater degree than did the various Christian denominations among themselves.

Assimilationist Reform Jewish leaders were especially sensitive to the impression Jewish synagogue worship made on the gentiles. They looked at the old-established Jewish conduct of services and the traditional Jewish behavior in the synagogue with imaginary gentile eyes, and, finding them ridiculous, decided to eliminate them. Thus Rabbi Isaac M. Wise (1819–1900), who did more for the establishment of Reform Judaism in America than any other Jewish spiritual leader, stated in 1854 that one of the basic principles of Reform was that "Whatever makes us ridiculous before the world as it now is, may safely be and should be abolished."[1] In the same year, Max Lilienthal (1814–1882), another leading Reform rabbi, wrote: "Reform has tried and tries to raise the dignity of our worship. No one will deny that the worship as conducted in the old synagogues is unsatisfactory. . . . How many prayers are there unbecoming the country we live in . . . ?"[2] Lilienthal, incidentally, arrived in

38

America in 1845; his Americanization must have been rapid indeed to lead him within nine years to the conclusion that "many prayers are . . . unbecoming" to America and must therefore be discarded.

The desire to achieve decorum and dignity of the French variety motivated the *Union Israélite Liberale* to declare, in a manifesto issued in response to the official separation of Church and State passed by the French legislature in 1905, that the Union was "persuaded of the necessity of placing the external forms of worship and the methods of religious instruction in more complete harmony with modern conditions of existence, knowledge, and conscience. . . ."[3]

For Jews of this ilk exile could not, and indeed did not, exist any longer. What did exist was the undeniable (and, for many assimilationist Jews, uncomfortable) circumstance that there were Jewish communities scattered all over the world, that there were Jews of many different citizenships and nationalities, and that sizable Jewish population aggregates in the East were considered by the majority populations and governments of the countries in which they dwelt as national minorities. Moreover, these Eastern Jewries themselves insisted on being considered as, and accorded the status of, national minorities, a point of view that the assimilationist Western Jews were simply unable to understand. The existence of these "unfortunate co-religionists" (as they would be referred to) in backward or reactionary countries on the pale of the civilized world tended to constitute a disturbing element in the picture the assimilationist Western Jews liked to paint of the Jewish dispersion for their gentile neighbors. Nevertheless, all individuals who followed the Jewish religion and who were organized into religious congregations all over the world were considered by the assimilationist Western Jews as members of a purely religious community to which they applied the term Diaspora.

Now "Diaspora," as we have seen, is a designation whose Hebrew equivalents have been employed, albeit rarely, ever since Biblical times. The very fact that the term was used but infrequently indicates that it was not felt to be sufficiently expressive of the quality of Jewish dispersion—namely, the

39

misery and suffering connoted in the term "exile"—as if the feeling had always been present that, whenever reference was being made to the scattered state of the Jewish people, the proper thing to do was to designate it clearly and unmistakably for what it was: exile. In addition, the difference in the theological-historical connotation of the two terms, also referred to above, played a part in the preference for the term "exile"; although the scattering of the Jews among the nations of the world was originally a divinely ordained punishment, the condition of exile, which has continued far beyond God's original intention, was due to the unrelenting gentile hatred of Israel. The Jews were in exile, which is a part of the human scheme of things, not in Diaspora which is (or, better: originally was) a part of the divine scheme.

It was precisely these very same connotations of the term "Diaspora" that made it more palatable to Reform Jews and induced them to accept it and use it to the total exclusion of "exile." When they spoke of the Jewish Diaspora they felt that the term did not imply in the least that the dispersion was a condition for which the nations of the world were responsible in any way. It did not contain even the faintest hint that the Jews might or could be dissatisfied with their condition as citizens of their respective countries. And it readily lent itself to the characteristic Reform-Jewish reinterpretation to the effect that it was God's will that the Jews should live in the lands of their disperion in order to fulfill the great mission of Judaism: to teach pure faith and morality to the nations of the world.

Mission versus Messiah

The logical correlates of pouring away the bitter cup of the exile and replacing it with the heady wine of Judaism's global mission were the flat denial of Jewish peoplehood and the emphatic rejection of both the Messianic expectation and the hope for a return to Zion. A very few examples will suffice to show how these Reform ideas were formulated on both sides of the Atlantic.

Most characteristic was a resolution adopted at the 1871 Augsburg Synod of Reform rabbis from Germany, Austria, Hungary, Galicia, and Switzerland (a total of fifty-two delegates), which stated that:

> the old Jewish political existence had passed altogether and the Jews were incorporated in the modern nationalities. . . . In the view of modern Judaism the destruction of Jerusalem was the end of the preparatory national existence of the Jews and the beginning of their larger mission as missionaries of the truth of the One God in all parts of the earth whither they were scattered. . . . Although we have long since been comforted for the destruction of Jerusalem, although we entertain no longer the wish to return to Palestine to found our own state, since we are citizens of our fatherland, and love it with all our heart and all our might, still, the first and second destructions of Jerusalem were sad events which cost so many lives and led our people into captivity; let the memory thereof be sacred to us. . . . The universalistic prophetic teachings of the faith . . . stand out all the more clearly since the fortunes of the religion are no longer bound up with the petty politics of a small country.[4]

More than a decade earlier, in 1860, an American Reform rabbi, Samuel Adler (1809–1891), stated that "the first and most important step for such a [Reform] congregation to take is to free its service of shocking lies. . . . Such are, the lamentation about oppression and persecution, the petition for the restoration of the sacrificial cult, for the return of Israel to Palestine, the hope for a personal Messiah, and for the resurrection of the body. . . ."[5]

In 1869 the Reform rabbis of the eastern United States convened a conference in Philadelphia and adopted a number of principles that were to guide the Reform movement. Among them was the following:

> We look upon the destruction of the second Jewish commonwealth not as a punishment for the sinfulness of Israel, but as a result of the divine purpose revealed to Abraham, which . . . consists in the dispersion of the Jews to all parts of the earth, for the realization of their high priestly mission, to lead the nations to the true knowledge and worship of God.[6]

41

Similar sentiments were voiced by the 1885 Pittsburgh Conference of American Reform rabbis:

> We consider ourselves no longer a nation but a religious community, and therefore expect neither a return to Palestine, nor a sacrificial worship under the sons of Aaron, nor the restoration of any of the laws concerning the Jewish State.[7]

In 1907 David Philipson, historian of the Jewish Reform movement, summarized the Reform point of view as follows: "If the reform movement teaches anything clearly, it is the repudiation of the political and national aspects of traditional Judaism and the clear declaration that Judaism is a religion with a religious mission. . . ."[8]

As a last example, let me recall to memory a personal experience of many years ago. In the summer of 1936, after having lived for more than three years in Jerusalem and obtained my Ph.D. degree from the Hebrew University, I returned for a few months to my native Hungary in order to sit for the final exams at the Francis Joseph National Rabbinical Seminary in Budapest and to be ordained as a rabbi. At the ordination ceremony, held that fall at the Seminary's synagogue, there was only one other candidate in addition to myself, my friend and colleague, Dr. István Molnár, who a few years later was among the hundreds of thousands of Jews killed by the Germans and their Hungarian henchmen. In the course of the ceremony it was customary for one of the candidates to express his thanks to the school and its masters, to vow efforts to follow in their footsteps, and the like. Of the two of us I was chosen to deliver the brief peroration. Although the Seminary at the time was headed by Professor Michael Guttmann, the famous Talmudic scholar, and it was he who conferred on us the traditional rabbinical *s'mikha* (ordination), the main address at the ceremony was given by Dr. Simon Hevesi, Chief Rabbi of the Jewish Community of Pest, a professor at the Seminary, and the most influential member of its board. A few days before the ceremony, Chief Rabbi Hevesi asked me to show him the text of my speech, and I took my prepared one-page manuscript to his apartment. He read it, then reached for a pen, inserted a half-sentence, asked me to read it, and made me promise that I would not skip it when delivering my speech. I have long since forgotten everything I said in my painstakingly composed short address, but I still remember *verbatim* the Chief Rabbi's emendation: ". . . living in our faith, we shall love the fatherland into which God implanted us and work for its weal. . . ." This feeling—that Magyar patriotism came above everything else in the life of Hungarian Jewry—remained characteristic of the spirit of most Hungarian Jews in the precarious years from Hitler's rise to power in neighboring Germany until well after the entry of Hungary into World War II as a German satellite. Incidentally, Court Councillor Samu Stern, President of the Israelite Community of Pest and of the National Bureau of Hungarian Israelites, was also present at that ordination ceremony, and addressed the gathering echoing the same sentiments.

The remarkable thing is that on both sides of the Atlantic Reform Jewish leaders felt it necessary to couple their patriotic fervor with the outright rejection of all historical and emotional connection with Zion. This feeling resulted in such pronouncements as the one made by a "minister" at the dedication services of the Reform Temple in Charleston, North Carolina, on March 19, 1841: "This country is our Palestine, this city our Jerusalem, this house of God our temple."[9]

In accordance with these sentiments, resolutions were passed by several Reform conferences to the effect that all references to a return to Zion, to the Messianic hope, to the rebuilding of the Temple of Jerusalem, and to Jewish peoplehood must be excised from the prayer books printed for and used by Reform congregations. The elimination of these traditional Jewish elements was considered so important that David Philipson, the historian of the Reform movement, singled it out as the greatest accolade in describing the prayer book of the Jewish Religious Union of England (revised edition, London, 1903), which, he stated, was "like the most advanced reform Prayer-Books; all petitions for a return to Palestine, a restoration of the Jewish State, and re-institution of the sacrificial worship are excluded."[10]

An Expurgated Prayer Book

A closer look at the *Union Prayerbook for Jewish Worship,*

edited and published by the (Reform) Central Conference of American Rabbis, is most instructive in this respect. In its newly revised edition, published in Cincinnati in 1942, not only are all references to a hope for a return to Zion and all supplications for a rebuilding of Jerusalem carefully excised, but the very names Zion and Jerusalem have been consistently deleted, with one or two exceptions where the names appear in Biblical quotations of a purely historical or theological connotation.[11]

But the editors of the *Union Prayerbook* went even farther in their rejection of the traditional Jewish claim of the chosenness of Israel. Even when they retained a traditional Hebrew prayer, they changed its translation almost beyond recognition. For instance, on page 13 one finds the prayer *Ahavat 'Olam* which, in literal translation, says in part: "With eternal love hast Thou loved the house of Israel Thy people. . . . And Thou shalt not remove from us Thy love for ever and ever. Blessed art Thou, O Lord, who lovest Thy people Israel." This has been paraphrased in the English translation of the *Union Prayerbook* (p. 12) to read: "Infinite as is Thy power, even so is Thy love. Thou didst manifest it through Israel, Thy people. . . . O that Thy love may never depart from our hearts. Praised be Thou, O Lord, who hast revealed Thy love through Israel." We note that, according to the translation-paraphrase of the *Union Prayerbook,* God no longer loves Israel, but merely "manifests" His love "through Israel." Even the request that God shall not remove His love from Israel forever is turned around in the translation, which asks God that His love "may never depart from our hearts."

This example of spiritual Bowdlerization can be multiplied indefinitely. On page 15 the Hebrew text says: "and we are Israel, His people." No trace is left of these words in the translation. On page 17 the Hebrew text praises God "Who performed miracles for us in Egypt, signs and wonders in the land of the children of Ham, and brought out His people Israel from among them to eternal freedom . . . and Moses and the children of Israel accepted willingly His kingship. . . ." In the *Union Prayerbook*'s English paraphrase this has become "Thy love has watched over us in the night of oppression; Thy mercy has sustained us in the hour of trial. And now that we live in a land of freedom . . . may Thy law rule the life of all Thy children. . . ." We note the careful omission of the key words: "miracles," "Egypt," "Ham," "Israel," "Moses," "kingship," without which the prayer loses its historical connotations.

The unmistakable general tendency of the *Union Prayerbook,* especially in its English paraphrase of Hebrew prayers, is to underplay any special relationship between God and Israel, to make the Jews assume the role of spokesmen for all humanity, and to direct prayers to God in this capacity only. For instance, on page 125 the following Hebrew prayer appears (in my literal English translation): "Rock of Israel! Arise to help Israel! Redeem us, O Lord of Hosts! His name is the Holy One of Israel! Blessed art Thou, O Lord, who redeemest Israel!" In the *Union Prayerbook*'s English version (p. 124) this has become: "O Rock of Israel, redeem those who are oppressed and deliver those who are persecuted. Praised be Thou, our Redeemer, the Holy One of Israel." The original prayer asks God to redeem Israel; the English version asks Him to redeem all those who are oppressed. The Jewish national-historical intent of the prayer has been changed to a general universalistic and humanistic one.

Even where a reference to Biblical history has been allowed to remain in the English version, it is turned into a mere introductory clause preceding the main point, which is made to apply to all humanity: "As Thou hast saved Israel from Egyptian bondage, so mayest Thou send Thy help to all who are oppressed" (p. 122). The second half of the sentence has no basis at all in the Hebrew original of the prayer. Another such invented addition in the same prayer is: "May the righteous of all nations rejoice in Thy grace and triumph by Thy power" (p. 122).

By means of such devices the *Union Prayerbook* actually succeeds in transforming the Jewish synagogue service from a familial colloquy between the Children of Israel and God their Father—which was its character throughout Jewish history—into a formal audience in which the Jewish worshipers appear before the Lord in their capacity of a self-appointed delegation to present to Him the petitions of all mankind.[12]

All this presents a view of Israel and the world that is diametrically opposed to the traditional Jewish outlook. The

45

traditional view of the Diaspora was (and, as we shall see below, has remained to this day, at least in theory) a deeply negative one: it was a misfortune, a calamity, a misery. It was *Galut*, exile. The new assimilationist Reform attitude, in contrast, considered the dispersion a condition brought about by God, not in order to punish Israel for its sins, but in order to manifest, to the Jews as well as to the world, the chosenness of Israel. God dispersed Israel in the world because He chose Israel to spread the knowledge of God among the nations and to teach them the lofty ethical ideas that He had revealed to the Hebrews, through their great prophets and teachers.

This ingenious combination of Mission and Diaspora made it possible for Reform Judaism to discard all national or Palestine-centered aspects of Jewish religion. The Jews who felt thoroughly at home in Germany, France, England, or America did not want to pray for a return to Zion. That was suited to, or even necessary for, Jews who were, in the past or at present, persecuted and oppressed, but not "us." The Russian, Polish, or Rumanian Jews, and likewise the Jews in various Arab and Muslim lands, were treated by the gentiles as strangers, as a foreign element in the body politic; because of this, and only because of this, they *were* strangers and foreigners in countries in which they had lived for hundreds of years. Not so in our own country, the Reform Jews felt; here we are at home, here we are as indigenous as any other segment of the population. With unexceptionable consistency, this was what they expressed in their conferences and resolutions, prayer books and sermons, social and charitable organizations. And this, they assumed or hoped, was how the gentiles in the land could be persuaded to consider them and feel about them.

In this manner, for the first time in Jewish history, assimilationism introduced a fragmentation into the community of Israel. In the eyes of the assimilationist Jews, the Jewish people was no more. The Jews, dispersed in the far corners of the world, now consisted, first of all, of two major categories: Jews who still suffered disabilities (mainly in Eastern Europe and the Middle East), and who therefore still had to fight for integration into the nations among whom they dwelt; and the Jews who had already achieved such integration. The latter, again, were divided into numerous communities, each with its own nationality. The only connecting link among the Jews of various nationalities was their religion. In this view the relationship between, say, German Jews and British Jews was the same in essence as that between German Catholics and British Catholics. And just as German Catholics or British Catholics would never dream of praying to God for a "return to Rome," although both acknowledged Rome as their spiritual center, so it was absurd for German Jews or British Jews to pray for a "return to Zion," even though Zion was the ancient spiritual center of Judaism.

This classic Reform Jewish position on Israel and the world and on the question of Exile versus Diaspora—whether one agreed with it or not—was clearcut and logically consistent. The same issues, as we shall see anon, caused a quandary and a great deal of equivocation among the tradition-abiding Jewish sectors.

Reform Judaism, to recapitulate, went officially on record denying the existence of the exile, and followed up this theoretical decision by eliminating from its ritual all reference to those aspects of Jewish religion which were directly or indirectly related to the exile—mainly, the hope for the coming of the Messiah, whose advent in the traditional Jewish view was expected to put an end to the exile; the return to Zion, which in the traditional Jewish view would be tantamount to a liquidation of the exile; the restoration of worship in the Jerusalem Temple, the reestablishment of the rule of the House of David and the ingathering of the Jews in the Land of Israel—all hopes and yearnings derived from the unhappiness and misery of the exile.

The Conservative and Orthodox Stand

The Conservative and Orthodox branches of Judaism were barred from this radical solution by the very framework of their religious outlook. Committed to a preservation of the traditional values of Judaism, Conservative and Orthodox Jews considered the Messianic expectation, the hope and prayer for the Return and Restoration, and all the rest, inviolable tenets. Similarly, the commitment to a way of life in which the Tora (i.e., the traditional Jewish law) was central, its commandments unchangeable divine ordinances, and its study the greatest achievement, was for them an immutable value. From these premises it followed inevitably that Jewish life in countries outside the Land of Israel had to be considered exile. In these, as in many other respects, there are, of course, differences between Conservative and Orthodox Jews, but, by and large, both trends, and all shadings within the two, subscribe to these tenets, albeit with varying degrees of intensity and stringency.

Then there is the problem of this-worldly attainments. In this realm, too, the position of Reform Judaism is consistent: we, it says, are at home in this country. Therefore, like all the other population elements in it, we shall try to achieve in it whatever God allows us to achieve—to attain a good life, acquire education, obtain position, accumulate wealth, build educational, social, and charitable institutions, and contribute the best of our talents to the welfare, well-being, prosperity, and advancement of our country in all fields. Conservative and Orthodox Judaism, committed as they are to the tenet of exile, should, if they wished to be consistent, negate all this. A people in exile, a community awaiting "every day" the coming of the Messiah who will lead them back to the land of their fathers, should refrain from striking material roots in the soil of the country in which it happens to live for the moment, even if historic experience has shown that moment to stretch into centuries. How can a Jew in exile, waiting, hoping, and yearning for the Redeemer, build houses, furnish them luxuriously, enjoy rich food and sweet wine (both, of course, of the strictly kosher variety), wear expensive and elegant clothes, and surround himself with the countless other material appurtenances and technical appliances whose loud clatter drowns out whatever subdued and quiet crying over the exile one would still be inclined to indulge in? Yet the fact is that most Conservative and Orthodox Jews do engage in just as eager a pursuit of worldly goods and creature comforts as Reform Jews. Even such a truly devout and God-fearing Jewish group as the Skverer Hasidim actually built for themselves a village not far from New York City, which certainly is a strange way of translating into action their thrice-daily expressed expectation of the Messiah and the return to Zion.

While the inner contradiction between what Conservative and Orthodox Jews profess and what they do is too great to be explained away, as some of them have tried, it is not too difficult to understand the psychological mechanism that brings it about. One factor is the gap that so often in life separates theory from action, the ideal from the real. We know what we should do, but are simply unable to do it. "The spirit is willing but the flesh is weak."

Then there is the encumbrance anchored in the very nature of Tora-directed Judaism. Traditional Jewish religion was crystallized in Talmudic times into 613 commandments, falling into 365 prohibitions and 248 mandates. While the exact identification of the 613 commandments varies somewhat in the codes of different authorities (e.g. Maimonides, Nahmanides, Moses ben Jacob of Coucy, Isaac ben Joseph of Corbeil), they all agree that only the first of both the do's and the don't's pertain to matters of faith: one must know that God exists, and one must not believe in the existence of any but the one God. All the rest detail the things that a Jew must and must not *do*. While it is patently impossible even for the most saintly of men to observe all the 613 commandments, a truly religious Jew will try to do his best to fulfill as many of them as he can. Hence, the religious framework in which Orthodox (and, to a lesser extent, Conservative) Jews live and function requires an enormous amount of unflagging attention to these commandments. It goes without saying that, ideally, a religious Jew must at least know all the 613 by heart, and must, at every step and turn, be aware of the possible applicability of a "do" or a "don't." Nor is this all. Over and above the 613 commandments, there are numerous so-called *dinim* (rules), which prescribe, in the greatest possible detail, how one must behave and what one must do when awakening in the morning, how to wash one's hands, how to put on the *tzitzit* and the *t'fillin*, how to say the prayers, and so on. All this is certainly enough to exhaust the religious virtuosity of even the

most pious Jew. Then, in addition to the practical commandments and rules of conduct, there are tenets of credo to which a
traditional Jew must subscribe. These were summarized as the
"Thirteen Articles of Faith" by Maimonides, which contain
credal details as to God, the prophets, the Tora, and the
resurrection of the dead. The twelfth article concerns the Messiah and it says: "I believe with a perfect faith in the coming of
the Messiah, and even though he tarry, nevertheless I wait for
him every day that he come." This every religious Jew must
believe. But nowhere in the voluminous Jewish religious literature is it authoritatively stated what do's and don't's derive from
this article of faith. And since the hands of the latter-day
religious Jews are sufficiently full with trying to observe as
many of the 613 commandments and the innumerable rules and
obligatory customs as possible under the objectively unfavorable circumstances of an environment cloyed with a tech-
nological hypertrophy, they are neither able nor willing to
increase the weight of the "yoke of the commandments" still
further by searching out additional do's and don't's that would
logically derive from the Messianic belief. In particular, as far as
the improvement of one's material status is concerned, including the acquisition of worldly goods and the enjoyment of a
good life (always, of course, within the strict limits set by the
explicit commandments, rules, and customs), very rare indeed is
the Jew in any of the Diasporas, be he otherwise as observant as
possible, who will refrain from these mundane enticements
simply because good life and exile are mutually preclusive and
because one cannot wait every day for the coming of the
Messiah and at the same time lead a *bale-batish* ("landlordish,"
i.e., well-established) existence.

The Issue of Civil Liberties

When it comes to such political issues as equal rights and civil
liberties, the inconsistency in the Orthodox and Conservative
Jewish position is even more obvious. That secularist Jews
should fight for the improvement of their civil, political, social,
and economic condition is more than understandable, it is
inevitable. In fact, as early as the turn of the century the secular

50

Zionists in Central and Eastern Europe incorporated into their program the struggle for the strengthening of the Jewish position as a national minority. They knew that the realization of the primary Zionist goal, the establishment of a Jewish national home in Palestine, was a long way off, and they were realistic enough to figure that, even after the establishment of the Jewish home or state, a great many Jews will remain behind in the lands of their dispersion. Therefore they called for *Gegenwartsarbeit,* "work for the present," an endeavor they also termed *Realpolitik,* by which they meant efforts to secure and improve the position of the Jews within the political structures of the Diaspora countries.

As far as religious Reform Jews were concerned, it was likewise inevitable that they should engage in campaigns for equal rights and against all forms of social and economic discrimination as well as against anti-Semitism in general. Having subscribed to the doctrine that the Jews differed from the other population elements in every country only in their religion, they embarked upon a course of advocating untiringly the principle of separation of church and state, and the scrupulous adherence to it in practice.

It was, therefore, perfectly logical for "enlightened" Jews in Germany to establish, as early as 1893, an organization called *Central-Verein deutscher Staatsbürger jüdischen Glaubens* (Central Union of German Citizens of the Jewish Faith) whose task was "to rally the German citizens of the Jewish faith, without distinction as to religious and political trend, in order to strengthen them in the effective defense of their civil and social equality as well as in the unswerving fostering of German mentality." At the time Hitler came to power in Germany, more than half of all German Jews had subscribed to these aims and were affiliated with the *Central-Verein.*[13]

Similarly, it was completely consistent with their view of Judaism and the relationship between Jews and gentiles that American Reform Jews, and modern, culturally assimilated Jews who have retained Jewish interests and a Jewish consciousness, should establish organizations whose primary purpose can be broadly defined as the improvement of the Jewish position in America and elsewhere.

51

This position was most clearly expressed by the American Jewish Committee (founded in 1906), which to this day is one of the most influential Jewish organizations in the United States and has a heavy preponderance of the Reform Jewish element in both its membership and leadership. Its aims, as described in its own publication, the *American Jewish Year Book* (1968), are:

Seeks to prevent infraction of the civil and religious rights of Jews in any part of the world and to secure equality of economic, social and educational opportunity through education and civic action; seeks to broaden understanding of the basic nature of prejudice and to improve techniques for combating it; promotes a philosophy of Jewish integration by projecting a balanced view with respect to full participation in American life and retention of Jewish identity.[14]

It is a common characteristic of many of these Jewish organizations that they do not wish to appear "too Jewish" in the sense of working exclusively for the benefit of the Jews. They therefore include into their general statements of aims two purposes: [1] Jewish and [2] general American or humanitarian. These twofold aims are clearly expressed in the aforementioned official description of the purposes of the American Jewish Committee. Similarly, the American Jewish Congress describes itself as an organization that "works [1] to foster the creative religious and cultural survival of the Jewish people; to help Israel develop in peace, freedom and security; [2] to eliminate all forms of racial and religious bigotry; to advance civil rights, protect civil liberties, defend religious freedom and safeguard the separation of church and state."

The Anti-Defamation League of B'nai B'rith "seeks [1] to combat antisemitism and [2] to secure justice for all citizens alike . . . [and] to achieve greater democratic understanding among Americans."

The Coordinating Board of Jewish Organizations conducts activities "[1] with respect to advancing and protecting the status, rights and interests of Jews [2] as well as related matters bearing upon the human rights of peoples."

The Jewish Labor Committee "seeks [1] to combat antisemitism and [2] racial and religious intolerance abroad and in the

U.S. . . . [It][1] aids Jewish and [2] non-Jewish labor institutions overseas; aids victims of oppression and persecution."

The Jewish War Veterans of the United States of America "seeks . . . [2] to combat bigotry and [1] to prevent or stop defamation of Jews. . . ."

The World Jewish Congress "seeks [1] to secure and safeguard the rights, status, and interests of Jews and Jewish communities throughout the world, within [2] the framework of an international effort to secure human rights everywhere without discrimination. . . ."

While it is clear that aim [2] of these and similar organizations is merely subsidiary or supplementary, its inclusion in the general statement of aims serves the important purpose of precluding the reproach of Jewish clannishness or ethnocentrism: one way of striving for the betterment of the Jewish position in America is to demonstrate, on an organizational level, the Jewish interest in the general American welfare.

In contrast to the position of the assimilated Reform Jews who seek "a philosophy of Jewish integration" in everything except religion, the maintenance of preservation of which they consider a "right," the position of the Conservative and Orthodox Jews on Jewish civil rights is beset by a deep internal inconsistency. Conservative and Orthodox Jews, as we have seen, continue to subscribe to the age-old Jewish tradition that considers the sojourn of the Jews in any country outside of the Land of Israel as exile. That tradition requires the Jew to hope and pray for the end of the exile, and to expect "daily" the coming of the Messiah who will put an end to the exile and will lead the Jewish people back to the holy land of their fathers. Yet the same Conservative and Orthodox Jews also fight for civil rights, either on their own or in conjunction with their Reform co-religionists, and they either close their eyes to, or actually remain unaware of, the incompatibility of their prayers and their acts. The fact is that Conservative and Orthodox Jews are just (or almost) as active in the present-day version of Jewish *Gegenwartsarbeit* as the Reform Jews. Thus, for instance, the Rabbinical Alliance of America, an organization of Orthodox rabbis, "seeks to elevate the position of Orthodox rabbis nationally, and to defend the welfare of Jews the world over." The Agudath Israel of America, Inc., an extreme Orthodox organization, "seeks to organize religious Jewry in the Orthodox spirit, and in that spirit to solve all problems facing Jewry in the United States, Israel, and the world-over." The National Council of Young Israel seeks "the advancement and perpetuation of traditional, Torah-true Judaism" among American Jewish youth. There is even a National Jewish Commission on Law and Public Affairs (founded in 1965) whose purpose is to "provide legal and legislative services to Orthodox Jewish organizations and individuals." These and similar efforts to improve the position of Orthodox Jews in a Diaspora country only make sense if sojourn in that country is tacitly recognized as a permanent or lasting condition. All this is certainly a far cry from the view of Rabbi Moses Sopher (Schreiber, 1763–1839), the great Talmudic authority of Pressburg, whom Orthodox Jews to this day consider as one of their guiding spirits, and who warned even against building houses in the lands of the exile lest it seem as despairing of redemption.[15]

The position, then, of secularist and Reform Jews on the question of the Jewish exile is one of flat denial: for them exile exists neither in theory nor in sentiment nor in reality. For Orthodox and Conservative Jews, exile does exist in theory and in tradition; in actual reality, however, their posture, their way of life, their attitude to the mundane, and their unceasing efforts to acquire all the trappings of modern Western civilization (within the limits of what they considered consonant with the *halakha,* the traditional Jewish religious law) bespeak a permanent rootedness in the realities of their temporal environment, or, as Moses Sopher put it, a "despairing of redemption."

A quarter of a century after Hitler, the reality of exile no longer exists for the majority of the Jews in the modern Western world. A minority still pays lip service to its old, traditional concept, while blithely living the life of non-exile. And even the small groups of Zionists who make the move of returning to the Jewish state, do so, not because they feel they are in exile in the countries of their birth, but because they want to share in the fullest Jewish life which, they feel, can exist only in the Land of Israel.

4

THE JEWISH "RACE"

What Is a Race?

For thousands of years little or no distinction has been made between human aggregates whose members shared such culturally determined and transmitted common features as occupation, religion, or language, and other human groups in whom the common element was due to the genetic fact of common descent. Josephus Flavius, for instance, writing in the first century CE, refers to the prophets as a "tribe."[1] The term "race," too, has been used so persistently in this nonbiological sense that even today one finds among the various definitions of the word given in *Webster's New World Dictionary, College Edition* (1966), the following: "Any group of people having the same activities, habits, ideas, etc.: as, the race of dramatists."

In the following discussion the term "race" will definitely not be used in anything like this sense. It will be employed in its modern scientific-biological meaning only: in this sense, *race is a population that differs from others in the incidence of certain genes.* The genes inherited from the parents are the basic determinants of the physical form of the offspring, although the latter is also modified to some extent by environmental influences. In general, it is more convenient to study the racial characteristics of a population by observing, measuring, classifying, etc., the visible varieties of its bodily form rather than its invisible, submicroscopic genes.

The Views

The study of human races has been rendered more difficult by the unscientific use to which nineteenth- and twentieth-century racists have put the race concept. Their primary interest in classifying mankind into races and describing racial differences

55

was to establish the existence of superior and inferior races within the human family. No people has been singled out as consistently as the Jewish for description as an inferior race by such nineteenth-century racists as Eugen Karl Dühring, Houston Stewart Chamberlain, Count Arthur de Gobineau, Vacher de Lapouge, and others,[2] and certainly in the case of no other people have these poisonous theories served as the basis for a state-sponsored systematic genocide like the one carried out by the Nazis against the Jews.

Racism apart, legitimate scholarship has in the last hundred years paid a great deal of attention to the problem of the Jewish race. The question whether or not the Jewish people constitute a race has been tackled literally by hundreds of physical anthropologists, whose findings can be grouped into four headings.[3]

1. There are those who maintain that the Jews constitute one single race. This view usually goes hand in hand with the assumption of the historical permanence and immutability of the Jewish racial character. Several reputable physical anthropologists subscribed to this view, among them Johann Friedrich Blumenbach, Josiah Clark Nott, Paul Broca, Friedrich Anton Heller von Hellwald, Paul Topinard, Richard Andree, Madison Grant, as well as Jewish scholars such as Joseph Jacobs, J. M. Judt, Arkadi Danilowich Elkind, and Ignacz Zollschan. In complete disregard of the easily observable differences between, say, Eastern European and Arabian Jewish features, the adherents of this view claimed, in Zollschan's words, that "the main features of the Jewish type reappear with the same clarity in every geographical longitude and latitude. . . . Even such important indices as hair and eye color are identical," which proves "the racial homogeneity of all major parts of the Jewish people. . . ."[4]

2. The second view, that the Jews comprise two distinct races or racial types, is held by Karl Vogt, G. Lagneau, M. Boudin, A. Weisbach, B. Blechman, Isidor Kopernicki, J. Majer, J. Deniker, F. Wagenseil, Hans F. K. Günther, Erwin Baur, Eugen Fischer, Fritz Lenz, Sigmund Feist, J. D. Brutzkus, Carleton S. Coon, and others. This view maintains that the Sephardi Jews constitute one race, in which much of the original Mediterranean character of the ancient Palestinian Jews has been preserved,

while the Ashkenazi Jews form another race, which shows, as Coon put it, "both a blending and a re-combination of Palestinian Mediterranean features with those of the populations among whom their ancestors have, for over two millenniums, lived on European soil."[5]

3. The third view holds that there are no less than three racial components in the Jewish people. This is the position of K. N. Ikoff (or Ikow), G. Lagneau (after he modified his earlier view), F. von Luschan, Fritz Kahn, Arthur Ruppin, Jan Czeckanowski, and others. The characterizations of the three Jewish races given by adherents of this view differ greatly, as do the Diasporas they assign to each of the three. Ruppin called them Babylonian, Sephardi, and Ashkenazi;[6] Czekanowski termed them Sephardi, Ashkenazi, and Caucasian-Armenian.[7]

4. The fourth view maintains that the Jews are not a race, nor do they comprise two or three racial groups. Interestingly, this view was put forward earlier than any of the other three, by the French traveler François-Maximilien Misson (1650–1722) after an extensive tour of several European countries. Both he and Georges Louis Le Clerc, Comte de Buffon (1707–1788), who followed him, argued that the Jews look in every country like the non-Jews. The same argument was put forth by Samuel Stanhope Smith (1750–1819), an early president of Princeton University, James Cowles Prichard (1786–1848), an English ethnologist and physician, as well as by the anthropologists Friedrich Ratzel, William Z. Ripley, Maurice Fishberg, Franz Boas, Roland B. Dixon, Eugene Pittard, Ernest A. Hooton, Louis L. Snyder, Carl C. Seltzer, Melville Jacobs, Alfred Kroeber, and Ashley Montague, and by experts from related and other fields, such as Karl Kautsky, Julian S. Huxley, A. C. Haddon, and Ellsworth Huntington. The conclusion of this school of thought can best be summed up by quoting two of its foremost exponents. Kroeber stated: "The Jews everywhere considerably approximate the local gentile type. . . . Normally a part of any Jewish population is physically indistinguishable, by measures or by observation, from the Christians or the Mohammedans of the same area. . . ."[8] And Montague concluded: "The fact is that there is not now nor was there ever a Jewish race. . . ."[9]

When one is faced with such a variety of contradictory views on the question of the Jewish race, several of them held by highly reputable, and indeed outstanding, anthropologists, the only path one can follow in an attempt to form an independent judgment is to collect, classify, present, and interpret as much factual evidence as is available. In doing so we shall present three sets of data from three widely disparate disciplines: historical, anthropometric, and serological.

THE HISTORICAL RECORD   Before turning to the anthropometric and serological evidence, let us throw a cursory glance at what the historical record has to say on the racial identity of the Jews. In doing so we must keep in mind that a (hypothetical) pure race is an isolated group which does not interbreed with other such groups. Only in such a group is the incidence of certain genes constant, and only in such a group can one, therefore, expect to find, throughout a historic period, the same range of bodily form, distributed along the same frequency curve.

Have the Jews, or their early ancestors, the Biblical Hebrews, ever been such a group? Scarcely, since it is known that, beginning with their first appearance on the stage of history, they received gene flows of varying intensity from other populations. That the Biblical Hebrews were the descendants of a mixed Amorite and Hittite ancestry was generally known, and the Prophet Ezekiel (who flourished in the early sixth century BCE) alludes to it in a brief reference as one does to a patent fact which requires no elaboration.[10] The Hittites were an Anatolian people who are shown in extant pictorial or sculptural representations as similar to the modern Armenoid type. As to the Amorites, the original meaning of their name, according to Professor N. H. Tur-Sinai, was "tall men," which indicates that they appeared to the Hebrews as a tall race as compared to themselves.[11] The Amorites were the original inhabitants of Canaan, the two names Amorite and Canaanite appearing interchangeably in Biblical usage.

Abraham himself, the traditional first ancestor of the Hebrews, was an Aramaean, and is so termed in the Bible.[12] His son Isaac married the daughter of Betuel the Aramaean, a close

58

kinsman of Abraham.[13] Isaac's son Jacob married the two daughters of Laban the Aramaean, his mother's brother.[14] Jacob's daughter Dinah was raped or seduced by Shechem ben Hamor, the Hivite prince of the city of Shechem, and although this led to a bloody revenge on the part of Jacob's sons,[15] according to later Jewish tradition Asenath, the daughter born out of this union to Dinah, was spared by Jacob, and ultimately became the wife of Joseph.[16] Also, according to Jewish tradition, after the killing of the Shechemites, the sons of Jacob took to wife the virgins whom they had spared.[17]

The Bible itself contains no information as to whom the sons of Jacob married, except in the case of one of the marriages of Judah: he married the daughter of a Canaanite named Shua.[18] He had three sons by her, and took Tamar, presumably also a Canaanite woman, as a wife for Er, his firstborn. Ultimately this Tamar became the mother of Judah's sons Perez and Zerah,[19] the first of whom became the ancestor of King David. By the time Jacob went down to Egypt with his family, each of his sons had offspring of his own.[20] Their wives, who were the mothers of these children, must have been Canaanite women: there is no reason to assume that Judah's marriage to a Canaanite woman was an exception; nor were other than Canaanite women available in the land of Canaan.

We do not know how much intermarriage took place between Egyptians and the children of Israel during Israel's sojourn in Egypt, but by the very nature of such a situation one must assume that some interbreeding occurred. Joseph himself, according to the Biblical account, married Asenath, the daughter of Poti-phera, priest of On.[21] His two sons, Ephraim and Manasseh,[22] were, therefore, racially half-Egyptians, while the sons of his eleven brothers were racially half-Canaanites.

Even before the Exodus, Moses married a Midianite woman and subsequently a Cushite woman.[23] These could not have been isolated instances of outgroup marriage; in fact, a union initiated between Zimri ben Salu, an Israelite prince, and Cozbi bat Zur, a Midianite princess, resulted in the death of both, at the hands of a zealous young priest, Phinchas, the grandson of Aaron.[24]

The offspring of Egyptian men and Israelite women, occasionally at least, were brought up by their mothers' families and joined the children of Israel when the latter left Egypt.[25] At a later time, legal provisions were made concerning the acceptance of the descendants of Egyptians and Edomites into the Israelite community: "The children of the third generation that are born unto them may enter into the assembly of the Lord."[26] Legal provisions were made also as to the circumstances in which an Israelite was allowed to marry a woman captured from the enemy: after letting her "bewail her father and her mother a full month," he could marry her.[29] Considering the long state of intermittent warfare that existed between the tribes of Israel and the Canaanites and other inhabitants of Palestine and the immediate vicinity, one must assume that this law merely gave religio-legal sanction to a practice in which the people of Israel had engaged for many generations, and which resulted in a considerable gene flow into the Israelite gene pool.

Individual cases of outgroup marriage come to our notice only when the protagonists involved were people of exceptional importance. Thus we are told about Uriah the Hittite, an officer in King David's army, who lived with his wife in the immediate vicinity of the royal palace.[28] The words and behavior of this Uriah clearly show that he had become totally assimilated to the Israelite nation and religion.[29] David also had other Hittite officers in his army.[30]

King Solomon married ("loved") many foreign women: "women of the Moabites, Ammonites, Edomites, Zidonians, and Hittites."[31] This royal example could not have failed to influence the court and other people as well. In other words, in the heyday of the Hebrew monarchy the Hebrew gene pool must have received a considerable gene flow from Canaanites and neighboring peoples. At the same time, remnants of the Amorites, Hittites, Perizzites, Hivites, and Jebusites still lived among or near the Hebrews,[32] which must have resulted in still more gene flow. After David's subjugation of Moab and Edom[33] and other population elements, such as the Keretites and Peletites,[34] the natural course of events was that the victors took concubines from among the women of the vanquished, and the offspring of such unions became part of the Hebrew population.

Intermarriage with the Moabites occurred long before the days of David; in fact, David himself was the descendant of such a marriage between an Israelite man and a Moabite woman,[35] Boaz and Ruth, whose son was Obed, whose son was Yishai, whose son was David.[36] Such marriages continued long after David. Among the palace servants of King Joash (836–798 BCE) were the sons of a Moabite woman and an Ammonite woman, whose fathers presumably were Judaeans.[37] These conditions continued after the return from the Babylonian Captivity, when the Judaeans intermarried with Ashdodite, Ammonite, and Moabite women, with the result that "their children spoke half in the speech of Ashdod and could not speak in the Jews' language, but according to the language of each people."[38] Even the son of Eliashib the high priest married a Horonite girl.[39] Men of Tyre dwelt among the Jews in Jerusalem.[40] Under the influence of Nehemiah, the Jews "separated from Israel all the alien mixture."[41] The book of Ezra contains long lists of those Jewish priestly men and Levites who had "married foreign women of the peoples of the land."[42] We are not told, at least not clearly, what happened to the children of these mixed marriages after their fathers "put away their wives,"[43] but in all probability, descent being reckoned patrilineally, the children remained members of the Jewish community and their genes thus entered the Jewish pool.

The legal reflection of a contrary situation which developed mainly after the Roman Exile—namely, the violation and impregnation of Jewish women by foreign conquerors, invaders, armies, bands, or marauders—was the Talmudic law that the child of mixed parentage follows the religion of its mother. In this manner the offspring of such unions was recognized as belonging to the Jewish people.[44]

Following the end of the Hebrew monarchies (the fall of Israel in 721 BCE and of Judah in 586 BCE) and even more during the period of the Second Commonwealth and after its destruction in 70 CE, conversion of individuals and groups to Judaism became, if not frequent, at least not exceptional. The documentary record of such events is far from complete, because, as a rule, only the conversion of outstanding individuals left its traces in the sands of history. Thus we know that the famous

Talmudic teacher Rabbi Meir was a convert (second century CE), as was the Edomite family of Herod the Great in the first century BCE. These and many more such conversions are part of recorded history. How many others converted in Egypt, Greece, Rome, and later in Europe we do not know, but whether known or unknown, their genes flowed into the Jewish gene pool and became a contributing factor in the racial picture of the Jews.

In Arabia in the centuries preceding the emergence of Islam (622 CE, the year of the Hegira), parts of the population converted to Judaism. In Southern Arabia this movement culminated in the rule of the Jewish king Dhu Nuwas in the sixth century.

In Central Asia in the eighth century the king of the Khazars converted with an unknown number of his subjects. In the seventeenth century a considerable proportion of the Transylvanian Sabbatarians became Jewish, as did smaller groups in subsequent centuries in many parts of the world.

As this rapid enumeration shows, there was frequent gene flow from the non-Jewish environment into the Jewish gene pool. In view of this, on purely historical grounds, a considerable variability must be expected in the physical types found among the Jews. One will expect, moreover, appreciable differences between the modal physical type in those Jewish populations which were exposed to gene flows from widely differing non-Jewish races.

Let us now turn to the anthropometric and serological data to see whether, whenever and wherever Jewish groups were measured, the results of such measurement can form the basis of a definite conclusion concerning the question of Jewish racial identity. In particular, two types of data will be presented: the cephalic index and the ABO blood group percentages. The reason for confining ourselves to these two categories of data is simply this: a much larger amount of information is available on the cephalic index and the ABO blood groups than on any other anthropological measurement.

THE CEPHALIC INDEX   The cephalic index is obtained by measuring the maximum width of the head from a point over

62

one ear to the opposite point over the other ear, then measuring the maximum length of the head from a point on the middle of the forehead between, or slightly above, the eyebrows to a point on the occiput (the back part of the head). The width is then divided by the length and the result multiplied by one hundred. Among the great majority of adult humans the cephalic index ranges from 70 to 85. It has been observed (on the basis of hundreds of thousands of measurements) that each human race has a particular range of cephalic indices. The characteristic range of the Mediterranean race is from 70 to 75: the true Mediterraneans are dolichocephalic or long-headed—the width of their heads does not exceed three fourths (75 percent) of its length. If a human group has an index range of 75–80, it is called mesocephalic or medium-headed; if it ranges from 80 upward, it is brachycephalic, or broad-headed.

Elsewhere[45] I have gathered all the data I could obtain on the cephalic indices of the Jews and compared them with the cephalic indices of the non-Jewish populations of the countries in which they lived. The results of this detailed comparison can be summarized as follows:

1. The cephalic index (CI) of the Jews ranges from an average of 72 (in the Mzab in North Africa) to an average of 87 (in the Caucasus). Between these two extremes there are dolichocephalic (North Africa, Yemen), mesocephalic (Turkey, Balkans, Palestinian Sephardim, part of Iraq, Iran, Egypt), and brachycephalic (part of Iraq, Kurdistan, Crimea, Central Asia, Poland, Russia, Lithuania, Galicia, Rumania, Hungary, Germany) Jewish groups.

2. The average CIs of Jewish groups approximate very closely those of the non-Jews in each country. The similarity between the Jewish and non-Jewish indices increases with the length of sojourn of the Jews in the locality in question. For instance, in Morocco, where the Jews have lived for about fifteen centuries, the Jewish index ranges from 74 to 78.2, while that of the Muslim Moroccans is 74.3 and 74.8. In Damascus, Syria (another old Jewish settlement) the Jews had an average cephalic index of 80.9, the Muslims 81.8. In Baghdad, the Jews ranged from 80.28 to 82.1, the Muslims from 77.7 to 82.2. In Bukhara,

the Jews averaged 84, the Muslims 84.2. In Baden, Germany, the Jews averaged 83.5, the Christians 84.1. In Galicia, the Jews averaged 83.6, the Christians 83.7. On the other hand, in places where the Jews were relative newcomers, there is a considerable difference between their average CIs and those of the non-Jews. For instance, in England the Jews had a CI of 80, while the Christians ranged from 77 to 79. The Sephardim in Turkey had a CI ranging from 76 to 79, while the Muslim Turks had a mean CI of 84. The Sephardi Jews in Turkey, who had arrived in the country after their expulsion from Spain in 1492, have evidently retained for four centuries their old CI, which was practically identical with that of the Christian Spaniards (77–79).

3. From the above two observations it follows that (a) the Jews do not have a typical range of CI of their own that could be considered a racial characteristic, and (b) as far as the CI is concerned the Jews have everywhere tended to assimilate to the non-Jewish majority.

BLOOD GROUPS   Coming now to the subject of blood groups in their bearing on the question of the Jewish race, some introductory explanation is necessary. During World War I two Jewish army physicians, L. and H. Hirszfeld, examined several thousand individuals of various ethnic backgrounds, and found that the frequency distribution of ABO blood groups varied from population to population. The blood group to which an individual's blood belongs depends on the presence or absence of one or both of two so-called agglutinogens (antigens that cause the agglutination or clumping together of the blood) designated A and B. If only A is present in the blood, it belongs to the group designated A; if only B, it belongs to B; if both, it belongs to AB; and if neither, it belongs to O. The four blood types are determined by three genes, one making A antigen, one making B, and the third making neither. Each individual has two of these genes, which may be the same. To simplify the handling of the data, the Hirszfelds devised a so-called "biochemical index" (BI) by taking all the people in a group studied, and adding the number of As and ABs, then dividing the result by the sum of the Bs and ABs:

$$BI = \frac{A + AB}{B + AB}$$

Every population group studied had thus one single index figure which could be readily compared to the indices of other populations. When the Hirszfeld biochemical index was calculated for a very large number of both Jewish and non-Jewish populations in many parts of the world, the overall results were, by and large, similar to those obtained from a comparison of the cephalic indices: on the one hand there were considerable differences among the BIs of various Jewish populations, while, on the other, there were marked similarities between the BIs of Jewish and non-Jewish populations in the same locality.

Subsequently, biometricians preferred to calculate the frequencies of the three genes whose combinations result in the four existing blood types. The frequencies of the genes determining A, B, and O were designated p, q, and r. Expressed as percentages, p, q, and r total 100. Utilizing all the data I could find, I assembled a large number of tables comparing the frequencies of these three genes in the Jewish and non-Jewish populations of many localities. Then, to make a comparison between them possible at a single glance, I devised a diagram of three coordinates on which I plotted two sets of data in triangular form: the gene frequencies of the Jews and of the non-Jews in the same place; or, the gene frequencies of two Jewish groups in two different places. Several samples of these triangular diagrams are reproduced here,[46] and they graphically illustrate the same two points that were made in the previous paragraph: the similarity between the Jewish and non-Jewish gene distribution in the same locality, and the difference between the gene distribution of the Jewish populations of two different localities.

Summing up our findings with reference to the Jewish gene frequencies, we note, firstly, that the difference in frequency distributions among Jewish groups are of the same order of magnitude as among non-Jewish groups. Secondly, the gene frequencies of the Jewish groups in most countries or places of their residence closely approximate those of the non-Jews in the same localities. This leads to only one possible conclusion: that the Jews in most places belong (as far as gene frequencies are

65

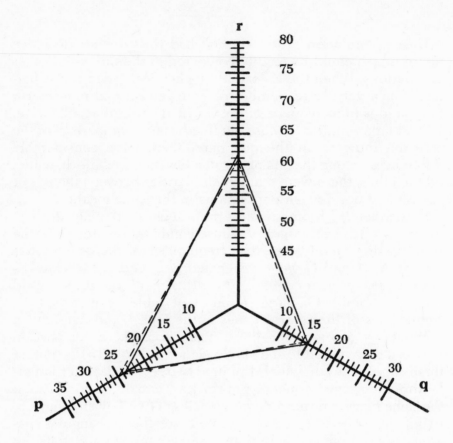

ALEPPO, SYRIA

pqr Gene Frequencies

	p	q	r
———— Jews(172)	23.66	15.03	61.31
--------- Arabs(933)	24.93	14.80	60.27

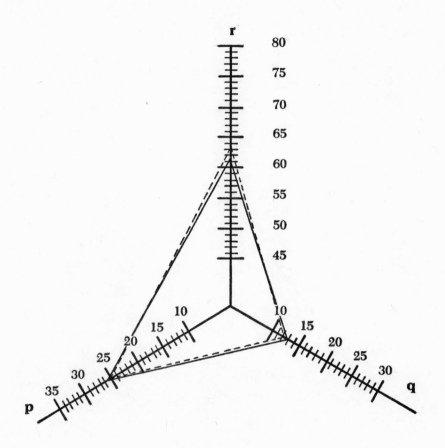

LITHUANIA

pqr Gene Frequencies

	p	q	r
——— Jews	25.52	13.00	61.48
----------- Non-Jews	25.20	12.45	62.35

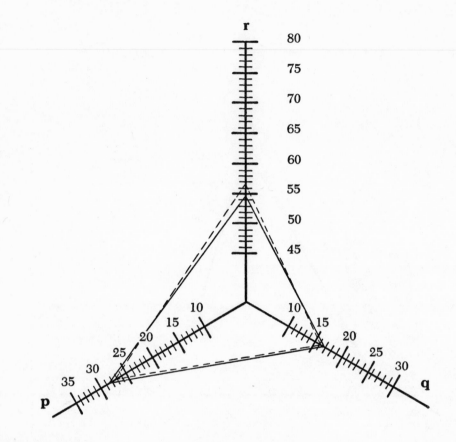

KHARKOV, UKRAINE

pqr Gene Frequencies

		p	**q**	**r**
——————	Jews(383)	28.66	16.41	54.93
--------	Non-Jews(2,075)	27.3	16.2	56.5

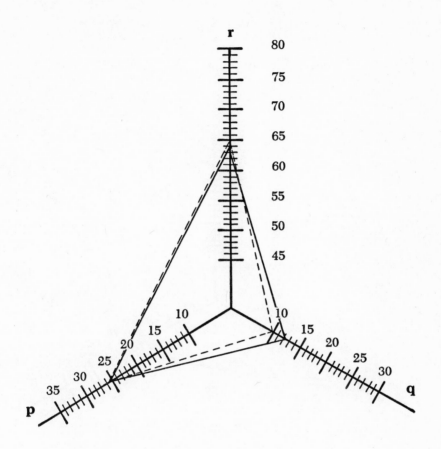

JASSY, RUMANIA

pqr Gene Frequencies

	p	**q**	**r**
—————— Jews(1,135)	25.47	12.14	63.39
- - - - - - - Non-Jews(2,740)	25.58	10.03	64.39

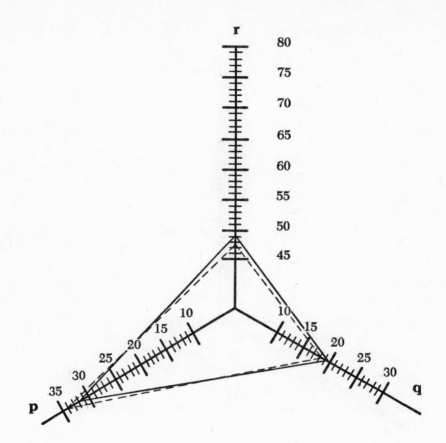

MARAMURES, RUMANIA

pqr Gene Frequencies

	p	q	r
——— Jews(211)	31.77	19.16	49.07
---------- Non-Jews(271)	34.14	18.18	47.68

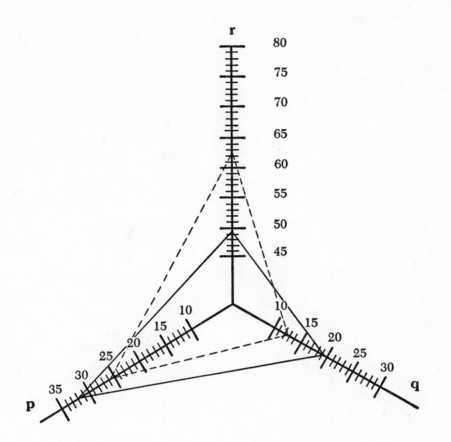

RUMANIA

Contrasting Jewish pqr Gene Frequencies

	p	**q**	**r**
——— Maramures(211)	31.77	19.16	49.07
- - - - - Jassy(1,135)	25.47	12.14	63.39

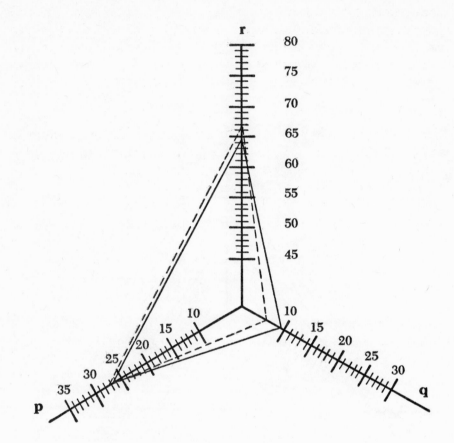

AMSTERDAM, HOLLAND

pqr Gene Frequencies

		p	q	r
————	Jews(1,077)	26.4	9.01	64.58
-------	Non-Jews(23,043)	27.02	6.39	66.59

concerned) to the same groups as the non-Jews, and that the Jewish groups resident in various localities do not belong (as far as gene frequencies are concerned) to one and the same group.

The absence or presence of homogeneity in a given population with respect to gene frequency does not, of course, constitute a sufficient criterion of racial identity. But it is one of the features—and one of the very few clearly determinable, inherited ones at that—which have to be considered in discussing the racial identity of any human group. Great variability in gene frequencies indicates that we are faced with different gene pools. The Christian Ukrainians of Dnetropetrovsk with gene frequencies of p=29.52 percent, q=18.30 percent, and r=52.18 percent are very unlikely to belong to the same group as the Christian Dutch population of Amsterdam with p=27.09 percent, q=7.62 percent, and r=65.29 percent. Similarly, the Jewish Ukrainians of Dnetropetrovsk with gene frequencies of p=31.63 percent, q=17.53 percent, and r=50.84 percent do not belong to the same group as the Jews of the Netherlands with p=27.10 percent, q=7.63 percent, and r=65.27 percent. Rather, the Christian and Jewish populations of Dnetropetrovsk belong, by this criterion, to the same group, and the Christian and Jewish populations of Holland to another group.

Conclusion

We have examined in some detail three sets of data, one historical, one anthropometric (the cephalic index), and the third serological (the gene frequencies), and found that all three point to the absence of common racial characteristics among the Jews. There are other data as well pointing to the same conclusions. Take, for instance, coloration. It is well known that the Jews of Yemen and other Arab countries are swarthy, with skin color ranging from light to dark brown, eyes and hair black. As against this, Rudolf Virchow (1821–1902), the great German pathologist and anthropologist, who conducted a survey extending over ten million schoolchildren in Germany, Austria, Switzerland, and Belgium, including 75,000 Jewish children. found that 18.65

percent of the latter had blue eyes, and 32.41 percent blond hair. Among adult Jews in Galicia, Little Russia, Rumania, Hungary, and Baden (Germany), fair eyes were found in more than 50 percent, and fair hair in about 20 percent.[47] All this points to one conclusion: the Jews are not a race. Or, to put it differently: the members of Jewish communities, scattered all over the world, exhibit disparate physical traits; in general, the Jewish group in each locality shows a marked similarity with regard to physical traits to the non-Jews of the same locality. It seems, moreover, that the longer the Jews and non-Jews have lived in the same locality, the greater this similarity.

 DEMOGRAPHY

While the ancient Egyptians, Babylonians, Hebrews, and Romans took population censuses, practically no such enumerations were carried out from the disintegration of the Roman Empire until the end of the eigteenth century. The significance of this observation for our present purposes is that it explains why we have no Jewish population figures, let alone other statistical data pertaining to the Jews, until the early nineteenth century, and why all statements as to the numbers of Jewish Diasporas prior to that time are nothing more than guesswork, and in many cases not even educated guesses at that. Since, moreover, statistics are the basis of all demographic studies, this means that Jewish demography (like demography in general) is a very young discipline that has little if anything to say about conditions prior to the nineteenth century.

In addition to this time limitation, Jewish statistics often encounter yet another specific difficulty: the very nature of a complete population census is such that it can be carried out only by governmental authority and machinery. This means that such a basic item of information as the number of the Jews in a country or a city can be obtained only from official censuses. However, these often do not contain data covering the religious affiliation of the enumerated population. The reason for not including this point in the census questionnaire is that in some countries, the United States among them, religious affiliation is considered a personal and private matter that an individual should not be asked to divulge. As a result, in many cases Jewish demographers trying to arrive at a reasonable estimate of the Jewish population are reduced to resorting to all kinds of secondary methods (such as that based on the number of children absent from public schools on Yom Kippur, or the number of Jewish burials in relation to all burials in a given period), none of which even approximates the reliability of an official census.

It would be too technical and, in our present context, unnecessary to describe the various methods developed for the purpose of estimating the number of Jews in various countries at the present time or in the past. As a general observation, however, we should mention that the farther back one goes in time, the less reliable the estimates become. With these cautions in mind, let us now have a look at what Jewish demography has to offer despite these and numerous other handicaps.

The Jewish Population

The general consensus of historians and demographers is that until the nineteenth century the number of Jews in the world increased at a very slow rate. There were, of course, temporary fluctuations, such as the sudden and catastrophic decrease of an entire Jewish Diaspora as a result of large-scale massacres (e.g., the Chmielnicki pogroms of 1648) or uncontrolled epidemics; but these shrinkages were, as a rule, made up again within the next generation. It is estimated that in the twelfth century there was a global Jewish population of 1,500,000, which by 1800 had gradually increased to 2,500,000. Thereafter, there was a rapid increase to about 16 million by 1939.

The breakdown between Ashkenazim and non-Ashkenazim shows that this more than sixfold increase within 140 years was due solely to the increase of the Ashkenazi Jews, whose demographic development paralleled that of the population in Europe in the wake of the industrial revolution, urbanization, and general modernization with improved living conditions, sanitation, etc. The non-Ashkenazi Jews remained almost entirely stationary in this period, as they had been in previous centuries. The reason for this absence of increase was not, as Arthur Ruppin surmised,[1] that the "high infant mortality and frequent epidemics decimated the population," because in the same period the Muslim populations in the countries of the Middle East, among whom most of the non-Ashkenazi Jews (i.e., the Oriental Jews) dwelt, did increase very considerably;[2] it lay in the fact that the Middle Eastern Diaspora consisted largely of urban aggregates, while the population increase in those countries took place primarily in the rural areas from which a constant stream of village-to-town migration replenished and augmented the urban sector of the population. Since the Jews were almost entirely urban, their total natural increase remained minimal, in keeping with the demographic characteristics of the Muslim urbanites.

To go back to the Middle Ages, it has been estimated by Ruppin and others before him, that of the 1,500,000 Jews who comprised the world Jewish population in the twelfth century, 1,400,000, or 93.3 percent, were Sephardi and Oriental Jews, and only 100,000, or 6.7 percent, Ashkenazi Jews. Of course, we must not forget that population estimates for as early a period as the twelfth century are extremely unreliable; but even if we take into account a very wide margin of possible error, we still get the picture of a Diaspora in which the Ashkenazi Jews constituted a numerically quite insignificant element. After 1170, however, this numerical relationship gradually shifted, so that by 1700, when the total number of Jews was 2 million, half of them were Ashkenazim and half Sephardim and Oriental Jews. During the next two hundred years the number of the Sephardi and Oriental Jews, with some fluctuations, decreased to about 950,000, while that of the Ashkenazim increased almost tenfold, to 9,550,000. From 1900 to 1939 both increased at about the same rate: the Sephardi and Oriental Jews reached about 1,300,000; and the Ashkenazi Jews, 14,900,000. Throughout this period more than 90 percent of all Jews in the world were Ashkenazim, and fewer than 10 percent Sephardim and Oriental Jews.

The Nazi holocaust of six million Jews altered this balance drastically and catastrophically in the years of World War II. After the war (1945) only about 9,500,000 Ashkenazi Jews were left alive, as against some 1,350,000 Sephardi and Oriental Jews, or a total of some 10,850,000. The Ashkenazi contingent was thus reduced to 87.6 percent, and the Sephardi-Oriental increased to 12.4 percent, of the total.

The large-scale immigration of Sephardi-Oriental Jews into Israel from 1948 on resulted in a continued relative increase of the Sephardi and Oriental divisions as against the Ashkenazi. The Ashkenazi division is characterized by a very low birthrate (see below), the Sephardi by a modest birthrate, and the Oriental by a high birthrate. Since in Israel infant mortality has rapidly been brought under control and reduced to almost the same low level among the Oriental Jews that it had attained among the Ashkenazim, the differential between Oriental Jewish mortality and fertility has considerably increased, resulting in a high natural increase among them. Due mainly to this factor, the total number of the Sephardi and Oriental Jews has increased considerably, and I estimate their number in 1970 at 2,300,000, of whom 1,360,000 were in Israel. Since the total global Jewish population in 1970 can be estimated at 14 million, the percentage of Sephardim and Oriental Jews in it had risen to 16.43 percent, while that of the Ashkenazim had eclined to 83.57 percent (see Table I).

The Jewish Birthrate

An important general characteristic of the European Diasporas for the last hundred years has been their continually declining birthrates. In this there was no difference between the Jews of Eastern Europe and Western Europe, although they contrasted sharply in many other respects. Reliable data are available only from the big cities, in which, however, was concentrated a considerable and increasing percentage of the Jews in each country. The data show that, already a hundred years ago, the Jewish birthrate was lower than that of the general population in the same place, and that subsequently both declined, with the Jews everywhere maintaining their lower rate. In Berlin, for instance, the Jewish birthrate in 1851–60 was 28.3, while that of the total population was 34.6. By 1921–23 the Jewish rate had gradually declined to 10.4, while that of the total population had declined only to 12.2. Similar declines, with the differential maintained, were found in those decades in Amsterdam, Vienna, Budapest, Warsaw, Lwow, St. Petersburg, and elsewhere. This leads to the conclusion that "among the Jews, as in the Western world at large, the birthrate is continually declining," and that

DEMOGRAPHY

TABLE I

Estimated Number of Ashkenazi and
Sephardi-Oriental Jews in the World 1070-1970

| Year | Ashkenazi Jews | | Sephardi and Oriental Jews | | Total |
	Number	Percent	Number	Percent	Number
1170	100,000	6.7	1,400,000	93.3	1,500,000
1300	300,000	15.0	1,700,000	85.0	2,000,000
1500	500,000	33.3	1,000,000	66.6	1,500,000
1650	700,000	40.0	1,050,000	60.0	1,750,000
1700	1,000,000	50.0	1,000,000	50.0	2,000,000
1800	1,500,000	60.0	1,000,000	40.0	2,500,000
1840	3,600,000	80.0	900,000	20.0	4,500,000
1860	5,200,000	86.6	800,000	13.4	6,000,000
1900	9,550,000	90.5	950,000	9.5	10,500,000
1930	14,600,000	91.8	1,300,000	8.2	15,900,000
1939	15,000,000	90.9	1,500,000	9.1	16,500,000
1945	9,500,000	87.6	1,350,000	12.4	10,850,000
1950	10,000,000	86.96	1,500,000	13.04	11,500,000
1960	10,900,000	85.16	1,900,000	14.84	12,800,000
1970	11,700,000	83.57	2,300,000	16.43	14,000,000

SOURCES: Arthur Ruppin, *Soziologie der Juden,* Berlin, 1931; *American Jewish Yearbook;* the author's estimates and calculations.

"for a considerable time the Jews in the Western countries have had a much lower birthrate than the non-Jewish population."[3]

In Russia in 1926 the Jews had the lowest rate of natural increase (15 per thousand of population) among all nationality groups (Germans—32, Ukrainians—24, Poles—21, Russians—18). It was lower than the general rate of the urban population.

From 1926 to 1939, the population of Russia as a whole grew by 15.9 percent, while the number of Jews increased by less than 13 percent. In Poland, too, the Jewish birthrate was consistently lower than that of the gentile Poles. As to Lithuanian Jewry, by the early 1930s it had no natural increase at all. Also in Latvia the Jewish birth and death rates were equal in 1934.[4]

In several other European countries the decline of the Jewish birthrate resulted in a minus figure prior to World War II. In Prussia, Germany, in 1926–27 there was an excess of 2.4 deaths over births per 1,000 of the Jewish population; in Hungary, there was such an excess of 0.7 in 1926–30, 3 in 1931–35 and 2.9 in 1936.[5]

The same situation developed in the Italian Jewish community on the eve of World War I: the rate of natural increase fell below zero in the five years of 1911–15, and continued to decline, until it reached the low of approximately −4 to −5 in which range it has remained since 1931, while the general Italian population in the same period had a natural increase ranging between +8 and +10.[6]

A very similar trend could be observed in the Netherlands. In the years 1946–53, the Jewish death rate showed a gradual increase (from 3.6, or according to a different source, from 7.6, to 8.2 and 8.6 respectively) while the birthrate declined from +23.5 to −1.4 or −1.8.[7]

The Jewish immigrants who had come from Europe to the United States and Canada brought along their demographic trait of low birthrate. Also in America, the Jewish birthrate remained lower than that of the white non-Jews and continued to decline at a faster rate than the latter.[8] After World War II, when the natural increase in the general population showed a rise, that of the Jews also rose, but not to the same high level. In the 1950s the general American natural increase was 17–18; the Jewish, 9–10. In Canada the general natural increase in 1936–40 was 10.6; the Jewish, 6.5; by 1946–50 the former rose to 18.2, the latter to 13.5.[9] In the 1956–66 decade, according to the estimate of the researchers of the *American Jewish Year Book,* the annual growth of the Jewish population was 10 per thousand, as against 15 per thousand for the general population.[10]

What are causes of this demographic trend, which, if it continues, can in the long run lead to a gradual melting away of the Jewish Diaspora?

First of all, there is the greater and earlier urban concentration of the Jews. The urban environment in itself is a factor conducive to a lowering of the birthrate. This result of urbanization may not show up within a few years, but its cumulative effect does not fail to make itself felt after one or two generations.

ce, on the average, the Jews have lived in cities (not necessarily in one and the same city) for a longer time than the non-Jews, they exhibit to a greater degree the fertility-reducing effect of the urban environment.

Secondly, both in Europe and the United States it was found that Jewish men and women marry, on the average, at a higher age than non-Jewish men and women,[11] and later marriages result in a reduction of fertility. The reasons for later marriage among the Jews are many: a stronger parental devotion to the children influences the children to postpone their marriage; the desire for a higher social and/or economic status motivates young men in their early twenties to concentrate on advancing themselves in business or to devote themselves to higher studies—while marriage can and must wait.

Thirdly, among Jewish parents there is a greater emphasis on providing their children with the best possible conditions for the fullest development of their talents, ambitions, and potential. Since the financial means at the disposal of middle-class parents are limited, they rather limit the number of children than have more children to whom they could not give all the advantages.

The combined effect of these factors is the lower birthrate among the Jews as compared to the non-Jews in each country and locality.

When we move over to the continents of Asia and Africa, we enter into countries in which to this day very few reliable demographic studies have been carried out among either the general or the Jewish population. Nevertheless, we have some knowledge of the situation with regard to the birthrates thanks to studies carried out in Palestine-Israel among the local Muslims and the Jewish immigrants from the Asian and African countries of the Middle East, and to some data available from North Africa. Although these Middle Eastern birthrates are much higher than those of European and American populations, here too the same differences can be found between the Jews and the non-Jews.

These differences can be measured by the gross reproduction rates of the specific populations in question. The gross reproduction rate represents the average number of female offspring born to a woman in her lifetime (regardless of mortality). For Israeli Jewish women born in Europe and America this rate diminished from 1.55 in 1949 to 1.19 in 1966. The same rate for Israeli Jewish women born in Asia and Africa was 2.17 in 1949, and after a maximum of 3.06 in 1951, diminished again to 2.17 in 1966. The corresponding rates for non-Jews (mostly Arabs) were 3.55 in 1955 and over 4.00 from 1964 on.[12] A gross reproduction rate of a little over 1 means that the population in question is neither decreasing nor increasing, because the place of each woman is taken by one daughter in the next generation. This was the case among the Jews of European and American extraction (i.e. roughly, the Ashkenazi Jews). Among the Oriental Jews (or, more precisely, Jews of Asian and African extraction), the rate was over 2, indicating something closer to a doubling of their number within a generation. Among the Arabs ("non-Jews") the rate was over 4, indicating a considerably greater population increase within one generation.

In the Middle Eastern countries, where the general birthrate is extremely high, the Jewish birthrate is also high, but lower than that of the general population. In Morocco, in the 1936–46 decade, the average Jewish birthrate was 37 as against a Muslim rate of 43. In Tunisia from 1934 to 1947 the Jewish birthrate increased from 30 to 38, while the Muslim rate increased from 29 to 39.[13] The reasons for this difference are the same as in Europe and America: greater urbanization, greater concern for the advancement of each individual child, and so on. That this, indeed, is the case, can be learned from the observation that the average number of children born to Afro-Asian Jewish women whose husbands were engaged in agriculture after their immigration to Palestine (5.61) was much higher than the average number of children born to Afro-Asian Jewish women whose husbands were engaged in public service and professions (2.66)—i.e., who successfully passed through the process of urbanization and Westernization.[14]

The Jewish Migrations

Every Diaspora is the result of one or more migrations of Jewish populations. Some of these movements from one country to another were voluntary, others were forced. The involuntary Jewish population movements again fall into two categories: transportation by force into a certain country, and expulsion from a country with the expellees allowed to go wherever they pleased, provided, of course, that the new country of their choice admitted them.

Voluntary movements from one country to another were, for instance, Abraham's migration from Mesopotamia to Palestine; the descent of Jacob and his family to Egypt; the exodus from Egypt and the immigration into Canaan; the migrations of Jews prior to the fall of the Second Jewish Commonwealth to Egypt, Phoenicia, Syria, Asia Minor, Cyprus, Greece, Crete, Italy (Rome), and North Africa; the frequent movements in the Middle Ages from one country of Europe to another, fleeing persecution or in search of better living conditions, especially from Western and Central Europe to Eastern Europe, or in the opposite direction; the migration in the nineteenth century to the Americas, and, on a smaller scale to South Africa and Australia, and, in the twentieth century, to Palestine-Israel.

Transportation by force to a definite country meant being taken into captivity or exile, as was done with the Israelites by the Assyrians, with the Judeans by the Babylonians, and again, 656 years later, by the Romans. Expulsion followed by a search for a new home was experienced by the Jews in almost every country of Europe from the seventh century on, in many of them several times. It was a fate shared also by the Jews in the Middle East, although not as frequently as in Europe.

As a result of all this, migrations have become an integral part of Jewish history and have resulted in periodic shifts of major Jewish population elements from one part of the globe to another. Until about the third century BCE, all Jews lived in western Asia and North Africa. Thereafter, until the eleventh century CE, only a minor part of them lived in Europe. In the eleventh century, with the peak of the Golden Age in Spain, the cultural hegemony in world Jewry was assumed by an European Diaspora, and remained in Europe until the twentieth century. At the time of the Spanish Exile (1492), the numbers of the Jews, some 1,500,000 in all, were about evenly distributed between Europe and the Middle East (including North Africa), although the Ashkenazi Jews still numbered only one-third of the world's Jewish population.

The subsequent gradual increase of the Ashkenazi division in three hundred years to three times its size (1500: 500,000; 1800: 1,500,000) was due, not to immigration of Jews from outside Europe, but to gradual natural increase. However, in these three centuries the Ashkenazi communities, or considerable contingents of them, migrated frequently across the length and breadth of Europe, carrying along cultural values developed by Polish Jewry in the sixteenth century, and making them dominant wherever they settled. In the same period the Sephardi and Oriental Jews led a less mobile existence, remaining mostly and largely in the same area, country, or province.

The largest and most dramatic migration ever to be undertaken by the Jewish people began in the nineteenth century and was concluded in the 1950s. Around 1850 some 72 percent of the Jewish people, which at the time numbered about 4,750,000, lived in Eastern Europe. The remaining 28 percent were distributed among Western Europe (14.5 percent), the Middle East (12 percent), and America (1.5 percent).

The Jewish migration that began, in fact, in the 1830s, had a consistently westerly direction: Jews from Central Europe (chiefly Bavaria, Posen, and Bohemia) began to move to France, England, and especially the United States. In the 1870s, after the German Jews had stopped going west, a sizable Eastern European Jewish migration had Germany as its target. In 1881 the large-scale Eastern European Jewish emigration to the United States began. By 1900 the number of emigrants surpassed 500,000; from 1900 to 1943 another 2,050,000 Jews, the great majority of them from Eastern Europe, reached the United States. In the same period another 930,000 Jews migrated to other countries outside Europe, giving a total of about 3,500,000 Jews who left Europe in the sixty-three years from 1881 to 1943. The magnitude of this migration becomes even more apparent if we remember that in 1881, when it began, the total Jewish population of Europe was about 6,200,000. That despite the emigration of half this number the total Jewish population of Europe not only did not diminish but even increased to

9,462,000 by 1939 (when the Nazi genocide began) was due to the considerable natural increase that characterized the European Jewish population of this period.

Nor was emigration to America and other overseas countries the whole story of Jewish migration in the six decades in question. In addition to this intercontinental movement, there was also an intra-continental trek which, from 1881 to 1943, brought 550,000 Jews from Eastern to Central Europe. It was partly as a result of this intra-European migration that the Jewish Diasporas of Central and Western Europe, which in the period in question were shrinking as a result of assimilation, mixed marriages, conversions, low birth rates, and emigration, were able to maintain their numbers, and, in several places, even chalk up some increases.

In comparison with the large overseas migration of the Jews from 1881 on, their immigration to Palestine, which began a year later, remained modest until the independence of Israel. The immigration to Palestine is usually divided into five 'aliyot, or immigration waves, which are presented, together with the much larger post-independence immigration, in Table II.

Following the end of World War II, and especially after the independence of Israel, the immigration to the Jewish State increased and represented about 78 percent of all Jewish migrations. In 1945–60 all other countries, including the United States, absorbed 300,000 Jewish immigrants, while Israel alone received 1,055,000. The role of Israel in global Jewish migration in the 80 years from 1881 to 1960 is summarized in Table III.

Westernization

The cultural consequences of the large-scale and frequent Jewish migrations were many, weighty, and far-reaching. As a result of migrations, the Jewish people—once upon a time one people, living in one country, speaking one language, and sharing one culture—split into ethnic groups whose number continuously increased, with a corresponding grwoth in linguistic and cultural diversity. As a result of migrations, moreover, the modality of the Jewish people as whole underwent

TABLE II

IMMIGRATION TO
PALESTINE-ISRAEL 1882–1966

'Aliya	Years	Ashkenazi Jews Total No.	No.	%[1]	Sephardi-Oriental Jews No.	%[1]	Of Unknown Origin
1st 'Aliya	1882–1903	25,000	24,000	96	1,000	4	—
2nd "	1904–1914	40,000	38,000	95	2,000	5	—
3rd "	1919–1923	35,183	29,000	92.4	2,400	7.6	3,783
4th "	1924–1931	81,613	64,000	86.7	9,800	13.3	7,813
5th "	1932–1939	224,785	170,000	91.6	15,600	8.4	39,185
World War II	1940–1945	54,109	25,000	61.7	15,500	38.3	13,609
Pre-State	1946–May 14, 1948	56,386	39,296	88.4	5,119	11.5	11,961
May 15, 1948–Dec. 31, 1966		1,231,023	551,558[2]	45.5	660,025[3]	54.4	19,440
Totals	1882–1966	1,748,099	940,854	56.9	711,444	43.0	95,791

[1] Percentages refer to the total of Ashkenazim and Sephardi-Oriental Jewish immigrants.
[2] Immigrants born in Europe and America.
[3] Immigrants born in Asia and Africa.

TABLE III

GLOBAL JEWISH MIGRATION 1881-1960

Period	Total	To Palestine-Israel Number	Percent	To Other Countries Number-Percent	
1881–1914	2,750,000	65,000	2.4	2,685,000	97.6
1915–1939	1,200,000	342,000	28.5	858,000	71.5
1940–1945	145,000	54,000	37.3	91,000	62.7
1946–1960	1,355,000	1,055,000	77.8	300,000	22.2
1881–1960	5,450,000	1,516,000	27.8	3,934,000	72.1

decisive changes the like of which could not be experienced by any people that continued to dwell in its own homeland. From the overwhelmingly Oriental people that the Jews had been until the twelfth century, they became by the sixteenth a predominantly Central and Eastern European people, and, in the twentieth, a primarily American people with a center of second magnitude in Israel, the same country whence their migrations had started some twenty-five centuries earlier. As a result of migrations the constituent aggregates of the Jewish people established themselves in many cases among populations which were experiencing a cultural ascendancy; they contributed their share to this cultural advancement, and, in turn, were carried up by it; the examples that readily come to mind include the Golden Age in Spain, the Renaissance in Italy, the nineteenth century in France and Germany, and the twentieth in the United States.

Once one Diaspora achieved a new plateau in cultural development, its members felt that the benefits it had acquired must be made available to other Diasporas as well, a feeling prompted by the persistent sense of brotherhood, of community of fate, that permeated many members of each Diaspora. Thus the French Jews established in 1860 the *Alliance Israélite Universelle* to make education and French culture available to their backward co-religionists in Muslim lands; the German Jews set up in 1901 *Hilfsverein der deutschen Juden* for similar purposes but with a German coloration; and, more recently, American Jews founded a series of overseas aid organizations the sum total of whose activities amounted to a large-scale exportation to other Jewish Diasporas of American values and cultural traits in such fields as health and hygiene, relief and reconstruction, vocational training, and so forth. Even the religious field has not remained untouched by this endeavor to let Jews in other countries share in the attainments of American Jewry, as shown by the efforts to introduce Reform and Conservative Judaism into Israel.

As a result of these procedures, the culture of one Diaspora, or parts of it, were often transplanted into other Diasporas—as best exemplified by the wholesale export, beginning in 1860, of

French Jewish culture to the North African Jewish communities. In that particular instance the culture was exported without accompanying migration; in most cases, however, migration was the primary factor and the transplantation of culture merely an inevitable by-product. This is how Sephardi Jews transplanted their culture into all the countries in which they found refuge after their expulsion from Spain; how Polish Jews brought their culture into Central and Western Europe in the seventeenth century; and how Eastern European Jews took their culture along to America and to Palestine from the late nineteenth century on. Jewish history can thus be viewed as a continuous process of cultural cross-fertilization among the Diasporas, with migration as its primary vehicle.

The last large-scale Jewish migration as of the time of writing (1970) was the emigration of North African Jews prior to and following the attainment of independence by the French domains of Tunisia, Algeria, and Morocco. As will be detailed in the chapter on North African Jews (Chapter XI), in the seventeen-year period of 1952–68 about 209,000 Jews emigrated from these three countries, most of them to France, others to Israel, the United States, and other countries. This migration, coming as it did soon after the earlier migration of another 200,000 North African Jews to Israel, reduced the total number of Jews in North Africa from more than 500,000 in 1947 to about 61,000 in 1969. A similar reduction of the number of Jews in other Muslim countries resulted in an almost complete liquidation of this oldest of the three divisions of the Jewish people in their home countries, in several of which they had lived for more than two and a half millennia. Of the estimated 1,800,000 Oriental Jews in 1970, 1,200,000 were concentrated in Israel; 200,000 had settled in France; 110,000 in the United States; 75,000 in the Asian regions of the Soviet Union; and about 50,000 in Latin America. This means that only 165,000 Oriental Jews were still living in their old home countries in Asia and Africa. Thus close to 90 percent of all Oriental Jews now live in countries where they are undergoing a rapid process of Westernization. We are today witnessing the last phase of the disappearance of the Oriental division of the Jewish people as a separate cultural entity, and with it the conclusion of the long historical process that began more than two thousand years ago and that has transformed the Jews from an Oriental into a Western people.

6 URBANIZATION

Urbanization is today a global socio-economic phenomenon that can be observed in all countries of the world. It is one of the three interrelated processes of transformation—the other two being modernization and industrialization—in which the spread of Western influences over the whole world primarily manifests itself. Modern urbanization began with the industrial revolution in England in the late eighteenth century. Soon thereafter, Central, Southern and Eastern Europe and the Americas followed suit. After the end of World War I came the turn of the Middle East. The rest of the world was caught up in the same movement in the aftermath of World War II. In statistical terms, this entire unprecedented global development can be summed up in a single observation: the percentage of urban dwellers in the population of the world has increased while that of the rural population evinced a commensurate decrease.

Jewish Urbanization

The same process could be observed in the Diaspora. However, Jewish urbanization paralleled the general global phenomenon neither in point of time nor in respect of its objective causes. As to the time factor, for many centuries before the industrial revolution the Jewish Diasporas had been much more urbanized than the non-Jewish majorities in the countries in which they dwelt. Statistics for past centuries are, of course, notoriously missing, but as an overall generalization one can say that whereas the populations of all countries prior to 1800 were overwhelmingly rural, the Jewish Diasporas were, ever since ancient times, overwhelmingly urban. This does not mean, however, that there were no Jews who lived in villages; on the contrary, many of them were village dwellers, especially in those countries in which they had lived for many centuries, although these Jewish villagers were in most cases not agriculturists but shopkeepers or had other service occupations. But the great majority of the Jews in every country lived in the towns, and most of them were concentrated in the major cities. This having been the case, whatever urbanization the Jews underwent in recent generations did not result in as significant an internal village-to-town migration as was the case with the gentile populations.

This predominantly urban character of the Jewish Diasporas for many centuries past had certain unexpected consequences for both the body and the mind of the Jews. Demographers and social pathologists have repeatedly observed a differential incidence of certain diseases in the Jewish and non-Jewish city populations, and attributed it to the difference in length of time elapsed since the ancestors of the two population elements had settled in cities. For instance, as a result of living in cities for many generations the Jews became more immune or resistant to tuberculosis than the gentiles, most of whose parents or grandparents had come up from the villages only one or two generations before; hence the lower rate of TB among the Jews—about one-third to one-half of that found among gentiles. On the other hand, the same circumstance is believed to account for the higher rate of certain mental and neurotic disorders among the Jews (about twice the rate of the incidence among gentiles); the longer exposure of the Jews to the strains and stresses of city life is taken to have contributed to a heightened neural and psychic sensitivity.[1]

Morbidity apart, the predominantly urban character of the Jewish Diasporas in almost every country (the Kurdish Jews were, until their immigration to Israel in 1950–51, a notable exception) had numerous other consequences as well. There were differences in occupational structure—that is, there was a typical range of occupations in which the Jews engaged in a given country and which in every place differed considerably from the typical gentile occupational range. To mention only one or two examples, the Jewish peasant or cultivator was a most exceptional phenomenon even in countries where the law did not bar Jews from owning or working land. In 1930, according to Ruppin's researches, there were 326,000 Jews in Eastern Europe, 76,000 in the Americas, 28,000 in Palestine, and 500 in Cyprus, Asia Minor, and Australia, or a total of 430,500, whose basis of subsistence was agriculture.[2] This figure constitutes 2.68 percent of the world Jewish population at the time (16,-000,000). Even if we add an estimated figure for Jewish agriculturists in certain Middle Eastern countries (whom Ruppin omits from consideration), we shall not reach a percentage higher than 3. Clearly, agriculture held no attraction for Diaspora Jewry.

Another occupation in which relatively few Jews could be found was unskilled labor. The percentage of day laborers and domestic helpers among the Jews was in most countries (except Poland and eastern Czechoslovakia) much lower than their percentage in the general population.[3]

Living in towns and cities, the Jews got early used to moving about in a large and often heterogeneous society, while the majority of the gentiles were accustomed to living only in the small, mostly homogeneous society of the village. Urban conditions of life forced the Jew to develop quick wit, alertness, and an ability to utilize suddenly arising chances, while most of the gentiles, peasants and the descendants of serfs, were slower, duller, and more complacent. Urban living added its own stimulus to the old Jewish valuation of learning, so that for many centuries the Jews were in every country a largely literate element in an almost entirely illiterate population.

The difference between the proportion of urban and rural residents among Jews and gentiles made itself felt in an unequal volume of village-to-town migrants supplied by the two population elements. Most gentiles lived in villages; therefore most gentile villagers were satisfied with staying in the villages with the majority of their kith and kin. Most Jews, on the other hand, lived in towns; therefore the village-dwelling Jewish minority was more sensitive to the pull exerted by the urban majority of their co-religionists and relatively more of them tended to move to the urban centers.

Motivations ————————————————————————————

As to the objective causes of the village-to-town migration among the Jews, one of them undoubtedly was the same as among the non-Jews: the opportunities to find a livelihood were greater and better in the town than in the village, a phenomenon that in itself was a function of industrialization. Among the non-Jews this was the major motivation; two or more surviving sons of a smallholder just could not all eke out a living from the same small parcel of land, so one remained while the others had to go to the city to seek a livelihood there. In the case of the Jews, other motivations were equally potent or even more so. Among these was, in the first place, the difficulty of living a full Jewish life in a locality where one was cut off from a Jewish community. (It was primarily this motivation that induced my grandfather, after having lived for forty years in the village of Pata, where there were only half-a-dozen Jewish families, to move in about 1920 to the town of Satmar where there was a large and vital Jewish community.)

Then there was the periodic upsurge of anti-Semitism which, of course, struck at relatively large urban Jewish aggregates as well (remember the Kishinev pogroms of 1903), but which often made it completely impossible for a few Jewish families to maintain themselves in a hostile village. Whether such waves of anti-Semitism led to a migration within the same country or to emigration to a country of the West (and especially America), the common feature in most cases was that the new place of residence chosen was a city with a large Jewish community.

The age-old Jewish emphasis on learning and the prestige accorded the learned contributed materially to the tendency to leave the village and seek the more congenial atmosphere of an urban Jewish community. It was the ambition of all good Jewish fathers to send their sons to the *yeshiva,* which was to be found only in towns; rabbis whose Talmud instruction and learned discourses were the source of both delight and self-advancement in understanding the Tora, could be listened to only in the larger urban communities. The urban *kehilla,* with its synagogue, house of study, *mikve* (ritual bath), *shohet* (ritual slaughterer),

94

hevra kadisha ("sacred society" whose main purpose was to take care of burials but also to help the needy and the ailing), acted as a veritable magnet attracting the village Jews from near and far.

The aforementioned factors were responsible for the Jewish village-to-town migration throughout many generations, and remained important motivations also after the industrial revolution. However, the industrial revolution considerably stepped up the pace of this population shift among the non-Jews as well as among the Jews. The growth of cities brought about by industrialization created many more work opportunities, including openings in numerous new types of occupations, and this made it objectively easier for more Jews to flock to the cities. As the Jewish community of a city increased, it needed more specifically Jewish services (rabbis, teachers, cantors, sextons, ritual slaughterers, circumcisers, makers of ritual objects and garments, scribes, restaurateurs, food processers, marriage brokers, and so forth), and since these could be supplied only by Jews, more Jews were enabled to find a livelihood in the growing community.

A few statistical data are available to illustrate this generalization. In the Ukraine in 1897 no less than 48 percent of the Jews lived in villages and small towns; by 1926 this percentage was reduced to 22.6. In White Russia in the same period the percentage of Jews in villages and small towns was reduced from 34 to 16.4 percent. Correspondingly, in the same period the number of Jews in the main cities of the Ukraine grew: from 32,000 to 140,000 in Kiev, and from 11,000 to 81,000 in Kharkov.

As a result of this specific Jewish tendency to concentrate in cities and towns, the ratio of the urban Jewish population to the entire Jewish population was considerably higher in every country of the Diaspora than the corresponding ratio for the non-Jewish population. In Central Russia (1926) 94 percent of all the Jews lived in cities and towns; in Latvia (1925), 92.4 percent; in both Bohemia (1921) and Asian Russia (1926), 91.3 percent; in Czechoslovakia (1921), 86.8 percent; in Carpatho-Ruthenia (1921), 86.1 percent; in Switzerland (1920), 85.3 percent; in the whole of Soviet Russia (1926), 82.5 percent; in the Ukraine (1926), 77.4 percent; in Poland (1921), 74.6 percent; in

95

Lithuania (1923), 63.5 percent.[4] Needless to say, in all these countries the percentage of urban dwellers in the general population was much lower than these figures for the Jewish population.

This tendency of Jews to concentrate in cities was not confined to the countries of the Ashkenazi Diaspora enumerated above (to which can be added Central and Western Europe as well as America), but was prevalent also in the Sephardi and Oriental Jewish Diasporas. Statistics for the latter are even more scarce than for the former, but it is known that in Egypt in 1917 no less than 90.7 percent of all the Jews lived in the two big cities of Cairo and Alexandria; that in Algeria (1927), 65 percent of the Jews lived in Algiers, Oran, and Constantine, the three biggest cities; that in Tunisia (1926), 56 percent of the Jews lived in the capital, Tunis; and that in French Morocco (1926), 44.2 percent of the Jews lived in Casablanca, Marrakesh, Mogador, and Fez, the four biggest cities. By 1947, 73 percent of all Moroccan Jews lived in the country's nineteen cities. Similarly, the Jews of Iraq, Iran, and Afghanistan were known to have been concentrated in the interwar years (and, in all probability, for a long time prior to that period) in the two or three biggest cities in each country.[5] A complementary feature of this picture is that in every country of the worldwide Jewish Diaspora, the biggest cities contained a much higher percentage of Jewish than of the general population. Let us conclude this statistical excursus by referring to the fact that, in the 1920s, there were numerous medium-sized and small cities in Eastern Europe in which the Jews formed a majority of the total population. In Russia (1923) the Jews constituted 74.6 percent (17,513 persons) of the population of Pinsk; 65.1 percent (28,381) of Berdichev; 57.2 percent (25,252) of Oman; and 53.4 percent (29,373) of Kremenchug, while in the whole of White Russia they constituted only 8.2 percent of the total population. In Rumania (1925) they were 60.2 percent (80,000) of the population of Kishinev; 60 percent (45,000) of the population of Jassy; and 58.4 percent (20,000) of the population of Botosani, while in all Rumania they constituted only 4.8 percent of the total population.[6]

By 1930, the centuries-old Jewish preference for urban re-

sidence had resulted in a situation that was decidedly anomalous in comparison with the position of the gentile population: a
concentration of 70, 80, 90 percent or more of the Jews in a few
towns and cities in countries where the majority of the non-
Jewish population was rural.

The Nazi Genocide

Then came two events, diametrically opposed in their nature
and significance for the Jewish Diaspora, both of which nevertheless had the same effect as far as the Jewish village and small
town population was concerned: that of practically putting an
end to its existence. The first, chronologically, was the Nazi
genocide; the second, the establishment of the state of Israel.

Most of the few Jews who survived the Nazi holocaust in
Europe found it impossible to continue to live in the environment in which their gentile neighbors were, at best, conve-
niently unaware of the horrors of the genocide and of the existence of extermination camps a few miles outside their places
of residence (such as Dachau near Munich), and, at worst, active
participants in it. Psychologically, the situation was especially
unbearable for the Jews in villages and small towns, because in
small population aggregates Jews and non-Jews used to know
each other personally, so that, after what had happened, it
became simply impossible for the Jews to stay in, or return to,
such an environment. Most of the survivors sought new homes
in new countries, in Israel, in America, in Western Europe. A
few, who for individual reasons of their own chose not to
emigrate, moved to the largest cities of the country. Thus the
remnants of the Jewish village population disappeared and
became concentrated in the cities.

In the countries that bore the full fury of the Nazi onslaught
the number of Jews in 1930 was estimated at 6,724,500. By 1945,
after the genocide of six million, only about 725,000 of them
were left. We do not know what percentage of the Jewish
population lived in villages and small towns in the period
immediately preceding the Nazi *Endlösung* (final solution) of
the "Jewish problem," but we know that there still were, in the

countries in question, many hundreds of villages and small towns with small Jewish communities or with a few individual Jewish families. Similarly, there are no data to show the percentage distribution of the postwar Jewish remnant between urban and rural residence, but whatever information is available seems to indicate that Hitler achieved at least one part of his diabolical scheme: he put an end to the last remnants of rural Jewish populations in the countries where his hordes held sway during World War II.

The evidence is indirect and circumstantial. It does not show that all the surviving Jews after 1945 were concentrated in cities and towns, but it shows that the number (quite apart from the size) of the Jewish communities was drastically reduced—from many hundreds to a few dozens or even fewer. This, together with all the factors that had made and continued to make for village-to-town migration among the Jews, leaves little doubt as to the almost total disappearance of the Jewish rural population in post-Hitler Europe. Of the three million Jews of prewar Poland only 25,000 were left, concentrated in about a dozen cities. Of Czechoslovakia's 400,000 Jews, 18,000 remained, in six cities. Of Hungary's 520,000, 80,000 were left, 90 percent of them in the capital, Budapest. Of Rumania's one million Jews, 100,000 survived; half of them in the capital, Bucharest, the other half in some seventy communities. In Austria, 11,500 were left of the prewar 250,000, 80 percent of them concentrated in Vienna. In Yugoslavia, of the prewar 70,000, only 7,000 remained, in thirty-four communities. Of the 50,000 Jews of Bulgaria, 7,000 escaped; of these 4,000 lived in the capital, Sofia, the rest in eight towns. In Germany itself, of the prewar 560,000 Jews, 25,000 remained, of whom 18,000 lived in the country's six biggest cities, the rest in sixty-five other communities.[7]

Israel and the Middle Eastern Jews

The countries of the Middle East (in which area we include all of North Africa in the west and Iran and Afghanistan in the east)[8] were touched only fleetingly and in a small part by Hitler's armies. There the emergence of Israel as an independent state brought about the virtual self-liquidation of the thousand-year-old tradition of indigenous Jewish village life. In the first half of the twentieth century, as we have just seen, the typical Middle Eastern Diasporas, like their European Ashkenazi counterparts, were predominantly urban; but next to the urban majority a certain percentage of Jews lived in villages where they were small traders, artisans, craftsmen, and occasionally even cultivators. Statistics, again, are lacking, but we know of numerous villages inhabited by Jews in Kurdistan (northern Iraq), Iran, Yemen, the Aden Protectorate, Saudi Arabia, Oman, Libya, Tunisia, Algeria and Morocco.[9]

A steady village-to-town migration characterized these Diasporas, as it did those of Europe, until the establishment of Israel on May 15, 1948, which event resulted in an unprecedented upheaval in their lives. As is well known, sporadic and small-scale fighting began between the Arabs and the Jews of Palestine soon after the United Nations General Assembly voted, on November 29, 1947, for the partition of the country and the establishment in it of a Jewish and an Arab state. The British Mandatory government of Palestine set May 15, 1948, as the date for the final withdrawal of all its forces. That day fell on a Sabbath and consequently the leaders of the Yishuv (the Jewish population of Palestine) advanced by a day the declaration of the independence of the Jewish State, for which they had chosen the name Israel. On the same day the United States recognized the new State, and soon Soviet Russia did likewise. No sooner was Israel born than several neighboring Arab states launched an attack across its borders, with the intent of snuffing out the life of the infant State before it learned how to defend itself.

Well-known and often told, too, is the story of Israel's War of Independence which thereupon unfolded and which ended (after several interventions by the UN) a few months later with Israel in control of not only all the area allotted to her by the UN, but also sizable sectors of the areas in which an Arab state should have been established. Whatever part of the former mandatory Palestine Israel did not control was occupied by Jordan (the so-called West Bank) and by Egypt (the Gaza Strip).

In the ensuing months Israel signed armistice agreements with its four immediate Arab neighbors, Egypt, Jordan, Syria, and Lebanon, who undertook in the agreements to respect the armistice lines and to proceed to the negotiation of peace treaties.

All these events, coming one after the other with great speed, shook the Arab countries, and, to a lesser extent, the non-Arab Muslim world. They had a particularly great impact on the Oriental Jews. It had happened more than once in the distant past—e.g., in the last decades of the Second Jewish Commonwealth—that clashes between the Palestinian Jews and their opponents (whatever the reason and whatever the outcome) triggered persecutions and massacres of those Jews who lived in countries allied or sympathetic to the elements the Jews fought in Palestine. This age-old community of fate between Israel and the Diaspora asserted its force once again during and after Israel's War of Independence. Anti-Jewish manifestations, occasionally of a violent nature, became the order of the day in the Arab countries. These events gave the impetus to most Jewish villagers in the Arab countries to leave the homes in which they and their ancestors had lived for many centuries and to seek the relative safety of the big cities with their police (whose notoriously late arrival at the scene of a mob attack was, after all, better than no arrival at all), their solidly packed and often quite large Jewish ghettoes, and their European residential quarters whose presence spelled the illusion of greater restraint on the part of the mob.

At the same time, the direct impact of the establishment of the State of Israel on the tradition-bound, religious, and in general unenlightened Jewish populations of Muslim (both Arab and non-Arab) countries was almost apocalyptic. This, too, is by now an oft-told tale, as is their naive identification of this great historical event with the even greater religious event, the onset of the Messianic days, for which the Oriental Jews, unlike many of their Ashkenazi brethren, never ceased to wait, to hope, and to yearn. The combined effect of Arab enmity and this Messianic upsurge, to which must be added the effective help in the organization of shelter and shipping rendered by outside Jewish agencies, was the transplantation to Israel of several Middle Eastern Jewish communities in their entirety and of the majority or a great proportion of others. Those who remained behind had all flocked to the biggest cities in each country. Jewish village life became a thing of the past in the Middle East, as it had in Europe.

Migration and Urbanization

Migration to new countries almost inevitably entails urban settlement. Villages rarely have an opening for precisely that skill which the newcomer happens to possess, and villagers have a strong ingroup feeling which goes hand in hand with distrust and dislike of foreigners. But in the city the newcomer finds people from the old country whose help he can claim, and who had, as a rule,—at least in the larger urban communities—set up institutions to aid the new immigrants. These general observations have a special bearing on Jewish migration in post-World War II Western Europe.

In France and Germany in the early periods of their settlement all Jews lived in the cities. Even when the prohibition that barred Jews from owning land was lifted in the early nineteenth century, few Jews felt that they wanted to move to a village and become cultivators. The fact that the same period also witnessed the growth of metropolitan cities under the impact of industrialization enabled the Jews to move from small towns to medium-sized ones, and from the latter to the big metropolises.[10] In the borderland between France and Germany, in Alsace, the trend was first from the country to the local capital, Strasbourg, and then from there to Paris.[11]

In 1939 the total number of Jews in France was 300,000. By 1945 this was reduced to 180,000. After some five years of gradual increase due to immigration (1950: 235,000) came the large-scale influx of Jews from Algeria, Tunisia, and Morocco, most of whom arrived between 1950 and 1952 but who still continued to come in the late 1960s. By 1969 the number of these immigrants was estimated at 250,000, or about half of all the Jews in France. As a result of this immigration, the trend

101

toward concentration in Paris was checked, at least temporarily. Although in 1969 about half of all the Jews in France lived in the greater Paris area, many of the newcomers had settled in the southeast of France where the climate was somewhat similar to the one they had left behind in North Africa. Others went to the Vendee, Brittany, Normandy, and even to Alsace.[12] French provinces from which, prior to 1950, the Jews had almost entirely vanished, again became centers of Jewish life. The newcomers, to be sure, did not settle in villages, but sought out large or medium-sized towns. In 1966 there were Jewish populations ranging from one hundred to one thousand in more than sixty cities, and Jewish populations of fifty to one hundred in another thirty. Moreover, it was estimated that more than 30,000 Jews in France were virtually isolated.[13] One can foresee that as the North African newcomers adjust to French life, both assimilation and a trend toward concentration in Paris will inevitably set in.

In Belgium on the eve of World War II there were about 90,000 Jews, including some 30,000 refugees. After the war only 18,000 were left; all the rest were victims of the Nazi genocide.[14] In the postwar years a renewed influx of displaced Jews from both Western and Eastern Europe raised the number of Jews in Belgium to an estimated 40,000 by the 1960s. Of these, 24,000 lived in Brussels, 13,000 in Antwerp, 1,500 in Liege, 1,000 in Charleroi, and 500 in various scattered communities throughout the country. Even in this small country there was, however, a continuing influx from the provincial towns to Brussels.[15]

In the Netherlands, where the prewar Jewish community of 120,000 (which included 22,000 refugees) was reduced by the Nazi genocide to about 23,000, their number increased in the subsequent years to about 27,000, or, according to other estimates, 30,000. Of these, 12,000 lived in Amsterdam (which in 1920 had a Jewish population of 68,758); there were large communities also in Rotterdam and The Hague.[16]

In Italy in the early nineteenth century there were still flourishing Jewish village communities, but by the end of the century they were replaced by urban concentrations. Around 1900, 63 percent of the Jews of Italy lived in cities with more

102

than 100,000 inhabitants; by 1931—76 percent. In 1932 there were 45,000 Jews in Italy; by 1939, as a result of emigration, their number had decreased to 35,000. During the war their number was further reduced to 29,000. Postwar immigration brought their number up to about 33,000, at which figure it remained in the 1960s. About 13,500 Jews lived in Rome, 9,000 in Milan, 1,661 in Turin, 1,438 in Florence, and about 1,000 each in Livorno, Genoa, and Venice, and the balance of about 4,400 in sixteen other cities. No information as to the presence or absence of a trend toward concentration in the two largest centers of Rome and Milan was available, but it is known that by 1965 almost 100 percent of the Italian Jews lived in cities with more than 100,000 inhabitants.[17]

In England the same process could be observed. As Cecil Roth has written:

> The "country town" and small port communities of the Hanoverian period (Canterbury, Exeter, Gloucester, Kings Lynn, Penzance, Falmouth, Yarmouth, Bedford and so on) had disappeared out of existence or almost so by the end of the reign of Queen Victoria. The early years of this century were the heyday of the "small town" Jewish community. But now, as in the other lands, the "small town" Jew has drifted more and more to the large towns. . . .[18]

In the mid-1960s the same trend continued. Some small communities in South Wales closed down, and the population trend was from the small provincial towns into the cities, while at the same time there was a movement from the central city districts into the newer outlying suburbs. The chief attraction was the greater London area where in 1966 there lived an estimated 280,000 Jews out of a total Jewish population of Great Britain and Northern Ireland estimated at 450,000.[19]

It has been pointed out above that one of the important factors that attracted Jews from villages and small towns to large urban centers was the absence in the former, and the availability in the latter, of those apputenances and amenities of Jewish life without which a traditional Jew could not feel that he led a full Jewish life, such as synagogues, Jewish schools, and so forth.

Cecil Roth has made an observation that ties in directly with this point—namely, that in England, France, Belgium, or Holland in the early twentieth century a Jewish community of, say, three hundred souls was "able to maintain not only its synagogue, which would be open for service daily, but all the ancillary institutions, and a full complement of officiants. Today on the other hand they will be content with only occasional (at the best, weekly) services and a single communal factotum. The minimal dimensions of the viable Jewish community, as one might put it, have become much larger."[20] In other words, while around 1900 a village Jew may have been attracted to a Jewish community of three hundred by its full complement of Jewish services, in the 1960s the still strongly Jewish-attached members of the same community of three hundred may be equally attracted to a larger community because only in it can they find all the Jewish institutions they feel they need. Of course, the reason for the decline of the Jewish institutions in small communities is to be sought in the decline of the interest of the average Jew in those small communities (as well as in the large ones) in matters Jewish, in his shrunken commitment to Judaism, which he expresses in his diminished support of his synagogue and "ancillary institutions." This is why only a much larger community than the turn-of-the-century three hundred can today maintain these institutions.

In contrast to the rest of the Jewish world, in America one cannot speak of Jewish urbanization for the simple reason that from the very outset the American Diaspora was a purely urban one. That is to say, the process of urbanization had taken place among the Jewish immigrants prior to their arrival in America. When they arrived they not only were determined to settle in cities, but had made up their minds to select the biggest metropolitan centers for their residence. By 1927, when the total number of Jews in the United States was 4,228,000, no less than 2,942,000 (or almost 70 percent) of them lived in the eleven biggest cities of the country.[21] Forty years later (1966), when the total Jewish population of the United States was estimated at 5,720,000, the same cities, together with several new metropolitan areas, had a Jewish population of 4,564,000, or about 80 percent of the total.[22]

Thus the process of the urban concentration of the Jews, that began many centuries ago, accelerated after the industrial revolution, and was completed in the middle of the twentieth century, has resulted in a Jewish Diaspora which, for all practical purposes, is completely urbanized and which evinces a pronounced tendency to congregate in the largest metropolitan areas of every country.

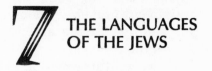

7 THE LANGUAGES OF THE JEWS

General Character

In general, one can observe an inverse correlation between the hold a national culture has on a people and the prevalence of the knowledge of foreign languages in its midst: the more a people is taken with its own culture, the less it is likely to know a second language in addition to its own national tongue. French and English can be adduced as examples of languages whose speakers (with few exceptions) are averse to learning other languages; the quasi-chauvinistic adulation of French culture by the French and of English by the British is, of course, proverbial. A contrasting example is that of eighteenth- and nineteenth-century Polish and Russian nobility, whose lack of appreciation of their own national cultures motivated them not only to learn French but also to speak it in preference to Polish or Russian.

Until the onset of the Enlightenment, the Jews formed an exception to this general rule, as they did to many other socio-cultural generalizations. Greatly devoted to their traditional religio-national culture, disdainful of other cultures, and insistent on cultural self-isolation from the non-Jewish environment, the Jews nevertheless learned and spoke other languages in addition to their own. In many ages and places they gave up Hebrew altogether. These linguistic developments in the history of the Jews were, of course, brought about by the Diaspora, but Diaspora conditions alone could not account for them, for often the Jews spoke languages which, while originally adopted from the non-Jews, were not the language of their actual environment (e.g., Yiddish in Eastern Europe, or Ladino in Greece and Turkey). It is as if, however foreign the origin of a language, once the force of circumstances made the Jews adopt it as their

107

vernacular, they came to consider it part of their traditional religio-cultural equipment and were therefore loath to give it up for another tongue among whose speakers they subsequently found themselves.

However, this aversion to linguistic change and the successful resistance to it date only from the latter part of the Middle Ages. Prior to that period, from late Biblical times down to the twelfth or thirteenth centuries, the Jews were always willing to give up their old languages and to adopt new ones in their stead. Thereafter, they refused to do so until the nineteenth century, when their entire situation underwent a basic change in consequence of the Enlightenment, emancipation, and assimilation.

One of the most interesting questions in Jewish history is: What was the reason for this disappearance of their old linguistic flexibility, as a result of which no new languages were acquired by Jewish Diasporas from about the thirteenth to the nineteenth century? Why did the Jews, who for centuries had been among the finest contributors to Arabic literature and culture, readily give up their Arabic for Spanish? And why, on the other hand, after their expulsion from Spain did they refuse to abandon their Ladino _or the languages of the countries in which they then settled? Why was the same process repeated by the Ashkenazi Jews, who acquired German in the Middle Ages but then clung to it for centuries in Polish, Lithuanian, Russian, Ukrainian, Rumanian, and other linguistic environments?

One explanation is that the cultures of the new environments in which the Jews found refuge after their expulsions from Spain and from German lands were considered by them as inferior to the ones they had left behind, and therefore they resisted them and their languages. This may have indeed been the case in Eastern Europe and in the lands of the Ottoman Empire, but this explanation cannot be applied to France, Holland, and England, where the Ashkenazi immigrants from Eastern Europe retained their Yiddish and the Sephardi immigrants from Spain and Portugal their Ladino. Most instructive in this connection is the case of the Ashkenazi Jews who had acquired German before they were forced to flee from Germany to Eastern Europe, where they retained their German vernacular and developed it into Yiddish. Yet when they came back to Germany in the seventeenth century, they refused to give up their Yiddish for German. Obviously, the theory that the cultural superiority felt by the Jews in relation to the non-Jewish environment prevented them from acquiring the language of a culture they considered inferior cannot be invoked to explain the Jewish reluctance to adopt the new form of the same language that a few centuries earlier conquered them without difficulty.

An alternative explanation is that up to the early Middle Ages contact between the Jews and the non-Jews had been more intensive than after the fourteenth century; and that, consequently, in the earlier period the Jews acquired the languages spoken by their host peoples, while in later times the objective circumstances of greater isolation resulted in the retention of whatever language they were speaking. This explanation, again, may be correct in a number of cases, but does not hold good in others. For instance, in Arab countries the amount of contact between the Jews and the Arabs has certainly not diminished appreciably in the last few centuries, and nevertheless the Jews in many places have retained a form of Arabic vernacular that is definitely archaic in comparison with the speech of their Muslim Arab neighbors. That is to say, up to a certain period the Jews adopted the idiom of the Arabs, then this process was discontinued, and while the colloquial of the Arabs continued to change, that of the Jews remained relatively unchanged and therefore appears archaic today.

Whatever the explanation, or the combination of explanations, the fact remains that, until their emancipation, all the languages spoken by the Jewish Diasporas were old tongues that had become rooted among them prior to the sixteenth century. From that time on the Jews no longer adopted new languages, even if they lived in linguistically foreign countries for centuries. The "Jewish languages," therefore, are those tongues or dialects spoken, and in most cases also written, by the Jews, which they adopted prior to the sixteenth century and then modified through the introduction of Hebrew words, usages, and syntactical forms, and into which they subsequently also incorporated

109

lexical elements from the languages of their actual environment, but whose basic stock they preserved in a somewhat archaic form.

The Hebrew lexical elements in the Jewish languages have in many cases something to do with Jewish religion and tradition. These aspects of Jewish culture have a rich Hebrew (and partly Aramaic) vocabulary in the Bible, the Talmud, the liturgy and the Jewish law codes, and it was inevitable that they should be retained in their original form, or with some dialectal modification, in all the Jewish vernaculars. Religious terms such as *Tora, Shabbat, Shekhina, kiddush, b'rakha, shaharit, mussaf, minha, ma'ariv, k'ri'at Sh'ma', Rosh HaShana, Yom Kippur, Sukkot, Pesah, Shavu'ot, Purim, Hanukka, bar mitzva, kasher, and t'refa;* historical-cultural terms such as *galut, mazal tov, tzarot* (in Yiddish: *tzores*), *hevra, hakham, bakhur* (Yiddish, *bokher*), *sh'tut* (Yiddish, *shtus*), *m'shuga',* and many others were incorporated into all Jewish vernaculars, in forms derived from the locally current pronunciation of Hebrew. In this connection it is interesting to note that the Hebrew names of God were not retained: God became *Allah* in Judeo-Arabic, *Khuda* in Judeo-Persian, *Dio* or *Senior* in Ladino, *Got* or *Oybershter* in Yiddish, etc.—all terms taken from the respective foreign tongues.

Another general characteristic of all Jewish languages is that many Hebrew words are incorporated into them in conjunction with a verb (often an auxiliary verb) taken from the foreign base language. Moreover, Hebrew words are treated as foreign words—i.e., prefixes and/or suffixes taken from the base language are appended to them. For example, in Yiddish *gepaskent* ("judged") is composed of the German verbal prefix *ge-*, the Hebrew verbal root *pask* (from *posek*, judge), and the German verbal suffix *-t.* Or the phrase *ikh bin ir moykhl dem to'es* ("I forgive her the mistake"), in which "I forgive" is expressed by using the German pronoun *ikh* ("I") and verb *bin* ("am") in combination with the Hebrew participle *moykhl* (literally "forgiving"). Of the two concluding words, the first, *dem,* is the German article, and the second, *to'es,* is the Hebrew noun "mistake."

The same procedure can be observed in Ladino: *gaviento*

("proud") is derived from the Hebrew *ga'ava,* pride, plus the Spanish nominal suffix *-iento; garonodo* ("glutton"), from the Hebrew *garon,* throat, plus the Spanish nominal suffix *-odo; diburiar* ("to speak a foreign language"), from the Hebrew *dibbur,* speech, plus the Spanish infinitive suffix *-iar; darsar* ("to talk a lot"), from Hebrew *darash,* preach, plus the Spanish infinitive suffix *-ar; zakhutiero* ("one who performs good deeds") from Hebrew *z'khut,* merit, plus the Spanish nominal suffix *-iero.* Countless other examples could be cited.

In Judeo-Arabic and Judeo-Persian, too, the same method is used for the incorporation of Hebrew words into the Arabic and Persian base languages. In Iraqi Judeo-Arabic, for example, they say *kayidrush* ("he will preach") from the Hebrew *darash,* preach, with the Judeo-Arabic colloquial verbal prefix *ka-,* followed by the Arabic third person prefix *yi-,* and the Hebrew verb vocalized in the Arabic imperfect form.

Aramaic

Aramaic was the ancestral language of the Hebrew patriarchs. The totality of the patriarchal family was ritualistically referred to as "a wandering Aramaean" (Deuteronomy 25:5). Those members of the family of Abraham who remained in Meso-potamia were consistently termed Aramaeans (cf. Genesis 25:20; 28:5; 31:20,24). Their language was Aramaic (cf. 2 Kings 18:26; Isaiah 36:11; Daniel 2:4; Ezra 4:7). Aramaic was also the mother tongue of Abraham, who, of course, is the mythical personifica-tion of that band of Aramaeans who settled in Canaan. In Canaan this group soon adopted the language of the country, which their descendants even centuries later still termed "the language of Canaan" (Isaiah 19:18), as well as "Jewish" (*Y'hudit,* cf. 2 Kings 18:26,28; Isaiah 36:11,13; Nehemiah 13:24; 2 Chronicles 32:18). Incidentally, it is interesting that while Abraham and his descendants are invariably called "Hebrew" and "Hebrews," the language they adopted in Canaan and developed into the classical Biblical Hebrew is never in the entire Bible termed *'ivrit,* "Hebrew."

After they adopted Canaanite (i.e., Hebrew) as their vernacu-

111

lar, the patriarchal Hebrew clan must have retained at least some knowledge of their ancestral Aramaic. This is implied in the stories about Eliezer and Jacob who seem to have had no difficulty in communicating with Abraham's kinfolk in Mesopotamia, which they could have done only through the medium of Aramaic. It is also reflected in the stories about the patriarchs' Aramaean wives and concubines (Sarah, Rebekkah, Leah, Rachel, Bilha, and Zilpa), all of whom had Aramaic as their mother tongue, which to some extent they must have passed on to their children. One can thus conclude that the members of the patriarchal family were imagined in Biblical times as having been bilingual—a remarkable mythical prefiguration of the bilingualism that was to characterize the Jews in most times and most places.

It must have been in the generation represented by the children of the twelve sons of Jacob that the Aramaic of the ancestors died out: This is the conclusion one is led to on the basis of the simple fact that most of the wives of the twelve sons were Canaanite women who knew only the "language of Canaan"—i.e., Hebrew.

During the period of Egyptian slavery the Children of Israel remained faithful to this language, and it was probably during that time that the dialectal differences between Hebrew and Canaanite developed. However, after the conquest of Canaan, and especially in the later monarchic period, Aramaic, which was the diplomatic *lingua franca* of the entire ancient Near East, was spoken in addition to their Hebrew mother tongue, at least by the leaders of the people (cf. 2 Kings 18:26; Isaiah 36:11). In the Babylonian exile (586 BCE) the Judean captives rapidly learned the Aramaic vernacular of Babylonia. Much of the post-exilic books of the Bible itself (Ezra and Daniel) is written in Aramaic.

During the period of the Second Jewish Commonwealth the Jews of Palestine knew both Hebrew and Aramaic, although a knowledge of the former became increasingly confined to members of the learned class who used either Hebrew of Aramaic in writing their religio-scholarly works. Among the uneducated people Hebrew was gradually displaced by other languages (cf.

Nehemiah 13:24), primarily by Aramaic. Eventually an Aramaic translation of the Bible became a necessity.

The same development led to the use of Aramaic in writing both the Palestinian (425 CE) and the Babylonian Talmuds (500 CE). In the Talmudic academies of both countries the local Aramaic dialects became the languages of tuition and discussion from the third century CE on, and thus it was inevitable that the same language should be used in writing down the "minutes" of these discussions, which came to form the texts of the two Talmuds.

While Aramaic remained the dominant vernacular of the Jews until its replacement in the seventh century by Arabic, it was by no means the only language in addition to Hebrew used by the Jews in antiquity. Although Aramaic still held sway in all of Western Asia, Greek became the Jewish vernacular, in Egypt exclusively and in Palestine side by side with Aramaic. Greek, of course, penetrated the East, and with it the Jewish world, in consequence of the conquests of Alexander the Great (356–323 BCE), which initiated the Hellenization of the lands ruled by his successors. In Egypt, where the Jews gave up both Hebrew and Aramaic, the Bible had to be translated into Greek (the so-called Septuagint, begun in the third century BCE) in order to make it again accessible to them. Subsequently Jewish authors wrote Jewish philosophical works as well as secular literature in Greek.[1] In Palestine, Hellenism was unsuccessful in replacing Aramaic with Greek, although individual Jews did learn and use Greek and even enjoyed the Greek authors. As a matter of fact, Rabbi Judah the Patriarch (ca. 200 CE), the author of the Mishna, was of the opinion that in Palestine the Jews should not speak Aramaic but either Hebrew or Greek.[2]

Another language spoken by Jews and, at least as far as Babylonia was concerned, preferred to Aramaic by some Talmudic sages, was Persian.[3]

After Arabic had replaced Aramaic as the Jewish vernacular, Aramaic itself acquired an aura of sanctity as the second holy tongue of the Jews after Hebrew. In the synagogue, the reading of the *Targum* (the Aramaic translation of the Bible) was continued although it had ceased to fulfil its original function—

namely, to permit the less educated members of the congregation to understand the Biblical portion read in Hebrew as part of the service; Aramaic verses were written by religious poets and added to the festival liturgies; Halakhic literature, including the Responsa of the *Geonim,* used Aramaic as its principal medium, as did Aggadic literature in the early post-Talmudic centuries, until this literary *genre* reverted to Hebrew. Since Aramaic was the language in which the Tannaim, the sages of the Mishnaic period, spoke if not wrote, Moses de Leon chose it over Hebrew as the language in which he wrote the *Zohar* (ca. 1280–85), pseudepigraphically attributed by him to the Tanna Rabbi Shimeon ben Yohai. The style of the *Zohar,* in turn, influenced both Kabbalistic and non-Kabbalistic literature produced by the Jews in subsequent centuries. Even prayers were written in Aramaic, so that in the synagogue the language retained an important position next to Hebrew.

Aramaic was retained as a living vernacular by one Diaspora only, that of the Kurdish Jews. The survival of the language among them was made possible by the fact that the Nestorian Christians (also known as Assyrians) who lived in the same area also retained Aramaic as their colloquial language. To be sure, the Aramaic spoken by the Kurdish Jews is identical neither with the ancient eastern Aramaic dialect in which the Babylonian Talmud is written nor with the Aramaic spoken by their Christian neighbors. It is, in fact, a language that has developed out of ancient Aramaic and is therefore rightly termed Neo-Aramaic. In addition to changes which a language is expected to undergo in the course of centuries, the Neo-Aramaic of the Jews of Kurdistan also has absorbed many words from Turkish (in Turkish Kurdistan), Arabic (in Iraqi Kurdistan), and Persian (in Iranian Kurdistan). As a result of these external influences, as well as of differential internal developments in the isolation of the rugged mountainous country, the vernacular spoken by the Kurdish Jews falls into several distinct dialects. In each they have produced a considerable oral literature, including a translation of the Bible, and a large amount of epic poetry. Selections from this rich religio-popular literature have been published in recent years by Professor Joseph J. Rivlin of Jerusalem and others.

A mixed Hebrew-Aramaic-Arabic dialect was discovered around the turn of this century by Nahum Slouschz among the troglodyte Jews in the Libyan mountains.[4]

Persian

Proceeding in chronological order, Judeo-Persian comes next after Aramaic. After the conquest of Babylonia by Cyrus the Great in 539 BCE, the Jews were drawn into the orbit of the Persian language, as attested first by many Persian proper names, titles, and nouns in the post-exilic books of the Bible, especially in Ezra and Nehemia. From the days of Cyrus to those of the Mongol invasion (1258 CE), most of the time Mesopotamia and Persia formed one single political unit. Consequently, in many periods, Mesopotamian ("Babylonian") Jewry was exposed to Persian influences, and Persian was its vernacular. The Babylonian Talmud contains a large number of Persian words, and as early as the Sassanian period (226–641 CE) there seem to have been Persian-speaking Jewish communities.

In Persia proper, Neo-Persian became the vernacular of the Jews in the tenth century, and subsequently it became modified in such a manner as to constitute separate Judeo-Persian dialects. These exhibit certain phonetic deviations from the dialects spoken by the Muslim Persians, containing an admixture of Hebrew words, more Arabic words than does standard Persian, as well as Aramaic elements. In writing Judeo-Persian, the Hebrew alphabet is used with the addition of certain diacritical marks.

In various places in Persia, and especially among the *Jedid al-Islam* (Marranos) of Meshhed, a kind of a secret language was developed for the purpose of allowing them to communicate with one another in the presence of Muslim Persians without being understood by them. The Jews of Meshhed called this language *Lo-Torai*—i.e., "not Tora-like"—because, while it contained, in addition to Persian, many Hebrew elements, it was not a pure Hebrew language like that of the Tora.[5]

The Jews who moved from Persia to Afghanistan, most recently from Meshhed in 1839, retained their Judeo-Persian until their emigration to Israel in the 1950s.

The Judeo-Persian spoken (and written in Hebrew characters) by Jews of Bukhara showed definite differences when compared to the Judeo-Persian in use among the Jews of Persia proper. For one thing, it contained Russian words and many words of Turkic origin, the latter borrowed from the language of the Turkman population of the area (although the majority population of the city of Bukhara itself consisted of Uzbeks who spoke Tajik—i.e., Persian). Apart from the lexicographic influence, it also exhibited some grammatical peculiarities.[6] In recent times the Jews of Samarkand published in this language a paper called *Roshnayi,* printed in Hebrew characters.

In the Caucasus, the Mountain Jews (*Dag Chufut*) speak (or spoke) a dialect called Farsi-Tat (i.e., Persian-Tat). This is an Iranian dialect, much modified by Semitic and Turkic influences. Up to the 1917 revolution the Mountain Jews wrote this vernacular in Hebrew characters; thereafter they switched to Latin characters. There are extant in the Farsi-Tat language liturgical and Kabbalistic manuscripts, as well as books printed from 1909 on.

Greek

Some two centuries after the adoption of Persian in the Mesopotamian-Persian area, Hellenization brought Greek to the Jews of Palestine and other countries conquered by Alexander. Greek became the second language, after Aramaic, into which the Bible was translated. Jewish authors living in Alexandria and Rome produced important works in Greek. Many Greek words penetrated into the Talmud and Jewish usage, among them the term for the supreme Jewish religious and legal council, the Sanhedrin (from Greek *synedrion*).

In contrast to other Jewish languages which differ from the corresponding languages as used by the non-Jews, in many cases to the extent of constituting a definitely separate dialect, the Greek spoken by the Jews from Hellenistic times down to the present has remained throughout practically identical with the language as spoken by non-Jews. The same observation can be made also with regard to the written language: it remained pure Greek. It was in this undiluted form that, beginning in the third century BCE, the Jews used Greek to produce Bible translations, historical writings, philosophical works, drama, poetry, liturgy, and other forms. First written in Greek characters, these works were transliterated several centuries later into Hebrew characters. The earliest extant Judeo-Greek writings in Hebrew characters date from the fifteenth century. Incidentally, the Karaites in Greece also used Hebrew characters for whatever literary works they produced.

Historical circumstances resulted in the disappearance of Greek as a Jewish vernacular in all Hellenistic countries, and even in Greece itself it was preserved, until the Nazi holocaust, in only a very few places. Up to World War II there were remnants of old Greek-speaking Jewish communities in Arta (Epirus), Chalcis (Euboea), Ianina, Prevesa, and Zante (an Ionian island). In 1900 the number of Greek-speaking Jews was estimated at about 5,000 in all Greece; most of the other Jews in Greece, whether of Spanish origin or descendants of ancient Greek Jewish communities, spoke Ladino. In some places, such as the island of Corfu, Jewish immigrants from Italy made the Apulian dialect dominant among the indigenous Jews.

After World War II the surviving remnants of Greek Jewry (approximately 6,500 in all), became rapidly Grecized.

Arabic

In pre-Islamic Arabia Jews wrote poetry in Arabic. In other countries they produced a rich and varied literature dating from the early eighth century, when they adopted Arabic as their vernacular soon after the Arab conquest of Iraq, the Levant, and North Africa. In all Arab countries Arabic has remained the vernacular of the Jews down to the present time. Colloquial Arabic itself, as spoken by the Muslims in the Arab countries, falls into numerous local dialects, several of which are mutually unintelligible. The greater the geographical distance between two Arabic-speaking peoples, the greater the dialectal difference. Thus Iraqis, Syrians, and Egyptians will understand one another, although there are differences in pronunciation as well as in vocabulary between their vernaculars. Moroccans and Syrians, or Moroccans and Yemenites, or Syrians and Yemenites will not, the differences in vocabulary, but especially in pronunciation, being too great.

Quite similar is the situation with regard to Judeo-Arabic. In addition, there are also differences between the Judeo-Arabic of any given locality and the standard colloquial Arabic of the same place. These differences are found in dialect (or pronunciation), in grammar, and in vocabulary. As to the dialectal differences, the Jews often use archaic word forms; the grammatical differences are due either to archaisms in the Judeo-Arabic or to the influence of Hebrew; the lexical differences are mainly the result of the incorporation of Hebrew words and phrases into Judeo-Arabic.

In writing their Arabic books and treatises, the Jews used Hebrew characters. The technical problems this procedure involved were easily overcome by adding diacritical dots above or below the Hebrew *gimel, dalet, tet, kaf, tzade,* and *tav,* in order to serve as the equivalents of Arabic *ghayn, dhal, ẓa, kha, ḍad,* and *tha.* Sometimes in place of the dots an apostrophe was inserted after the letter. Apart from these variants, the Hebrew and Arabic alphabets are identical and the first can thus readily be substituted for the second.

The custom of transliterating Arabic into Hebrew characters brought about a widening of the distance between the written forms of Arabic used by the Muslims and those employed by the Jews. The Arab populations remained throughout their history largely illiterate. As centuries passed, the dialects that developed among them in their far-flung countries became increasingly unlike the original, classical Arabic as exemplified by the language of the Koran. In writing they retained the classical form with minor modifications and, of course, with the addition of new lexical elements, and thus modern literary Arabic, identical in all Arab countries, emerged. Systems of putting colloquial Arabic into writing, however, did not develop. As a result, for the illiterate Arab masses in any country the literary Arabic used in books and newspapers has become almost like a foreign tongue which they have difficulty in understanding. The

118

rich oral literature (folk poetry, folk tales, proverbs) produced by the Arabs employed everywhere the local spoken idiom, and there was (and is) no way in which it could be put into writing in Arabic characters. Let me illustrate this with two simple examples. The well-known Biblical name Solomon (Hebrew, *Sh'lomo*) has in classical Arabic the form *Sulayman,* which is written *SLYMAN* (in Arabic, as in Hebrew, only consonants and the *matres lectionis alif, waw, ya,* and *ha* are written). In the Moroccan Arabic colloquial dialect this has changed to *Sliman.* If one wanted to write the word *Sliman* in Arabic, one could do so only by writing *SLYMAN,* which, however, would be read *Sulayman.* Or take the word for "house": in classical Arabic it is *baytun* (written *BYT*); in literary Arabic, it is pronounced *bayt* (like English "bite"; with the omission of the ending, the so-called nunation); in Arabic colloquials this has become *bet* or *bit* (as in English "bate" and "beat"). If one wants to write *bet* or *bit* in Arabic characters, one can do so only by writing *BYT,* which, of course, would be pronounced by everybody who knows how to read as *bayt.* Only recently has colloquial Arabic begun to be utilized in the publication of plays, in minutes of meetings, and the like. The problem with these publications, as with private letters which always have been written by the semi-illiterate in colloquial language, is that they represent merely an approximation of the actual pronunciation, and are read differently in every country. Because of this difficulty in using the Arabic alphabet in putting to writing dialect stories or other pieces of oral Arabic literature, when linguists collect and publish such material they as a rule resort to a transliteration system of Latin characters adopted for the purpose by the addition of diacritical marks.

The utilization of Hebrew characters for the writing of the Judeo-Arabic vernaculars had a similar function. It enabled the Jews to reproduce in writing the language as they spoke it with its dialectal peculiarities. For example, the classical Arabic word *sulṭān* (spelled *SLTAN*), is pronounced in Moroccan Judeo-Arabic, *tzlṭān,* and, in writing, is spelled צלטאן , which reproduces the spoken morpheme quite accurately.

In this manner the Jews in Arab lands were able not only to

read and write Hebrew but also to read and write their own Judeo-Arabic vernacular in Hebrew characters. As a result of this development, we possess written texts (in Hebrew characters) faithfully reflecting the Judeo-Arabic dialects of various Arab countries, some of them going back to the eighteenth century or even farther, while no corresponding literary documents were available for the various local Arabic dialects as spoken by the Muslim majority until modern times when European Arabists began to take an interest in them and devised their precise system of transliteration into Latin characters.

The literature produced by the Jews in Arabic is voluminous. They translated the Bible into Arabic; following the first translation by Saadia Gaon in the early tenth century, several more translations were made because Saadia's classical Arabic became unintelligible when spoken Judeo-Arabic changed. They wrote studies in Arabic of Hebrew language and grammar. They produced Bible dictionaries. They wrote philological works comparing Arabic, Aramaic, and Hebrew, the three Semitic languages in which Jewish scholars living in Arab lands were fluent. They authored important medical, mathematical, astronomical, philosophical, and other works, all in Arabic. They wrote poetry in both Hebrew and Arabic. And, in modern times, they published Judeo-Arabic newspapers, weeklies, and monthlies, some of which in the Iraqi and Tunisian dialect were among the earliest periodicals to appear in Arabic.[7]

Ladino

Ladino is the most commonly used designation for the vernacular spoken by the Sephardi Jews. It is also referred to as Spaniolic, Judeo-Spaniolic, or Judeo-Spanish. The early Jewish inhabitants of Spain used a Roman dialect which they carried along with them to Mauretania when they were expelled by the Visigoths in the seventh century. After the Arab victory in Spain (711), there were in the Iberian Peninsula itself both Spanish- and Arabic-speaking Jews. During the long centuries of Arab rule the Jews of Spain became increasingly Arabicized, until the trend was reversed in consequence of the territorial advance of the Christian Spaniards from north to south.

Under Spanish influence the Jews readily gave up their Arabic vernacular and adopted Spanish, or Castilian, which they spoke in its standard form until the expulsion in 1492. In this respect, as in many others, the history of Ladino closely parallels that of Yiddish. From the period preceding the expulsion from Spain practically no literary documents written in Judeo-Spaniolic are extant. However, from the early sixteenth century on, Ladino writings are increasingly plentiful. After the expulsion, the transformation that led from fifteenth-century Castilian to Ladino began. The Jews retained the fifteenth-century base form of Spanish, while the Spanish spoken in Spain evolved into its modern form. As a result, a distance developed between the two tongues, Ladino remaining "archaic" as compared to modern Spanish. Thus in modern Spanish "h" came to replace Castilian "f" and "g"; in Ladino, however, both "f" and "g" were retained. For example, Castilian and Ladino "fijo" has become modern Spanish "hijo"; "agora" has become "ahora."

As was the case in Yiddish, Ladino too incorporated many Hebrew words into its vocabulary. These are in most cases religious terms or terms pertaining to the special Jewish socio-cultural heritage. In addition to the Hebrew elements, lexical elements from the vernaculars of the countries in which the Sephardi Jews settled after their expulsion from Spain also were incorporated into Ladino from the seventeenth century on; in this manner Turkish, Greek, Bulgarian, Italian, and other elements entered Ladino. After 1860 the French influence, exerted by the schools of the Alliance Israélite Universelle, began to be felt. The words of Arabic origin which Ladino also contains may be due to survival from pre-Spanish times in Muslim Andalusia, or to more recent accretion after the settlement of Sephardi Jews in Arabic-speaking lands.

The Hebrew and the other foreign lexical elements are often treated in Ladino (again as in Yiddish) as if they were Spanish words—that is, they are Spaniolized, e.g., by appending Spanish endings to them. Some examples of this process have been adduced above in the introductory section of this chapter. A few more can be added: from Hebrew *hanaf,* to flatter, comes Ladino *hanifero* (flatterer); from Hebrew *haver* (friend)—Ladino *havransa* (partnership); Hebrew *hole* (sick)—Ladino *holitico* (sick ly); Hebrew *herem* (ban)—Ladino *enharimado* (person under a ban). In some cases the Hebrew words were changed in pronunciation so as to make them fit Spanish phonetics. For example, Hebrew *bet hayim* (cemetery, literally "house of life") became in Salonican Ladino *bedahi;* Hebrew *ba'al bayit* (master of the house)—Ladino *balabai;* Hebrew *shalosh s'udot* (the third meal on Sabbath)—Ladino *salisudo.*[8]

A characteristic development in Ladino was the considerable use to which it was put in connection with Jewish religious life. Not only were the traditional Hebrew prayers translated into Ladino (and often printed in Latin characters—see below), but new prayers were composed in Ladino and gained great popularity. One of them was the bedtime *Sh'ma'* which became an indispensible part of the daily home ritual.[9]

Like the other Jewish languages, Ladino is most often written in Hebrew characters. To make this possible, certain adaptations of the Hebrew alphabet had first to be worked out. The Hebrew *aleph* was adopted for the Spanish *a;* the *he,* for the *a* at the end of words; the *waw* for *o* and *u;* the *yod,* for *i* and *e;* the *zayin* with an apostrophe for the *j;* the *gimel* with an apostrophe for the *ch;* and so on. In this connection it must be added that no standardization of spelling, such as has developed in Yiddish, has taken place in Ladino, so that variations in the latter are greater than in the former.

In print, the so-called "Rashi" script is used most commonly, while in cursive handwriting there is a general Sephardi style, with several local variants.

From the early sixteenth century on, a rich literature was produced in Ladino. It began with translations from the Hebrew (the ritual laws of slaughtering, Bible translations, prayer books, etc.) printed either in the Hebrew so-called "square" characters, or in Hebrew "Rashi" script, or else in Latin characters. Somewhat later, original Ladino works began to appear, including apologetic writings, ethical studies, philosophical works, religious manuals, an exegetic-midrashic-homiletic encyclopedia (entitled *Me'Am Lo'ez*), poetic works (both religious and secular, including the famous folk-poems known as *romances*), and a compendium in defense of the Hebrew language. In the eighteenth and nineteenth centuries, mystical, kabbalistic, and moralistic books were added, including a Ladino translation of extracts from the *Zohar* and a biography of Israel Ba'al Shem Tov (Belgrade, 1852). The literary crop of the second half of the nineteenth century indicates a certain influence of the Ashkenazi Haskala (Enlightenment), as expressed in Ladino books on subjects such as Hebrew grammar, juvenile and popular books on Biblical history, geography, astronomy, astrology, arithmetic, a history of the Ottoman Empire, and numerous other general histories, biographies of famous men, and translations of novels, stories, and dramas from French, Arabic, and Hebrew. Also a number of periodicals were published in Ladino.

The cities in which these Ladino works were published from the sixteenth to the nineteenth centuries read like a list of the main places of the Sephardi Diaspora and include Constantinople, Smyrna, and Salonica in Turkey; Venice, Pisa, Ferrara, and Leghorn in Italy; Belgrade in Serbia; Vienna and Budapest in the Austro-Hungarian Empire as well as Hamburg, Amsterdam, and London.

To conclude this brief discussion of Ladino, it should be mentioned that the Sephardi Jews who spoke it found it relatively easy to acquire modern Spanish (and, to a lesser extent, Portuguese), which in turn facilitated their adjustment in the countries of Latin America.

Yiddish

The most widely used Jewish language is Yiddish, or Judeo-German, which until the Enlightenment was *the* vernacular of the entire Ashkenazi Diaspora. Yiddish emerged about the eleventh century among Jewish immigrants who had come from Northern France to the Rhine area. In France they had spoken a language based on Old French (see section Other Jewish Languages in this chapter). In the Rhineland they adopted the local Germanic dialects, while retaining much of both the phonemic quality and the vocabulary of their old language.[10]

At first they called their new language *"L'shon Ashk'naz,"* i.e.,

"Language of Germany." Later they referred to it by many different names: *Taitch* (i.e., *Deutsch*), meaning "German," *Ivre-Taitch* (Hebrew German), *Yiddish-Taitch* (Jewish-German), or simply "our language." Popularly it came to be referred to as *mame-losh'n,* i.e., "mother tongue."

By the twelfth century "Yiddish was a distinct fusion language with Germanic as its main component." Some historians attribute the emergence of the differences between Yiddish and the other medieval German dialects to "conscious efforts made by the Jews to keep apart in their religious and social life, and in almost all other areas, except trade and commerce."[11]

In the thirteenth century Yiddish, already comprised of Hebrew, French and German elements, began to absorb a fourth component: Slavic. Czech words and forms appeared first, then Polish, later White Russian and Ukrainian, and much later—in the nineteenth century—Russian. These new influences resulted in a considerable distinction between Eastern Yiddish as it developed in the Slavic countries, and Western Yiddish as spoken in the German lands. In addition, Yiddish absorbed minor but distinct contributions from practically every locality in which Yiddish-speaking Jews settled: Dutch words in Amsterdam, Lithuanian words in Lithuania, Moldavian words in Rumania, and, from the nineteenth century on, English words in the English speaking countries and Spanish words in Latin America.[12]

The incorporation into Yiddish of all these diverse lexical elements was effected by means of a simple device: they were treated as loan words and absorbed as such without affecting in any way the basic grammatical and syntactic structure of the language which remained Germanic. This meant the unhesitating affixing of German prefixes and suffixes to the non-German lexical elements, whether these were of Hebrew origin and thus very old constitutents in the Yiddish language, or recent neologisms absorbed from English. As examples of the former we can mention forms such as *er hot gepaskent* ("he decided") from the Hebrew *posek,* decide, with the addition of the German prefix *ge-* and suffix *-t;* or: *rayen* ("to look"), from the Hebrew *ro'e,* look, with the addition of the German infinitive ending *-en.*

124

English verbs, absorbed in recent decades in America, are treated in the same manner: *Ikh hob gemuvt* (or even *gemuft*)—i.e., "I have moved"; or *dzshetn*—i.e., "to fly by jet."

In the seventeenth century, as a result of contact between East European and Central European Jews, and primarily of reimmigration of the former into Central Europe, Yiddish became dominant also among the Jews of the German lands. In the meantime, standard German itself had developed, so that the Yiddish of the Jews now appeared as quite a different language containing many antiquated German words and forms, quite apart from its Hebrew and Slavic lexical elements. This is, in fact, how it appeared to such non-Jewish German scholars as Johannes Buxtorf (1564-1629) and Johann Christoph Wagenseil (1633-1705), who studied and wrote about the Yiddish language.

One important factor in the spread of Yiddish from Eastern Europe into Germany was the virtual monopoly of the Jewish scholarly and religious fields enjoyed by the Polish rabbis and teachers from the sixteenth to the eighteenth century, not only in Eastern Europe but in German lands as well. It was they who were called to officiate in most Jewish congregations in Germany, and it was due to the prestige they enjoyed as exponents of Jewish scholarship that the vernacular they spoke, Yiddish, was accepted in Germany, from where it spread also into Western Europe.

Before long Yiddish not only became the common vernacular in all parts of the Ashkenazi Diaspora (including the United States) but also acquired an aura of sanctity, so that to speak any other language was considered by tradition-minded Ashkenazi Jews (and is so considered to this very day by the most Orthodox) as a manifest sign of deviation from the straight but narrow path. From the nineteenth century on, however, side by side with the rich religious literature produced in Yiddish, enlightened and secularist Yiddishists put the language to completely nonreligious use, published in it secular (and occasionally even antireligious) books and newspapers, established a Yiddish stage for which they wrote melodramas, comedies, and musicals, and, in general, treated the language like any other medium of everyday communication.

Needless to say, Yiddish, like the other Jewish languages, is written in Hebrew characters. In order to make the Hebrew alphabet adequate for the transliteration of the German vocabulary of Yiddish, the convention developed in the early nineteenth century of using the Hebrew *aleph* for the phonemes *a* and *o*, the *waw* for the *u*, the *yod* for the *i*, the 'ayin for the *e*, the double *waw* for *v* (so that the *bet* always stands for *b*), the double *yod* for *ay* or *ey*, and the *waw* followed by a *yod* for *oy*. To distinguish between *p* and *f*, the פ stands for the former and the ף for the latter, while the *khaf* stands for *kh*, and *qof* for *k*. (The *kaf* is not used.) The English *j* phoneme causes some difficulty and is usually transliterated by no less than three Hebrew consonants, *d*, *z*, and *sh* (דזש), although in Judeo-Arabic the same phoneme, which exists also in Arabic, is transliterated simply as ג or ג'. The French *g* is transliterated as זש, *zsh*—e.g., *mirazsh* (mirage).

One more peculiarity of Yiddish must be mentioned. This is the change of gender as compared to German. Words that in German are masculine can become feminine in Yiddish; e.g., German *der Spargel*, becomes Yiddish *di Sparge*; German *der Pomp*, Yiddish *di Pompe*; German *der Kolben*, Yiddish *di Kolbe*. German feminine nouns can become masculine in Yiddish— e.g., German *die Pistole*, Yiddish *der Pistol*; German *die Neurose*, Yiddish *der Neuroz*; German *die Sorte*, Yiddish *der Sort*. German neuter nouns can become masculine in Yiddish—e.g., German *das Wunder*, Yiddish *der Wunder*; or feminine—e.g., German *das Weib*, Yiddish *di Weib*, German *das Nest*, Yiddish *di Nest*, German *das Schiff*, Yiddish *di Shif*.

From at least the seventeenth century, the Yiddish language area and the extent of the Ashkenazi Diaspora were coterminous. The Yiddish language had thus become the most reliable criterion for differentiating between Ashkenazi and non-Ashkenazi Jews. It also had become a veritable international (or, to be more precise, inter-Diasporal) Jewish language, a circumstance with far-reaching consequences. First of all, the very fact that until the Enlightenment almost all Ashkenazi Jews spoke Yiddish enabled them to maintain communications throughout Europe as if the continent were not broken up into numerous national and linguistic units. An Ashkenazi Jew could start out from Moscow, and in every city on the way all across the continent as far west as London he could talk to the Jews in his own mother tongue which was also theirs, could transact business with them, settle among them, and easily feel at home with them.

The internationalism of which the Jews were often accused by anti-Semites was in fact nothing but the existence of a Jewish religio-national culture with the Yiddish language as both its basis and main vehicle, and with carriers spread out all over the Ashkenazi Diaspora.

Yiddish played an important, and often crucial, role in the great historic events and movements that the Ashkenazi Diaspora experienced or initiated. It was the Yiddish language that enabled Hasidism to be carried by traveling preachers and *Maggidim* ("tellers" of moralistic tales) to all parts of the Ashkenazi Diaspora. True, printed tracts, which also spread the new doctrine, were mostly in Hebrew, rarely in Yiddish. But the printed word is cold, and converts are made everywhere and in all times by the power of oral suasion. This is why Hasidism, unable to cross the boundaries of Yiddish, remained confined to the Ashkenazi Diaspora.

In the spread of Haskala (Enlightenment), too, Yiddish had a significant enabling role. The fact that it was basically a German dialect made it easy for Ashkenazi *maskilim* (enlighteners) to proceed from *Taitch* to *Deutsch,* and to acquire a sufficient mastery of that closely related tongue, which enabled them to read and understand German *Bücher* (books), called in Yiddish *bikher.* Other factors also entered the picture, but it cannot be doubted that the linguistic affinity between German and Yiddish importantly contributed to making the acquisition of *German* culture, rather than of French or English, the prime goal of the Haskala.

Since Haskala was a Yiddish-based movement, the assimilationist trend and the religious reform that derived from it *eo ipso* grew out of the Yiddish subsoil. Of course, by the time these modern Jewish movements developed, Yiddish had been largely replaced by German in Germany, by French in France, and by English in the English-speaking countries, as well as by other

127

national languages in other lands. It was this breakup of the linguistic unity of the Ashkenazi Diaspora that deepened the cleavage between the Western and Eastern Ashkenazim. The latter, who retained Yiddish as their colloquial, now found that a formerly unknown language barrier was separating them from the Jews of the West.

In spite of this linguistic fragmentation, Yiddish, or rather a mixture of Yiddish and German, humorously referred to as *Kongressdeutsch,* still served until World War II as the *lingua franca* of the Zionist Congresses, the most important international Jewish gatherings in modern times. Even Hebrew had difficulty in making headway against *Kongressdeutsch* until the time when the Zionist Congresses were transferred to Israel.

It is difficult to give in a few sentences even the barest indication of the richness of the literature created by the Ashkenazi Jews in the Yiddish language. Following the early translations of prayer books and Biblical books in the fourteenth and fifteenth centuries, ethical works were written and printed in Yiddish in the sixteenth and seventeenth centuries, as well as *tehinnot,* prayers for women who, although able to read the Hebrew alphabet, could not understand the Hebrew prayers. The most popular of Yiddish women's books, the *Tz'ena UR'ena* (commonly pronounced *Tzenerene*), a paraphrase of the Bible embroidered with explanations, legends, and the like, was first printed in the late sixteenth century and remained the favorite reading matter of Ashkenazi women down to the nineteenth century. From the seventeenth century on a great number of Yiddish folk-medicine books, dream books, lot books, and similar popular works were produced, as well as a few secular works, especially poetical descriptions of persecutions and imitations of German epics.

In the eighteenth and nineteenth centuries the range of literary works printed in Yiddish matched that of any other national language. It included poetry, drama, short stories, novels, satire, scientific works, history, criticism, dictionaries, grammars, daily and weekly papers, magazines and other genres. Many modern Yiddish writers have become known to the general public through English, German, French, Russian, and other translations of their works, which in the original too had a readership in all parts of the Ashkenazi Diaspora. Despite the inroads made by the Enlightenment, assimilation, the Nazi genocide, the ingathering in Israel, the revival of the interest in Hebrew, the adoption of new languages by the Jews, and several other factors, Yiddish still has a sizable following and will continue to have one for at least another generation in all communities of the Ashkenazi Diaspora.

Other Jewish Languages

In the foregoing survey of the Jewish languages, a number of old tongues spoken by Jewish Diasporas in various ages and places have not yet been touched upon. Among them were several Italian dialects (Venetian, Apulian) as well as standard Italian. Some of these dialects survived until recently on the island of Corfu.

In Italy itself, until their emancipation (which took place in Rome in 1870), all Italian Jews used Judeo-Italian as their vernacular. This was an Italian dialect with numerous archaic forms and with the usual addition of Hebrew lexical elements. As was the case with other Jewish languages, Judeo-Italian, too, used to be written in Hebrew characters. Its literature was not very rich, but it comprised translations of the Bible and of liturgical texts (fifteenth and sixteenth centuries) as well as original liturgical poems and glossaries, elegies, and, later, sonnets, plays, and so on. Following the emancipation, the upper layers of the Italian Jewish community rapidly substituted Italian for Judeo-Italian in vernacular use. The Jewish dialect, however, survived among the poorer elements, and especially in the ghetto of Rome.

French dialects, and especially Provençal, were spoken by the Jews in medieval France.[13] The French vernacular was carried from France to the Rhineland and even as far east as Regensburg by French Jewish migrants in the eleventh to thirteenth centuries. It became the dominant Jewish colloquial in these regions until its gradual replacement by German.[14]

In all their languages, and, in addition, in Latin as well, the

Jews of the Middle Ages wrote secular poetry; however, these poems are not part of Jewish literature, but are early forerunners of the contributions made by Jewish authors to the literature of every nation among whom Jews lived, especially in the wake of the Enlightenment and assimilation. From the nineteenth century dates the beginning of the gradual disappearance of the old Jewish languages and their replacement by the vernaculars of the host countries, as a result of which process the Jews have, in most places of their Diaspora, become linguistically identical with the general population.

On the peripheries of the Jewish Diaspora this process of linguistic assimilation has been going on for many centuries. Thus the Falashas in Ethiopia have adopted Amharic, Tigrinya and some Agau dialects—the languages of the non-Jewish populations among whom they have lived for many centuries. The Jews of India spoke Marathi and Malayalam; those of China, the local Chinese dialect. Similarly the Krimchaks, the pre-Ashkenazi indigenous Jews of the Crimean Peninsula, spoke a Tatar dialect. Berber dialects survived among the Jews of Mzab, and in other places in North Africa. On the Somali coast the Jews spoke a South-Arabian dialect.

Hebrew

We shall conclude this chapter on the languages of the Jews with a brief statement about Hebrew, the Jewish language *par excellence*. The tenacity of the hold which Hebrew, once the family of Jacob acquired it, exercised over the Jewish people in every time and place is nothing short of phenomenal. Despite the dispersion, and the penetration of the local vernaculars discussed above, Hebrew, until the Enlightenment, remained everywhere the language of the synagogue, of religious life, and of traditional Jewish literature. In addition, records, minutes, and resolutions of meetings, and all kinds of official documents were written in Hebrew. Diaries were kept in Hebrew. Hebrew was the language of correspondence conducted by Jews across countries and continents, in connection with business transactions or learned religious questions and answers, the latter

130

known as *Responsa* literature. Prior to the Enlightenment, private letters too were frequently written in Hebrew, and this not only when Hebrew was the only common language known to the correspondents, but even when the writers did have a common vernacular in which they were more fluent. I still have in my possession Hebrew letters written in the 1890s from the village of Pata by my grandfather, who was a learned Talmudist and Hasid and was very far from being a Maskil, to my father, who was then a student in the Yeshiva of Nyitra (Neutra). Undoubtedly it would have been simpler for them to correspond in Yiddish, the language in which they conversed, but the very act of writing a letter seemed to have had a solemn aspect for my grandfather, as it had for countless other traditionally educated Jews all over the Diaspora, and the use of the holy tongue added weight and significance to the written communication.

Hebrew as a spoken language is not encountered as frequently as it is in writing, but data from many ages and places show that it was quite frequently used as a vernacular. The evidence has been assembled and presented by Simon Federbusch in a learned volume,[15] and it is, therefore, unnecessary to recapitulate it here. Only a few interesting data should be mentioned.

In the Middle Ages there were Hebrew-speaking Jewish tribes in Arabia. In the eleventh century medical lectures were held in Hebrew at the University of Montpellier. Joseph Caro, in his Kabbalistic book *Maggid Mesharim* states that the angel who was his spiritual mentor spoke to him in Hebrew. Caro's contemporary, Moshe Cordovero, commanded his disciples to "speak among themselves in the Holy Tongue at all times." Rabbi Isaiah Horowitz (1555–1628) records that the pious observed the custom of speaking only Hebrew on the Sabbath. The same custom was observed by Kabbalists, Hasidim, and *Mitnagdim* and other Jews in various countries down to the present time: they all felt that on this sacred day only the holy tongue must be used. Horowitz also reports that the Jews of Aleppo spoke Hebrew and that he delivered a sermon at the Aleppo synagogue in Hebrew. One of the aims of the Jewish Enlightenment, the Haskala, was to modernize the Hebrew language and make it a medium suitable for a discourse on any subject. Even before Eliezer Ben-Yehuda, usually referred to as "the father of modern Hebrew," arrived in Jerusalem, there were many Jews in that city who spoke Hebrew among themselves. Sir Moses Montefiore mentions somewhere in his diary that he encountered young Sephardi girls in Jerusalem chatting in Hebrew among themselves.

From its very inception the Zionist movement embraced the cause of Hebrew and gave a powerful impetus to the study of Hebrew wherever Zionist groups were established. While not all Zionists managed to become Hebraists, it is certainly true that all Hebraists became Zionists. Religious Jews, even those who were not Zionists, recognized the promotion of Hebrew by the Zionists as a positive Jewish value. Only the ultra-orthodox fringe, represented by some of the Hasidic rabbis and their followers, opposed Hebrew. In 1930 I heard the Rabbi of Munkač, in a Sabbath morning sermon in Marienbad, execrate the Zionists who spoke *"b'loshn hebraish, Rahmone litz'lon"* ("in the Hebrew language, God preserve us"). And in the 1950s the rabbi of the Satmarer Hasidim, Joel Teitelbaum, issued from Brooklyn a ukaze prohibiting his followers from learning and speaking Hebrew.

Despite such efforts, the growth of the Yishuv (the Jewish population of Palestine) and the modernization of Hebrew proceeded apace. When the League of Nations Mandate for Palestine provided (in 1922) that Hebrew was to be one of the three official languages of Palestine (the other two being English and Arabic), Hebrew had been used for decades as the vernacular of an ever-increasing Jewish population in the country. Within a relatively short time Hebrew had become transformed from the "sacred tongue" of Judaism into the national language of the Jewish people, the language of the Yishuv in Palestine, and, ultimately, the language of the State of Israel. In the concluding chapter of this book we shall see that the very idea of Zion underwent a similar metamorphosis from the religious-mythical-sacred to the secular-national.

What this transformation of Hebrew into the secular, everyday language of the Jews of Israel has meant for the Diaspora could be observed on several levels. In Jewish education it has brought about a greater emphasis on Hebrew as a living language taught in an increasing percentage of all Jewish schools with the Israeli pronunciation (the so-called "Sephardi" accent). Also many Ashkenazi synagogues and Reform Temples follow the trend to replace the traditional pronunciation of Hebrew with the Israeli-Sephardi one. Hebrew (both the language and literature) is being taught at an increasing number of universities. Thousands of Jewish students from many parts of the Diaspora go to study at one of the Israeli universities, in all of which Hebrew is the language of instruction. Intensive, Ulpan-type Hebrew courses are being conducted in many Diaspora communities. The scientific works written in Hebrew by Israeli scholars in such fields as Biblical studies, Palestinian archaeology, Jewish history, literature, religion, philosophy, make it necessary for specialists in these disciplines (whether Jewish or gentile) in all parts of the world to learn Hebrew to a degree sufficient to be able to peruse this Israeli research output. International Jewish gatherings (such as the World Zionist Congresses) are using Hebrew increasingly as the language in which their business is transacted. A growing number of Jews, who either visit Israel or meet Israeli visitors in the Diaspora, become familiar with the sound of Hebrew speech even if they do not understand it. While one cannot say that the Diaspora has become or is becoming Hebraized, it is unquestionably true that Hebrew has become part of the intellectual and cultural horizon of Diaspora Jewry.

Next to language, it is the culture of the common folk that makes for the most important difference among the three major divisions of the Jewish people. In fact, a good case could be made for arguing that the differences in folk culture are greater and deeper than the linguistic ones, for with regard to language both the Ashkenazim and the Sephardim have since the fifteenth century shown a remarkable resistance to assimilation to the tongue of the nations among whom they lived, while they showed no such resistance when it came to culture traits outside the tabooed and sacrosanct domain of religion. And, even in the latter, as we shall see, certain gentile influences could not be avoided.

Separatism

Cultural adaptation cannot be measured as easily and accurately as linguistic assimilation. The latter can even be expressed in percentages. For instance, if it is found that the Yiddish spoken by Polish Jews in the nineteenth century contained words of Polish derivation amounting to 10 percent of the total vocabulary, then this finding can be used as an index figure for the linguistic adaptation of the Jews to the language of the Polish environment in which they have lived since the sixteenth century. With regard to culture, on the other hand, it would be extremely difficult, if not impossible, to approximate such accuracy in the measurement of adaptation. One is, instead, reduced to weighing—i.e., evaluating—random observations made mostly by anthropologically untrained observers or recorders, and thus concluding as best one can to what degree the Jewish community in question has been influenced by the culture of its non-Jewish environment.

Again, such an evaluation will depend on the perspective from which one looks at the culture of a Jewish community. By way of illustration, let me mention that some time ago I began working on a study reconstructing the life of my grandfather and his family in the Hungarian village of Pata in Heves county where they lived from about 1880 to about 1920. My attention was focused on the almost complete separation that existed between the life forms of that Hasidic Orthodox Jewish family and the other five equally religious Jewish families of Pata, on the one hand, and those of the hundreds of Christian Hungarian families of the village, on the other. As I began to reconstruct the life of my grandfather's family by assembling it piecemeal from the written record left behind by my father (who was the eldest son) of his childhood at home, and from the reminiscences I had gathered in conversations with my uncle in Gyöngyös, Hungary, two uncles in Jerusalem, and one in Brooklyn (all long since dead), I received the distinct impression that the life of my grandfather and that of the Hungarian peasants of Pata had practically nothing in common. My grandfather had a grocery and general store which for most of the day was tended by my grandmother, while he sat all day long in the dining room behind the store and studied the Talmud. Only when grandmother had to leave her post to prepare the meals, or for some other reason, did grandfather emerge to mind the store. It goes without saying that the store was closed on Saturdays and Jewish holidays; I do not know whether it was open on Sundays and Christian holidays. The contact between my grandparents and the peasants of the village was confined to the occasions when the latter stopped by the store to make their small purchases. To this may be added the twice-daily trips my grandmother had to take to the village well until about 1902 when my father—who was by then a university student in Budapest—spent his first meager earnings on having a well dug in his parents' courtyard to spare his mother this exertion.

Life in the village, of course, necessitated the knowledge of at least some elementary Hungarian on the part of my grandparents. Whether they had a Yiddish accent when speaking Hungarian, and whether they knew how to read and write in that language, I do not know. But apart from this, my grandfather lived entirely in the world of Jewish tradition, primarily that of the Talmud. He knew nothing of the cultural traditions of the Pata peasants. (Later, from reading Hungarian village studies, I discovered that the peasants in those villages had quite a rich and colorful folk culture of their own, even though most of them were still illiterate at the time.) Even in the realm of material equipment there was very little similarity between grandfather's way of life and that of the Christian peasants of his village. His house, of course, whether he bought it or had it built for himself by the local craftsmen, was identical in appearance and layout with the houses of the other villagers: it had a mud floor, a thatched roof, and whitewashed walls—whether of mud bricks or burnt bricks I could not ascertain on the single occasion when I visited the house, in 1925, several years after my grandfather had moved away from the village, first to Satmar, where he became a Hasid of the Satmarer Rebbe, and then to Jerusalem, where he died in 1928. But, both grandfather's and grandmother's clothing was different; so were their hair styles and the food they ate, and, because of the strict separation of milk from meat dishes, even the arrangement of the kitchen. If one adds the differences between the intellectual interests of a learned and traditional Jew and those of a Hungarian peasant, and between the ethos of the one and of the other, one reaches the conclusion that this Hungarian Jew lived in practically complete cultural isolation from his purely Hungarian environment.

The World of Custom

Yet if one shifts one's point of view and asks: Was the admittedly 100-percent-Jewish life of my grandfather identical with the likewise 100-percent-Jewish life of similarly religious and tradition-bound Jews in Galicia, in Poland, in Lithuania, in Bukovina, in the Ukraine?—the answer will tend to be in the negative. And if one further asks: Was his life identical with the likewise 100-percent-Jewish life of Jews in the villages of Morocco, Kurdistan, or Yemen, even disregarding the linguistic differences?—the answer, evidently, will have to be an even more emphatic no. Even between my grandfather's life (or culture) and that of other Ashkenazi Jewish villagers there were palpable differences; between his life and that of Oriental Jewish villagers, the differences were not merely palpable but quite considerable. It is in these differences that the cultural influence of the non-Jewish environment, and/or the locally evolved Jewish cultural specificity express themselves.

The first thing to consider here is the all-pervading world of *minhag,* or custom. As in language, so in custom there are strictly local developments, which, however, the tradition-bound mind considers as having the same importance as, or even precedence over, the *halakha,* the traditionally transmitted mandatory religious law that is believed to go back to the revelation Moses received on Mount Sinai. "Custom overrides *halakha*" is an old rule, which itself already occurs in the Talmud.[1] From a conspectus of the customs of the localities within one larger area one can derive, or better recognize and establish, the common custom of an entire country, say the Lithuanian Diaspora. By the same token, all variants of all the Ashkenazi Diasporas together give the Ashkenazi *minhag.* The Lithuanian *minhag* will, of course, differ from the Galician *minhag.* But both will appear quite similar when compared with the Sephardi *minhag,* from which the Ashkenazi differs to a much greater degree. A very few examples will have to suffice from a realm of traditional life that is as wide and varied as the Jewish Diaspora itself.

In connection with birth, marriage, and death, the great stations of human life, there are innumerable customs which differ from place to place but which can be grouped together by contrasting the Ashkenazi with the Sephardi versions. For instance, among the Ashkenazim it has been customary to name a child after one of its deceased relatives but never after a living one. Among the Sephardim, on the other hand, a son is customarily named after a living grandfather or even father.[2] The Ashkenazi Jews preserved the Talmudic custom of placing ashes on the head of a bridegroom in memory of the destruction of the Temple,[3] while among the Sephardi Jews it became customary to substitute a wreath of olive leaves, "since olives are bitter and thus remind us of the mourning for Jerusalem."[4] Since polygyny and concubinage remained legal among Sephardi Jews, the custom developed to insert a clause into the *ketubba* (marriage contract) in which the bridegroom undertakes neither to marry another woman nor to take a concubine.[5] Among the Ashkenazi Jews, on the other hand, polygyny has been outlawed since ca. 1000 CE, so that there has been no need for such a clause in the marriage contract. The Sephardi *minhag* requires not only the bride and the groom but also the officiating rabbi to drink from the wine at the marriage ceremony; among the Ashkenazim only the bride and the groom drink.[6] The letter of divorce *(get)* differs among the Ashkenazim and Sephardim with regard to textual variations, the spelling of names, and the style of the script.[7] During the ritual of cleansing of the dead or during the funeral the Sephardim blow the shofar—a custom not practiced by the Ashkenazim.[8] The employment of professional wailing women, not practiced by the Ashkenazim, was retained by the Sephardim until the sixteenth century and was found among the Jews of Baghdad as long as they lived in that city.[9] The custom of putting earth from the Holy Land into the grave seems to have been practiced among the Ashkenazi Jews only during the Middle Ages.[10] Many more examples of Ashkenazi-Sephardi differences could be mentioned, but these will have to suffice in the present context. Let us instead proceed into a traditional realm contiguous to that of custom—namely, "superstition."

"Superstition"

In general, anthropologists have a strong aversion to using the term superstition, because of its definite derogatory connotation. Superstition is defined in Webster's *New World Dictionary* as "any belief or attitude that is inconsistent with the known laws of science or with what is generally considered in the particular society as true or rational; especially such a belief in charms, omens, the supernatural, etc." Equally valid and psychologically more telling is the anthropological semi-jocular definition: "superstition is what you believe and I don't; what I believe is religion." In any case, in every Jewish community, as in every other human group, there are or were beliefs and attitudes upon which the learned frowned but to which the simple folk nevertheless adhered with undiminished fervor. There were also beliefs and attitudes frowned upon by the learned people of one group but fervently followed by the learned of another group, and so on. As a broad generalization one can state that the influence of the non-Jewish environment on popular Jewish beliefs and practices (as we prefer to call them, rather than superstitions) has been much greater always and everywhere than the non-Jewish influence on officially sanctioned traditional doctrine and ritual. Moreover, the influence on the popular level has been not only intensive but also reciprocal; on the higher, doctrinary level, the mutual attitude has leaned more toward exclusivity. This observation was classically formulated by Edward William Lane in his incomparable *Manners and Customs of the Modern Egyptians* (written in Cairo between 1825 and 1835), where he said: "It is a very remarkable trait in the character of the people of Egypt and other countries of the East, that Muslims, Christians and Jews adopt each other's superstitions, while they abhor the leading doctrines of each other's faiths."[11]

Had Lane been a student of other countries as well, he would have undoubtedly substituted the word "world" in place of "East" in the above sentence. For it is a remarkable trait of folk cultures all over the world that popular beliefs and practices very easily cross national, religious, and ethnic boundaries, and even fly in the face of the general rule that, by and large, such traits are accepted only from those cultures that are considered superior by members of the group on the receiving end.

The Gentile Influence

The immediate relevance of the foregoing observation for the subject on hand is that when it comes to popular beliefs and practices, the Jewish Diasporas in every country received considerable influences from the non-Jewish environment, even when and where they regarded the culture of the latter as inferior. As a result, the cultural physiognomy of the Jewish ethnic groups showed greater variations in this area than in any other nonmaterial realm. As to material equipment and features, such as buildings, furniture, clothing, utensils, food, and so forth, the local availability of raw materials exerted its limiting influence everywhere and thus inevitably imparted a special, local character to the Jewish products over and beyond the cultural influence of the host peoples. Even popular beliefs and practices very frequently have a material basis, or a material, tangible aspect, so that the limitations and variations imposed by the physical environment often make themselves felt here as well.

This is true particularly in folk medicine, that widely ramified and ubiquitous combination of belief and practice which played an exceedingly important role in the life of all the peoples among whom the Jews were dispersed, and in which the latter learned more from their neighbors than traditional Jews at present care to admit. "Folk medicine," says Dr. Zimmels, the most outstanding authority on the medieval and later Jewish Responsa Literature, "was the channel through which a continuous flow of such [i.e., "superstitious"] ideas and practices" penetrated the Jewish communities from the outside.[12]

Folk medicine flourished, especially among the semi-learned but pious (i.e., tradition-abiding) Jews. Even as late as our own century, a great many books, usually small booklets, have appeared in print, written by rabbis and containing collections of charms, remedies, and recipes, not only for all kinds of aches and pains, but also for such purposes as averting dangers and demons, evoking love, increasing sexual powers, conferring fertility, and assuring easy childbirth, success, and safety. Usually these books of remedies and charms also contain instructions of how to perform divinations and interpret omens. In brief, they cover all areas of life which prescientific man desperately tried to bend to his will and which only too often elude our control even today. In many cases the learned rabbis wrote and published these handbooks in Hebrew, with many abbreviations, quotations from former authorities, and refer-

141

ences to the sacred books of Judaism, so that the recipes contained in them could be prepared only by other rabbis or at least by semi-learned individuals. The background and basis for these books of remedies and charms and other similar literature was the solid Jewish tradition; they addressed themselves to those who knew the tradition and were bound by it; those who, from the nineteenth century on, considered the entire 3,000-year-old structure of Jewish tradition as no longer valid in its ritual-legal aspects could see in this remedy book literature (if they knew about it at all) nothing but the outgrowth of a ritualistic-formalistic hypertrophy, or, as they would have put it, sheer, nonsensical superstition.

Differences Between Ashkenazim and Sephardim ————

Since, as stated above, many of the remedy books, collections of charms and incantations, and related writings were written in Hebrew, they were accessible to, and inevitably came to the attention of, the rabbis and the learned of communities belonging to a division of the Jewish people other than the one in which they had been composed and to which they primarily addressed themselves. So long as they remained in their original environment, the non-Jewish influences reflected in this literature went unnoticed, because they were the result of gradual seepage from the outside through the ghetto walls over the course of many generations. But they came as a shock to the rabbis of spatially and ethnically remote communities, who often gave vocal expression to their disapproval. "I am greatly astonished," writes Rabbi Moses ben Nahman (Nahmanides, 1194–c.1270), the Sephardi Talmudist, exegete, and physician, and one of the greatest minds of medieval Jewish Spain, "at the habit of the (pious) people of Allemagne [Germany] of occupying themselves with demons, conjuring them, and using them for various purposes."[13]

However, while Nahmanides thus objects to the German (i.e., Ashkenazi) Jewish custom of turning to demons, nonetheless he himself also believed in them. This becomes evident from his enumeration of the various types of idolatry which he considered prohibited under the Biblical injunction: "Tnou shalt have no other gods before Me."[14] He writes: "And the third type of idolatry [is that of those who] serve demons which are spirits . . . which hold sway over the nations, to make them the rulers of their lands, and to harm their enemies . . . as is known from the science of *nigromansia* [necromancy] also in the words of our rabbis . . . the demons are not at all *eloah* [divine], that is to say they are not like the angels who are called *eloah* but they are gods [*elohim*] . . . in whom no divinity [*elohut*] can be found. . . ."[15] In his commentary on Leviticus 17:7 Nahmanides further explains:

> The truth is, as I wrote above . . . that they are called demons [*shedim*] because their dwelling is in a desolate [*shadud*] place, such as the desert, and they are mainly found in corners, such as the northern one which is deserted because of the cold . . . and [it is as] our Rabbis said,[16] in three respects the demons are like the ministering angels and in three like the sons of man: they have wings like the angels, and they fly like the angels, and they know the future as the angels do; . . . but they eat and drink like humans, they multiply sexually like humans, and they die like humans . . . and while flying in the air of heaven they receive [information] from the guardian spirits of the constellations which dwell in the air . . . but [the demons] do not know what will happen in the distant future . . . and they only inform [the necromancers] of what is going to happen in the near future . . . and there is no need whatever in [appealing to] the demons because they cannot prevent the damage that is going to occur and they help in no way, nor do they inform one well in advance so that one should be able to take preventive measures. . . ."[17]

These explications of Nahmanides make it clear that when he reproached the Ashkenazi rabbis he did so not because they believed in demons, since he himself believed in their existence, but only because his Ashkenazi colleagues engaged in attempts to control them and to get help from them, which, Nahmanides believed, was futile.

While in this case the Sephardim took a more reserved position than the Ashkenazim, there were numerous other instances in the wide field of popular beliefs and practices in which a reverse relationship obtained. And there were, of course, popular customs that were observed equally among both

Sephardim and Ashkenazim. One of these was reported by Nahmanides himself: "It is known that on the 'night of the seal' [i.e., of Hoshana Rabba] the head of a man who will die that year will have no shadow."[18] He refers to the custom, described by numerous Sephardi and Ashkenazi rabbinical authorities (usually without any disapproval), of stepping out wrapped only in a blanket into the moonlight on the night of Hashana Rabba, letting the blanket drop, and observing carefully whether each and every part of one's naked body casts its proper shadow. If the shadow of the head was missing, the person could expect to die within a year; if that of a finger was not visible, a relative of his would die; if the entire right hand cast no shadow, it presaged the death of a son; in the case of the left hand, it presaged the demise of a daughter.[19]

In general, Polish Jewry was considered by Sephardi savants the most superstition-ridden community. About 1700, Tobias HaKohen (1652–1729), the Polish-Jewish physician and medical author who was the personal physician of five successive Turkish sultans, remarks in his encyclopedic *Ma'ase Tuvya* concerning the Polish Jews: "There is no country in the world where people occupy themselves with demons, amulets, incantations, conjurations, and dreams more than in this country."[20]

However, while in concrete detail the Polish (or, in general, Ashkenazi) popular beliefs and practices differed from those of the Sephardi Jews, the continued fascination exerted upon all of them in like manner by what outsiders would not hesitate to term superstition was a factor common to both Ashkenazim and Sephardim as well as to the Oriental Jews. And, what is particularly significant for our present considerations, the non-Jewish environmental influence made itself strongly felt in each division of the Jewish people and in each community within each division. The preoccupation of the Jews with the control of the supernatural continued until the nineteenth century, when the Enlightenment pried loose an increasing proportion of both the gentile and the Jewish populations from the grip of "superstition."

144

"Custom Overrides Law"———————————————————

No systematic study of outside influences on Jewish popular beliefs and practices has as yet been undertaken, nor has an extensive comparison between the Jewish and non-Jewish varieties of popular culture been attempted. But from the glimpses I gained during my four decades of studying Jewish and Middle Eastern cultures I have gathered the definite impression that popular beliefs and practices constitute the area in which the outside world most effectively penetrated the age-old defenses of traditional Jewish separatism. "Keep apart from the gentiles!" the *halakha,* the traditional, sacred, religious law, has consistently warned. "To approach them or to let them come near you can lead to one thing only: your submersion among them, culturally as well as ethnically."

However, "custom overrides law." The great truth of this ancient insight into the working of cultural dynamics has asserted itself in this area perhaps more decisively than in any other: custom, in the sense of popular beliefs and practices, even if of foreign origin, could not be prevented from penetrating and conquering Jewish life. This, too, was clearly recognized, although not as early as the previous cultural law: "Wie es sich christelt, so jüdelt's sich" is a German-Jewish saying that can be translated only in pale approximation: "Like Christian, like Jew." And, of course, as far as the Sephardi and Oriental Jews, who lived in a Muslim environment, were concerned, it was "like Muslim, like Jew." The deep truth in this ironically intended observation is amply borne out by any study conducted in any part of the Jewish Diaspora. This, in turn, means that the the overall differences between Ashkenazi, Sephardi, and Oriental Jewish ethnicity correspond, to a considerable extent, to the ethnic differences between the cultures of the three world areas in which the three major Jewish divisions lived for many centuries: Central and Eastern Europe (the main areas from which the Ashkenazim absorbed cultural influences); Mediterranean Europe and Turkey (the source of much of Sephardi ethnicity); and the Muslim world of the Arabs and

145

Persians (the origin of the main influences upon the Oriental Jews).

Under the influence of non-Jewish popular beliefs and practices that were too powerful to resist, all the three major divisions of the Jewish people nonchalantly disregarded not only general Jewish religio-legal principles, such as the prohibition against following the ways of the gentiles *("hukkat hagoy"),* but also explicit concrete commandments, such as dietary laws. As to the rabbis, in some cases they warned their flock that a certain popular practice was forbidden by Jewish law; in other instances they would find a loophole in the law to render it permissible. But in either case, the people would persist in the practice.

"HOLLEKREISCH"   Examples illustrative of this general thesis abound. One of the more remarkable of them was the German Jewish Hollekreisch ceremony, performed, at least since the fifteenth century, in connection with bestowing a secular name on a child. This was done in addition to, and at a later date than, the giving of a Jewish name to a boy at circumcision and to a girl on the first Sabbath after her birth. The infant would be lifted into the air three times, and each time the guests present shouted his secular name in unison, in response to a shouted, stereotyped question such as "Hollekreisch! What shall this child's name be?" or "Holle! Holle! This child's name shall be . . ." In certain parts of Germany this custom was religiously observed by the Jews down to the present century.

"Hollekreisch" means "Holle shout," and Holle herself is an ugly, hairy, old Teutonic witch (also called euphemistically Holda or Hulda—i.e., "beautiful"), who was feared by the German folk down to modern times. Of the several explanations of the meaning of this custom, the most likely is the one that views the shouting of the witch's name as an attempt to frighten her away so as to keep her from harming the child.[21] The power of German influence is specially apparent in this custom, because the Jews had their own Lilith, an old, indigenous night demon who lay in wait to harm the newborn child and therefore

146

also had to be kept at a distance by religio-magical means. [22] And yet it was the German witch, not the Jewish she-demon, who figured in connection with the giving of the secular name to the child. It appears that once the custom of calling the child by a non-Jewish (German) name was adopted, it brought with it the attendant non-Jewish belief in the Teutonic she-devil. Needless to say, this German-Jewish custom never struck root among Sephardi and Oriental Jews. To the latter, Holle was unknown, and thus, even if they heard about the Hollekreisch ceremony, they would have considered it still another manifestation of the foolishness of their superstitious German-Jewish brethren. So much for an example of a German "superstition" adopted by German Jews only.

NAMING PRACTICES   As a direct continuation of the Hollekreisch ceremony, let us now discuss the Jewish naming practices in general, an area in which strong non-Jewish influence has been manifest in all ages and places. In Biblical times the naming of a child had no specific religious connotation; it was at first the mother's prerogative, but later was taken over by the father. It was a religious act only to the extent that all important acts were part of the overall religious tenor of life. There was certainly no religious ceremony connected with it. [23]

In post-Biblical times the naming of the child gradually assumed a religious character with a ceremony performed in the synagogue.

As to the names themselves, they have always been subject to environmental influences and to changing fashions. Most Biblical names, as one would expect, have Hebrew nouns or verbs as their roots (e.g., *Yitzhak,* Heb. "he laughs"; *Binyamin,* Heb. "Son of the right hand"; *Y'sha'yahu* (Isaiah), Heb. "God helps," etc.). However, already in Biblical times, foreign names, too, appear (e.g., *Moshe,* which is of Egyptian origin; *Mord'khai,* from the name of the Babylonian god Marduk). In the Hellenistic period many Jews, including not only kings but also Talmudic sages, had Greek names, while Aramaic names remained equally popular. In the Talmud we find such Greek names as Tarphon (Tryphon), Pappos, Avtalion (Eutalion), Euridimos,

Horkenos (Hyrcanos), Antigonos, Symmachos. In the post-Talmudic period the custom spread of calling the first child by the name of his paternal (more rarely maternal) grandfather, as well as the practice of giving a child an additional name for civic purposes. The secular name was, in many cases, the translation of the Hebrew name into the language of the country (e.g., in Italy *Hayyim* was called also Vita; *Manoah*—Tranquillo, *Asael*—Diofatto, etc.); or names were chosen which in sound were similar to the Hebrew name (e.g. Menahem—Mann, Moshe—Moritz, Levi—Leo, etc.).

It was in the latter type of names that American Jews evinced much ingenuity in choosing names for their children which both resembled the traditional Hebrew name of the grandfather and at the same time sounded sufficiently Anglo-Saxon to satisfy their desire to ease the boy's or the girl's way in American society. Thus a man whose father had the Biblical name *Moshe* and was called by the civil name Moritz in Germany (or Mieczyslaw in Poland), would call his first born son *Moshe* in Hebrew and Morris or Max in English; more recently these two names had fallen in disfavor and little *Moshe* became Marvin, Murray, or Merwyn. However, totally un-Jewish names, such as Christine and Christopher, also are given to Jewish children in more obvious attempts to give them a Christian coloration. As Duker remarked,

> preference is always given to Anglo-Saxon and Celtic names (Barry, Dennis), and only a few Biblical names are acceptable (David, Daniel, Judith), more among women than men. It is presumed that changes of family names occur more frequently among Jews than among other ethnic groups. A study during the Second World War revealed that 50 to 60 per cent of names of Jews in the armed forces were of Anglo-Saxon or Celtic origin.[24]

What prompts Jewish parents to choose typical Anglo-Saxon or similar names for their children? It is not as if they wanted to make it easier for their children to assimilate. The Jewish father or mother who called their son Pierpont would have been horrified at the idea that the boy, upon reaching the age of discretion, could decide to leave the fold of Judaism. The Anglo-Saxon name was intended, in all probability, merely to

148

facilitate Pierpont's getting ahead in the outside world, among gentiles with whom he had only business or professional contact, and who, when learning what his name was, would not suspect that he was Jewish. At the same time, his parents piously hoped, Pierpont would remain a good Jew at home, marry a Jewish girl, become a member of a Jewish congregation, and bring up his children as Jews. Thus we recognize in the choice of non-Jewish-sounding names a manifestation of Marranism: of the endeavor to appear outwardly as non-Jewish while in fact remaining Jewish; to be indistinguishable from John Doe in his capacity as a member of his civic, business, or professional community, while continuing to be a solid member of his Jewish community or congregation.[25]

MUMIA   Our next example is a folk practice adopted by Sephardi Jews from their historical environment in the circum-Mediterranean area. One of the most popular remedies among the Sephardi Jews was the *mumia* (i.e., mummy). This consisted of a piece of a mummified human body, which was pulverized and taken internally (often with honey-water), as a cure against all kinds of complaints. Its origin goes back to antiquity, when Pliny, Virgil, Josephus Flavius, and others considered bitumen a potent drug. The bitumen of the Dead Sea was called *mumia* in old Syriac medical books, as well as by the Persians and Arabs. The same term *mumia* was also applied by them to the material used by the ancient Egyptians for embalming the dead, hence the medieval Latin *mumia,* from which is derived the English mummy. In this way the belief in the medicinal value of bitumen was transferred to mummies, and by the twelfth century, in response to growing demand, the Jews of Alexandria had developed a lively mummy trade. Among the Sephardi Jews *mumia* continued to be taken internally down to the present time, even among Sephardim living in Seattle, Washington. The rabbis, throughout the ages, gave the practice their official sanction.[26] But although in Christian Europe *mumia* was a popular drug from the sixteenth to eighteenth centuries, with traces of it even in the nineteenth century,[27] the Ashkenazi Jews never adopted this particular folk remedy.

SAINT WORSHIP   Our final example illustrates the dependence of Oriental Jews on their Muslim environment in the field of popular belief and custom. In the Arab Middle East there are two countries in which the veneration of saints is a more prevalent feature of folk religion than in any other Muslim country: they are Morocco and Iraq. The saint is usually a person of great piety who may have lived in the distant past or as recently as within the memory of the older people. His tomb or shrine is the center of his cult which is expressed in popular festivities celebrated on his birthday, and in individual or group pilgrimages to his shrine, often in fulfillment of a vow, or in order to present a request for health, fertility, good fortune, safety, and the like. Stories about the miracle-working powers of the saints are innumerable and serve to spread their fame far beyond the immediate vicinity of the shrine, and also across religious lines.

As to the veneration of saints among the Jews, there are several unmistakable signs indicating Muslim influence. Among the Jews, just as among the Muslims, the two countries in which saint-worship is most prevalent are Morocco and Iraq. The external forms of the practice and the types of legends told about the saints are very similar in both religions. Most important is the fact that there are numerous Muslim saints equally venerated by Jews, and vice versa, there are Jewish saints venerated also by Muslims. In some cases, where both Jews and Muslims visit the same shrine, the Jews claim that the saint buried in it was Jewish, while the Muslims make an equal claim for his having been a Muslim.[28]

L. Voinot, who made a special study of the subject in Morocco, reports about the veneration of thirty-one saints by both Muslims and Jews, fourteen cases of Muslim saints worshiped by Jews, and fifty cases of Jewish saints invoked by Muslims.[29] The evidence on this subject is so rich that André Chouraqui, in his history of North African Jewry, states categorically: "The cult of the saints is one of the most characteristic traits of Judaism in North Africa. . . . The Jews, intimately intermixed with the Muslims, had to adopt [these] customs. . . . The same *Tzaddik,* the same *Marabout* often receive, without distinction, the pious offerings of both Jews and Muslims."[30]

While the veneration of saints is most frequent in Morocco and Iraq, other Middle Eastern countries also supply examples of this form of popular religion as well as of the joint worship of the same saint by members of diverse faiths. Thus, for instance, two miles from Dumahou in Egypt is the shrine of Abu Hassira, a Jewish saint who is venerated equally by Jews, Muslims, and Copts. In rare cases, the saint thus venerated is a woman, such as Sol Ha Sadiqa, or, briefly and more familiarly, Soliqa, a Jewish girl who, in 1834, at the age of seventeen, chose a martyr's death rather than convert to Islam and become a member of the imperial harem.[31]

The Attitude of the Leaders

The foregoing examples give us an inkling as to the extent and depth of non-Jewish influences on popular Jewish life everywhere and in every time down to the present. And they serve to illustrate the differences that developed in the Diaspora among various Jewries under the influence of the gentile environment. Nor has this influence been confined to folk life—i.e., to popular beliefs and practices, which, at least occasionally, were frowned upon by the rabbinical authorities. On the contrary, it ranged from material culture all the way to ethos and values. If, despite these influences, the total configuration of Jewish culture seemed nowhere markedly similar to that of non-Jewish culture, the reason for this was that in the officially accepted Jewish religious codes there was a sufficient number of specific rules and regulations to introduce a clear demarcation between the Jewish and gentile ways of life. It was the adherence to these rules and regulations that made the Jews "a people scattered and separated," as phrased in the ancient Hamanic accusation.[32]

Thus far we have discussed two trends that worked at cross purposes: the *intention* of the Jews to remain isolated from the non-Jewish environment, an intention stressed primarily by the rabbis who in most places and times were the spokesmen of Jewish separatism; and the impact of the non-Jewish environment which, again in most places and at most times, proved a force that could not be turned aside. That the latter factor should have exerted such a strong influence is the more remarkable

151

since not only the Jewish leadership, but also the Christian and Muslim religious authorities, in most times and places, did everything in their power to prevent contact between members of their own flock and the Jews. From the days of the Emperor Constantine (280–337) down to the French Revolution, Christian Church leaders, individually and in councils, issued bulls, decrees, and edicts in endless sequence prohibiting the Christian people from having contact of even the most cursory and superficial nature with Jews. One of the latest of these instructions issued in Rome on the eve of the French Revolution was entitled *Edict Against the Jews,* and contained, among other things, the following: "Jews and Christians are forbidden to play, eat, drink, hold intercourse, or exchange confidences of ever so trifling a nature with one another."[33]

Yet despite this effort sustained over centuries by both the Jewish and the gentile authorities to keep the two peoples apart, the acculturative processes continued. No matter how negatively weighted the outgroup stereotype, each group absorbed cultural influences from the other. In the case of the Jews this ongoing process resulted in an increasing variety in the cultural physiognomy of their Diasporas.

Internal Development

Another factor that contributed significantly to the differentiation among the Jewish Diasporas was the internal development of each of the Jewries. It is not easy to keep external (i.e., non-Jewish, environmental) influences apart from internal developments, because these two factors, in turn, act upon each other. A cultural trait received from the outside may trigger an internal development; and vice versa, a trait that developed internally may result in specific receptivity to an outside feature.

As an example of the former, we may refer to the penetration of mystical ideas from medieval German Christianity into early German-Jewish mysticism. As Fritz I. Baer and Gershom Scholem have shown, the *Sepher Hasidim,* the most important literary monument of the German-Jewish mystical movement, which contains mostly the writings of R. Jehuda HeHasid (died

152

in Regensburg, 1217), clearly shows its dependence on German Christian mysticism.[34] Foreign influences affected the Kabbalistic movement in numerous other ways as well. Elsewhere I had occasion to show, for instance, that the Kabbalistic doctrine of a divine tetrad—consisting of Father, Mother, Son, and Daughter—as found in the *Zohar,* is simply the thirteenth-century Spanish-Jewish version of a much more ancient tetradic mythology found in many ancient Near Eastern cultures, in India and elsewhere.[35] And yet, after absorbing these outside influences, the Kabbala developed, internally, into a most original and powerful Jewish mystical movement which, for more than half a millennium, decisively influenced Jewish religious developments, and is at present still a potent force in certain Jewish circles.

For an example of an internally developed Jewish trait that has created a specific Jewish receptivity for an outside feature we may turn to the familiar scene of American Jewish life. One of the characteristics of modern American culture is the great emphasis on higher education. Statistically this finds expression in the percentage of college-age youth actually attending college and in the percentage of college-trained individuals in the general population; both percentages are considerably higher in the United States than in any other country in the world. Both percentages within the American Jewish community, however, are again considerably higher than in the American population in general. The reason is not hard to find: it is the traditional Jewish, internally developed trait of according first priority to learning. True, in the traditional Jewish environment from which most of the American Jewish immigrants came, learning meant "Tora study,"—i.e., primarily, the study of the Talmud—while what America offered was a strong incentive for secular studies. But there can be no doubt that the traditional emphasis on Tora study was responsible for the equally strong new emphasis on secular studies. It was simply a matter of extending or generalizing an old attitude to apply to a new situation. The common feature was the value of learning as such, the preference for using one's brain rather than one's brawn as an instrument of achievement.

This, then, is part of the background against which the present diversity in the cultural physiognomy of the Jewish Diaspora must be viewed. Both external influences and internal Jewish developments were at work for centuries carving out the individual features, and what we see today is the end result, so far, of these complex and intricate processes. We shall next have a closer look at some of the more characteristic features of the Jewish cultural physiognomy in the various Diasporas, and, in particular, at the influence of the gentile environment on the specific directions taken by the Jewish drive for cultural excellence.

ETHNICITY
AND
EXCELLENCE

In the foregoing chapters we have discussed the major characteristics of the Jewish people: the shared religious basis of its
life and the diversity of the religious customs in the various
Diasporas; the disparate views on the concept of Diaspora held
by the various religious trends that have developed in Judaism
following the Enlightenment and emancipation; the problem of
the Jewish "race" and the demographic differences among the
Diasporas; the phenomenon of urbanization common to all of
them and the languages of the Jews; the issue of the Jewish and
non-Jewish components in the folk cultures of the Diasporas. In
the course of these discussions we have repeatedly had occasion
to point to the influences exerted by the non-Jewish environment on the Jewish Diasporas—in each case an influence from
the majority on a minority in its midst.

Having done all this, one question now inevitably presents
itself: in view of the differences among the Jewish Diasporas
and of the similarities between each Diaspora and its gentile
environment, can the Jews still be considered an ethnic group?
In order to answer this question about Jewish ethnicity, we shall
have, first, to define as clearly as possible what is meant by an
ethnic group, and, second, to see whether the terms of that
definition are applicable to the Jews.

In studying human populations it has been found that, in
addition to differing in such more easily discernible traits as
physical type and language, they also differ in what anthropologists call "culture patterns." The patterns of a culture consist of
the traditions of the group, its values, ethos, expectations, and
behavior, as well as the tangible (i.e., material) expressions of
these factors. Moreover, localized human groups are often found
to focus their group identification around these elements that
constitute their culture patterns, and this identification itself is a

very significant factor in differentiating among them. Often group identification amounts to group loyalty, but whether it does or not, a group characterized by the sharing of common forms of the features that constitute a culture possesses an ethnicity of its own. An ethnic group, then, can be defined as a group that possesses shared culture patterns which include traditions, values, ethos, expectations, and behavior, and which are primary foci of group identification.[1]

Diaspora and Cultural Physiognomy

Let us now see to what extent this definition of an ethnic group is applicable to the Jews.

It goes without saying that the question of Jewish ethnicity is greatly complicated by the fact of the Diaspora and all its attendant circumstances. First of all, to live in a Diaspora inevitably means to be exposed to cultural influences emanating from the majority population that surrounds the Jewish community. However intent the Jews were on preserving their own identity, however ingenious the religious barriers they erected between themselves and their host peoples, they could not prevent being affected by these influences. For one thing, rarely if ever was a Jewish community economically self-sufficient. Economic interdependence meant that the Jews had to learn the language of the host people in order to be able to communicate with it, and had to acquire at least a modicum of its manners and values in order to render commercial and other types of contact at all possible. The locally available nutrients of a vegetable (and less frequently animal) origin could not fail to influence the Jewish food habits in the direction of those of the host people, although, of course, religious proscriptions made commensality impossible. The climatic conditions forced upon the Jews the adoption of locally developed styles of clothing, although, again, religious laws imposed certain restrictions in this area as well. When it came to housing and furnishing, the adoption of local materials and styles was rarely limited by religious rules. The sum total of these adaptive processes was considerable cultural similarity that developed in each Diaspora community with respect of the non-Jewish environment.

An inevitable concomitant of this development was the emergence of commensurate differences among the various Jewish communities. These differences were most apparent in external features. A German Jew visiting Yemen would be struck by two things: that Yemenite Jews were very different from German Jews, and that they were very similar to Muslim Yemenites. The houses, furniture, utensils, clothes, food, the ways of earning a livelihood, the arts, the pastimes, the family life, the social forms, the gestures, behavior patterns, speech, etc., of the Yemenite Jews were, in the eyes of the German Jew, much closer to their Muslim Yemenite than to their German Jewish counterparts. And, of course, a Yemenite Jew visiting Germany would make exactly the same observation in reverse.

Even the realm of religion, this most specifically Jewish of all traditional Jewish cultural attainments, exhibited some degree of local non-Jewish influence, resulting in a variety and diversity as between one Jewish community and another. The common Jewish tradition was there, but the manner in which religion was observed bespoke external influence. The Yemenite Jews, for instance, would leave their shoes at the door of the synagogue and would sit down on mats or flat, hard mattresslike cushions spread on the floor of the synagogue. They would use all kinds of strange bunches of herbs. They would pronounce the Hebrew prayers with a complement of phonemes identical with those of Arabic, and chant the Bible and the prayers to tunes which appear very much like the Arabic melodies of the country and certainly are built on the identical micro-tonal elements.

Outside the synagogue, the German Jewish visitor would notice that religious life revolved around much of what he, in all good conscience, would have to brand sheer superstition: demons, spirits, the evil eye, other supernatural forces and influences, and the innumerable ways and means of combating, propitiating, or otherwise influencing them. Before long he would find that in all this there was a striking similarity between the beliefs and practices of the Jews and the Muslims. When the Yemenite Jew repays the visit, he makes exactly the same observations with reference to the German—i.e., Christian— influence on the German Jewish religious beliefs and practices both in and out of the synagogue.

Thus one reaches the conclusion that every Diaspora has a cultural physiognomy of its own, which includes even religious features not shared by others. In each a balance is struck between what is traditionally Jewish and what is assimilated into Jewish life from the culture of the non-Jewish environment.

Hukkat HaGoy—*Gentile Custom*

It has been pointed out by historians and social scientists that throughout the long history of their dispersion, the Jews tended to assimilate to those cultures which they considered superior to their own, and conversely, to resist assimilation in cultural environments they found inferior. There can be no doubt as to the general correctness of this observation, as, for instance, the considerable degree of Jewish assimilation to German culture as against the much more limited assimilation to Polish or Ukrainian will readily show. Assimilation, which, in this context is more accurately termed acculturation, is, after all, but the acquisition of something the cultural environment has to offer; and groups, just like individuals, acquire only things they want, things they value. This generalization, however, does not tell the whole story.

For, in addition to the free decision to acquire something because it appears desirable, individuals or groups often are induced or even forced by circumstances to adopt cultural traits which in themselves hold no attraction whatsoever for them. To put it differently, considerations that have nothing to do with the trait itself may motivate its adoption. An example can be seen in the prohibition of polygyny introduced among Ashkenazi Jews about the year 1000 CE., in all probability primarily because in Christian Europe monogamy was considered the only proper and moral form of marriage.[2] When Rabbenu Gershom's synod passed the enactment banning polygyny, it did so not because monogamy in itself was considered a more desirable form of marriage—for tradition-bound Jews who look upon the polygynous Biblical patriarchs as their ideal this would be an impossibility—but because the adoption of monogamy was deemed necessary in order to remove the Gentile reproach of sexual immorality leveled against the Jews.

Another case in point is the papal decree of 1555 (modified in 1560 and renewed in 1776) according to which the Jews in Avignon and the Papal States had to wear a green or black hat of a certain shape. The decree was abolished in 1792, but the Jews continued to wear the hat out of habit.[3]

The fear of adopting the customs of the gentiles was a strong motivation in Jewish religion for centuries. The Biblical admonition, "Ye shall not walk in the customs of the nations which I am casting out before you, for they did all these things, and therefore I abhorred them,"[4] was interpreted as a general prohibition against behaving in the manner of idolaters and practicing their rites. It was incorporated by Maimonides among the 613 commandments, as prohibitive commandment number 30. *Hukkat HaGoy,* "gentile custom," became forbidden, not because it was necessarily wrong in itself, but because it would contribute to a rapprochement between the Jews and the gentiles, and that was anathema. Rabbi Moshe Isserles in his glosses to the *Shulhan 'Arukh* decrees: "He [a Jew] must be different from them [the gentiles] in his clothing and the rest of his doings," although then he goes on to limit this obligatory self-differentiation to clothing used and acts performed for immoral purposes.[5] Nevertheless, and despite the constant warnings of the rabbis from Talmudic times down to the nineteenth century, the *Hukkat HaGoy,* which term we may take as referring in general to non-Jewish cultural traits, penetrated Jewish life everywhere, even entering those circles that imposed upon themselves the strictest isolation. To mention but one characteristic example, the Hasidic garb (black knee breeches, white stockings, and long black caftan, topped by the fur-brimmed *shtrayml* on Saturdays and holidays), the discarding of which is considered to this very day by the Hasidic Jews as the equivalent of becoming a renegade, was adopted by their ancestors in the sixteenth century in imitation of the costume worn by the Polish and Russian upper classes. The very word *shtrayml,* incidentally, is derived from the Polish *stroj,* meaning costume.[6]

Thus, whatever the reason for adopting traits from the gentile cultural arsenal, the fact remains that a certain degree of acculturation to the non-Jewish environment has taken place in every Jewish Diaspora. In view of these acculturative processes which have been very considerable, especially since the Jewish Enlightenment and emancipation, it is quite clear that the Jewish people as a whole cannot be termed an ethnic group. There are marked cultural differences among the Diasporas, and everywhere the traits in which one Diaspora differs from the others are the traits in respect of which it is similar to its non-Jewish environment. On the other hand, no Jewish Diaspora is culturally identical with its non-Jewish host people; or, to put it positively, every Diaspora differs from its gentile environment in several respects, of which Jewish religion and tradition and Jewish group identification are the most important. In relation to the gentile majority, the Jewish Diaspora of every country thus constitutes a different ethnic group, but the Jews as a whole constitute not one but several ethnic groups.

Each of these Jewish ethnic groups exhibits its own specific combination of Jewish and non-Jewish traits. The Jewish traits themselves are of two kinds: old ones, going back to earlier ages and countries of Jewish sojourn, including some—and these are often precisely the most important ones—that date back to Biblical Hebrew origins; and new ones, which themselves may be several generations old, but which were developed locally and therefore are likely to represent a certain divergence from corresponding traits that are the results of other local developments.

What we have referred to as "non-Jewish traits" are either traits directly borrowed from the non-Jewish environment in an unchanged form, or traits coming from the outside but modified to varying extents within the Jewish context.

However, the actual situation in a given Jewish Diaspora is much more complex than one would gather from this simplistic dichotomy into Jewish and non-Jewish traits. A Jewish community, as we shall see—e.g., in Chapter XIX, which deals with American Jewry—may exhibit a "Jewish" trait in a form and with an intensity that reflect the influence of the non-Jewish environment. Whether such a trait can or cannot be considered Jewish may be a theoretical issue, but the implication it has relative to the survival chances of the community in question is not.

Such problems aside, the Jewish—non-Jewish scale alone yields a wide spectrum of Diasporas, and, within them, of communities, congregations, and individuals ranging from the overwhelmingly Jewish to the almost entirely non-Jewish. In addition to the dispersion itself and to the differences in concrete cultural content, it is this great variety in the relative weights of the Jewish versus the non-Jewish cultural components that make the Jewish Diaspora a unique phenomenon from the cultural point of view among the peoples of the world.

Cultural Excellence

The foregoing discussion of the cultural physiognomy of the Jewish Diasporas and the varying relative weights of the Jewish and gentile elements in their cultural configurations leads us directly to a consideration of the phenomenon in which the relationship of the Jews to the cultures of their host countries most remarkably expresses itself. The phenomenon I am referring to is the frequently observable tendency of the Jews to direct their attention, talent, and élan primarily into areas that represent cultural foci in the lives of their host peoples. This tendency to aim at excellence precisely in the focal concerns of the host cultures recurs with such regularity in the Jewish Diaspora that it can be taken as a manifestation of yet another trait characterizing Jewish ethnicity. It is, of course, evident that such a correlation between Jewish and general cultural specialization could manifest itself only in places and ages in which the Jews were enabled by their own attitudes, on the one hand, and the external, objective circumstances, on the other, to participate intensively in the life of their non-Jewish environment. Such conditions obtained only rarely prior to the Enlightenment and emancipation. They existed in Hellenistic Alexandria, in medieval Muslim Spain, and to some extent in Renaissance and post-Renaissance Italy. From the nineteenth century on, they existed in the countries of Central and Western Europe. Examples illustrating the earlier historical periods can be found in Chapter VII, "The Languages of the Jews" (Hellenistic Greek culture), Chapter XIV, "The Sephardi Jews" (medieval Arab culture), and Chapter XXI, "Five Exceptional Communities" (Renaissance and post-Renaissance Italian culture). In looking over those examples drawn from various periods of intensive Jewish participation in the focal cultural concerns of the non-Jewish environment, one gets the impression that the Jews had an uncanny sense that enabled them to discern at an early stage the specific character of the cultural developments upon which their host peoples were about to embark, and then, considering this a supreme challenge, had immediately risen to meet it.

In no other cultural surrounding has this challenge been as great and manifold as in the modern Western world, and nowhere have the Jews met it as successfuly. Country after country can be cited to show to what extent the Jews, once they obtained emancipation and passed through the processes of Enlightenment and acculturation, literally threw themselves into the pursuit of excellence in those fields that were most highly regarded in the culture of their host countries.

The close correlation between the Jewish and gentile cultural endeavor could be most completely and convincingly demonstrated by going through a large general encyclopedia and noting the number of Jews and non-Jews in various fields of art, literature, science, etc., in one country after another. Instead of embarking on such an extremely time-consuming and unattractive exercise, let us rather rely on a few illustrative examples. Take mathematics, for instance. That Jews have a special talent for mathematics has been so often stated that it almost amounts to a commonplace. Yet only rarely has it been noted that Jewish mathematical genius has emerged precisely in countries in which mathematics has been a focal cultural interest on the general scholarly scene. A. A. Roback touched upon this issue in passing in his study on "The Jew in Modern Science" when he remarked: "England has not been productive of great mathematicians; and, of course, there were few Jews who distinguished themselves in this field as compared with German or Italian Jews. . . ." Further, "Only those who are conversant with Jewish biography will appreciate to what extent German mathematics is in large part Jewish mathematics. . . ." As for France, Roback went on to say: "In France mathematics has had a glorious following, but as is well known, the arts and humanistic subjects have been far better cultivated; and as the saying goes *Wie es sich christelt so jüdelt sich es* [i.e., "like Christian, like Jew"] is true here."[7]

In England in the nineteenth century (when, as a result of their emancipation, the Jews could fully participate in the life of the country) the nation as a whole focused much of its attention on parliamentarianism at home, colonial expansion overseas, mercantilism (including the mass production and distribution of consumer goods), finance and money management, and sports (including pugilism). In each of these activities the English Jews took a prominent part.[8] Their participation in science began later, but by the early decades of the twentieth century they were represented in it well beyond their proportion in the urban population of the country.

On the other hand, in the various fields of British artistic creativity, including the fine arts, music, and the performing arts, the Jewish participation has remained scanty down to the present day. Anglo-Jewry has nothing to show that would be comparable to the role Jews played in German painting, poetry, literature, and music, in Russian musical performance, in French painting, literature, music, and theater, or in the press and journalism, literature, and art in the United States. The meager Jewish share in these areas appears to have something to do with the fact that these fields of endeavor, with the possible exception of the novel, played a relatively smaller role in British culture as a whole.

Or take Germany in the century or so that elapsed between the Jewish Enlightenment and the rise of Nazism, and during which the Jews were able to participate fully in the cultural life of the country. An early forerunner of this period was Moses Mendel-sohn (1729–1786) who became an important figure in the galaxy of the eighteenth-century German philosophers, earning the designations "the German Plato" and "the German Socrates." In the nineteenth century the German genius expressed itself primarily in poetry, literature, music, and science, and in each of these fields some of the greatest names were those of German Jews.

Additional insight into the correlation between Jewish and gentile scholarly and intellectual excellence in specific fields can be reached from a comparison of the numbers of Nobel Prize winners in various countries with the numbers of Jews among them. Of the total of 393 Nobel Prizes awarded from 1901 to 1969, ten Peace Prizes were given to institutions and organiza-tions. Of the 383 prizes awarded to individuals, 58, or 15.2 per cent were given to Jews (including a few who were of mixed Jewish-gentile parentage). The 383 Prizes went to citizens or residents of thirty-four countries. Of these countries, twelve were the countries of citizenship or residence of one Nobel Prize winner each; four additional countries were the homes of two Nobel Prize winners each. In none of these sixteen countries (except Israel) did a Jew receive the Prize. Among the four countries which were the countries of citizenship or residence of three Nobel Prize winners each, there was one, Hungary, in which one of the three was Jewish. Four more countries re-ceived from four to seven Prizes each—none of these went to Jews. One country, Denmark, received nine Prizes, including one given to a half-Jew. The remaining nine countries were the countries of citizenship or residence of no less than 318 Nobel Prize winners, or 83 percent of all Prizes awarded to individuals. Of these 318 Prizes, 51 or 15.8 percent, went to Jews. Again, within these nine countries there were four (the United States, Great Britain, Germany, and France) which, among them, accounted for 257 Prizes, or 67.1 percent of all Prizes awarded to individuals. Of these 257 Prizes, forty-three, or 16.7 percent, were awarded to Jews. In three of these four countries, the number of Jewish Nobel Prize winners in relation to the total of the country was high (in Germany 28 percent; in the United

States 20.6 percent; in France 15.8 percent). In the fourth, Great Britain, there was not a single British-born or British educated Jew among the sixty Prize winners (see below). A more detailed comparison of the Jewish and total numbers of Nobel Prize winners in the eleven countries in which Jews were among the winners of the Prize can be made by perusing Table IV.

The figures contained in the table confirm the tentative conclusion we reached on the basis of other observations: namely, that the greater the stimulus provided by the cultural atmosphere and attainments of the gentile environment, the higher the level of the Jewish performance. This observation could even be refined and formulated as follows: the greater the stimulus provided by the cultural attainment of the gentile environment *in a given field,* the higher the level of Jewish performance in that field. At least some support for this specific correlation can be found in Table IV in the figures pertaining to Germany, Hungary, Russia, and the United States.

A word has to be said about the conspicuous absence of Jews among the sixty Nobel Prize winners in England. In view of the Jewish record in other countries with high numbers of Nobel Prize winners (i.e., more than ten), this is a definitely anomalous phenomenon that must have specific reasons. Perhaps it can be attributed to the fact that Anglo-Jewry concentrated its attention on those fields in which the genius of Britain most essentially expressed itself—namely parliamentarianism, commercialism, and colonialism—fields in which no Nobel Prizes are awarded. In doing this, the best talents of the small and newly acculturated Anglo-Jewish community expended themselves in keeping abreast of, and, indeed, often leading, Britain in these areas of primary cultural concern and concentration. Anglo-Jewry thus perforce neglected those fields which were secondary within the British cultural configuration: physics, chemistry, physiology, medicine, literature, and work for world peace. It could not muster enough strength to supply Britain with top-ranking men in these fields as well. Britain herself, on the other hand, had enough genius left in its population of 50 million to make it the second ranking country after the United States in its number of Nobel laureates, and to become thus a world leader even in those fields which within its own culture lay somewhat outside the focal interest.

This explanation of the absence of Jews among Britain's Nobel Prize winners becomes even more plausible if one considers that in the other three major Nobel Prize winning countries the Jews won their Prizes in those fields which were areas of prime concern for the country as a whole: physics, chemistry, and medicine in the United States, Germany, and France, and literature in France, Germany, and Russia. All this again reconfirms our conclusion, that, to put it differently this time, the more important a cultural field in the totality of a nation's culture, the more intensive the Jewish participation in it.

TABLE IV
JEWISH AND TOTAL NOBEL PRIZE WINNERS BY COUNTRY AND FIELD, 1901–1969

Country	JEWS						TOTAL					
	Physics	Chemistry	Medicine	Literature	Peace	Total	Physics	Chemistry	Medicine	Literature	Peace	Total
Austria	1	–	2	–	1	4	2	1	2	–	2	7
Denmark	1	–	–	–	–	1	1	–	4	3	1	9
France	1	1	2	1	1	6	8	6	6	11	7	38
Germany	4	4	6	2	–	16	16	22	11	5	3	57
Holland	–	–	–	–	1	1	5	2	2	–	1	10
Hungary	–	1	–	–	–	1	–	1	2	–	–	3
Israel	–	–	–	1	–	1	–	–	–	1	–	1
Italy	2	–	–	–	–	2	2	1	2	4	1	10
Russia	2	–	1	1	–	4	6	1	2	3	–	12
Switzerland	–	–	1	–	–	1	–	3	4	2	3	12
United States	10	1	10	–	–	21	28	16	38	6	14	102
Total	21	7	22	5	3	58	68	53	73	35	32	261

TWO

10 THE ORIENTAL JEWS

Jews under Islam

The origins of the Oriental Jewish communities and their early history until the destruction of Jerusalem (70 CE) were briefly sketched in Chapter I. Here we shall continue the story of these communities which constitute the most varied and most fragmented of the three divisions of the Jewish people. But first a few words of general characterization are in order.

Since the rise of Islam and its spread over the entire Middle East, the Oriental Jews have lived in a Muslim environment. This historical circumstance in itself has been unquestionably the most important external factor that influenced their destinies and development. Ever since Islam was founded by Mohammed (570–632), accepted by Arabs, and carried by them to the Atlantic in the west, Central Asia in the north, and India in the east, the official Muslim attitude to the Jews has been one of toleration and scorn. The Koran itself enjoined the Muslims to allow the Jews (as well as the other two "Peoples of the Book," the Christians and the Zoroastrians or Parsis) to live in the lands of Islam and to extend to them the protection of Islam's conquering sword—a privilege for which, in most Islamic countries and ages, the Jews were made to pay in the form of a special head-tax called *jizya*.[1] About a century after Mohammed, the duty of the Muslims to treat the "People of the Book" in this manner was reconfirmed by the so-called "Testament of Omar" attributed to the second Caliph of Islam: ". . . I commend to your favor the people under 'protection.' Do battle to guard them and put no burden on them greater than they can bear, provided they pay what is due from them to the Muslims, willingly or 'under subjection, being humbled.' . . ."[2]

Since they were placed under the "protection" of Islam, the

169

People of the Book were called *dhimmi*—i.e., "protected people." Since they refused to recognize Mohammed as the prophet of Allah and to accept his teachings, they were "unbelievers," and had to suffer contempt and abuse.

There were, of course, better times and worse times, better places and worse places for the Jews under Islam. However, in contrast to their fate in Christian Europe, there were fewer cases of active persecution or of massacres; such outbreaks as did occur were of a local character and on a relatively small scale. By and large, the life of the Jews in Muslim countries ranged from pleasant, through tolerably unpleasant, to miserable. They never experienced anything like the Crusaders' massacres, the tortures and stakes of the Inquisition, the countrywide expulsions that hurled Jews from one part of Christian Europe to another and then back again, the bloodbaths of Chmielnicki's Cossacks, the Russian pogroms, or the Nazi holocaust. On the other hand, neither did they experience the elation with which the Jews of Christian Europe greeted their emancipation, nor the gratification (however illusory it proved to be in some cases) over finally having achieved civil equality with the gentiles in their own lands.

Up to the twentieth century Western observers tended to regard the East as "immovable." One of the manifestations of Eastern conservatism has been that the position once assigned to the Jews by Mohammed had remained largely the same for thirteen centuries, until the establishment of the State of Israel.

This position, to be sure, entailed frequent humiliation and degradation. The Jew in Muslim lands was treated with rude condescension, was cursed to his face, slapped and buffeted, forbidden to wear shoes, made to wear special badges, limited in his occupations, forced to move out of the way of a Muslim even if it meant stepping into the filth of the gutter, compelled to allow any Muslim who commandeered him to jump on his back to be carried across the mud or sewage of the street, and to suffer many more small and great indignities.

Throughout history, abuse and humiliation heaped on the heads of the lower classes have been an integral part of Middle Eastern behavior patterns. This is one side of the coin; the

170

reverse is exaggerated and elaborate formality of polite manners among equals and obsequiousness toward those of higher status. This being the case, the Jews, who in their capacity as *dhimmis* occupied the lowest rung in the social scale, could not, and in fact did not, expect any other treatment than the one that was meted out to them.

Rudeness and purposeful humiliation apart, some observers of Jewish life in Muslim lands and some students of Jewish history under Islam feel that "the lot of the Jews . . . was no worse than that of the lowest classes in the Moslem society who were exploited with equal harshness by the dominating feudal system."[3]

Minorities in the Muslim World————————————

To understand the position of the Jews under Islam, one must know something of the nature of minorities in Muslim countries. The Muslim view is that a religious group constitutes a "nation." With reference to the Muslims themselves this view is expressed in the early charter drawn up by Mohammed which states that the community of believers constitutes one *umma* (i.e., "nation") over against mankind;[4] or in the proverb which states "There are no nations in Islam." Similarly, all Muslim domains constitute, at least in theory, one world, the "house of Islam" *(Dar ul-Islam).* The tolerated and protected minorities within Muslim countries form, likewise, religio-national groups, which have been called for many centuries by the Arabic term *millet,* "nation." Following the conquest of Constantinople in 1453, Mehmed II confirmed the autonomy of the Greek Orthodox *millet,* the Armenian Gregorian *millet,* and the Jewish *millet,* each headed by its own *millet bashi,* or community chief, who was officially accredited to the Ottoman government, had his residence in Istanbul, and served as liaison between his community and the government. Each *millet* was authorized to use its own language, maintain its religious, cultural, and educational institutions, collect from its member the taxes levied by the imperial government, and exercise juridical, civil, and religious autonomy in disputes among its members.[5] The Jewish *millet* comprised all the Jews who lived in the far-flung Ottoman domains, and was headed by the *Hakham Bashi* (chief rabbi) who resided in Istanbul. In Persia the Jews (as well as the Christians and Parsis or Zoroastrians) enjoyed a religious autonomy comparable to that of the Ottoman *millets.*

This *millet* system, developed and elaborated by the Ottoman Turks, was based on the old Koranic tradition of affording toleration and protection to the members of other monotheistic faiths who, while refusing to convert to Islam, were willing to accept Muslim overlordship. The Koran enjoins the Muslims to "fight against those who have been given the Scripture [i.e., Jews and Christians] . . . until they pay the tribute readily, being brought low."[6] Consequently, whether a particular Muslim country was under Turkish control or not, the position of the Jewish (and other) religio-national communities that dwelt in it was essentially the same.

After World War I, the *millet* system remained in force in all the Arab states that were carved out of the Ottoman Empire, while in Turkey itself it was abolished soon after the creation of the republic. This meant that the position of the Jews in the Arab countries remained basically the same in the twentieth century as it had been in the days of Mohammed. After having been "brought low" they were kept low, but they were "not to be wronged," as Mohammed had put it in his charter.[7] They were favored with safety of life and property, to the same degree that such safety was enjoyed by the Muslims; however, violations of these rights were common—and more common in the case of the Jews than in that of the Muslims.

Since to "bring the *dhimmi*s low" was an old and venerable Muslim tradition, the Jews could never dream of obtaining equal rights in any country in which Muslim law and tradition were operative. The entire mentality dominating the highly tradition-bound culture of the Middle East precluded all thought, let alone action, in the direction of introducing such a basic change in the position of the Jewish *dhimmi*s as granting equality to them would have entailed. Since Islam, as has been pointed out innumerable times, is (or was, until very recently) not only a religion but a total way of life, it was crystal clear to both Jews and Muslims that the Jews, whose own religion too is (or was) a total way of life in the Middle East, could by no stretch of imagination hope to attain equality with the Muslims.

In fact—and this requires careful consideration—equality between the religio-national minorities and the Muslim majority is impossible in principle as well as in practice within the traditional Middle Eastern cultural configuration. Muslims are subject to Muslim religious law; Jews to Jewish religious law. Both of these legal *corpora* cover not only the conduct of religious services and the performance of those duties that come under the heading "religious" in the modern Western world, but also all areas of jurisprudence which constitute in modern Western legal development such varied specialties as criminal law, civil law, family law, land law, business law, and so forth. In the Middle East all these are subsumed under "religious law" called *Shari'a* (literally "path") in Islam and *Halakha* (literally "walking") in Judaism. All these, as well as all other, areas of life are regulated by rules which each religion developed for itself, which have religious sanction, and which are part and parcel of the domain of religion. This is one of the meanings of the observation that religion in the Middle East is a total way of life.[8]

This being the case, it becomes apparent that the total way of life of the Muslims must be very different from that of the Jews, and that for a Jew it would be possible to obtain legal equality with the Muslims only at the price of giving up his ethno-religious identity for the one conferred by Islam upon the Muslims. To do this in a cultural environment whose traditional outlook had not been modified by Enlightenment and its attendant weakening of the religious hold would be tantamount to apostasy, to embracing Islam. The alternative devised by assimilationist Jews in the West—to become like the non-Jewish majority in everything except religion—could not be applied to the Middle Eastern situation where religion has been "everything" and determined a man's status, ethnic belonging, way of life, and even the range of occupations open to him.

173

Between Christians and Jews ——————————————

In this respect there has been a subtle difference between the positions of the Jews and the Christians in the Arab states. Although no love has been lost between the Muslims and the Christians, and in the Ottoman Empire the same *dhimmi* status was accorded to both Christians and Jews, nevertheless a certain assimilation of the Christian Arabs to the Muslim Arabs has taken place ever since the establishment of the Arab successor states after World War I. This has been expressed primarily in the former's identification with the national aspirations of the latter. In fact, in Syria, Lebanon, and Transjordan, and in Palestine under the British Mandate (i.e., up to the establishment of Israel in 1948), the spokesmen and protagonists of Arab nationalism were Christian Arabs far beyond their proportion in the population. The Christian Arabs in all Muslim countries were (and still are) a more literate, more educated, more urbanized, and more prosperous community than the Muslim Arabs, and thus there were relatively more individuals among them able to give oral and written expression to the ideas and aims of Arab nationalism as it developed in the Middle East in the post-World War I era. Although the differences between Muslim Arabs and Christian Arabs were incomparably greater than those between, say, Protestant and Catholic Englishmen, there were enough common interests between the Arabs of the two religions to make a certain rapprochement to the Muslims seem desirable in the eyes of the Christians. As to those relatively few Christian Arabs, and even fewer Jews, who achieved membership in the cabinets of Muslim countries or became deputies in their legislatures, their characteristic attitude was to act more Muslim than their Muslim colleagues and to represent but rarely the interests of their respective communities.[9]

Some Christian communities in the Arab world are referred to, and refer to themselves, by an ethnic designation—e.g., Armenians, Assyrians (or Nestorian Christians). These were originally non-Arabic-speaking groups, and in many cases they have preserved, to some extent, their old languages. That is to say, they are neither Arabs nor Muslims, and are considered definitely separate ethno-religious minorities. Then there are Arabic-speaking Christians who belong to various Christian churches (such as the Greek Orthodox, the Maronite, and the Syrian Orthodox) but who in occupational structure, rural-urban distribution, cultural attainments, and so forth, are quite close to the Muslim Arabs. These are called by both the Muslim Arabs and themselves "Christian Arabs."

The Jews unquestionably are similar to the first of these two categories of Christians. Even though in most Arabic-speaking countries the Jews too speak Arabic, neither they themselves nor the other populations ever refer to them as "Jewish Arabs," except in the case of small and vanishing groups of semi-nomadic and almost totally un-Jewish tribes on the Tunisian-Algerian border who are called, probably contemptuously, by this name (see Chapter XI). In other words, it is felt everywhere that the Jews, even if Arabic-speaking and autochthonous, are nevertheless not part of the local population to the same extent as are the "Christian Arabs." They are considered, and in fact are, indigenous foreigners, like the Armenians, Assyrians, and other non-Arabic-speaking Christians.

Assimilation to the Muslims?

Another question that has to be touched upon briefly is whether there is (or was) any inclination or intention among the Jews of the Middle East to assimilate to the Muslim majority. The answer is unequivocally and emphatically no. No, because for the Jews to have assimilated to Muslim Arab culture (quite apart from the insurmountable religious barrier already referred to) would have meant a lowering of their own cultural standards. Once, in the faraway days of the Middle Ages, the Jews achieved a close acculturation to Arab civilization; they were among the outstanding contributors to the great Arab achievements in many areas of cultural endeavor. When the decline of Arab culture set in, the Jews declined with it, but managed to retain their own traditional values (which they had never given up, even in the Golden Age of Spain), and continued to foster such traditional Jewish preoccupations as Tora study. Since the

175

Middle East never experienced a movement like the European Enlightenment, the overwhelming majority of the Muslim population in all countries of the area remained illiterate until the end of World War I, when modernization and Westernization began to penetrate it. To this day there is no single Middle Eastern country (except Israel) in which as many as 80 percent of the school-age population is enrolled in elementary schools. In the more remote countries, such as Yemen, South Yemen, and Saudi Arabia, this percentage ranges from 6.91 to 17.71; in Algeria, Iran, Iraq, Libya, Morocco, the United Arab Republic, and Turkey, the range is from 38.80 to 59.71 percent.[10]

It is evident that a Muslim culture which was characterized by such a high degree of illiteracy and all the concomitant features of civilizational backwardness had few enticements to offer to the Jews among whom most males were able to read not Arabic or the other local languages, but Hebrew, the sacred tongue of their religion. The reason for this widespread Jewish literacy was religious; to be able to read the Bible and the prayers was as much a religious prerequisite for Jewish males as to be circumcised on the eighth day after birth. This contrasted sharply with the Muslim religious duty that consisted of nothing more than the recitation of a short prayer five times a day. Thus pious Muslims could, and most of them did, remain illiterate; pious Jews—and in the Middle East until very recently all Muslims and all Jews were pious—could not. In this difference between the Muslim and the Jewish religious requirement in respect of literacy lies much of the explanation of the reluctance of the Middle Eastern Jews to assimilate to the majority culture of the Muslim environment. Later on we shall see what role this negative opinion of the value of Muslim culture played in the emigration of Jews from North Africa at the time the Maghribi states achieved independence.

The Position of Women

Since the position of women in the Oriental Jewish communities is so different from their position in the other two sectors of the Jewish people, it seems appropriate to discuss it here. We

176

may begin by stating that, in general, the position of women in the Middle Eastern Diaspora has remained largely similar to what it was in Talmudic times, and even earlier, in the era of the Hebrew kings and patriarchs. This peculiar longevity of a very important element in social and family organization is due to the extremely conservative nature of Middle Eastern society in general, and, in particular, to the early incorporation into the religio-legal systems of both Jews and Muslims of rules governing the position of women, rules which thenceforward were regarded as inviolable religious tenets. The essential features of this position—largely identical among Jews and Muslims—can be enumerated briefly.

The woman is considered as a person who stands under the tutelage of a male next-of-kin most of her life; while she is a girl, she is dependent on her father, or, if she is an orphan, on her brother or other close kinsman; after marriage, her husband becomes her master. Only if she is divorced or widowed does an Oriental Jewish woman acquire a more or less independent status, although even at that stage her womanhood places her in a position of some dependance on male relatives, such as brothers or sons. As Briggs and Guède put it with reference to the extremely conservative Jews of Ghardaia in the Algerian Sahara: "There could never be any question of real independence for her because it was a woman's destiny always to be practically a slave to one man or another, father, husband, son or brother according to circumstances."[11]

A woman must be segregated from all men who are not her first-degree relatives, as well as secluded and often veiled (these provisions, however, generally were less stringently observed by the Jews than by the Muslims). A man can have more than one wife simultaneously; a woman can have only one husband at a time. A wife may be divorced by the husband without her consent, in an easy and rapidly performed ceremony—among the Muslims, an oral pronouncement before two witnesses and in the case of Jews, a written bill of divorcement *("get")* signed by two witnesses. The woman cannot initiate divorce nor can she force her husband to divorce her.[12] The children, unless they were very young, remain with or are returned to, the father.

177

During her menstrual period (and, among the Jews, for seven days thereafter), and for a longer period after childbirth, the woman is impure and her touch defiles. Since women, in the Talmudic view, are not only loquacious and addicted to eavesdropping but also lightheaded, it is a wise father who marries off his daughter well in advance of puberty so as to preclude all possibility of her lightheadedness bringing disgrace upon her family. According to the Muslims, "men stand superior to women in that Allah hath preferred the one over the other" (Koran 4:34); Jewish ritual requires a man to express in his daily prayers his thanks to God for not having created him a woman.[13]

A legislative break in the continuity of this religiously codified Ancient Near Eastern tradition concerning women occurred in the Ashkenazi sector of Jewry about 1000 CE when a synod under Rabbenu Gershom, "the light of the Exile," outlawed polygyny and made the consent of the wife a prerequisite for divorce. However, these *takkanot* (Rabbinic enactments) were binding on Ashkenazi Jews only. Sephardi Jews adopted the custom of inserting a clause into the marriage contract (the so-called *ketubba*) to the effect that the husband undertook not to marry a second wife or live with a concubine during the lifetime of the woman he was about to marry.[14] Some Sephardi communities adopted the prohibition of compulsory divorce, but it remained merely a local communal rule.[15] Among the Oriental Jews there were communities—e.g., those of North Africa—where the clause precluding polygyny was included in the *ketubba,* although not very frequently. In other Oriental Jewish communites—e.g., those of Yemen or Iran—it was not used at all, and, in theory at least, the number of wives was not even limited to four as it was among the Muslims. Divorce without the consent of the wife remained a general practice in the Oriental division. Likewise, child marriage, with the brides being eight or nine years old, continued to be practiced occasionally down to the present day, while the marrying off of girls immediately upon puberty remained the rule. In Ghardaia, for instance, until the very end of the community's existence (the community migrated to Israel in 1962) daughters would be married off when they were eleven or twelve, as soon as they

178

began to menstruate, while the grooms were usually seventeen or eighteen.[16]

It was a general rule, among both Jews and Muslims, that a girl was not consulted in connection with her marriage and a boy only rarely; the decision lay entirely in the hands of the father.

It is difficult to compare the position of the Jewish woman in the Middle East with that of her Muslim sister, since among the Muslims her position ranged from that of a virtual chattel to that of great freedom.[17] Nevertheless, one can state in general terms that everywhere in the Middle East the position of the Jewish woman, while strongly influenced by that of the Muslim woman of the immediate environment, was on the whole better. Better, in the sense that the Jewish woman had a little more freedom, a little more social intercourse, and enjoyed a little more respect as a wife and mother. As to divorces, to judge from the scanty reports available, they occurred with the same high frequency among the Jews as among the Muslims. Among the Jews of Ghardaia, in the period 1916–25, 189 marriages and 123 divorces took place; and over half (51 percent, of the persons who got married had been married at least once before.[18] As to the incidence of polygyny, no information could be obtained on which a comparison between the two religious groups could be based.

Elsewhere I have shown that in the Middle East in general the subordinate position of the woman is closely correlated with the differential treatment accorded to boys and girls from the very moment of their birth. To sum it up as briefly as possible, the basic pedagogical principle is to pamper the boy but not the girl, and to accustom the boy to the dominant position he is destined to occupy in the family, and the girl to the servile position that will be her lot.[19] Precisely the same principles and aims are expressed in the early socialization of children among the Oriental Jews. Well in advance of the birth of a child, and in fact even prior to conception, magic efforts are made to make sure that the child to be conceived, or, in the case of a pregnant women, to be born, should be a boy. The means used are innumerable, and of interest only to the folklorist, but a specifically Jewish one must be mentioned. In many Oriental Jewish communities the women swallow the foreskin of a boy cut off at circumcision; this is believed to be the most reliable method to ensure that she will give birth to a son.[20] The birth of a son is greeted with great rejoicing; the birth of a girl, by contrast, is received with a sense of disappointment. If the firstborn child of a couple is a girl, the father is comforted by the Talmudic saying, "A first girl is a sign that boys will follow."[21] If, instead, the second child is also a girl, the father is derisively called *abu banat*, "father of daughters." Among both Muslims and Jews this differential attitude toward sons and daughters goes so far that when a man is asked, "How many children do you have?" he will answer by giving the number of his sons and will make no reference to his daughters. However, in evaluating such responses, one has to take into account that neither Arabic nor Hebrew has a neutral noun such as the English "child"; there are only words for "son" and "daughter." Therefore, when one asks, "How many children do you have?" one actually asks, "How many sons do you have?" and the answer goes accordingly.

The pampering of a boy child as against the strict attitude toward a girl begins even before the child is able to express any desire except by crying. The general Middle Eastern custom to breast-feed boys for a much longer period (two to three years) than girls (one to one-and-a-half years) is a typical expression of the greater concern a mother has for a son than for a daughter.[22] I have no information as to whether this custom obtains among Oriental Jews as well; I strongly suspect, however, that this is the case. Once the child is able to walk and talk, the mother gives incomparably more freedom to a boy than to a girl. A boy can exhibit the rudest, unruliest, naughtiest behavior, and will hardly ever receive as much as a rebuke; a daughter, on the other hand, would never dream of being anything but demure and obedient. At a very early age a daughter must begin to help her mother with household chores, and with the unending task of caring for, or watching over, the younger brothers, who, in return, treat her "as dirt."[23] The father and the other men in the house, as a rule, ignore a young daughter, who is inured in this manner, in her own parents' house, to taking subsequently an even more subservient position in the home of her husband under the thumb of his mother.

Apart from this daily routine, the lives of the male and female children are differentiated at an early stage by a series of popular-religious ceremonies performed for a boy, for which there is no counterpart in a girl's life. A firstborn boy must be "redeemed" by the payment of a symbolic price for him to a *kohen,* a descendant of the Biblical priesthood; this is usually a festive ceremony. Also, in many communities when the boy is two or three years old, his hair is cut for the first time, a rite which affords another occasion for festivity. When the boy reaches the age of five or six, he is sent to the Hebrew school (called in Arab countries by the Arabic name *kuttab* or its variants); and his induction into the school is accompanied by yet another ceremony. From that time on the greater importance of the male sex receives its institutionalized stamp. The boy is introduced to the intricacies of Jewish religious life—the rhyme and reason for the very existence of the community—while the girl remains outside. She is neither expected by tradition nor enabled by local custom to participate in or to observe most of the *mitzvot* (religious commandments), except for those few which fall into her specific domain as a wife, mother, and cook. Then, at the age of thirteen comes the Bar Mitzva ceremony which, as far as religious ritual is concerned, makes the boy a full member of the adult community, and which has no counterpart in the girl's life.

Female literacy was almost as exceptional among Middle Eastern Jews as it was among Muslims. However, while among the Muslims both men and women were equally illiterate (although the very few literate persons in Muslim tribes or villages were, of course, invariably men), among the Jews there was a sharp contrast between the almost wholly illiterate female half and the largely literate male half of the population. This put the Jewish women at a greater relative disadvantage in relation to the Jewish men than was the case with Muslim women vis-à-vis Muslim men. That the Jewish women nevertheless enjoyed greater respect from their menfolk than the Muslim women did from theirs was due to the differences in the female stereotype as it crystallized in the religious traditions of the two peoples. In Muslim tradition the attitude to women is overwhelmingly negative; the superiority of men over women is stressed; the Koranic rule whereby a refractory woman should be admonished and even beaten by her husband (Koran 4:34) has remained in force.[24] In Jewish tradition the negative traits attributed to women (as mentioned above) are counterbalanced by attractive portraits of the "woman of valor" (Proverbs 31:10–31), and of heroic and wise women (Judges 4:4–22; 2 Samuel 14:2–20), by the commandment to honor both father and mother (Exodus 20:12; Deuteronomy 5:14), and by the Talmudic precept according to which a man should listen to his wife, honor her, and refrain from offending her.[25] The Talmudic attitude to women is summed up by Maimonides, whose words became and have remained law for the Oriental Jews: "The sages have commanded that a man should honor his wife more than himself, and love her like himself. If he is a man of substance, he should bestow favors upon her according to his means. He should not intimidate her and should always talk gently to her. . . ."[26] In view of these instructions, which formed part of the mandatory religious rules observed by traditional Jews everywhere, it goes without saying that the idea of physically disciplining a wife was totally foreign to Judaism.

This difference in religio-legal tradition between Jews and Muslims not only has secured a better position for the Jewish woman even in the most conservative Jewish communities in the Middle East, but also has created a greater predisposition among the Jews than among the Muslims for letting their daughters, too, benefit from modern education when it became available. While among the Muslims in all the Middle Eastern countries the number of girls attending schools is much lower than that of boys,[27] among the Jews of the Middle East one of the important results of modernization was that the number of girls in the schools (e.g., in the school system of the Alliance Israélite Universelle) was roughly equal to that of the boys.[28]

Nevertheless, instead of improving the women's position, incipient Westernization at first brought a change for the worse.

By the nature of the circumstances, of the society, and of the economy, men were much more frequently exposed to Westernizing influences than women, and thus an even more considerable cultural gap developed between them. Many Westernized or semi-Westernized husbands became dissatisfied with their "unenlightened" wives (*"non-evolué"* was the French term used in North Africa) and made use of the possibility offered by traditional Jewish family law (which was recognized as valid by the government) of summarily divorcing them.

By 1970 most of the Oriental division of the Jewish people had become concentrated in Israel (see Table V). This made the problem of the Oriental Jewish woman part and parcel of the broader issues of the economic, social, and cultural absorption of the Oriental Jewish half of Israel's population into the modern Israeli scene. Since, however, the present book deals with the Diaspora and not with Israel, we shall say only this much: compulsory general elementary education for eight years, compulsory army service for two to three years, the gradually increasing incidence of interdivision marriages, the growing number of Oriental Jewish members in the Histadrut (Israel's General Federation of Labor), the sustained psychological pressure represented by the unrelenting Arab hostility to Israel—these are the major factors that contain the promise of a considerable measure of integration between the two halves of Israel's Jewish population and with it the transformation of the special problems of the Oriental Jewish women into part of the general problems women still face in Israel as they do in all other countries of the modern world.

TABLE V

MIDDLE EASTERN JEWISH IMMIGRANTS TO ISRAEL
MAY 15, 1948–DECEMBER 31, 1960

Country	1948–1951	1952–54	1955–57	1958–60	Total 1948–60
Morocco	30,750	15,903	70,053	9,236	125,942
Algeria	1,523	396	2,483	529	4,931
Tunisia	13,139	5,902	15,267	2,149	36,457
Libya	30,482	1,609	198	94	32,383
Egypt (U.A.R.)	16,508	3,203	14,562	1,051	35,324
Yemen	45,199	698	10	55	45,962
Aden	3,155	151	7	95	3,408
Syria & Lebanon	2,898	461	—	—	3,359
Turkey	34,213	861	2,650	1,316	39,040
Iraq	121,512	1,382	361	233	123,488
Iran	24,804	5,750	2,035	7,472	40,061
Total	324,183	36,316	107,626	22,230	490,355

184

11

THE ORIENTAL
JEWS: NORTH
AFRICA

Before the Muslim Conquest —————————————————

By the seventh century, when the Arabs conquered North Africa
and turned it into a Muslim world area and a part of their
far-flung empire, the Jews could look back upon a history of a
thousand years in that part of the ancient world. We have
already heard of the earlier phase of this long period that began
with the flight of Judeans into Egypt in 586 BCE. By the third
century BCE Jews lived also in Cyrenaica, to the west of Egypt.
In 96 BCE the city of Cyrene and its environs came under Roman
rule, and from that time on there was contact between the Jews
of Cyrenaica and Rome. Their numbers were augmented by
many Jewish refugees who fled from Judea during the Jewish-
Roman war of 66–70 CE and after the defeat of the Jews, when
many of the survivors sought refuge there. According to Philo of
Alexandria (first century CE) there were in his days one million
Jews in North Africa, a figure modern scholars do not consider
exaggerated.[1] The languages spoken by the North African Jews
in this period were Greek and Latin. In the early second century
CE the Jews of Cyrenaica staged a large-scale uprising (115–
117), which was put down by Trajan. Many of those Jews who
remained alive after this war sought safety farther west in
Mauretania (today Tunisia, Algeria, and Morocco), or went
south, into the Sahara desert, beyond Roman reach. This is the
origin of the Jewish tribes in the Sahara whose way of life and
fate after the encounter with Islam resembled in many respects
those of the Jewish desert tribes of Arabia. For seventeen
centuries thereafter their numbers were to be augmented by
Jewish refugees fleeing into the desert from the sword of
conquerors who periodically took one or the other of the North
African cities.

185

Prior to the Arab conquest the Jews spread out, albeit very thinly, all over North Africa, and, again paralleling events in Arabia, they made many converts among the tribal population. Especially among the tribes of the Botr moiety of the Berbers (this moiety was composed mostly of nomadic tribes, while the other Berber moiety, that of the Beranes, consisted largely of sedentary groups), many became Jewish proselytes—at least this is what Ibn Khaldun, the fourteenth-century Arab historian, reports.[2] According to an old tradition first recorded by Procopius (ca. 500–565), the Berbers originally had come from Palestine after their king Thalut killed Jalut (i.e., Goliath).[3] Other Berber traditions attribute Ishmaelite—i.e., Abrahamic—origins to the Botr moiety.[4] These origin myths may have created a predisposition among some of the Botr tribes to adopt Judaism. For a time there seems to have been an alliance in the Algerian hinterland between pagan, Christian, and Jewish Berbers, brought together by the menace of Muslim-Arab advance from the east. In 613, and again in 622, the number of the Jews was augmented by the arrival of co-religionists expelled by the Visigoths from Spain. In the late seventh century an army composed of the aforementioned three population elements and led by a Jewish-Berber seeress-queen, Dahia, surnamed al-Kahina or al-Kahiya, defeated the Muslims and blocked their westward advance for five years, until she in turn was vanquished in a second Muslim onslaught. Soon thereafter the Jews must have adopted Arabic as their vernacular, as well as their second literary language (next to Hebrew), for, in the ninth century, Yehuda ibn Quraysh became the first non-Arab to write a treatise (on grammar) in Arabic.[5]

Jewish Scholarship in the Maghrib

The rise of Muslim scholarship in the Maghrib (i.e., Northwest Africa) was paralleled by that of Jewish learning. The main centers of Muslim religious studies were the universities of Kairuwan in Tunisia, Tlemcen in Algeria, and Fez in Morocco, and it was in the same three cities that the most important early Maghribi rabbinical academies were established; it was from

186

these academies that Jewish scholarship subsequently was passed on to the Spanish Jews. By the end of the eighth century, the Jewish scholars of Kairuwan were engaged in learned correspondence with the Geonim of Sura and Pumbedita in Babylonia. In 880 the Jewish traveler and adventurer Eldad HaDani visited Kairuwan, which occasioned additional correspondence between the heads of the community and the Babylonian sages. The scholars of Kairuwan conducted halakhic, haggadic, philological, and exegetic studies in the Jewish field, and excelled also in such secular endeavors as medicine (several of them were court physicians), astronomy, and intercontinental trade between Spain and Syria and Babylonia, through North Africa and Egypt. In the middle of the eleventh century the city was overrun by the Beni Hillal Bedouins, and the Jewish community disintegrated; in the thirteenth century the few Jews who had remained were forced to leave. Even in modern times, no more than a handful of Jews has returned to live in Kairuwan.[6]

Fez (Arabic, *Fas*), one of the most important cities of northern Morocco, was founded in the late eighth century. In the early ninth century, Imam Idris II, finding that his nomadic subjects were averse to urban living, settled the city with several thousand Muslim and Jewish Andalusians, allocating a special quarter to the latter. This was the origin of the old *mellah*, or Jewish quarter, that has remained the ghetto of Fez to the present day. By 900 the Jewish scholars of Fez had established communication with the *Geonim* of Babylonia. In 1146 the Jews of Fez were given the choice of exile or conversion to Islam; many chose Marranism, others fled to Spain, Italy, and Palestine. However, a short while later, the Jewish community, and even Jewish scholarship, again flourished in Fez, so that the father of Maimonides and his family, fleeing persecution in Cordova, Spain, were attracted to the Moroccan city in which they spent the years from 1152 to 1165. Such rapidly changing ups and downs remained characteristic of Jewish life in Fez in the following centuries. In 1492 many Jews expelled from Spain fled to Fez, only to be expelled from there, too, by the natives who feared they would cause inflation. Many Jews were en-

187

slaved, then set free and given a new quarter to live in. The Spanish Jews gradually returned, and from the sixteenth century on Ladino became a dominant Jewish vernacular next to Judeo-Arabic. Until the end of the nineteenth century Fez was alternatingly a place of refuge for Jews expelled from other cities, and a place from which the Jews were expelled. About 1900 their number was estimated at 8,000, they had nineteen synagogues, and a synod of rabbis.[7]

Tlemcen, the third important Jewish center in North Africa, had its own rabbinical academies from the tenth to the twelfth centuries. After 1145, when the city was sacked by the Almohads, Jewish cultural life practically ceased, but it was renewed in 1391 with the arrival of famous scholars among the Spanish Jews who at that time found refuge in the city. In the fifteenth and sixteenth centuries Tlemcen was the home of Jewish poets, commentators, philosophers, preachers, moral theologists, Kabbalists, and physicians, some of whom, after their death, became the object of popular veneration as saints. In the middle of the nineteenth century there were in Tlemcen some 2,000 Jews who maintained three synagogues in the city.[8]

Kabbalism

Kabbala mysticism, whose origin in Spain, development in Safed, Palestine, and spread all over the Jewish world will be outlined in Chapter XIV, held sway over the North African Diaspora to an unparalleled extent. It reached the Maghrib as early as the sixteenth century, and was propagated most effectively from the sixteenth to the twentieth centuries by emissaries from the holy cities of Palestine who regularly visited the Maghribi communities. The primary purpose of the rounds made by such an emissary, or *Hakham Kolel* (literally, "foundation sage"), as he was called, was to collect funds for the maintenance of the Kabbalistic-Talmudic schools of Palestine. The actual effect of his visits was to spread the knowledge of the Kabbala, to fan the belief in its holy book, the *Zohar,* and to perform miraculous cures. The belief in these *Hakhme Kolel* (plural) was general and unshakable even as late as the twentieth century, as attested, for instance, by the following footnote, written in the 1960s, by Dr. André N. Chouraqui, historian of North African Jewry and graduate of the University of Paris: "The present author owes his life to *Haham Kollel* Rabbi Franco of Jerusalem who cured him as a child in Aïn-Témouchent (Algeria) when all hope for his life had been given up and preparations made for the funeral."[9]

The *Zohar* was considered more holy and played a more important role in the life of the Maghribi Jews than even the Bible itself. In their synagogues, they devoted up to one hour three times daily to a reading of sections from the *Zohar* prior to the morning, afternoon, and evening prayers. In many communities there was a fraternity of *Zohar*-readers known as the *Hevra* ("Society"). In the large and partly very modern port city of Casablanca "there were until recently at least five places where the *Zohar* was chanted 24 hours a day." In all parts of the Maghrib the *Zohar* readers functioned at every Bar Mitzva, marriage, and burial. They were unable to understand the difficult Aramaic text of the book, but this did not diminish the efficacy of the reading in securing divine rewards for those to whom it was read as well as for those who did the chanted reading. Printed copies of the *Zohar,* as behooves such a sacrosanct book, were kept in many synagogues in the Holy Ark next to the Tora scrolls; if put under the pillow of a patient or a barren woman, cure was believed to follow unfailingly. Magic incantations quoted from the *Zohar* were hung on the walls of rooms in which the mother and the newborn child lay until the circumcision, and, of course, *Zohar*-inspired amulets were used for the most diverse purposes. In contrast to the Ashkenazi Diaspora of Eastern Europe, where the Hasidism that developed out of Kabbalism in the eighteenth century provoked the strongest opposition of the *Mitnagdim* (see Chapter XV), in the Maghrib there was no opposition to the Kabbala, which completely dominated rabbis and laymen alike.[10]

Hand in hand with this intensive preoccupation with the Kabbala went the unquestioning reliance on folk medicine consisting of spells, counter-spells, good-luck charms, talismans, amulets, the figure of a hand or the number five, the figure

189

of a fish and concoctions administered by wise women, or incantations by healers and sorcerers. The religious lines were as blurred with respect to these dispensers of popular cures as they were in the case of the veneration of saints: Jews and Muslims alike flocked to the same healers of renown irrespective of their religions. The theory behind these treatments was that all illness was caused by demons (*jnun;* sing. *jinn*), or by God himself, who inflicted disease and suffering as a punishment for the violation of some ritual rule (especially the menstrual taboos by women, and the Sabbath laws), or for some sexual sin (adultery, prostitution, shamelessness).

Some Demographic Changes

The Kabbalistic beliefs and practices discussed above, combined with the appalling lack of the most elementary hygiene and the great overcrowdedness in the urban *mellahs* and *haras*, resulted in a high infant mortality which for centuries effectively counterbalanced the equally high fertility of the North African Jewish women. To give only one example of the magnitude of these uncontrolled rates of mortality and fertility, let us refer to the Tunisian Jews. Among them, as recently as 1919–23, the general mortality rate averaged 21.9 per 1,000 of Jewish population, which was considerably higher than the corresponding rate among the Muslims (16.3). In the same period, the birthrate of the Algerian Jews was 37.3 (as against 22.9 of the Muslims), giving a gross rate of increase of 15.4. This indicates, to say the least, that in those four years the health situation among the Jews was worse than among the Muslims; it must have been still worse in earlier years, because it was only after the war that the European influence had begun to make a real impact, bringing about an amelioration in the health conditions. As to Tunisia, in the 1911–21 decade the total Jewish Population of the country remained roughly stationary at about 50,000.[11]

Following World War I, incipient modernization and the gradual improvement of living conditions resulted, in the first place, in a reduction of infant mortality and an increase in general life expectancy. In Tunisia, for example, by 1944–46 the infant mortality among the Jews was reduced to about 120, (as against 234 among the Muslims and 107 among the Europeans). The general Jewish mortality rate diminished from 21.9 in 1919–23 to 16.6 in 1934–38. As always happens in such situations, there was no commensurate decrease in the birthrate, which resulted in a marked upswing in the natural increase (22.1 by 1945–47). In addition, the *mellahs* and *haras* of the larger cities had to cope with an influx of migrants from the south and the rural areas who came in search of a better livelihood, and, after the establishment of Israel in 1948, were attracted by the greater security (real or imaginary) of the large cities. These factors created an incredible overcrowding, with more filth and putrefaction than the *mellahs* had ever before known. In the early 1950s, when one acre in the shantytown *(bidonville)* of Casablanca held 374 inhabitants, in the *mellah* there were 870 Jews per acre. In the old *hara* of Tunis there were 1,000 per acre; in Sefrou, 1,680 per acre. Inside the crumbling houses the situation matched this incredible overcrowdedness: often eight to ten people of a three-generation family lived in a single room. What all this meant for health, nerves, morals, and character can easily be imagined. As in all situations of traumatic social upheavals, many lost their traditional occupations and became beggars in the cities, which in turn necessitated the development of welfare agencies. The number of Jewish prostitutes, usually of the "unregistered" or clandestine variety, increased. That Jewish criminality and juvenile delinquency remained at their former low level despite these worsened conditions speaks volumes for the staying power of the Jewish ethos.[12]

In the nineteenth century (and, to a great extent, well into the twentieth) the Jews of North Africa (and of the Middle East in general) exhibited a peculiar combination of two contradictory sets of traits. On the one hand, they lived in material circumstances that were, in general, worse than those of the Muslims. The Moroccan Jewish *mellahs*, the Tunisian Jewish *haras*, the Algerian Jewish ghettos were filled with incredible filth, nauseating stench and refuse, were infested with rodents and vermin, and their inhabitants were unwashed and unkempt to a greater extent than was the case in the quarters inhabited by the

Muslims. Yet, as against this, the Jewish men in the cities were all literate, while the Muslims were illiterate, and this difference in literacy, of course, meant that the Jews on the average were an intellectually superior group. As André Chouraqui put it, "the Jews regarded themselves as superior to their Moslem neighbors, and . . . paradoxically, the Moslems regarded the despised *dhimmis* as a cultural elite."[13]

Jews in the Desert

In a large world area like that of North Africa, where, as one proceeds southward, the cultivated zone gradually gives way to the desert, it was inevitable that marked cultural differences should emerge between the populations of the cultivated strip near the sea and the primitive desert hinterland. Such differences developed also among the Jews. In contrast to the literate and, in recent decades, French-influenced Jewish population of the northern towns, there were Jewish groups, occasionally not very far away from the former, who had remained untouched, not only by French culture, but even by the cultural attainments brought into the Maghrib by the Sephardi exiles from Spain or developed locally in the centers of North African Jewish life. Some of these groups were those called *Yahud al-'Arab*—that is, "Arab Jews"—or *BaHutzim*—i.e., "outsiders"—possibly of Berber origin, who were found down to the twentieth century in the el-Kef area in northwestern Tunisia, and, across the border, in the Kabyle region of Suq Ahras, as well as between Constantine and Khenchela in northeastern Algeria. Originally, these *BaHutzim* were nomads or semi-nomads (they had been known by this Hebrew name since at least the fifteenth century), but by the twentieth century most of them had settled in the towns of Algeria and Tunisia.[14]

However, Jewish communities have existed, down to the present time, much farther south as well—in fact, as far as the very heart of the Sahara. Due south of the city of Algiers, at a distance of some three hundred miles, lies the Mzab area whose chief city is Ghardaia. In the 1950s, when Lloyd Cabot Briggs studied the Saharan tribes, he still found some 1,200 Jews in Ghardaia, who used Arabic as their vernacular, but all men aged

192

fifteen or older could also speak Hebrew. Moreover, Hebrew was for them not merely a ritual language but a living tongue. In the nineteenth century the trans-Saharan trade of the Mzab was in the hands of the Jews; in the 1950s, although their importance had declined, they were still in the front rank of sedentary Saharan merchants.[15]

Elsewhere I discussed in detail the remarkable phenomenon in social structure called "dual organization," which divides many population aggregates in the Middle East into two mutually hostile moieties (halves), often claiming related but separate descent, and individual and antagonistic character traits, traditions, and customs.[16] The Jews of the Middle East have remained relatively unaffected by this form of social duality, but in Ghardaia they were as sharply divided into two opposing factions as any Muslim social group characterized by such a dichotomy. Briggs found that they were "split into two bitterly opposed factions which disagree violently on nearly all questions of general policy." One of the two moieties was headed by the rich, powerful, and large Balouka family or clan, the other by the Sulams, to whom originally also the Baloukas had belonged. The Balouka moiety was associated with the West, was conservative, and was called *Khabiya* (the name of the huge jar in which dates are usually stored). The Sulam moiety was associated with the East, was progressive, and was called *Filala* (recalling the Tafilalet region, in which is situated the town of Tamentit from where, in the sixteenth century, a group of Jews had migrated to Ghardaia). The members of some of the other powerful families were divided between the two moieties. On the feast of *Shavu'ot* the boys and girls of the two moieties used to squirt or pour water on the opposition of the same sex; even young married men took part in these playful but energetic proceedings. The two moities were endogamous.[17]

Some thirty miles east-northeast of Ghardaia lies Guerrara, the second-largest town of the Mzab. In it Georg Gerster found in the 1950s the shrunken remnants of a Jewish community. According to this traveler, the Jews in the Mzab have for centuries "been regarded as unclean and shunned. A Mozabite will even refuse to employ manure from a Jewish house for his palm-trees. . . ."[18]

However, Jewish settlements were found much deeper still in the Sahara than the Mzab area. In Timimoun, roughly 350 miles southwest of Ghardaia, Briggs found a Jewish group called *Mehadjeria*—i.e., "ostracized"—most of whom had converted to Islam and married sedentary Arab neighbors, but whose "hard core of diehards" he still found to "cling tenaciously to their original religion and marry only among themselves." They were jewelers, smiths, and woodworkers, and also engaged in other crafts.[19] According to R. V. C. Bodley, who spent seven years in the Sahara in the 1930s and 1940s, "In every Sahara oasis, there were many Jews. In ours [i.e., the oasis of Kourdane] there were over thirty." He goes on to describe the appearance and way of life of these oasis Jews:

From the Arabs they were almost indistinguishable. To a tourist a Hebrew in his robes or an Arab in his were the same. The features, the build, the calm were similar. There was a slight difference in the intonation of Arabic. The Jew's gait was less easy than the Arab's, inclined to shuffling and more rapid. The clothes had a difference too, which I could not describe unless I had an Arab and a Jew before me. . . . Some of the oasis Jews wore European clothes in the street, but in the house they always went back to their robes. . . . The Jews in the oasis, then, were sedentary people. . . . They had gardens and shops, but they were chiefly merchants. They imported grain, they exported sheep. They were our main contact with the outer world. The Jews of the oases depended on the nomads of the desert for livelihood. The nomads depended on the Jews. Without the nomads, the Jews would have had no sheep to buy; without the Jews, the nomads would have had no one to sell their sheep to. Or, if they had found Arab dealers, it would have been an uncertain and vague undertaking. The sheep business in North Africa was important. Something like five million sheep left the Sahara every year for distribution to Algeria and France. The Jews handled the whole thing admirably. During the time I was living in the Sahara I never heard Madani, or Daylis or Jelloul or Ali [the head shepherd] complain of a deal made with Jews. They observed the current market prices, they knew what they wanted, they paid cash. When we came to the market with our lambs, we knew that the Jewish merchants would be there to take our goods, pay us for them and absolve us from all further worry. How the sheep got to Algiers or France was the buyer's business.[20]

194

Another type of primitive Jewish group, at least as far as their physical accommodations are concerned, is the cave dwellers in Tripolitania. In the villages of Garian (some fifty miles south of Tripoli), Ben 'Abbas, and Tigrinna the Jews lived in caves, as reported by Israel Joseph Benjamin. They were organized in a community, had their rabbi, and led what appeared to be a normal Jewish life in North Africa.[21] A traveler who visited them in the 1940s described these troglodyte Jews as wearing Arab dress, "save for the fez which is black instead of red. Their women are resplendent in Berber jewellery, but are secluded, Moslem fashion: they farm their land in Arab style, and they speak Arabic. They have an ancient synagogue, partly under-ground. . . ." By 1949 "they gradually drifted for safety to a ghetto-like area in Tripoli."[22]

The Coming of the French

Some improvement in the condition of the North African Jews took place even before the advent of the French, partly because they obtained the protection of foreign consuls, partly because of the general penetration of European influences, and partly because they managed to establish themselves in middle-class occupations which were needed in the changing economy of the Maghribi countries. In the conservative south, on the other hand, the traditional humiliating restrictions remained in force well into the twentieth century. In Marrakesh, for instance, the Jews had still to wear the blue, white-flecked headkerchief, to walk barefoot, and to hug the walls when they entered the Arab town.[23]

ALGERIA   The French gained control of Algeria in 1830, more than half a century before they made Tunisia into a French protectorate (1881), and more than eighty years before they achieved the same position in Morocco (1912). In all three countries the French presence was beneficial to the Jews, although not in equal measure. The greatest share of these benefits were reaped by the Algerian Jews who obtained French citizenship under the Crémieux Decree of 1870. Thus, the French governmental public schools that were established in

195

the country, as well as the educational work of the Alliance Israélite Universelle, which had begun almost a decade earlier, opened the door for Algerian Jewry to a considerable assimilation to French culture in general and to French Jewry in particular. Only a small percentage of the Algerian Jews, those who lived in the remote Saharan oases in the south, were not included in the famous Decree.

It was an unforeseen development that the Crémieux Decree, instead of leading to a rapprochement between the Algerian Jews and the French colons, resulted in an increase in the anti-Semitism of the latter. After a temporary improvement in the situation during World War I, in which many more Algerian Jews fought and fell than would have been expected on the basis of their proportion in the population, the anti-Semitic sentiment increased again under the influence of the German Nazi movement. After the French defeat in World War II, the Vichy government abolished the Crémieux Decree, reducing the Jews to the status of natives without civil rights. The Jews suffered many vicissitudes and thousands of them were concentrated in labor camps. As a reaction, many Jews participated in the underground resistance movement, especially in connection with preparations for the invasion of Algeria by American forces late in 1942. Thereafter the position of the Jews gradually improved and returned to the antebellum level.

The urbanization of Algerian Jewry continued both during and after these political ups and downs. By the 1950s, when the total number of Algerian Jews was about 140,000, 35,000 of them lived in the capital, Algiers, 30,000 in Oran, and 15,000 in Constantine—i.e., about 57 percent of the total lived in these three big cities.

The occupational structure of the Algerian Jews was similar to that of the Jews in Morocco and Tunisia. In the 1940s about one-third of all the breadwinners were small shopkeepers and itinerant peddlers, others were craftsmen, low-grade officials, clerks; many were unemployed, especially in the south of the country; and only 3.8 percent of the earners were professional people and senior officials.[24]

Despite the French leanings of the Algerian Jews, their

French citizenship, French education, and French language, neither the French colons nor the Algerian Muslims considered them Frenchmen. They were Algerian Jews, occupying a middle position between the Muslims and the French and having practically no social contact or intercourse with either. However, culturally, from the point of view of values, ideals, endeavors, and aspirations, the Algerian Jews completely identified themselves with the French, a tendency that was accompanied by a commensurate alienation from Jewish traditions, religion, and cultural values.

The establishment of Israel changed this picture to some extent, for it led to an intensified Jewish consciousness, especially in the young generation, and in many cases awakened the desire to become part of the ingathering of the exiles in the Jewish State.

TUNISIA   Even prior to the establishment of the French Protectorate in Tunisia, Mohammed Bey, the ruler of the country, yielding to the threat of French armed intervention, promulgated the so-called "Fundamental Pact" (1857) that in effect granted equality before the law to Muslims and non-Muslims. The Fundamental Pact was, however, swept away by the Tunisian revolt of 1864, after which the Jews had to resort to the long-tried method of obtaining "protection" either from the Tunisian authorities or from foreign consuls. After 1881 the Jews remained subjects of the Bey and retained their internal communal autonomy, while the French presence had the effect of a liberalizing influence. However, it was not until 1910 that a decree was issued enabling Tunisian Jews to renounce their allegiance to the Bey and accept French nationality.

An interesting insight into the closeness and frequency of the relations between Tunisian Jews and the representatives of European powers in Tunisia as early as 1905 is afforded by the enumeration of Tunisian Jews who stood under the protection of European consuls. At a time when the total Jewish population of Tunisia was less than 50,000, a total of some 1,450 enjoyed the protection of foreign powers and counted, in effect, as foreign subjects (although in religious matters they were under the jurisdiction of the Tunisian rabbinates). In addition to these 1,450, there were many Italian Jews (the so-called *Gomeyim*) who had lived for generations in Tunisia and had become Tunisian citizens while retaining their Italian cultural traditions, as well as numerous Algerian Jews who had moved to Tunisia while retaining their French citizenship acquired under the Crémieux Decree of 1870. All in all, the leading element among the Tunisian Jews was thus characterized by definite European leanings and orientations. These, as well as the concrete advantages that accrued from French citizenship, impelled many Tunisian Jews to obtain French citizenship when this was made possible by the successive easings of requirements enacted by the French from 1910 on. By 1950, an estimated 35,000 Tunisian Jews, or about one-third of their total number, had acquired French citizenship.[25]

With the control over Tunisia passing into the hands of the Vichy government, the situation of the Jews did not deteriorate markedly until the German and Italian armies occupied Tunisia (November 1942). As it happened in other places as well, the relationship of the Italians to the Jews was incomparably better than that of the Germans. In May 1943 Tunis was liberated by the British.

The occupational structure of Tunisian Jewry was similar to the one found in many other Middle Eastern Diasporas. Most of them (according to the 1946 census) were small shopkeepers, tailors, and shoemakers. In the ghetto of Tunis, more than half of the economically active Jewish population consisted of unskilled laborers. With this low economic base it was difficult to introduce improvements. Nevertheless, by the late 1940s, more than half of the Jewish school-age population of Tunisia attended the schools of the Alliance Israélite Universelle and the ORT (Organization for Rehabilitation through Training). This achievement was made possible because by that time most Tunisian Jews had become concentrated in the capital, Tunis, and another few cities (Sfax, Sousse, Gabes, Jerba). In the first four years following the independence of Israel some 20,000 Tunisian Jews migrated to the Jewish State.

In Tunisia, as in Morocco and Algeria, world Jewish organizations, led by the World Jewish Congress, entered into negotiations with the leaders of the independence movement and obtained the promise of equal rights for the local Jews. After independence (1955), the promise was, in fact, fulfilled, and the Jews began to participate in the politics and administration of the country. However, increasing nationalism and anti-Israel sentiments made the position of the Jews difficult, and led to economic and other types of discrimination, as well as to periodic outbreaks. Added to other problems (such as the difficulties the Jews experienced when suddenly Arabic replaced French in all walks of life), these factors resulted in a renewed wave of emigration, and from 1956 to 1966 some 80,000 to 90,000 Jews left Tunisia, with only 20,000 remaining.[26]

MOROCCO   In Morocco the establishment of the French Protectorate in 1912 was followed within three weeks by one of the worst massacres perpetrated in that country: sixty Jews in Fez were killed, fifty seriously injured, women were raped, and one third of the *mellah* was burnt down, leaving 10,000 Jews homeless. However, this remained an isolated incident. In general, during the forty-four years of the Protectorate (1912–1956), the Jews were able to occupy an intermediary position between the French rulers of the country and the Muslim subject colonials. A goodly proportion of them, especially in the northern part of the country and in the coastal cities, received a French-oriented education in the schools of the Alliance Israélite Universelle. With regard to occupational structure they were middle-class, and as to cultural status they stood somewhere between the French and the Muslim natives. An extraordinarily high proportion of them were rabbis; according to one authority, one out of every six adult males Jews.[27]

However, in the south, and in the conservative inland cities, the Jews engaged mostly in crafts, with a few in the retail trade and service occupations. For example, in the city of Meknes, in 1900, there were about 1,000 gainfully employed Jews divided

199

among the following occupations (listed in diminishing order of numbers): lace and button makers (150), tailors (136), druggists and hardware mongers (102), shoemakers (81), dressmakers (62), cobblers (59), public criers (55), tinsmiths (52), goldsmiths (48), money changers and lenders (25), ritual slaughterers and clerks of the rabbinical courts (24), flour merchants (22), rabbis and teachers (18), gardeners (15), waxmakers (15), carpenters (14), hairdressers (14), weavers (13), embroiderers on velvet (11), distillers (10), scribes (7), silk thread retailers (7), grocers (7), wool carders (6), furnace operators (6), muleteers (6), dyers (5), cotton goods retailers (5), bellows makers (4), gold and silver stirrup inlayers (4), bookbinders (3), clockmakers (3), scabbard makers (3), masons (2), snuff makers (2), furnishers, kiln operators, suppliers, stokers, and wagoners.[28]

In the north, one of the results of the French occupation was a significant change in this age-old occupational structure of the Jewish community. Instead of concentrating in small trades and handicrafts (as exemplified by Meknes), many of the Jews were able to engage in new types of work, including the professions, officialdom, and, to some extent, even agriculture. French and American Jewish philanthropic organizations, such as the Alliance Israélite Universelle, the ORT, and the American Jewish Joint Distribution Committee, had a major share in providing education and raising the living standards of Moroccan Jews.[29]

Since the Moroccan Jews in general saw in France their protector under whose benevolent government their civil condition has steadily improved, they could not sympathize with the Moroccan Muslim aspirations for independence. Although the Moroccan independence movement emphasized its secular-national (i.e., non-Muslim and nonsectarian) character and tried to gain the sympathy and help of the Jews, the latter were understandably apprehensive of the dangers that lay ahead for them in the course of a Moroccan struggle for independence and after its eventual achievement. In this situation important help was given to the Moroccan Jews by the World Jewish Congress, which reached an agreement with the leaders of the Moroccan independence movement to the effect that the Congress would give its support to the independence movement, while the latter undertook to give full equality to the Moroccan Jews and to see to it that no harm befell them in the increasingly frequent riots and clashes. With the independence of Morocco in 1956, the Jews were, in fact, accorded equal rights.[30] However, the developments of the subsequent years proved that a law on the books is a far cry from its enforcement in real life.

Until 1947 Morocco was, except for Israel, the Middle Eastern country with by far the largest Jewish population. In that year, the estimated number of Jews in Morocco was 280,000. By 1958 this number was reduced to 200,000, and by 1969 to 50,000. Since the Moroccan Diaspora constituted a typical Middle Eastern population with a high birth rate (37 in the 1936–46 decade), while emigration reduced its numbers, natural increase (birth rate minus death rate) added about 1.8 percent annually. It can, therefore, be assumed that at least 250,000 Moroccan Jews emigrated from 1947 to 1969. Of the emigrants, about 117,000 went to Israel between 1948 and 1960. The rest went to France and other countries.

Under the Italians in Libya

The ancient autochthonous Jewish community in Tripolitania (the western part of Libya, bordering on Tunisia) received a considerable influx of Italian Jews beginning with the seventeenth century. These immigrant *Gorneyim* were encouraged to settle in Tripoli as a result of the increased influence of the foreign consuls in the city. They engaged in trade and commerce with Europe, as well as in medicine; a certain Abraham Michael Cardozo, a Marrano and adherent of Shabbatai Zevi, who had come from Spain via Leghorn, became the personal physician of the Bey of Tunis about 1660.[31]

. Jewish scholarly and intellectual activity of any significance began in the eighteenth century, although even prior to that time emissaries from the holy cities of Palestine had engaged in teaching *Halakha*. Most of the rabbis of Tripolitanian birth devoted themselves to Kabbalistic studies and writings while the teaching of other branches of religion was entrusted to rabbis invited from Palestine or other countries.[32]

The Lausanne peace treaty of 1912 gave Italy the right to control Tripolitania, as well as Cyrenaica to the east and Fezzan to the south—the three provinces constituting Libya. This was the culmination of a protracted process of gradual Italian penetration into Libya. The first Italian school was founded by the Italian government in Tripoli in 1876: its organizer, as well as most of its pupils, were Jews. Before the end of the century the Alliance Israélite Universelle established a network of schools. All this resulted in a split between the poorer, tradition-bound, Arabic-speaking Jews, and the well-to-do, enlightened, Italian- and/or French-speaking and oriented Jews, a split that had its origins in the seventeenth century when the *Gomeyim* first arrived in Tripoli.

After 1912 the Italian government encouraged the founding of Italian schools and newspapers in Libya, activities in which the Tripolitanian Jews took a leading part. Italian rabbis were invited to serve as chief rabbis of Tripoli. The interwar years were relatively uneventful. During World War II the Jews of Libya suffered much less than those of the Maghribi states. Following Libya's conquest by the British (1943), members of the Jewish Brigade (a unit of Palestinian Jews in the British army) were active in the reconstruction of Jewish life in the country.

In 1945 a wave of anti-Jewish outbreaks swept the country: 135 Jews were killed, 300 wounded, many of them seriously, and much Jewish property was looted or destroyed. These events prompted the Jews to set up a self-defense organization, which gave a good account of itself in the summer of 1948 when, in connection with the War of Independence in Israel, an Arab mob attempted to repeat the feat of 1945.

In the four years that elapsed between the independence of Israel and that of Libya (January 1, 1952), some 15,000 Libyan Jews emigrated to Israel. Thereafter, the emigration increased, spurred on by periodic outbreaks of anti-Jewish violence. By 1969 not more than a hundred Jews were left in Libya out of a community that only twenty-two years previously counted 38,000.[33]

202

Westernization and Assimilation

While neither the Enlightenment nor religious Reform, nor the Science of Judaism—the three great movements that transformed the life of the Ashkenazi Diaspora and touched off the assimilationist trend—reached them, the Jews of North Africa nevertheless experienced a development leading away from the traditional confines of Judaism and in the direction of modernization. Modernization in the entire Middle East meant Westernization, a powerful movement that influenced the populations of all countries in the area, albeit to varying degrees. This influence was felt strongly after World War I, and its impact was greatest on the large urban concentrations.[34]

Since the Jews in the Middle East were a much more urbanized population element than the Muslims, they were caught up in the Westernizing movement to a greater extent than the latter.

In North Africa, additional factors were present pushing the Maghribi Jews in the same direction. There was, first of all, the educational effort of the Alliance Israélite Universelle which, since 1862, maintained a large network of schools in the Maghrib, enabling a sizable proportion of Jewish children, especially in the cities of the north, to acquire a basic knowledge of Hebrew and secular subjects, with strong emphasis on French language and civilization.

Another factor that decisively influenced the cultural development of the Jews, especially in Algeria, was the arrival, following the French conquest of the country, of considerable numbers of French Jews, many of whom gained leading positions. As a result of the influence of these modern and assimilationist Jews, despite the strenuous opposition of the native Algerian conservative Jewish leaders, a decree was issued in 1867 placing the three Consistories of Algerian Jews under the General Consistory of Paris, the highest religious institution of the French Jews.

Thirdly, the French influence, after the French occupation of Algeria in 1830 and the establishment of French Protectorates over Tunisia in 1881 and Morocco in 1912, resulted in a greater assimilation to French culture among the Jews than among the

Muslims. The Jews, having been treated for centuries as second-class subjects by the Muslims, made use of the arrival of the French to improve their position by engaging in occupations that became necessary to bridge the gap between the new French rulers and the largely illiterate, uneducated Muslim majority. To be able to do so, it was necessary for the Jews to acquire a knowledge of the French language and to approximate French behavior patterns, in addition to attaining a proficiency in the administrative, commercial, financial, and other professional fields they wished to enter. In Algeria the Crémieux Decree gave French citizenship to the Jews, thereby introducing an important legal distinction between them and the Muslims. In all three Maghribi states the Jews rapidly developed into a population element that, while native to their respective countries, was yet set apart from the Muslim majority, occupying a half-way position between it and its French overlords.

These conditions obtained in particular in the north and in the port cities where the French presence was most strongly felt. In the south, in the mountains and the desert, the Jews were as little touched by the French influence as they had been four centuries earlier by the arrival of Sephardi exiles from Spain. The difference between the two situations was that in the sixteenth century no village-to-town movement was touched off by the cultural changes introduced into North African Jewish life by the Sephardim, while in the nineteenth and twentieth centuries the modernization brought by the French into the Maghrib resulted in industrialization and urbanization. After the establishment of Israel, the Jewish village-to-town trend intensified to such an extent that the great majority of the small Jewish communities all over the Maghrib simply disappeared.

The changes in the internal character of Jewish life were equally far-reaching. Maghribi Jewry, for the first time, was faced with the blandishments of one of the greatest cultures of modern Europe, possessed of an ethos and a set of values and ideals of great attractiveness, which was further enhanced by the fact that its carriers were the prestige-laden rulers of the country. The old-fashioned rabbis, with their Talmud Tora schools and their emphasis on the rigid adherence to ritual minutiae, had no effective way of counteracting the French cultural enticements. Their continued ministrations to the sick, the unfortunate, and the barren came to be regarded by those who had acquired as much as the barest rudiments of modern education or outlook as benighted superstition. The number of those who were drawn at least to the peripheries of the magic circle of French culture steadily increased. Whether they were conscious of it or not, the fact was that assimilation to French culture and the concomitant abandonment of traditional Jewish life were the price the young Jewish generation had to pay, and was only too eager to pay, for economic and social advancement and for liberation from the appalling conditions of the *mellah* or *hara.*

Once they loosened the ties to their traditional frame of life, Maghribi Jews were in a worse position, as far as the chances of their group survival were concerned, than the Jews of the Ashkenazi Diaspora. In the case of the latter, there were the new Jewish movements of Enlightenment and Reform Judaism, and the new approach to Jewish history, religion, and culture represented by the Science of Judaism, that could, to an extent, fill the void that developed in Jewish life when it was emptied of its old traditional contents.This meant that Ashkenazi Jews could, and many actually did, remain Jewish without being Orthodox in the old, pre-nineteenth-century manner and sense. For the Jews of the Maghrib there was no such thing as a Jewish Enlightenment *(Haskala),* no reform of Jewish worship had ever been introduced among them, and no Science of Judaism had ever reached them. For those who managed to shake off the shackles of traditional Jewish ritualism and to discard the popular beliefs and practices to which Kabbalism had degenerated in the Maghrib, there was no new Jewish content that they could have substituted, and thus the move out of the *mellah* often became the equivalent of a move out of Judaism. Some adopted Christianity (none converted to Islam because that would have been, in their eyes, a step backward and downward), others turned to communism, many simply became secular, worldly, and French in their general orientation. This was the background whose aftereffects were felt for a long time even among those Maghribi Jews who settled in Israel and who, when asked where they had come from, would answer: "From Paris."

Emigration

The two historic events that brought about the almost total liquidation of Maghribi Jewry were the achievement of independence by Israel and by the North African states.

In 1948, when Israel gained independence, the French were still in control of the three Maghrib states and the British still held Libya. Yet despite the presence of these European powers with their armies, and despite appeals issued by such moderate native leaders as the Sultan of Morocco, sporadic anti-Jewish outbreaks occurred in Morocco and in Libya claiming several dozens of victims in each country. These events contributed their share to the mass emigration of Jews from North Africa that began in 1948.

Another factor that made for the emigration of North African Jews was their economic insecurity and widespread poverty. Poverty was the fate of most North African Jews, as it was of most North African Muslims, ever since the Diaspora existed. But, in the past, the possibility of emigration was simply not present. After the coming of the French, the idea slowly spread that in France one might do better. Following the independence of Israel the belief that in the Jewish State they would fare better economically was as important a motivation for moving there as was the desire to be rid of the indignities they had to suffer from the Muslims. And, after the independence of the Maghribi states, the economic upheaval that followed resulted in a worsening of the economic position of the Jews, which, of course, added its own weight to the desire to emigrate.

The third factor was cultural and it requires a somewhat more detailed explanation. The Maghribi Jews in general, and those of Algeria in particular, were perhaps the most typical examples of Jewries caught in the insoluble dilemma of a twofold cultural affiliation. Their roots were sunk deeply into the soil of the Maghrib. Their language was the local Arabic vernacular (with certain idiomatic differences); their ethos and values were those of the Maghribi Muslims; their personality traits and other characteristics were largely similar to those of their Muslim neighbors; even the Jewish and Muslim attitudes to the super- natural—with the all-pervading belief in magic, evil eye, saints, amulets, apotropaic utterances and gestures—were practically identical, as was the personality of the God whom the Muslims called Allah and the Jews by one of his several Hebrew names. This approximation to the Muslims in so many basic cultural and psychological characteristics, while at the same time re- maining as a group sharply separated from them, was the result of a symbiosis of more than a thousand years, and, in all probability could have continued for many generations to come. But then the French arrived, and the appeal of their physical presence combined with that of their culture, suddenly put an end to this age-old equilibrium. In Algeria the Jews became the main beneficiaries of the French colonial system; in Tunisia and Morocco the attraction emanating from everything French was no less overwhelming. In all parts of the Maghrib, with the exception of the remote Saharan south, acculturation to the French and what they represented proceeded apace. The ac- quisition of French culture became the central motivating desire that gripped especially the younger generation of Jews.

In view of the strength of this trend it was inevitable that the prospect of having to reintegrate into an Arabic culture, society, and state structure should be a most unattractive one for the French-oriented Maghribi Jews, as well as for the Jews of Libya who were exposed to both French and Italian cultures. Quite apart from the actual and not inconsiderable lowering of living standards this would have entailed for the educated sector, there was the double-edged feeling of superiority as Jews and as carriers of French culture (or, at least, its rudiments) that made it most undesirable to even as much as consider the possibility of assimilating into the newly emerging Muslim Arab states of the Maghrib. The answer, evidently, lay in emigration.

The fourth (and last) factor was the quasi-Messianic fervor sparked by the establishment of an independent Jewish State in the Holy Land of Israel 1878 years after the destruction of Jerusalem by the Romans. While the early immigrants who came from the Ashkenazi Diaspora to Palestine up to 1933 were nationalistically and idealistically motivated, and those who came from Europe thereafter did so primarily in search of safety, the Jews of North Africa (and of the Middle East in general) were still too close to the traditional Jewish and Kabbalistic influences that had dominated their parents, and partly their own generation as well, to see the reestablishment of Israel in any but religious terms. As far as I know, no study has been made to find out how they reconciled their age-old Messianic expectation with the realities of an actual Jewish State which, to boot, was dominated and governed by an irreligious majority; but eyewitness accounts of their initial reaction to the emergence of Israel leave no doubt as to the general religio-enthusiastic quality of their response.

All these factors together set in motion two waves of emigration from the Maghrib: one after the independence of Israel, and the other before and after the independence of the North African states. As soon as the gates of Israel were opened to Jewish immigration, the movement started. Many North African Jews moved from the villages to the cities, from the cities to transit centers near the ports, then were shipped to another camp near Marseille, and from there were taken to Israel. The first wave of emigration from North Africa took about four years before it subsided, and during that time it brought more than 100,000 immigrants to the shores of Israel.

Two or three years after this 'aliya (immigration) had petered out, it became clear that the Maghribi states would gain independence before long, and this prospect set off a new wave of emigration. This time, however, only part of the emigrants chose to go to Israel; others (especially the Algerian Jews) preferred France or other countries. All told, emigration reduced the number of North African Jews from 548,000 in 1947 to 61,600 in 1969, of whom 50,000 were in Morocco, 1,500 in Algeria, 10,000 in Tunisia, and 100 in Libya.

In Israel, to which some 200,000 of them had moved from 1948 to 1960 (see Table VI), North African Jews have become part of the Oriental Jewish half of the population. On them are focused many of the problems and issues resulting from the presence in that small country of two greatly differing types of population elements: Ashkenazi and Oriental Jewish.[35] In other countries, such as the United States and Canada, the North African Jewish arrivals were too few in relation to the established Jewish community to create any problem. In France, where the North African Jewish immigrants doubled the size of the Jewish community, their absorption and integration occasioned considerable difficulties which will be discussed in Chapter XVI dealing with French Jewry.

TABLE VI
JEWISH EMIGRANTS FROM NORTH AFRICA TO ISRAEL
1948–1960

Country of Emigration	1948–51	1952–54	1955–57	1958–60	Total 1948–60
Morocco	36,344	16,047	70,052	9,282	131,725
Algeria	721	414	2,483	481	4,099
Tunisia	8,035	5,928	15,267	2,149	31,379
Libya	30,865	1,571	198	94	32,728
Total North Africa	75,965	23,960	88,000	12,006	199,931

Source:–Private communication from Mr. Z. Rabi, director, Demographic Section, Central Bureau of Statistics, Government of Israel, Jerusalem.

12 THE ORIENTAL JEWS: EGYPT AND SOUTHWEST ASIA

Introduction

A glance at the map suffices to indicate the great geographical differences between North Africa and the eastern half of the Middle East. North Africa constitutes one solid land mass stretching from the Red Sea to the Atlantic, bordered on the north by the Mediterranean and on the south by the Sahara Desert with its large uninhabited stretches. Ancient trade routes running along the Mediterranean coastline have for many centuries connected, and to a certain extent unified, North Africa, as did sea lanes hugging the same coast. More difficult and more dangerous were the trans-Saharan routes that cut through the desert from north to south. But they, too, enabled cultural influences, soon after they had become established in the north, to spread into the vast regions of the Sudan belt to the south of the desert. The north itself, despite regional differences, was characterized by an overall unity, which stamped this entire enormous land expanse, excluding Egypt, with a character of its own, that of the Maghrib, the Muslim west.

In marked contrast to this unity, the eastern half of the Middle East is broken up into many separate land masses by both seas and deserts. Egypt, actually nothing more than the Nile valley and delta, is isolated by deserts on both east and west. The Arabian Peninsula is surrounded on three sides by the sea, while the inhabited lands of the Fertile Crescent to the north are cut off from it by the desert, which also separates and isolates the various coastal areas of the peninsula itself. Turkey is similarly surrounded by the sea on three sides, while on the fourth, eastern, side a most difficult mountainous terrain has made communication between Turkey and her eastern neighbors tenuous and hazardous. Syria, Lebanon, and Jordan form a geographical unit bounded by the Anatolian Plateau in the north, the desert in the east and the south, and the sea and Israel in the west. Iraq is isolated from the west by the desert and from the east by the Zagros and other mountains of Iran. Iran and Afghanistan, while forming one large land mass, are so greatly broken up by mountains and deserts that cultural isolation characterizes their various subareas. And, lastly, the Turcoman-Uzbek area to the north of Iran and Afghanistan is geographically part of the vast steppe region that stretches from the Caspian Sea and the Ural Mountains in the west to the Altai Range in the east.

This difference in geographical character between the North African and the eastern halves of the Middle East is reflected in the cultural picture of the two areas. The Maghrib, wedged in as it is between the sea to the north and the Sahara to the south (within which the oasis settlements form islandlike outposts in the uninhabited wasteland of the desert), is something of an overall cultural entity. In contrast, the eastern half of the Middle East is broken up into numerous cultural units, corresponding to the geographical areas mentioned above, or, in several cases, to parts within them. Thus, as against the three basically similar culture areas found in North Africa (counting only that part in which Jewish communities are or were found), the eastern part of the Middle East has no less than fifteen culture areas, many of which exhibit marked dissimilarities.[1]

The same observation holds true with regard to the Jewish Diasporas. In North Africa the Jewish communities present an overall similarity as against the marked diversity found in the Jewish groups inhabiting Egypt and Southwest Asia. All the Jewish communities of North Africa can be subsumed, and usually are, under the generic term Maghribi Jews, or, as they are known in Israel, *Mughrabim.* The Jewish Diasporas of the eastern half of the Middle East, on the other hand, have no such generic designation. Each of them has its own specific name, its own specific history and traditions, and its own specific character.

These differences can be illustrated by listing the Jewish community organizations (the so-called *Kehillot*) that were established by Oriental Jewish immigrants in Jerusalem in the late nineteenth and early twentieth centuries and were registered up to 1938 with the District Commissioner's Office as separate public bodies:[2]

Community	Date of Registration
Mughrabim (from North Africa, mainly Morocco)	1844
Gruzinim (or Gurjim, from Georgia in the Caucasus)	1863
Bukharans	1868
Persians	1877
Halabim (from Aleppo, a city in North Syria)	1880
Yemenites	1883
Daghestanim (from Daghestan, a district in the Caucasus)	1887
Bavlim (from Bavel, i.e., Baghdad, Iraq)	1888
Afghans	1900
Urfalim (from Urfa, a town on the southern border of Turkey)	1902
Crimeans	1909
Hararim (i.e., mountaineers, from the Caucasus)	1912
Jarmuklim (from Cermik, a town in Turkey)	1920
Sviriklim (from Siverek, a town in Turkey)	1922
Urmiyim (from Urmia, a town in Iranian Kurdistan)	1923
Damaskim (from Damascus in Syria)	1925
Meshhedim (from Meshhed, Khorasan, N. E. Iran)	1928
Iranim (a separate community of the Persians)	1931
Kurdim (Kurds, mainly from Amadiya, Dehok etc., in Iraqi Kurdistan)	1931
Targum (another group of Kurdish Jews)	1932
Arbelim (from Arbel, a town in Iraqi Kurdistan)	1936

Diarbekrim (from Diar Bekr, a town in Turkish Kurdistan)	1936
Asshurim (i.e., Assyrians, mainly from Mosul, N. Iraq)	1938
Zakhoim (from Zakho, a town in Iraqi Kurdistan)	1938
Nesibin and Kamishlu (from the twin towns, Nusaybin in Turkey and Kamechlie in Syria)	1938
Adenim (from Aden Colony)	1938

As we can see from this list, the North African immigrants formed one single community, while the immigrants from the eastern half of the Middle East tended to organize not merely according to their countries of origin but on the basis of the individual towns from which they had come. Thus the Syrian Jews were organized into an Aleppan, a Damascan, and a Kamechlian *kehilla,* the Kurdish Jews into an Urfa, a Chermik, a Siverek, a Diarbekr, and a Nusaybin (all in Turkey), an Arbel, a Mosul, and a Zakho (all three in Iraq), and an Urmia (Iran) *kehilla,* in addition to two general Kurdish communities called *Kurdim* and *Targum.* This tendency, known also among Jewish immigrants of East European origin in the Western world and especially in the United States, indicates the extent of cultural isolation in which these Middle Eastern Jews had lived and which had resulted in a local specificity in socio-cultural development and in a separatism that were carried over into Palestine and effectively precluded the banding together of these communities into more comprehensive organizations.

The various languages that served as the vernaculars of these communities were discussed in Chapter VII. Let us nevertheless mention here that linguistically, too, the diversity in the eastern half of the Middle East was greater than in North Africa. In the Maghrib the dominant vernacular was Arabic, with small isolated Jewish groups speaking Berber, while some Sephardim had preserved their Ladino. In the east, in addition to Arabic (which itself was broken up into several mutually unintelligible local dialects), the Jews spoke several Persian dialects, several Arama-

214

ic dialects, and also Ladino (especially in the coastal cities of Turkey), while smaller groups spoke several other languages.

While the list of the Middle Eastern *kehillot* shows the great number of places from whence Jews had immigrated to the Holy City prior to 1938, the entire immigration prior to the establishment of the State of Israel was on a small scale compared to the great immigratory wave after the emergence of the State that resulted in the complete or virtual liquidation of most Middle Eastern Diasporas. Table VII shows the number of Jews in Middle Eastern countries in 1947, 1958, and 1969—that is, prior to the independence of Israel and ten and twenty-one years after it. While not all the Jews who left their native countries went to Israel, most did. Thereby, at least as far as the Oriental Jews were concerned, the two-thousand-year-old process of increasing dispersion was suddenly halted and reversed in this the greatest "ingathering of the exiles" ever in Jewish history.

TABLE VII

THE ORIENTAL JEWS IN THE
MIDDLE EAST (OUTSIDE ISRAEL), 1947, 1958, 1969

Country	1947	1958	1969
Morocco	280,000	200,000	50,000
Algeria	130,000	140,000	1,500
Tunisia	100,000	85,000	10,000
Libya	38,000	3,750	100
Egypt	75,000	40,000	1,000
Yemen	50,000	3,500	–
Aden (incl. Protectorate)	8,000	800	–
Lebanon	6,000	6,000	3,000
Syria	13,000	5,000	4,000
Turkey	80,000	60,000	39,000
Iraq	110,000	6,000	2,500
Iran	90,000	80,000	80,000
Afghanistan	5,000	4,000	800
Total	985,000	634,050	191,900

Egypt——

In the geographic dichotomy outlined above, Egypt occupies an intermediary position. It lies in North Africa, and is thus the fifth and easternmost political unit in the chain of countries bordering on the Mediterranean coastline of Africa. However, in contrast to the overall similarities that characterize the four North African countries that lie to the west of it, Egypt is a compactly settled riverine country with intensive irrigated cultivation, 80 percent of whose population comprise the most typical *fellahin* found in the entire Middle East, and whose affinities lie with other riparian agricultural *fellah*-areas, such as that of Mesopotamia.[3]

The history of the Jews in Egypt until the first century CE was sketched earlier in Chapter I. In Alexandria alone there were 110,000 Jews in the seventh century, of whom 40,000 remained after the Arab conqueror Amr ibn al-As took the city in 641 CE. After the Arab conquest of Egypt the position of the Jews was, in general, tolerable; they constituted a recognized religio-national community headed for many centuries by an official, called *Nagid,* whose status and influence paralleled those of the Babylonian *Resh Gelutha.* Maimonides, and after him his son Abraham, were among the *Negidim,* who were also known in Arabic as *Ra'is al-milla* (i.e., "head of the [Jewish] Nation"). Both before and after Maimonides, Jews were in the service of the court, especially as physicians and ministers, as well as in other capacities. They had important Talmudic academies which flourished until the early fourteenth century. By the fifteenth century the number of the Jews had declined to five hundred families in Cairo and sixty in Alexandria; however, the office of the *Nagid* continued until it was abolished by the Turkish conquerors of Egypt (1517). In the sixteenth and seventeenth centuries the position of the Jews improved, their numbers grew, and their influence at the viceregal court increased. For a while the office of treasurer was held by Jews, among them Raphael Joseph Chelebi, the wealthy friend and patron of Shabbatai Zevi, whose Messianic movement caused a great stir among the Egyptian Jews.

In the first half of the nineteenth century, when Mohammed Ali (1805–49) encouraged the influx of foreign capital, European Jews began to settle in Egypt. They prospered and contributed substantially to the economic development of the country. By the middle of the nineteenth century there were some 6,000 indigenous Jewish families in Cairo, as well as 200–250 "Italian" Jewish families; in Alexandria there were 500 indigenous and 150 Italian Jewish families.[4] By 1866 there were fifty Jews of East European extraction in Alexandria, and in 1892 a German-Italian congregation was founded in Port-Said. As they were in other parts of the Ottoman Empire, these foreign Jews were under the protection of European consuls. The official census of 1897 put the number of indigenous Jews at 12,693 and that of the foreign Jews at 12,507, or a total of 25,200. These figures indicate not so much a sizable immigration of foreign Jews into Egypt, as the extent to which the Egyptian Jews sought and obtained the protection of foreign consuls, thereby making themselves officially foreigners.

Napoleon's invasion and the French occupation of Egypt (1798–1801) signaled the beginning of French influence in the country. However, several decades had to pass before the first modern Jewish schools were established in Cairo and Alexandria as a result of the initiative of Adolphe Crémieux (1796–1880) who, together with Sir Moses Montefiore (1784–1885) and the French Jewish orientalist Solomon Munk (1802–1867), visited Egypt in 1840. These "Crémieux schools," however, were shortlived and were closed down in 1842. In 1860 a modern Jewish girls' school was opened in Alexandria, and in 1892 a second girls' school was added. The first boys' school, established with funds supplied by Baron Yacoub de Menasce (or Menache), an Egyptian Jewish notable and philanthropist (1800–1884), was opened in Alexandria in 1885. The Alliance Israélite Universelle entered the Egyptian Jewish educational field a decade later. Its first boys' and girls' schools in Cairo were opened in 1896 and in Alexandria in the following year.[5] In the years that followed, numerous additional Jewish schools, including trade schools, private schools, and high schools leading to the French *baccalaureat,* were established in Egypt.

The result of these educational efforts was to transform, within two generations, most of the Egyptian Jews into an educated, middle-class community with a considerable professional sector, a common knowledge of French, and a leaning away from the Arab culture of the environment and toward French culture. The latter trend was expressed, among other things, in the publication of several papers (*Aurore, Israel,* and others) in French. Numerous literary, sports, and Zionist associations were founded, as were youth and philanthropic organizations, B'nai B'rith lodges, and *Landsmannschaft*-type organizations of Sephardi, Corfiote, and Italian Jews.[6] Thus, in the early twentieth century, irrespective of their historical background and origin, the Jews of Egypt were largely a European or Europeanized urban population which had its niche in the Egyptian economy and state structure but which was a foreign element as far as its culture, language, interests, and tenor of life were concerned.

No significant change occurred in the position of the Jews in Egypt under British rule (1882–1922), except that their French orientation was somewhat modified in favor of an assimilation to British culture, and that many of the younger generation learned English. In the 1920s and 1930s Egyptian Jews achieved important positions in public life, high officialdom, the parliament, and even in the government.[7] At the end of the British Protectorate the number of Jews in Egypt reached 72,000; thereafter it increased somewhat (to 75,000) until 1947, when it began to decline as a result of emigration. During this period most of the Jews in Egypt were not Egyptian citizens, but either foreign citizens or stateless. Even those whose ancestors had lived in Egypt for many generations preferred to retain the citizenship, and with it the protection, of a European country. The number of such "foreigners" was put at 30,000 in the 1940s. Those who had no European citizenship remained stateless, Egyptian laws making it almost impossible for a non-Egyptian to acquire citizenship; their number was estimated at 40,000. This left only about 5,000 Jews who were Egyptian citizens.[8]

After the independence of Egypt, and especially following the end of World War II, Egyptian nationalist sentiment grew and with it rose the anti-Jewish feeling. The first anti-Jewish outbreak occurred on the twenty-eighth anniversary of the Balfour Declaration, on November 2, 1945. Several Jewish public buildings were burned but there was no loss of life. From 1947 on anti-Jewish legislation was enacted leading to mass dismissals of Jews from their jobs, sequestration of Jewish property, and the exclusion from practice of non-Egyptian professionals, to which category most of the professional men in the Jewish community belonged. Within a year the economic basis of the entire Jewish community of Egypt was thus effectively destroyed.[9]

Israel's declaration of independence (May 14, 1948) was followed by mass arrests of Jews. In June a renewed mob attack resulted in twenty Jewish dead. On July 15 the Israeli Air Force attacked Cairo; this was followed by more outbursts, bombings, and murders. At the same time the Jews were prohibited from leaving Egypt, even as their ancestors had been more than three thousand years before.

In August 1949 the ban against emigration was lifted, and immediately a large-scale exodus began. Within three months more than 20,000 Jews left the country. Thereafter, with a certain improvement in the situation of the Jews, emigration continued on a diminishing scale. The overthrow of the monarchy (July 1952) was followed by a period of relative quiet, but after the ouster of President Mohammed Naguib by Colonel Gamal Abdel Nasser in February 1954, the anti-Jewish measures and agitation were renewed, and, especially after the Israeli Sinai Campaign late in 1956, there were mass arrests of Jews. Whatever property still remained in Jewish hands was confiscated and pressure was put on the now penniless Jews to leave the country. Between November 1956 and the end of 1959 more than 36,000 Jews actually left. By the mid-1960s, no more than 3,500 Jews remained, and after the Six-day War of 1967 this number was further reduced to 800 (many of whom were in prison). At the same time the number of Karaites, too, has shrunk from 4,000 in 1947 to 500 in 1968.[10] These were the last remnants of the Jewish Diaspora in the country which had been the original "house of bondage" of the Children of Israel, and in which, despite explicit Biblical prohibition, they had lived uninterruptedly for 2,500 years.

Some 40,000 of the Egyptian Jewish refugees settled in Israel; more than 30,000 went to other countries, mainly to England, France, Italy, the United States, Canada, and other American countries.[11]

Arabia

The beginnings of the Jewish dispersion in the vast Arabian Peninsula are reflected in legends current among the Yemenite Jews, according to which their first ancestors settled in South-west Arabia at the time of the first fall of Jerusalem (586 BCE). Historical evidence begins about a thousand years later, when powerful Jewish warrior tribes were spread over large areas of Southern Arabia, and founded a kingdom in Himyar (fifth-sixth centuries CE). The last Jewish king of Himyar was Yusuf Ash'ar Dhu-Nuwas, who came to power in 523 CE, conducted large military operations against the Christians and Abyssinians in which 14,000 men were killed and 11,000 taken prisoners, and was killed in a second campaign led by the Negus of Abyssinia against Yemen.[12]

In the days of Mohammed (570–632), some Jewish tribes adopted Islam, others followed suit later. Still others, however, remained faithful to Judaism and for centuries led the life of *dhimmi*s already familiar to us. Scattered evidence indicates that Jews managed to maintain themselves in Arabia, in addition to their main concentration in Yemen, and also in the central, western, southern, and eastern parts of the peninsula.

In north-central Arabia, as late as the end of the nineteenth century, Charles M. Doughty, that greatest of all British Arabians, found numerous traditions among the Arab tribes about Jews who were said to have lived in several oases. In fact, one of the largest of these oases, that of Kheybar (about a hundred miles north of Medina) was considered as having belonged to the Jews in the past.[13] Also the oasis of Teyma (another 140 miles to the north) was reputed to have been owned in the past by Jews, headed by a prince named Beder ibn Joher, the ruins of whose castle were pointed out to Doughty.[14]

In the southwestern part of Saudi Arabia, in the province of Asir, small Jewish communities managed to maintain themselves until the establishment of Israel. The latest and most reliable evidence comes from H. St. J. B. Philby, the famous British Arabian and confidant of King Ibn Saud, who visited the area in 1920, 1931, and 1936. On these trips Philby met with the Jewish inhabitants of Najran, a township some 120 miles from the Red Sea coast and about ten miles north of the Yemeni border; of another town, Dhahran, to the west of Najran; of Habauna; and of villages on their outskirts. In 1920 Philby reported four Jewish families in Najran; in the 1930s he found eighty Jews there. At this time they asked him to help them get transferred from Saudi Arabia to Palestine, and, by 1950, all of them had actually emigrated to Israel. The Jews of Najran made jewelry and trinkets for the women and dagger-sheaths for the men, and they were the only gunsmiths and armorers in the district. They owed, Philby remarks, "their continued existence in the midst of wild and intolerant Muslim tribes to the special services which they alone are capable of rendering to their neighbors in peace and war."[15] In fact, "they had lived for generations in Najran on terms of perfect amity with some of the most ferocious tribes in Arabia and had had little to complain of." Occasionally, Jewish girls embraced Islam to marry an Arab.[16]

The Jews of Najran had come partly from Haraz (in the Yemen), partly from San'a, the capital of Yemen, and partly from Iraq. On the other hand, Philby informs us, some of the Jews of Sa'da in Yemen were emigrants from Najran.[17] Arabian Jews seem to have been traveling from one country to another, occasionally or regularly, and Philby mentions that prior to World War I "a Jewish leech, famous for his skill as a camel-doctor, used to come down to Najd [central Arabia] from Damascus every spring season to cure the camels; but of late [this was written in 1920] he had not been at Riyadh [the capital of Saudia Arabia], with the result that last year there had been a very heavy mortality among the camels. . . ."[18]

Along the southern coast of the peninsula scattered Jewish communities were found, until their emigration to Israel, in many parts of the Aden Protectorate (now Southern Yemen). Thus in the town of Dhala, the capital of the Amiri country north of Aden town, and in the surrounding villages,

> there used to be a considerable Jewish population . . . which earned a living by weaving ornate clothes and making bracelets and necklaces out of silver coins. The Jews of Dhala were easily distinguished by the curls and caps of the men and the bright yellow make-up used by the women; but they have all now [1953] emigrated to Israel.[19]

To the northeast of the city of Aden, at a distance of some fifty to one hundred miles, lie several provincial towns which harbored small Jewish communities for many generations. In 1939 the Dutch explorer D. van der Meulen visited this part of the then Western Aden Protectorate and described his meetings with local Jews and the impression they made on him. In al-Jof, he reports having

> seen some Jews, living among the Arabs and looking as poor and dirty as they, but immediately recognizable by the two ringlets that dangled in front of their ears. More still their whole attitude and the quiet expression of their face spoke of their being Jews. Centuries of oppression and of silently suffered disdain had deeply pressed their stamp on this ineradicable race. . . .[20]

In Lodar (or Lawdar) van der Meulen visited the Jewish quarter in which lived thirteen families. All gainfully employed Jews were craftsmen, mostly silversmiths, "making elegant jambiyat [the south Arabian J-shaped daggers] for the men and belts, girdles, earrings, bangles and anklets for the women and girls." The houses of the Jews, he found, were like those of the Arabs, "except that they were a little cleaner inside." Ascending to the second floor of a Jewish silversmith's house, van der Meulen found that the women "were dressed and had their hair made up in exactly the same way as the Arab women, and even their faces were also painted yellow." The men and the boys wore skullcaps.

> They had good intellectual qualities that were continually cultivated thanks to their marvelous faithfulness to the religion and traditions of their forefathers. They studied the Hebrew language; they read the books of the Old Testament; they raised their

spirit from scorn and oppression by recourse to their election as God's chosen people, by holding on in unshakable belief to the promise of a national restoration. . . .[21]

In the villages of the area van der Meulen also encountered some Jewish silversmiths.

In 1949 the total number of Jews in the western Aden Protectorate was put by the British Agent at 2,600 to 2,750. Over half of them lived in the 'Awdhali sultanate, the others in seven of the nineteen emirates, sheikhdoms, and sherifates of the Western Aden Protectorate. In 1949, most of them left for Israel.[22]

Farther to the east, some 300 to 350 miles east of Aden, lies the well-known Hadhramaut Valley, identified with the *Hatzar-mavet* mentioned in the Bible (Genesis 10:26). In the Hadhrami (the adjectival form of Hadhramaut) town of Haban there was in 1946 a Jewish community of 450, while in five surrounding villages there were another 250 Jews. Prior to their settlement in Haban and its villages, the Jews lived in the mountains and caves of the Hadhramaut. Their traditions have it that they had arrived in the Hadhramaut prior to the destruction of the Second Temple of Jerusalem (70 CE). Thanks to their contact with Yemenite Jews, however, the basic works of Jewish religion produced in subsequent centuries became familiar to them: they knew the Talmud, the Codes, and the Kabbala. In the twentieth century most Jews in Haban were silversmiths. They lived in many-storied houses, typical of Yemen and south Arabia, with the ground floor serving as workshop, the second as storage space, the third contained the living rooms, the fourth and fifth the bedrooms of the family head and his sons. Married sons lived with their father, in accordance with the widespread Middle Eastern custom of maintaining the unity of the extended patrilineal family. The women were veiled like the Muslim women of Haban, and they observed all the other rules of sexual segregation.[23]

Until their emigration, the Habani Jews had to pay an annual poll tax to the sultan of Haban. In 1950, 321 of them were "ransomed" by an emissary of the Jewish Agency with a payment of a lump sum to the sultan, taken in six trucks to Aden, and thence flown to Israel.[24]

The liquidation of the Jewish communities in Oman, in the easternmost corner of the Arabian Peninsula, took place half a century earlier. The Jews at that time emigrated to Bahrain and Baghdad. In Sahar (or Suhar), a town on the Batina coast of the Gulf of Oman, a Jewish cemetery, seen by Bertram Thomas in the late 1920s, still bore mute testimony to their presence for many generations past.[25]

In the city of Aden, at the opposite, southwestern, corner of the peninsula, there was an old Jewish community whose origins are unknown. A British possession from 1839, Aden was inhabited in the late nineteenth century by some 3,500 Jews (within a total population of 42,000) including 1,000 Jews from Yemen and some 150 from the Bene Israel community in Bombay.[26] In the wake of the establishment of Israel, anti-Jewish outbreaks in Aden in December 1947 (eighty-two Jews were killed, seventy-six wounded; Jewish shops were looted, houses burned) induced the Aden Jews to join their Yemenite brethren in going to Israel. Within a few years practically all Aden Jews were transferred to Israel.

We left the Jews of Yemen to the last in this rapid presentation of the Arabian Diaspora because they were the largest and by far the most important Jewish community in the entire Arabian Peninsula, and because it was their mass transfer to Israel that put an end to the long history of Arabian Jewry. In the sharply demarkated class system that characterized Yemeni society in general, the Jews occupied the lowest position. They had to put up with all the humiliations referred to earlier (see Chapter X) in a most pronounced form. If other Jewish communities were "brought low," the Yemenite Jews were brought lowest. The special harshness with which the Yemenite Jews were treated was perhaps due to the fact that the Yemeni Arabs of the central (highland) area are Shi'ite Muslims, followers of the so-called "Sevener" sect of the Shi'a, and the Shi'ites in general have been much more intolerant in their attitude to the Jews (and other "people of the book") than the Sunni Muslims.

In any case, a Yemenite Jew was not allowed to raise his voice against a Muslim, to discuss religion with him, to ride on horseback, to touch a Muslim in passing, to wear new or good clothes, to engage in money transactions. He had to pay *jizya* (head tax), to rise in deference whenever a Muslim passed him, to be humble and self-effacing. One of the laws that hurt the Jews most was a decree issued in 1922 according to which every Jewish child whose father died before he reached the age of thirteen was taken from his home (even if his mother was alive) and reared as a Muslim.

The rigid class system of the Muslim environment left its mark on the internal social structure of the Jews as well. The Jews of the capital, San'a, considered themselves the elite of Yemenite Jewry, and regarded the Jews of other towns, and especially of the villages, as low-class people with whom they refused to intermarry.[27]

Like their co-religionists in other Middle Eastern countries, the Yemenite Jews were great believers in the Kabbala and were given to many magic beliefs and practices. One of the tasks of their rabbis (a rabbi among them had the title *mori*, "master") was to dispense magical remedies, write or otherwise prepare amulets, and thus to minister to the psychological needs of a people who had to have supernatural comfort to be able to suffer silently the hardships of a life of incessant humiliation. Only in his home and in the synagogue did the Yemenite Jew find respite from his troubles, and it was in home and synagogue that his interests were centered: wife (or wives) and children in the former, and the prayers and the study of the *Zohar* in the latter.

It is nothing less than remarkable that under these conditions the Jews of Yemen nevertheless were able to produce an impressive list of Jewish scholarly works. In addition to commentaries to the Bible, Masoretic studies, and glosses on the Code of Maimonides, the Yemenite Jews compiled Midrashim, wrote Kabbalistic and philosophical works, and produced fine Hebrew poetry. They maintained contact, even though only sporadically, with the centers of Jewish life, and it was in reply to an inquiry sent by the Yemenite scholar Yakob ben Netanael al-Fayyumi that Maimonides wrote his famous *Iggeret Teman,* or Yemen Epistle. However, by the seventeenth century the notable intellectual activity of the Yemenite Jews had come to an end, and thereafter their energies seem to have been exhausted by the very difficult task of simply keeping alive.

Yet despite all humiliation and degradation, the quarters of the Yemenite Jews were kept scrupulously clean, in contrast to the filth of both the North African *mellahs* and *haras* and the Muslim quarters in the Yemeni towns. Inside, their houses were even cleaner. The cleanliness of the Yemenite Jews has been noted by numerous travelers in Yemen, and is a trait that has contributed to making them the most liked Oriental Jewish community in Israel.

Another characteristic of the Yemenite Jews was the emphasis they placed on religious education. They had numerous Talmud Tora schools, and, in addition, fathers taught their sons not only their trades but also Tora. While in many other Diasporas there was a certain percentage of illiteracy even among the men, all Yemenite Jews could read and understand Hebrew and were well versed in the Bible and other Jewish religious source books, including the *Zohar*.

In the last century or so prior to the liquidation of their Diaspora by emigration to Israel, the Yemenite Jews were primarily artisans and craftsmen. The most important single craft they engaged in was silversmithing; they were the sole producers of silver and gold filigree and other jewelry, including the characteristic daggers with the J-shaped sheath that all Yemenite men wore in their belts. I recall that in 1952 my colleague and friend Professor Philip K. Hitti told me in Princeton that, on a visit he had paid to Yemen shortly before, he found that the price of silver jewelry had skyrocketed, and, what was worse, practically none was available: the Jews having emigrated to Israel, there were no silversmiths left in the country.

In addition to working as silversmiths, the Yemenite Jews were also coiners, tinsmiths, coppersmiths, blacksmiths, armorers; makers of lamps and water-pipes (narghilehs); cabinet makers, sieve makers, and wicker workers; leather workers, bucket makers, shoe makers, cobblers, saddle makers, furriers, tanners, and flayers; tailors, weavers, spinners, cushion makers, makers of decorative ribbons from silver threads, cotton workers, carpet weavers, dyers; potters, millstone chamferers, charcoal burners, pulvermakers, soapmakers, pharmacists; millers, bakers, seed roasters, candy makers, slaughterers, butchers, wine makers, distillers, snuff makers; building workers, stonecutters, carpenters, house painters, plasterers; ovenbuilders, gypsum makers; cuppers, barbers, servants, guides, donkey drivers, porters, woodcutters; manure collectors, cleaners of latrines, sewers, cisterns, and courtyards, animal corpse removers (these occupations were forced upon them by the Muslims); peddlers, shopkeepers, merchants in cloth, oil, and spices; moneylenders; bookbinders, and, of course, scribes (i.e., Bible copyists). All these occupations were usually inherited from father to son. The Jews' share in the commerce of the region was small; Jewish wholesalers and exporters-importers were practically nonexistent.[28]

The first Yemenite Jews to return to Palestine arrived in 1881, shortly before the first Jewish immigrants from Russia. Thereafter, the number of those who followed in the footsteps of these pioneers gradually increased. By 1908 there were some 3,000 Yemenite Jews in Palestine; from 1919 to 1948 some 30,000 more arrived.

After Israel's independence Yemenite Jews arrived in growing numbers in the port city of Aden and were put up in two refugee camps operated by the American Jewish Joint Distribution Committee. From the camps they were flown to Israel in an airlift that soon acquired popular fame as "Operation Magic Carpet." Since it was impossible to work out a close coordination between the arrival of Yemenite Jews in Aden and the rate of their transfer to Israel by the airlift, by September 1949 there were as many as 13,000 of them in the two camps. However, within a year all of them (a total of 45,126) were flown to Israel. The number of the Jews who remained in Yemen is unknown; estimates range from two thousand down to two hundred. In Israel, by the end of 1950, their number reached approximately 112,000.[29]

Syria

The history of the Jews in Syria is essentially that of two urban communities that have resided for many centuries in Damascus and Aleppo (Halab), the two large cities of the country.

As early as the first century CE there were some 10,000 Jews living in Damascus. They were governed by their own ethnarch. During the Jewish rebellion against the Romans in Palestine (66–70 CE), the pagan inhabitants of the city who sympathized with the Romans attacked and killed many Jews.[30] The community continued into Talmudic times, survived the Persian (614) and Arab (635) conquests of the city, and flourished in the subsequent centuries. Benjamin of Tudela, the intrepid Jewish traveler who visited most Jewish Diasporas in the twelfth century and whose name we shall frequently encounter in these pages, reported in 1170 that there were three thousand Jews there (as well as two hundred Karaites), while according to Petahia of Regensburg (Benjamin's Ashkenazi counterpart, about the same time), their number was ten thousand. They had an important Talmudic academy and, in the late twelfth century, a Damascan rabbi became the *Nagid* of Egypt.

The community continued to flourish; in 1481 Menahem of Volterra found 450 Jewish families in it, "all rich, honored and merchants," and headed by a physician. In 1492 Sephardi exiles came from Spain, established themselves in the city, and built a synagogue of their own. A few years later an anonymous traveler relates that Damascan Jews who dealt in dress-goods, or engaged in handicrafts, lent money at 24 percent interest to the Venetians (not at all exorbitant for those days), and counted five hundred households. They were grouped around three synagogues: one belonged to the Sephardim, the second to the indigenous Jews called by the Sephardim *Moriscos,* and the third to the Sicilians. Among the Damascan rabbis of the sixteenth and seventeenth centuries there were outstanding scholars. Hayim Vital (1526–1603), the famous Kabbalist, was for many years the chief rabbi of Damascus. His son Samuel, who transcribed and circulated his father's Kabbalistic writings, lived there, as did Moses Najjara (d. 1581) and his son Israel, the well-known poet (flourished in the late sixteenth century); Josiah Pinto (1565–1648) the author of numerous homiletic commentaries; and many others.

In the mid-nineteenth century there were about four thousand Jews in Damascus,[31] headed by a chief rabbi and represented by one of their leaders in the municipal government. In 1840 the Jews of Damascus were brought to the attention of the Western world in connection with a ritual murder accusation; the release and acquittal of the nine accused was obtained after personal intervention by Sir Moses Montefiore, Adolphe Crémieux, and Solomon Munk with Mohammed Ali in Egypt and Sultan Mahmud in Constantinople. Twenty years later, two hundred Jews of Damascus were accused of having participated, with the Muslims and Druzes, in the massacre of the Christian Maronites. The Grand Vizier, Fuad Pasha, had five hundred Muslims punished by hanging; the two hundred Jews narrowly escaped the same fate, and finally were released against a payment of a fine of four million piasters which was defrayed by the whole Jewish community.

About 1900 there were ten thousand Jews in Damascus; they had nine synagogues with several officiating rabbis. Most of the breadwinners were engravers on copper and wood, weavers, carpenters, and smiths; a few were bankers and small merchants; half a dozen worked in government offices. The various schools of the Alliance Israélite Universelle, the first of which was opened in 1880, had about two thousand pupils.

Most of the Jews lived in abject poverty which was barely alleviated by the work of the four benevolent societies organized by the well-to-do Jews of the city.

Aleppo, in northwestern Syria, also had a very old Jewish community. Benjamin of Tudela and Petahia of Regensburg, who visited the city between 1170 and 1180, estimated the number of Jews at 1,500. A leading member of the community was Joseph ibn Aknin, for whom the great Maimonides wrote his *Guide of the Perplexed.* Jewish scholars and poets from Aleppo were known throughout the centuries. Aleppan Jews maintained commercial relations with Italy in the west, and India in the east, where they had specially close contact with the Jews of Cochin.

In the mid-nineteenth century there were 1,500 to 2,000 Jewish families in the city.[32] The first modern Jewish school was

229

opened by the Alliance Israélite Universelle in 1869. By 1900 the Alliance schools had about five hundred pupils. The total number of Jews at the time was about ten thousand.

In the course of time the Sephardi Jews, who had settled in both Damascus and Aleppo after 1492, merged with the indigenous Jews, the *Moriscos,* giving up Ladino and adopting Arabic instead. The entire Jewish community assimilated to the Arab environment culturally and morally, as well as linguistically, which, in general, meant a decline in both areas, and which resulted in a peculiar combination of moral laxity with continued religious rigidity.[33]

The occupational structure of the Syrian Jews remained largely the same from the beginning of the twentieth century to World War II. In Damascus, 20 percent were peddlers, 20 percent engravers on metal and marble, 15 percent merchants, 10 percent craftsmen, and 15 percent were living on charity.[34]

Both the economic and the civil conditions of the Syrian Jews improved under French mandatory rule (1920) but worsened again considerably under the short-lived Vichy regime (1940), which was replaced a year later by the Free French administration. Under the latter, civil rights were restored to the Jews, but with the growth of Arab nationalism the anti-Jewish feeling among the Arabs increased, especially after Syria gained independence in 1945. The resulting tensions led to an increase in the Jewish emigration that had been sizable even prior to World War II. It is estimated that from 1919 to 1939 some 27,000 left for Palestine, Lebanon, and Latin America. By 1943 about 10,000 Syrian Jews had settled in the United States, leaving, in the same year, according to the census, 29,770 Jews in Syria (17,000 in Aleppo and 11,000 in Damascus). By 1947 only 13,000 had remained, prompting the Syrian government to launch an investigation into the "disappearance" of 17,000 Syrian Jews within the preceding four years.[35]

In that same year anti-Jewish outbreaks occurred, in the course of which eight Jews were killed in Aleppo and hundreds of Jewish shops were looted and destroyed. In 1948 the Syrian government prohibited the emigration of Jews, concentrated the Jewish villagers of the Jezirah district (in northeastern Syria) into closed ghettos in Damascus and Kamechlie (near the Turkish border), and transformed the entire remaining Jewish community of the country into an indigent group that had to be kept alive by charity from the neighboring Lebanese Diaspora and the American Jewish Joint Distribution Committee. Despite the ban on emigration, Jews intermittently were allowed to cross the border into Lebanon, and others left illegally, so that by 1970 only an estimated 3,000 remained of this old and once large community.[36]

Lebanon

Lebanon is exceptional among the Arab and other Middle Eastern countries on many counts. It is the only Arab country in which the Muslims do not constitute an overwhelming majority; in fact, according to the last official census, now twenty-six years old, they are slightly in the minority. Of all the Middle Eastern countries (except Israel), Lebanon is the most Westernized, urbanized, educated, and literate. It is equally exceptional in its treatment of the Jews.

The relatively comfortable position the Jews have had in Lebanon can be attributed partly to the presence in the Lebanese population of numerous minorities which obliged the country to maintain a balance among them—in particular, between the Christian communities (who officially still count as the majority) on the one hand, and the non-Christian (Muslim, Druze, etc.) communities on the other. As a result of this situation, and of some other factors, the Jews have throughout enjoyed a much better position in Lebanon than in any other Arab country.

The known history of the Jews of Lebanon begins with a catastrophic event: in 502 CE their synagogue in Beirut was demolished by an earthquake. In 1173 Benjamin of Tudela found fifty Jews in the city. Jewish travelers who passed through Beirut from the fourteenth to the sixteenth centuries say nothing about Jews living there. On the other hand, local Jewish tradition claimed that the synagogue and Jewish cemetery dated from ca. 1300. In 1840 there were only twenty-five Jewish

231

families in Beirut; in 1889 there were 1,500 Jews, and in 1901 there were 5,000. The 1932 census registered 3,588 Jews in Lebanon; the 1944 census 6,261. The community in Beirut had a number of schools, in most of which French was the language of tuition; an Arabic-language weekly, *El-'Alam El-Isra'ili (Jewish World)*, was published. The Beirut Jewish community council represented all Lebanese Jews, including the community in Saida (Sidon) and the few Jews scattered in other parts of Lebanon.

As the position of the Jews deteriorated in neighboring Syria, refugees began to arrive in Lebanon. By 1949 their number reached four thousand. Subsequently, foreign Jews were forced to leave Lebanon, so that the number of Jews remaining in the 1960s was estimated at six thousand. The emigrants went mostly to Italy, France, and England, as well as to Latin American countries and the United States. The position of those who remained is, while far from pleasant, at least tolerable. As the Lebanese Jews themselves put it, they suffer only from the "conventional forms of anti-Semitism."[37]

Turkey

For about four centuries the Ottoman Empire dominated the Muslim world. After World War I the victorious Allies detached all Arab territories from Turkey and carved out of them the successor states whose Jewish Diasporas are discussed in other sections of this chapter. The Republic of Turkey was left essentially with Asia Minor and a small corner of Europe to the north of the Sea of Marmara.

Jews had lived in this area for some fifteen centuries prior to its conquest by the Ottoman Turks. In all major Turkish cities the history of the Jews had, in the main, the same general outline: early evidence as to the presence of Jews in the Byzantine period and their persecution or harsh treatment by the emperors; several centuries of historical silence with almost no data concerning the Jews; the development of the community following the Turkish conquest, its recognition as a *millet*, and a relatively peaceful period (fourteenth and fifteenth centuries);

the arrival of Ashkenazi refugees from Central and Eastern Europe (in the same two centuries); the arrival of the Sephardim (from 1492 on) and the subsequent rapid Sephardization of the entire Jewish community; the rise of individual Jews influential with the Porte and local governments; the development of Yeshivot, scholarship, and religio-literary activity; the Shabbatian upheaval (seventeenth century); decline and decadence (eighteenth century); European influence (nineteenth century); new problems and large-scale emigration (from 1948 on).

This pattern can be discerned first in the capital city of the Empire, Constantinople (today Istanbul), which in the early twentieth century had a Jewish population of 65,000. It can be followed also in Smyrna (today Izmir; 25,500 Jews in 1900) and Salonica (today Thessalonica in Greece; 75,000 Jews in 1900); Brusa (today Bursa, in Asiatic Turkey, south of the sea of Marmara; 3,500 Jews); as well as in a number of other places with smaller Jewish communities. Since the Sephardi culture became predominant in all these cities, from the sixteenth century on, whatever the pre-1492 composition of their Jewish communities, they will not be discussed here but in Chapter XIV, which deals with the Sephardi Jews. (Thessalonica, however, will be dealt with in the section on Greece.) Nor will the Kurdish Jews, who lived in the southeastern corner of Turkey and who, together with the Iraqi and Iranian Kurdish Jews, form a separate ethnic group which is discussed in another section of this chapter.

However, we cannot leave ancient Turkish Jewry without giving at least one example of its history as reflected in the ups and downs of one typical Turkish-Jewish community. We take as this example the old community of Adrianople, which in 1900 had a Jewish community of about 17,000.

The history of the Jews in Adrianople (today Edirne, on the Turkish-Greek border) begins with the Byzantine period, and their oppression by the Byzantine emperors in the fifth and sixth centuries. In 1361, when Murad I conquered Thrace and Thessaly, the impoverished Jewish community of Adrianople welcomed the new Turkish rulers and asked their co-religionists in Brusa to come over and teach them Turkish. Soon the com-

233

munity was flourishing, and its Yeshiva attracted students not only from all parts of Turkey but also from the Ashkenazi Diasporas of Hungary, Poland, and Russia. In 1376 a group of Jews expelled from Hungary settled in Adrianople and founded the Budun (i.e., "of Buda") Synagogue. In the middle of the fifteenth century Jewish refugees from Bavaria, Swabia, Bohemia, Silesia, and other European countries flocked to Adrianople and founded an Ashkenazi synagogue. A little later came Jews from Italy and, in 1492, the Sephardi exiles from Spain, all of whom founded several synagogues of their own. The Sephardi influence soon became dominant, and all Jews in Adrianople adopted Sephardi customs and manners and the Ladino language, and took to the study of Kabbala. It was here that, in 1522, Joseph Caro began writing his great commentary on Jacob ben Asher's *Turim,* and his Kabbalistic diary, the *Maggid Mesharim.* From this time on the history of Adrianople Jews is part of the Sephardi history and therefore does not belong to this chapter.

The boundaries of present-day Turkey were established in the Lausanne Peace Treaty of 1923. Within those boundaries the 1927 Turkish census registered 81,872 Jews; the 1935 census 78,730 Jews; and the 1948 census 82,622 Jews. Of these, some 55,000 lived in the European corner of Turkey (almost all of them in Istanbul), and about 26,000 in Asian Turkey (Anatolia).

The new republican government of Turkey under Kemal Ataturk inaugurated an energetic policy of Turkization, which resulted among the Jews in a rapid adoption of Turkish in place of the traditional Ladino spoken by most of them. In 1927, 84.1 percent of the Jews in Turkey spoke Ladino; by 1935 this was reduced to 54.1 percent.

Following the outbreak of World War II, pro-Nazi sympathy in the country (Turkey and Germany had been allies in World War I) led to the introduction of some antiminority measures, including the dismissal of Jewish employees and the introduction of an extremely high special taxation that resulted in the financial ruin of numerous Jews and impoverished the community as a whole. This was the gravest anti-Jewish step taken in Turkey. On the other hand, Turkey played an important role in the rescue of European Jews during the period of the Nazi holocaust. True to its centuries-old tradition of hospitality to Jews fleeing from persecution in Christian Europe, this time, too, Turkey allowed close to 19,000 Jews to pass through its territory on their way from Rumania, Lithuania, Hungary, Yugoslavia, and Bulgaria to Palestine.[38]

In the years after the end of World War II the economic position of the Jews gradually improved. The property tax law was abrogated in March 1944 (after it had been in force for seventeen months), and, with the help of the American Jewish Joint Distribution Committee, the Jews regained much of their former economic positions, engaging in commerce and handi-craft, as well as in academic professions. The civil position of the Turkish Jews remained unharmed, even in the days of Israel's War of Independence. Turkey and Israel maintain diplomatic relations, and the Solel Boneh, the large building construction company owned by the Histadrut (Israel's General Federation of Labor) received and carried out sizable construc-tion contracts in various parts of Turkey.

Nevertheless, immediately upon the establishment of Israel, large-scale Jewish emigration from Turkey began, reducing the Jewish community by 1970 to 39,000. Of the emigrants, the overwhelming majority went to Israel (in 1948–60, 38,548). The motivations of this large-scale emigration were quite different from those that prompted the Jewish Diasporas in the Arab lands to leave their homes in masses. The emigration from the Arab countries was a response to persecution, discrimination, and acute danger. In Turkey it was primarily a result of the continuing economic hardships; the desire to live a life of, not only legal, but actual and social equality, with others; the wish to join relatives; and, last but not least, the fascination exerted by the idea of becoming part of the free and independent Jewish State.

In Turkey itself the emigration resulted, first of all, in the disappearance of rural and small-town Jewish communities, a phenomenon familiar to us from many other countries. Most of those who left their homes either emigrated to Israel or settled in the biggest urban centers of Turkey. Secondly, even in the

235

largest community, that of Istanbul, whose numbers were reduced from 55,000 in the 1940s to 33,000 in 1958, it was as a rule the poorest element that left, so that those who remained behind came to constitute on the average a better-to-do group than the Jewish community prior to the onset of mass emigration.[39]

At the same time, the spiritual and intellectual impoverishment of Jewish life continued. The Turkization process went on; the Ladino vernacular was being increasingly replaced by Turkish which had become the language of tuition in the remaining Jewish schools (with some hours weekly devoted to the study of Hebrew); and about half of the Jewish children were sent to Turkish public schools.[40] In brief, those Jews who chose to remain in Turkey were well on the way to becoming Turkish in everything but religion, in the sense in which this phenomenon is so well known to us in the modern Western world.

Mesopotamia (Iraq)

Next to Palestine, Mesopotamia, the Land Between the Rivers, was the scene of the greatest religious-literary achievements of the Jewish people. In Chapters I and II we touched upon the emergence and general significance of the Babylonian Diaspora. Let us, nevertheless, reemphasize that from the conclusion of the Mishna (ca. 200 CE) to the end of the Gaonic period (1038), the Jewish spiritual and cultural hegemony belonged to the Babylonian Exile, although toward the end of this eight-hundred-year period the ascendancy of Iberian Jewry was clearly visible.

In the eight centuries in question, the most important religio-legal works that were destined to become the basic building blocks of the Jewish cultural edifice for all ages came from Babylonia. The Babylonian Talmud, as its name shows, grew out of the Babylonian schools. It was brought to conclusion about 500 CE, and it so overshadowed the smaller and less complete Jerusalem Talmud, compiled in Palestine about 425 CE, that when, in Jewish literature and Jewish life, the term "Talmud" is used, it always refers to the Babylonian Talmud.

Talmudic academies continued their work after the completion of this *magnum opus,* and carried on important Halakhic studies for another half millennium. It was to the heads of these academies, located in the towns of Sura and Pumbeditha, that the title *Gaon* (literally "excellency"; plural *geonim*) was given, and it is due to the centrality of the religious authority of the *geonim* that the five centuries following the close of the Talmud have become known as the Gaonic period.[41]

The typical form in which the *geonim* carried on the exposition of the Law was that of *t'shuvot* (responsa, or answers) which they wrote to religious questions sent to them by rabbis from all parts of the Diaspora. The gaonic responsa had the authority of unappealable legal decisions, and it was primarily due to them that Babylonia remained the preeminent religio-legal center of the Jewish world throughout this period.

However, the *geonim* left their mark on other areas of religio-literary creativity as well. They exercised judicial functions as the heads of the higher court *(Bet Din Gadol),* and presided over the assemblies (called by the old name Sanhedrin) which discussed, and decided on, the authoritative interpretation of Talmudic problems. They compiled codes of law such as the *Halakhot P'sukot* and *Halakhot G'dolot* of Yehudai Gaon (760–69); composed Midrashim such as the *Midrash Esfa* of Haninai Gaon; (769–77); wrote Talmudic dictionaries, such as the 'Arukh of Zemah Gaon (872–90); authored analytical and historical works on the Talmud such as *M'gillat S'tarim,* and the famous epistle of Sherira Gaon (968–1000); and penned legal treatises, such as those on purchases, conditions, mortgages, oaths, etc., written in Arabic by the last of the *geonim,* Hai Gaon (1000–1038).

The most outstanding of all *geonim* was undoubtedly Saadia Gaon (born in Dilaz, Upper Egypt, 892; became Gaon of Sura in 928; died in Sura, 942). He wrote the first important Jewish philosophical work since Philo of Alexandria eight centuries earlier: the book known in the Jewish world by the title of its Hebrew translation (Saadia himself wrote it in Arabic), *Sepher Emunot V'De'ot,* or Book of Beliefs and Opinions, prepared by Judah ibn Tibbon (1120–c. 1190). Saadia himself translated the

237

Bible into Arabic, and compiled a *Siddur* (prayer book) to which he added his own Arabic explanations and his own Hebrew synagogal poetry. Until the death of Saadia the entire Diaspora was guided by the Jews of Babylonia. Thereafter, coinciding with, and probably precipitated by, the breakup of the Muslim caliphate, the Babylonian Jewish spiritual hegemony came to an end within a century.

Another type of scholarly activity, engaged in by both Babylonian and Palestinian scholars, was the *Masora,* that is the determination of the exact pronunciation of the Biblical text by developing a system of vocalization. The Masoretes, as these scholars were called, also added marks to indicate the traditional musical phrases to which the sacred books had to be chanted in the synagogue. This work was carried out in Babylonia and in Palestine in the eighth and ninth centuries, and it was the Palestinian system that became adopted in the entire Jewish world. In the eighth century, in the very midst of the Gaonic period, Karaism ("Scripturalism") emerged in Babylonia to become one of the few religious movements that split off from the body of Judaism. The followers of this movement denied the validity of all rabbinical interpretation and development of Jewish tradition, basing themselves exclusively on the Bible.

With the death of Hai Gaon (1038) the Gaonate came to an end, but the exilarchate—i.e., the officially recognized secular leadership of the Jewish community of Babylonia—continued for another four centuries. However, while the spiritual hegemony of Babylonian Jewry was definitely over by the early eleventh century, the Mesopotamian Jewish Diaspora remained and even enjoyed periods of prosperity or at least tranquility. According to Benjamin of Tudela, who visited Iraq prior to 1170, there were at the time forty thousand Jews in the country, among them many scholars and rich people.

As in other Muslim countries in the period, the position of the Jews in Iraq had its ups and downs, depending on the whims of the caliphs and the high court officials. At times they were left alone and could live in peace, and their leaders, the exilarchs, who internally always wielded considerable power, were highly respected by the rulers; at others, they were discriminated against in numerous painful ways: the men had to wear special Jewish clothes or badges, yellow hats, and a bell around the neck; the women had to wear a yellow mantle, one white and one black shoe, and an iron chain around the neck when going to the public bath; the children were excluded from the Muslim schools; the Jewish houses had to be marked by wooden figures in front of the entrance, and more of the like.

In the first half of the thirteenth century the position of the Jews was good, but at the time of the Mongol invasion they were forced to defray the cost of the foreign mercenary army that defended Baghdad, which caused them to welcome the Mongol conquest of the city in 1258. The Mongols, still pagans at the time, massacred hundreds of thousands of Muslims but did no harm to the Jews and the Christians.

In the late thirteenth century a Jew by the name of Sa'd ad-Daula ("Joy of the Kingdom") ben Moshe, a physician, financier, and administrator, and a man of great ability, beauty, and charm, became the personal physician and confidant of Arghun Khan. In 1289 the Khan appointed him head of the government ("diwan") of Iraq, and, still in the same year, Grand Vizier of the entire Mongol empire. Sa'd ad-Daula elevated his relatives to high government posts in many parts of the empire, and ruled from the Caucasus to the Indian Ocean and from the Syrian Desert to Afghanistan. In 1291, after having wielded the supreme power under Arghun for two years, during a serious illness of the Khan, ben Moshe was assassinated by his enemies two weeks before the Khan himself died. His death was the signal for an attack on the Jews of Baghdad and of the rest of Iraq. This time, however, the Jews defended themselves, and both sides suffered heavy casualties.

In the fourteenth century there were again periods in which Jews held high office and the position of the community as a whole was satisfactory, alternating with periods of cruel persecutions. The overlordship over Iraq changed hands several times: in 1336 the Jalairi dynasty took Iraq; in 1379 the Turkmen Kara-Koyunlu ("those of the Black Sheep") tribal federation conquered it; in 1393 Timur Lang; and thereafter, throughout the fifteenth century, every few years the city (which, in fact, meant the country as well) was taken by a new conqueror. That most of these conquests meant massacres, from which the Jews were not exempt, goes without saying. In these times of troubles many Jews fled from Baghdad and sought refuge in the Kurdish mountains, replenishing the numbers of the old Jewish communities of Kurdistan (see next section). For close to a hundred years (until the end of the fifteenth century), no Jews seem to have lived in Baghdad. However, from 1470 on, under the Turkmen Ak-Koyunlu ("those of the White Sheep") federation of tribes, the Jews began to return to Baghdad, and after 1492 several Sephardi exiles from Spain found their way to the city. Under the Persian dynasty of the Safavids, who took Baghdad in 1508, the Jews had at first a period of respite, followed, from 1524 on, by persecutions under Tahmasp Shah.

In 1534 the Turks conquered Iraq and established their rule that was to last, with a short interruption, until the end of World War I. The Jews were glad to come under Turkish dominion, which was liberal and friendly toward them. They soon established intellectual and commercial relations with Jewish communities in other parts of the Ottoman Empire, including Istanbul and Safed. From 1623 to 1638 the Persians again held Baghdad, but this time the Jews did not suffer from the change of control over the city. In the Turkish army of 150,000 men that took Baghdad back from the Persians in 1638 there were ten thousand Jews, including high officers. Some thirty thousand Persians were massacred by the Turks in the conquered city; the Jews were not harmed.

Under the Turks the position of the Jews in Baghdad depended largely on the personal whims of the pashas who were appointed by the sultan as governors of the city. (On the average, the tenure of a pasha was less than two years in the seventeenth century.) There were decent and just pashas, and there were cruel and rapacious ones. From the seventeenth century on, the pashas of Baghdad would appoint one of the leaders of the Jewish community to serve as "chief treasurer" (*Sarraf bashi*) of the local government and as *nasi*—i.e., duke—of the Jews. Until the early eighteenth century this position was filled by men who, according to geneological tradition, were the descendents of

King David. When the Jewish duke rode out on his white horse, criers ran before him shouting "People, give honor to the son of David!" and he was popularly referred to as "the King of the Jews." His authority, which extended over all the Jews of Iraq, included the imposition of fines and corporal punishment *(bast)*. The position of Jewish duke was abolished in 1849 and his place as leader of the Jewish community was taken by the chief rabbi, the Hakham Bashi.

While the economic conditions of the Jews of Iraq improved from the middle of the nineteenth century on, and they took a leading part in commerce and foreign trade, their civil and social situation was varied. In the eighty-six years from 1831 to 1917 no less than forty-two *valis* (governors) were appointed and again recalled by Istanbul and, as in the case of the pashas who preceded them, much depended on their personal attitude to the Jews.

The number of Jews in Baghdad was estimated at 16,000 in 1845, 20,000 in 1860, 24,000 in 1884, 25,000 in 1899, 45–50,000 in 1909, and 50,000 in 1917 as well as in 1928. These numbers do not mean much except that they show a general, slow trend of increase. The official census of 1933 found 59,000 Jews in Baghdad and its immediate environs. The total number of Iraqi Jews in the 1937–47 decade was variously estimated from a minimum of 87,500 to a maximum of 180,000.

For centuries the Iraqi Jews maintained traditional Tora schools, and in the nineteenth century there was in Baghdad a famous rabbinical seminary. Modern education among the Jews was initiated by the Alliance Israélite Universelle, which opened its first school in Baghdad in 1864. Thereafter, although strong objections were raised by the rabbis to the opening of schools for girls, Jewish education advanced gradually, and by the 1930s practically the entire Jewish school-age population actually attended schools, either Jewish or governmental.

The British conquered Iraq in 1917, from which time, until Britain relinquished her mandate over Iraq in 1932, the position of the Iraqi Jews improved. In 1921 when Feisal was crowned King of Iraq, he declared: "We all are of one common origin, sons of our father Shem. We all belong to this noble race, and

241

there is no difference between Muslim, Christian and Jew."[42]
The Anglo-Iraqi treaty of 1922 stipulated that the King of Iraq
agreed "to frame an Organic Law" which

> shall ensure to all [populations inhabiting Iraq] complete free-
> dom of conscience and the free exercise of all forms of worship.
> . . . It shall provide that no discrimination of any kind shall be
> made between the inhabitants of Irak [sic] on the ground of race,
> religion or language, and shall secure that the right of each
> community to maintain its own schools for the education of its
> own members in its own language . . . shall not be denied or
> impaired.[43]

During the British mandatory period the Iraqi Jews came to
occupy positions in the government administration. An increasing proportion of them obtained higher education and special-
ized in the professions. Others developed the international trade
of Iraq. In 1932 it was estimated that 800 of the country's 1,000
importers were Jews, as were 400 of the 500 exporters, 2,500 of
the 3,000 merchants, 40 of the 50 money changers, 170 of the
200 real estate agents, and so on.[44]

Soon after the independence of Iraq (1932) the position of the
Jews began to deteriorate. True, the Jews were not massacred as
were the Nestorian Christians (Assyrians) in 1933, nor were they
persecuted as were the Kurds and the Yezidis in Iraqi Kurdistan.
But Jewish officials were dismissed from government offices
(1935), and several youth organizations, such as the *al-Futuwwa*
and *Kataib ash-Shabab,* engaged in anti-Jewish activities.

A turn for the worse came in 1941, after the coup of Rashid
'Ali al-Gailani, when Iraq openly joined the Nazis. This was a
signal for the mob to attack the Jews: in three days of rioting 150
Jews were killed, 500 wounded, and about 1,500 Jewish homes
and shops burned or looted. The excesses were stopped by the
British army, but the anti-Jewish trend continued and intensified in a manner familiar from other Arab countries. In the mid
1940s an Arab authority on minorities observed that "In the past
few years, many Iraqi Jews, aware that their future in Iraq is
dark, have emigrated to Palestine and America. . . ."[45]

In 1950 the Iraqi parliament passed a law allowing the Jews to
emigrate on condition that they gave up their Iraqi citizenship

and left all their property to pass into government receivership. Within a year more than 120,000 Iraqi Jews left the country via an airlift from Baghdad to Cyprus and then from Cyprus to Israel. By 1960 another 5,000 Iraqi Jews had settled in Israel.

The position of the roughly ten thousand Jews who remained in Iraq eased somewhat, until 1967 when, in the wake of the Six-Day War, their persecution was resumed and even intensified. Secret spy trials and spectacular public executions of several Jews were staged, arousing widespread indignation and inspiring protests all over the world. By 1970 no more than 2,500 Jews were left of this once large and distinguished Jewish Diaspora that had lived in Mesopotamia for about twenty-seven centuries.

The Kurdish Jews

The Kurdish Jews constitute a separate group among the Oriental Jewish communities with characteristics of their own, not shared by any other Middle Eastern Diaspora. In physical appearance they assimilated to a great extent to the Kurds. They speak a language, Neo-Aramaic, not spoken by any other Jewish community; (until about 1920) a high proportion of them was engaged in agriculture and lived in villages of its own—a phenomenon not found to this extent in any other country of the Middle East; and they had a mentality of peasants and a self-assurance bordering on ferocity that contrasted sharply with the subservience exhibited by many Jewish groups in Arab countries and especially with that of the Persian Jews. The women among them (as among the Muslim Kurds) had much more freedom than the women in the Arab countries: they were unveiled, and monogamy was the rule.

Kurdistan, the name of the country in which the Kurdish Jews lived until the recent emigration of most of them to Israel, is not a political entity but a compact geographical area that is divided among three states, Turkey, Iraq, and Iran, and bordered roughly by the Tigris River in the west, Lake Van in the north, Lake Urmia and the Zarineh River that flows into it in the east, and the thirty-fifth parallel in the south. It is a rugged, mountainous country centering on the Zagros and Taurus mountains. Its total area is, very roughly, about 40,000 square miles. The majority population in Kurdistan are the Kurds, who are Sunni Muslims, speak Kurdish (an Iranian dialect), and whose history goes back to ancient Assyrian times. In the midst of the Kurds live two minorities, both Neo-Aramaic-speaking: the Nestorian Christians and the Kurdish Jews.

As usual, historical data concerning the origins of the Kurdish Jews are lacking, but it is reasonable to assume that they, or some of them, are the descendants of the exiles from Israel who were settled in Assyria (2 Kings 17:23; Isaiah 11:11; 27:13). Apart from rare and inconclusive references, the first reliable information on the Jews of Kurdistan stems from the twelfth century, when, according to Benjamin of Tudela and Petahia of Regensburg, there were in Mosul 6,000–7,000 Jews, in Nesibin 1,000, and in Jeziret el-'Omar, 4,000. In 'Amadia there were at the time 25,000 Jews. Half a century after these two travelers, the wandering poet Judah Alharizi visited Kurdistan (in 1230) and in one of his famous *maqamat* (rhymed prose writings) he described the ignorance in Jewish matters and the general crudeness of the Jews of Mosul.[46]

Three centuries later, it is again a poet, this time the Yemenite Yahya Alzahiri, whose *maqamat* give us information about the Kurdish Jews. Alzahiri visited the Kurdish town of Arbel in the sixteenth century and described his meetings and conversations with the learned Kabbalists of the community.[47] One wonders whether the Jewish knowledge among the Kurdish Jews actually increased so considerably in the three centuries between the visits of Alharizi and Alzahiri, or whether the difference lay more in the eyes of the beholders: the satirical, haughty point of view of the Sephardi Alharizi as against the appreciative, humble approval of the Yemenite Alzahiri.

Another source for our knowledge of the Jews of Kurdistan in the sixteenth century is a series of letters sent by the head of a Jewish school in Mosul to various Kurdish-Jewish communities asking their support for the maintenance of the school. The numerous and large communities mentioned in these letters were all located in the 'Amadia area, and in each of them the size of the Jewish group has greatly shrunk between the sixteenth and twentieth centuries. In those centuries, during which the Kurdish area changed hands several times, the Kurdish population suffered greatly from the intermittent fighting between Turkey and Persia. In the period of 1832 to 1847 there were numerous Kurdish uprisings against the Turkish rule, and whenever the Kurds were defeated the heavy hand of the conquerors pressed on Muslims, Nestorians, and Jews alike. The Turks also managed to incite one indigenous population element against the other, and often the Kurds and the Nestorians went at each other with a cruelty that exceeded that of the Turks. That the Jews did not suffer more in this situation than they did, that they were not wiped out entirely in this intercommunity warfare, was due to the fact that they had no political organization whatsoever, but stood under the protection (or "were owned by," as the local expression had it) the Kurdish chieftains. Since the Jews had no political power nor any political or territorial ambitions, neither the Turks nor the Kurds paid any attention to them, and simply did not bother to attack them at a time when they needed all their forces to fight each other.

According to Benjamin II, in the mid nineteenth century there were 450 Jewish families in Mosul, 70 in Khoi Sanjak, 150 in Urfa, 4 in Siwerek, 100 in Chermuk, 250 in Diar Bekr, 50 in Mardin, 2 in Nisibin, several more in largely Jewish villages around Jebel Sanjak, 20 in Jezireh on the Tigris, 200 in Zakho on the Khabor, 50 in Sandur, 40 in Deik, 30 in Tanura (Betanura), 100 in Akra, 200 in Sindu. This gives a total of 1,710 families, or about 10,000 persons, not counting the villages.[48]

The tripartite division of Kurdistan after World War I into an Iraqi, a Turkish, and a Persian area influenced the situation of the Kurdish Jews in that they now had a new third government, that of Iraq, to contend with. On the other hand, the warfare between the Turks and the Persians, and between the Turks and the Kurds ceased, which gave some surcease to the Jews as well. The twofold population movement, one from the villages into the urban centers, and the other from the country as a whole to Palestine-Israel, which we encountered in other Diasporas, began here, too, in the 1920s and gathered speed after the independence of Israel. In fact, the first Kurdish Jewish immigrants, originally just a few individuals, arrived in Palestine in 1812; between 1920 and 1929 no fewer than 1,900 arrived.

After the establishment of Israel the situation of the Kurdish Jews became difficult. In Iranian Kurdistan twelve Jews were murdered in various villages in March 1950. This event triggered the large-scale emigration of Jews, and by October of that year an estimated 6,000 of them had moved to Teheran.[49]

THE ORIENTAL JEWS: THE IRANIAN-SPEAKING DIASPORAS

The three Diasporas to be discussed in this chapter comprise the Jewish communities of Persia, Bukhara, and Afghanistan. All three share the Persian language (although they speak it with dialectal differences), and this circumstance in itself is evidence of their common historical roots. Some of the Jewish migratory movements from Persia to the north into the Bukhara and Central Asia, and to the east into Afghanistan may have taken place as early as the eighth century (precise historical information is lacking); the latest occurred in the first half of the nineteenth century.

Iran

In turning to the Jewish community of Iran (formerly Persia) we leave behind not only the Arab world but also that of Sunni Islam to which most Muslims belong, and enter the realm of Shiʻism. The historical and doctrinary differences between the Sunnis and the Shiʻites do not concern us in the present context except insofar as they bear on the Muslim attitude to the Jews (and other *dhimmis*). In this respect there is, indeed, a difference that can be summed up succinctly by stating that the Shiʻites, in general, have been less tolerant to the "people of the book" than the Sunnis. As a result, forced conversions of Jews to Islam were a more frequent occurrence in Persia than in Arab countries.

After Babylonia and Egypt, Persia is the third Biblical country in which there was a Jewish Diaspora since antiquity. After conquering Babylonia in 539 BCE Cyrus, king of Persia, permitted the Jewish exiles to return from Babylonia to Judea. This was the beginning of the history of Jews in Persia, for Babylonia having become a province of Persia, Jews were able to, and actually did, move from Mesopotamia eastward, settling in

Persia proper. The anecdotal story told in the Biblical Book of
Esther of the danger and deliverance of the Jews of Persia under
King Ahasuerus (i.e., Xerxes, reigned 486–465 BCE) captures
much of the atmosphere at the court of an absolute but benevolent Persian despot. More than eight centuries later, a Sassanid
king of Persia, Yezdegerd I (reigned 399–420 CE), actually had a
Jewish wife, who became the mother of his successor, Bahram V
(reigned 420–38).

Detailed information about the Jews of Persia is available
from the time of the Arab conquest, in the middle of the seventh
century. In the twelfth century Benjamin of Tudela reports
having found 50,000 Jews in Hamadan, 15,000 in Isfahan, and
10,000 in Shiraz.[1] These figures, especially the first, seem
exaggerated in view of the much smaller numbers of Jews found
in these cities in subsequent centuries: e.g., in Hamadan in 1818
there were only 600 Jewish families; in 1840, 200; in 1900,
1,000. Persecutions, expulsions, and forced conversions to Islam
(especially in the seventeenth and eighteenth centuries) occurred relatively often; those who converted became known and
remained identified as *Jedid al-Islam,* or "new Muslims," with
whom neither the Jews nor the "old" Muslims intermarried.

The Jews of Persia embarked at an early date on the production of a rich and varied literature of their own in Judeo-Persian,
the special Jewish dialect that has remained their vernacular
down to the present day. The earliest Judeo-Persian literary
documents date from the eighth century; the second oldest, from
the year 1020. The hiatus of almost three centuries is indicative
of the fragmentary nature of historical evidence for this early
period. From the thirteenth century down to the twentieth there
was a remarkably rich and varied literary output in Judeo-
Persian, falling into the several major categories: Bible translations, translations of Apocrypha, of the *Pirke Avot* (Sayings of
the Fathers), and of Midrashim; commentaries; dictionaries;
liturgical works; the story of Eldad HaDani; books of charms
and dream interpretations; epic poems; translations of liturgical
poetry; *diwans* (anthologies of songs); poems describing the
persecutions of the seventeenth and eighteenth centuries or
celebrating the martyrdom of pious individuals; and so on.[2]

248

Shi'ite intolerance was expressed with increasing harshness in the eighteenth and nineteenth centuries even in those places where no actual anti-Jewish outbreaks occurred. The Jews were considered unclean, had to take the utmost care not to touch a Muslim, were confined to overcrowded ghettos, and had to eke out a meager living in a few narrowly delimited occupations. Although Persian Shi'ism, with its belief in twelve Imams, is a different sect from Yemeni Shi'ism, which believes in seven Imams, the two share this extreme intolerance toward the Jews and other "people of the book."

A typical manifestation of this fanaticism occurred in 1839 in the city of Meshhed, capital of Khorasan, the northeastern province of Persia, and the holiest city of Shi'ite Islam, into which Nadir Shah had brought a group of Jews in 1747, just before he was assassinated.[3] The inflamed mob killed thirty-two Jews; the rest were given a choice between leaving the city and embracing Islam. Most of them became Marranos, and managed to keep the Jewish faith in secret until they had a chance to escape from Meshhed. Some moved to Teheran where they were able to join the local Jewish community and live again openly as Jews; others crossed the border into neighboring Afghanistan and settled in Herat; still others went north to Bukhara; several decades later many reached Jerusalem.

As in most countries in which a Jewish Diaspora established itself, in Iran, too, the largest Jewish community grew up in the most populous city. As Teheran, the new capital of Iran (since 1788), grew, so did the Jewish community in it. Under Nasr ad-Din Shah (whose personal physician from 1855 to 1860, Dr. Jakob Eduard Polak, a German Jew, wrote a most instructive book on Persia and its inhabitants) the city grew into the largest of the country. According to the 1956 national census there were 35,101 Jews in the capital.

By the nineteenth century, restrictions, discrimination, and persecutions had reduced the Jews of Persia in Teheran, as well as in their other urban centers, to a sad state of ignorance and misery. They were forced to wear a special garb or mark on their clothes, and a hat of a certain color; they were considered unclean to such an extent that their touch, especially when their

249

bodies or clothes were wet, was believed to contaminate the Muslims, and they were therefore commanded to avoid most carefully all accidental contact with Persians. In some places and times these restrictions were so severe that when it rained Jews were simply forbidden to go into the streets outside their own ghettos.

A peculiar Persian development in the relationship between Muslims and Jews was the offer made by various rulers, among them Shahs Abbas I (r. 1587–1629) and Abbas II (r. 1642–1667), to pay a substantial amount to every Jewish man converting to Islam. While these inducements seem to have had little effect, in some places and periods the persecutions were so cruel that many Jews, unable to endure them and equally unable to emigrate, embraced Islam. One of the most recent occurrences of such large-scale conversion took place in Shiraz in 1830, when, according to the Jewish traveler Benjamin II, 2,500 of the 3,000 Jews of the city became Muslims, so that when he visited there in 1850 he found only 500 Jews.[4] The forcibly converted Jews in most cases continued to adhere in secret to their old religion, but within two generations the memory of Jewish traditions faded away and they became Muslims not only in name but also in fact. The Marranos of Meshhed, mentioned above, remained the only known exception to this rule.

The difference between the Spanish Marranos and the Persian *Jedid al-Islam* in respect of the ability to maintain a secret allegiance to Judaism lay in the respective cultural level, economic standing, and mentality of the two Diasporas. The Spanish Jews of the fifteenth century were a highly cultured, well-to-do, and proud group. When forced to adopt Catholicism, the values of their Jewish life, religion, and traditions were strong enough to provide an internal resistance to actual, as against nominal, acceptance of Christianity for several generations. Yet even in the Spanish orbit, true conversions, too, did occur, as was the case, for instance, among the Chuetas of Majorca.[5]

The Persian Jews of the eighteenth and nineteenth centuries, by comparison, were a weakened, often broken, community whose vitality had been sapped by persecutions and humiliation. By the time they were forced to convert to Islam, no strength had been left in them to continue with the very difficult and highly dangerous task of internal resistance in the form of secret adherence to Judaism.

The traditional occupations of the Jews in Persia were primarily small-scale commerce and handicrafts. Many were small merchants and peddlers, dealers in old clothes, skins, or rugs; others were jewelers (mostly silver workers), glass cutters, silk weavers, blacksmiths, shoemakers, tailors, masons. Some manufactured opium and wine (Shi'ite Islam, in contrast to Sunni, tolerated the drinking of wine). Some were physicians, the last disciples of the great Avicenna (Ibn Sina, 980–1037) whose *Canon of Medicine* was early translated into Hebrew and printed at Naples in 1491, and who is buried at Hamadan. Others ministered to the mental well-being of Jews and Muslims alike by telling fortunes and preparing amulets (either written on parchment and paper, or engraved on small copper or silver plates). In several places the Jews had to work as scavengers and in other unsavory jobs, a situation that again reminds us of that of the Jews in that other Shi'ite country, Yemen.

In addition to these occupations in most of which Jews typically engaged in all Muslim countries, in Persia they had a specialty which was quite exceptional for them in the entire Middle East: they were musicians and dancers, and as such were in great demand by the Muslims on such occasions as weddings and Ramadan nights entertainments. In the course of my study in the early 1940s of the Meshhed Jews, who were represented by a large community in Jerusalem, I came across several members of this group who were able to recite endless lines from Firdausi's monumental *Shah Name* in the traditional Persian fashion, with two men sitting opposite each other and rhythmically swaying back and forth as they chanted the cadences—monotonous to the Western ear—of that great epic poem, the longest of world literature.

Toward the end of the nineteenth century the cultural level of the Persian Jews began to improve, due to the establishment of modern schools by the Alliance Israélite Universelle (from 1898 on) and later by the *Otzar HaTora,* the Jewish Agency for

Palestine, the Joint, and the ORT. These organizations had to wage a long fight, not only to obtain governmental permission for the operation of their educational institutions, but also to be accepted by the Jewish community, most of whose members were unable to grasp the significance of modern education, and were opposed especially to sending their daughters to school. Finally, the struggle was won, and by mid 1960s about 14,000 Jewish children attended Jewish schools (in all of which, since 1926, the language of tuition has been Persian), in addition to 4,500 who went to governmental schools.[6] Since the total Jewish population of Iran in 1966 was an estimated 80,000, it appears that practically all Jewish children of school age did attend school. In the same year only 41.17 percent of the total Iranian school-age population, aged 6–13, attended school.[7]

A considerable improvement in the civil status of the Jews resulted from the reform measures introduced by Riza Shah Pehlevi (r. 1925–1941). The influence of Nazi Germany that was strongly felt in Iran from 1936 on reversed this trend temporarily, but it was resumed after the British and Soviet troops occupied Iran in 1941. Since those days and down to the present, the official attitude of the Iranian government to the Jews has remained consistently benevolent. The Jews enjoy legal equality, Zionist organizations can function undisturbed, and in 1950 the Iranian government became the second Muslim country (after Turkey) to extend *de facto* recognition to Israel.

At the same time, it has to be stated that this official attitude of the government is not matched by the feelings most Iranians harbor about the Jews. Age-old prejudices have a tendency to persist, and the attitude of contempt for the Jews that was for generations an integral part of Iranian popular tradition is still widely felt. Nor has the economic position of the Jews improved to the point where most of them could earn a decent living. On the contrary, poverty is widespread; according to one report in 1945 almost half of the 25,000 Jews in Teheran had to be supported by the community, and two thirds of Isfahan's Jews were destitute.[8]

Under these conditions it was inevitable that many Iranian Jews should seek relief in emigration. Following the establishment of Israel, two migratory tendencies were noticeable: one, to leave smaller cities and concentrate in the capital; and the other, to go to Israel. Old Jewish centers, such as Shiraz, Yezd, Isfahan, Hamadan, Kermanshah, have lost most of their Jewish inhabitants, and this process of disintegration still continues. About 50,000 Iranian Jews immigrated to Israel from 1948 to 1966, most of them in the first few years after the establishment of the State (from 1948 to 1960, 37,049 went to Israel). If the estimate of 80,000 for the number of Jews left in Iran in 1966 is not exaggerated, as some sources maintain, then, paralleling the large-scale emigration, there must have been an exceptionally strong upsurge in natural increase since the 1940s, as a result of which a new generation largely replaced those who had left the country. By the same token, one can expect that, if conditions remain normal, Iranian Jewry will continue to increase in numbers, and, in any case, will remain one of the last representatives of a Jewish Diaspora under Islam.

Afghanistan

Afghanistan, the easternmost country of the Middle East, has a population of 15,400,000 (1966 estimate), the overwhelming majority of whom are Sunni Muslims. The history of the Jews in Afghanistan begins with a long chapter of legends telling of their arrival in the days of Cyrus the Great. However, even this legendary claim gives them no priority in the country, because according to other local legends the Afghans themselves are the descendants of Afghana, the son of King David and his wife Iramiya, daughter of King Saul.[9]

Historically, on the other hand, the presence of Jews in Afghanistan is not attested prior to the nineteenth century. This is a surprisingly late date, because in the neighboring countries (Iran, Bukhara, etc.) Jews have had a much longer history. Moreover, as pointed out by the ethnologist Erich Brauer, the Jews of Afghanistan are rather similar in physical type to the Muslim Afghans, which points to a lengthy period of sojourn in the country, and are quite different in many of their customs from the Persian Jews, which again indicates a separation between the two groups which must lie much farther back than the nineteenth century.[10]

The fact that the Afghan Jews retained Judeo-Persian as their vernacular does not militate against this theory, since the Jews are known for their tendency to retain old vernaculars in new countries of residence even after several centuries; besides, the fact that Pashtu, the language of Afghanistan, is itself an Iranian tongue related to Persian, would have facilitated the retention of Persian by the Jews. Also the periodic waves of Jewish immigration from Persia into Afghanistan contributed to the preservation of Judeo-Persian in the Afghan Diaspora.

According to Joseph Wolff, a Jewish-born German Christian missionary who visited Afghanistan in 1832, there had been in Kabul sixty Jewish families brought there by Ahmad Shah from Meshhed about 1772, but they had gone back to Meshhed prior to Wolff's visit. After the anti-Jewish outbreak of 1839 in Meshhed, a sizable group of Jews left Meshhed and settled in Herat in Afghanistan. Another part of Afghan Jewry came from Bukhara; some of these arrived prior to 1850, others joined them later.

Prior to the Bolshevik revolution, some well-to-do Afghan Jews had extensive business interests in Russia, but in 1917 they lost everything they had there. This development contributed to the pauperization of the community, a process hastened also by the Afghan government's policy of monopolizing foreign trade, in which many Afghan Jews had been engaged. In view of this situation, and of the anti-Jewish restrictive government policy, by 1947 the Afghan Jews felt that their only hope was to emigrate to Palestine. Within a few years after the independence of Israel almost all the Jews who were still in Afghanistan managed to leave and to reach Israel via Iran.

The number of Jews in Afghanistan in the mid nineteenth century was estimated at 40,000. Emigration reduced this number to 12,000 in the early twentieth century, and further to three or four thousand in the 1930s. In 1949 their number was estimated at 3,500, of whom more than 2,000 lived in Herat, most of them engaged in the karakul and Persian carpet trade. As a result of persecutions, many fled to India.[11] By the mid

1960s a mere few hundred Jews remained in Afghanistan.[12] The estimate for 1966 was 800.[13] According to Afghan Jews in New York, among whom I made inquiries in December 1969, by that time no more than a few dozen Jews were left in Kabul and Herat. These figures tell the gist of the story: within the last hundred years Afghanistan has become practically *Judenrein*.

Bukhara and Central Asia

To the north of Iran and Afghanistan lies the territory named after its chief city, Bukhara. For twelve centuries, from the eighth to the nineteenth, Bukhara was ruled by Muslims. In 1868 the Emir of Bukhara had to accept Russian overlordship, and after the Russian revolution of 1917 Bukhara became a part of the Uzbek SSR with Tashkent as its capital.

The Persian dialect, called Tajik, spoken by the Jews in Bukhara and other towns and villages of the Turkmen and Uzbek areas of Soviet Russia, is the clearest evidence of their Persian origin. The precise time of their migration from Persia up into Transoxania is unknown, but it must have taken place, probably in several waves, between the eighth century, when the area was conquered by the Muslims, and the twelfth, when our old friend Benjamin of Tudela reported about his Central Asian co-religionists.

According to him, there were some fifty thousand Jews in Samarkand, headed by an exilarch of their own, and about eight thousand Jews in Khiva, to the northwest of Bukhara. Soon thereafter, in the early thirteenth century, the Mongol invasion destroyed these cities and it is not until the late seventeenth century that we again hear of Jewish life in the area: in 1688 a Bukharan poet, Yusuf Yehudi (i.e., "Joseph the Jew"), completed a long Persian poem, titled "The Seven Brothers" (the reference is to the seven martyrs mentioned in 2 Maccabees 7:1), which remains popular among Bukharan Jews to this day. The Bukharan Jews loved poetry; they transliterated into Hebrew characters the famous classics of Persian poetry, such as the poems of Nizami, Hafiz, Jami, and Sadi, and translated Hebrew poets (e.g., Israel Najjara) into Persian. At a much earlier time

255

(exact date unknown) they translated the Pentateuch into Persian. Another type of scholarly activity which attracted them was the compilation of dictionaries. The earliest work of this kind was a Hebrew-Persian dictionary completed in 1338 by Solomon ben Samuel in Gurgang (or Urhenj) in the country to the west of Bukhara bordering on the Caspian Sea.

In 1839 the numbers of the Bukharan Jews were replenished by an influx of refugees from Meshhed, Persia, who chose emigration rather than conversion to Islam. Soon thereafter Bukharan Jews began to settle in Jerusalem, where they established their own community in 1868. They continued their literary and lexicographic activities in the Holy City, and by 1936, when their number had grown to 2,500, they had published no less than 170 volumes.[14]

Following Bukhara's annexation by Russia in 1868, the country was allowed to retain self-government under its emir; hence the old Muslim rule that obliged Jews to wear a badge continued in force. Around 1900 the Jews numbered 20,000 in the entire *khanat* of Bukhara, with some 4,000 to 5,000 living in the city of Bukhara itself, where they inhabited a special quarter. The Bukharan Jews were great travelers, going as far as India, and even China, in the east, Moscow, Paris, and London in the west, and many of them making the pilgrimage to Jerusalem.[15]

Many Bukharan Jews Russianized their names by adding the suffix "-of" or "-ef" to the Hebrew or Persian name of the father and using it as a family name—e.g., Aminof, Davidof, Abrahamof, Suleimanof, Yehudayef, Musayef.

The disabilities from which the Bukharan Jews suffered were the ones imposed upon them in other Muslim countries, with some local variations. They included the prohibition against living outside their ghetto, entering the Muslim part of the city after sunset, riding a horse, and sometimes even a donkey, exposing more than their heads to Muslim customers when squatting in their shops, and building a new synagogue or even a new dwelling within the ghetto. They also included the duty of wearing a rope over their outer garment and a special type of hat, and, occasionally, black robes only; of having houses and shops that were lower than those of the Muslims, and of hoisting

256

a rag over their buildings to mark them as Jewish-owned; and of paying a poll tax (the *jizya*), upon whose delivery the payer received a slap in the face as a token of degradation. In addition, the testimony of a Jew concerning a Muslim was inadmissible in a court of law.[16] While most of these disabilities were of a humiliating nature rather than constituting a serious menace to life and limb, they were sufficient to make life quite miserable. As against all this, the Bukharan Jews enjoyed the protection of the law as to person and property, again in accordance with general Muslim tradition. As *dhimmi*s, they had their own rabbinical courts which exercized jurisdiction in disputes between Jews, and whose decisions, if the need arose, were enforced by the government of the Khan.

The establishment of the Bukharan Soviet Republic in 1920, three years after the Bolshevik revolution, was greeted by the Bukharan Jews with a sense of liberation. At that time there were 15,000 Jews in Bukhara City, 12,000 in Samarkand, and several hundred in smaller towns. In the city of Tashkent, there were, in addition to 6,000 Bukharan Jews, also 4,000 Ashkenazim. Committees, societies, Communist party youth groups, and similar organizations were formed, and hopes ran high for a better future. Schools with Hebrew as the language of tuition were established and Zionist groups were allowed to function. A Zionist youth league, *Tarbut*, was organized as early as 1917–18, with branches in six cities. However, these improvements were short-lived. From 1921 on (at various dates in various towns) the Yevsekzia (the Jewish Department of the Soviet Commissariat of Internal Affairs) began to eliminate Hebrew and replace it with Tajik (i.e., Persian) as the language of tuition (in Tashkent this took place in 1926); Friday was substituted as the day of rest instead of the Sabbath; the only Zionist newspaper in Tajiki, the *Rahamim*, was closed down; in Tashkent, the Ashkenazi synagogue was shut down in 1926, the Bukharan in 1929; the *Tarbut* league was dissolved. The Bukharan Jews had thus become the object of a ruthless, effective, and rapid Sovietization.[17] Simultaneously, the economic position of the Bukharan Jews was undermined, since the well-to-do among them had been engaged in the international trade that came to a halt with the

Bolshevik revolution. Nevertheless, in comparison with the fate of the Jews in European Russia, the Bukharan Jews suffered less under the new regime.

According to the 1926 census there were 38,000 Jews in the Uzbek SSR, of whom 18,000 were Bukharan Jews. Their largest concentration was in the city of Samarkand, in which 7,740 Jews lived in their own separate quarter called *Mahane Yisrael* ("Camp of Israel"); in Tashkent there were 1,350 Bukharan Jews. In 1939 the estimated total number of Jews in Uzbekistan was 51,000, and another 19,000 (almost all of them European-Russian Jews) had settled in the Kazakh SSR to the north of Uzbekistan.

According to the 1959 Russian census, the number of Jews in the Central Asian Socialist Soviet Republic was as follows: in the Uzbek SSR, 94,344; in the Kazakh SSR, 28,048; in the Tadzhik SSR, 12,415; in the Kirghiz SSR, 8,610; and in the Turkmen SSR, 4,078.[18]

14 THE SEPHARDI JEWS

No Jewish Diaspora could boast of a more glorious period of efflorescence than the Sephardi. None was more filled with pride in its own ethnic excellence, a haughtiness which suggested a reflection of the Spanish national character with its famous *grandezza* that often bordered on arrogance. In the ten or eleven centuries that passed between the close of the Talmudic period and the beginnng of the modern era, no Jewish community has contributed more to Jewish life and letters, religion and scholarship, or to human achievement in general in such varied fields as poetry, philosophy, statesmanship, medicine, and the sciences. None had stronger emotional ties to its Diaspora home, loved it—despite persecutions, tortures and *autos da fé*—with greater patriotic fervor, or considered expulsion from it a more cruel exile. And none has sunk more deeply into the morass of mediocrity during the last three hundred years, after the exile from Spain had taken most of its sons to countries which themselves were outside the mainstream of modern Western civilization. Such, in brief, was the position of Sephardi Jewry, this remarkable smallest division of the Jewish people to which we now turn our attention.

History

The adjective Sephardi (from the Hebrew *S'fardi,* plural *S'fardim*) is derived from *S'farad,* the medieval Hebrew name for Spain. Thus Sephardim are the Jews whose ancestors lived in Spain and Portugal until their expulsion in 1492 or until their voluntary emigration prior to it, or their subsequent escape, after a period of precarious existence as Marranos or crypto-Jews.

Jews lived in the Iberian Peninsula since Roman times (cf. above, Chapter I). Under the Arabs, who conquered Spain in

259

711, their position became at first incomparably better; they obtained full religious liberty. Their numbers, at the same time, were augmented by Arabic-speaking Jews who came in with the Arab conquerors. Quite rapidly Arabic became not merely the colloquial language of the Jews in Spain, but also the medium in which they wrote literary, philosophical, medical, and scientific works of great importance, not only from a Jewish but also from a general human perspective.

The Arab conquest of Spain ushered in the period called by historians the Jewish "Golden Age." It took about two centuries before the Jews consolidated their position to a sufficient degree to be able to turn to science, literature, poetry, philosophy, and statesmanship. During those two centuries, under the relatively mild rule of the Muslim kings, the Jews gradually established themselves in various fields, became local and international merchants, and took an increasing interest in all the cultural activities that developed among the Moors of Spain who, in turn, had been influenced by the cultural flowering and upsurge of scholarship in the newly Islamized but culturally mature lands of the east. Before long the Jews made great advances in all those fields of learning and intellectual activity to which the Muslims themselves had been attracted, and vied with them in scientific studies, especially in medicine, astronomy, and geometry, in which branches of learning they wrote important treatises in Arabic.

Arabic was also the language in which the Jews wrote their philosophical works, although—since philosophy in those days was a religious pursuit—their writings were, of course, contributions to Jewish, not Muslim, religious thought. Under the influence of Arab grammarians, who in that period initiated the scientific study of the Arabic language, Jews wrote, in Hebrew, grammatical studies of the Hebrew language. Emulating Arab poets and borrowing the metrical forms they employed, the Jews wrote great Hebrew poetry, some of which is considered to this day the finest in the three-thousand-year history of Hebrew literature. Most important was the role of Jewish translators in the chain of renderings through which Greek (and even Hindu) works reached Christian Europe. The originals were often translated first into Arabic in the east, then from Arabic into

Hebrew by Jews in Spain, then from Hebrew into Latin by other Jews in the Christian Provence.

In addition to these intellectual pursuits in which the Jews of Spain reached unsurpassed excellence in the Golden Age, they also achieved outstanding positions as diplomats, viziers, and statesmen at the courts of the Moorish kings. What impresses us most in looking at the great Jewish figures of this age is their many-sidedness, their accomplishments in several different and unrelated fields of endeavor, which in Christian Europe remained unparalleled until the Renaissance. Take Hasdai ibn Shaprut (ca. 925–975), an early figure in this epoch, who was a physician, chemist, diplomatist, patron of Jewish scholars, and the Western "discoverer" of the Jewish Khazar kingdom to the north of the Caucasus. In the next century, the versatility of Samuel ibn Naghdela (993–1056) similarly anticipated that of the Renaissance man: he was a linguist (he addressed a poem to the king of Granada consisting of seven stanzas, each in a different language), a mathematician, a philosopher, a trusted advisor to the king, and a general of the royal army, while in the Jewish field he was a Hebrew poet, Talmudist, author of a Hebrew dictionary, head of a Talmudic academy, patron of poets and scholars, and *Nagid* or chief of the Jews.

Solomon ibn Gabirol (1021–1069) was a great poet and philosopher; Moses ibn Ezra (1080–1139) an outstanding poet; Judah Halevi (1086–1145) a great poet, philosopher, and physician; Abraham ibn Ezra (1092–1167), a poet, philosopher, grammarian, astrologist, and Bible commentator; and, of course, Moses Maimonides (1135–1204) who, as is generally agreed, was the greatest in this splendid company of talent, was a philosopher, codifier, physician and medical author, statesman, and Jewish communal leader.

Instead of adding more and more names to this list, let us sum up the Sephardi Jewish record of the tenth to thirteenth centuries by making one blanket statement: If one were asked to name the greatest Jewish poets, philosophers, scientists, codifiers, and mystics of all time, almost all would be Sephardi Jews of this period. No other Diaspora and no other age has ever achieved or even approximated such a galaxy of greatness.

Not that Jewish life in Spain did not have its dark side as well.

Persecutions and forced conversions occurred from 1066 on, although they were neither as frequent nor as widespread as under the Christians. In 1086 Spain became the first country in the world in which the Jews experienced the tragedy of fighting in the armies of two opposing powers, and thus of being arrayed brother against brother in the battlefield; this occurred in the battle of Zallaka which established the Almoravides as the rulers of the southern part of the Iberian peninsula.

Faced with the Moorish enemy in the south, the Christian kings and princes of central and northern Spain (Castile, Leon, Aragon, and Navarre) offered privileges to the Jews who, in turn, placed themselves at the service of the Catholic rulers. Thus, while the Jews in southern Spain (Granada) remained an Arabic-speaking element throughout the Middle Ages, those of central and northern Spain acquired Spanish and assimilated to the Christian Spaniards in custom and culture.

This early attempt at cultural assimilation, however, did not prevent the reemergence in Catholic Spain of a Jew-hatred the fires of which were diligently stoked by the popes from Rome. The Holy Office of the Inquisition was introduced into Aragon early in the thirteenth century. In the fourteenth century there were renewed persecutions and massacres of Jews, the worst of which occurred in 1391. To escape death, many Jews fled abroad, and tens of thousands converted to Christianity, only to become helpless prey for inquisitorial hunters for generations thereafter.

By the middle of the thirteenth century all of Spain, with the exception of the Kingdom of Granada in the southernmost part of the peninsula, was again in Christian hands. In Granada, where the Jews were so numerous that the city was sometimes referred to as "Granada of the Jews," the Nasrid dynasty managed to maintain itself for another two and a half centuries (1238–1492), until its last ruler, Boabdil, was defeated in 1492 by Ferdinand of Aragon and his wife Isabella of Castile. A few months thereafter the two *reyes catolicos* (Catholic kings) issued their decree of expulsion against the Jews of all Spain. Some fifty thousand Jews preferred baptism to exile and embraced Christianity. Perhaps four times as many left,[1] some going to neighboring Portugal where they were soon forced to convert to Christianity, this time without the option of emigration. The day on which the last groups of Jews left Spain was the very same day on which, 1422 years earlier, the Romans had destroyed the Second Temple of Jerusalem and on which, another 656 years before that, the Babylonians had conquered Jerusalem. It was also the day, Friday, August 3, 1492, by the Christian calendar, on which Columbus sailed from the Port of Palos near Seville, with several Marranos in his crew, on the voyage that led to the establishment of Spanish colonies in the New World and ultimately to the development of the largest and best-established Diaspora that has ever been witnessed by Jewish history. A long time before that, however, the Inquisition followed the Jewish emigrants to the New World, where from the sixteenth to the eighteenth centuries some sixty persons were burned alive in *autos da fé.*

Long before the expulsion from Spain, Sephardi Jews who settled elsewhere achieved positions of undisputed leadership in their new countries. Maimonides comes to mind as the outstanding example. Less known is the fact that, from the early fifteenth century on, almost all the rabbis in the Jewish communities of Algeria were Sephardi emigrés.

For almost two centuries after the expulsion of 1492, all the greatest developments in Jewish history were initiated by Sephardi Jews: the final codification of the law—by Joseph Caro; the Kabbalistic movement—by the Safed circle; and the greatest pseudo-Messianic movement—by Shabbatai Zevi. The first of these has already been discussed; the second will be dealt with when we come to talk about Safed in the sixteenth century; the third requires a few words right here.

Shabbatai Zevi (1625–1675), born in Smyrna (today Izmir), Turkey, the scion of Sephardi family, believed, probably in all sincerity, at least in the earlier part of his life, that he was the long-awaited Messiah. A Kabbalist, he practiced asceticism and mortification of the flesh, and at the age of twenty-two revealed himself to a few friends as the Redeemer. Three years later, the rabbis of Smyrna banished him and his followers. Shabbatai thereupon embarked on a period of wandering, entered a most unusual marriage, and in the year 1665 which, according to the Kabbalists was the year of Redemption, proclaimed himself publicly as the Messiah in the synagogue of Smyrna.

Shabbatai's early followers included numerous rabbis whose names read like a roster of the prominent religious leaders of the Sephardi world. His fame rapidly spread far beyond the Sephardi Diaspora and evoked a veritable Messianic hysteria in the Ashkenazi and Oriental Jewish communities as well. The fact that Shabbatai soon thereafter was imprisoned by the Turkish authorities in the castle of Abydos did nothing to dampen the enthusiasm he had aroused. Individuals and entire communities began preparations to emigrate to the Messianic Kingdom which, they believed, Shabbatai Zevi was soon about to found in the Land of Israel. Still in the year 1666, Shabbatai embraced Islam to escape the death penalty.

Despite this dismal end of the pseudo-Messiah's career, many continued to believe in him and some even followed him into apostasy. In the entire movement, Sephardim were the initiators and the leaders, while the followers were recruited among all the three divisions of the Jewish people. Once again, as in the case of the Kabbala, Ashkenazi resistance to Sephardi doctrine, teaching, and innovation totally broke down. Never again did a comparable initiative issue from the Sephardi world. The Shabbatian movement was the last flame to blaze into the sky before the Sephardi fire began to die down.[2]

However, for almost two centuries, from the Spanish expulsion until the collapse of the Shabbatian movement, Sephardi creativity shone brilliantly in all countries where the Spanish exiles sought and found refuge: first of all in the lands of the Ottoman Empire, which at the time included, in addition to Asia Minor, the Balkans and the greater part of Hungary in Europe, Syria and Palestine in Asia, and Egypt in Africa; then in North Africa, Italy, Holland; and later also in England and America.

From the early or middle seventeenth century the Sephardi communities, which by then were dispersed in many parts of the world, began to go into a decline. Their absolute or relative number diminished everywhere, their creative genius seemed exhausted, their rigidity increased, and their proud demeanor became hollow. The once most fruitful branch on the tree of Diaspora Jewry seemed destined to wither away. Let us survey rapidly the rise and decline of the Sephardim in the principal countries of their Diaspora, beginning with a small Galilean town which for a century was the brightest star on the Sephardi horizon.

Safed in the Sixteenth Century

From the viewpoint of inner Jewish development, the small Sephardi community of sixteenth-century Safed (Palestine), in which we must include Isaac Luria, although he was of Ashkenazi extraction, made a more valuable and more lasting contribution than any other Jewish group in any other century since the conclusion of the Talmud. It was here that Joseph Caro (born in Spain, 1488; died in Safed, 1575) wrote his *Shulhan 'Arukh* ("Prepared Table"), the final codification of the totality of Jewish law which is considered binding upon traditional Jews to this day. The *Shulhan 'Arukh* is the one religio-legal *magnum opus* that prevented the Jewish Diaspora from breaking up into fragmented schools, each following its own legal code and system (as was the case, e.g., in Sunni Islam with its four religio-legal schools, the Hanafi, Hanbali, Maliki, and Shafi'i). It was the literally unprecedented authority enjoyed by the *Shulhan 'Arukh* in the entire Diaspora that prevented such a development, although it also crystallized the differences between the Sephardi and Oriental Jews (including the Italian and Greek communities) on the one hand, and the Ashkenazim, on the other. While the former followed the decisions of Joseph Caro as laid down in his *Shulhan 'Arukh,* the latter considered as valid the emendations made by the Polish rabbi Moshe Isserles (1520–1572) which are printed interlineally in all standard editions of the *Shulhan 'Arukh.* The fact that Isserles made his emendations codifying Ashkenazi custom while Caro was still alive, and that the *Shulhan 'Arukh* spread into most parts of the Diaspora as soon as it was published, shows the extent of the cohesion and unity of the sixteenth-century Jewish world despite the slow, primitive, and hazardous communications of the time. There can be no doubt but that it was the work of the Sephardi Joseph Caro more than that of any other rabbinical authority which was responsible for the maintenance of the basic religio-legal unity of world Jewry down to the period of the Enlightenment and assimilation.

The other great and lasting influence that emanated from sixteenth-century Sephardi Safed was the spread and popularization of Kabbalism, the mystical trend in Judaism. Jewish mysticism had its roots in antiquity; Kabbalist schools, however, developed only in twelfth- and thirteenth-century Germany. Kabbalism sprang into full bloom in Spain where the Sephardi Moses de Leon (who lived in the little town of Guadalajara in Castile, and died in 1305 in Arevalo) wrote the *Sepher HaZohar* ("Book of Splendor") between 1275 and 1286. In order to assure its acceptance as an authoritative work, de Leon attributed the *Zohar* to the second-century Palestinian sage and mystic Rabbi Shimeon ben Yohai. It was actually accepted as the work of Ben Yohai, and not only overshadowed all the other documents of Kabbalist literature, but as Gershom Scholem put it, it "alone among the whole of post-Talmudic rabbinical literature became a canonical text, which for a period of several centuries actually ranked with the Bible and the Talmud."[3]

And yet Kabbalism did not become a popular religious movement, nor a real historical factor, until almost three centuries after the completion of the *Zohar*. That it finally did become one was due to the work of several Sephardi Kabbalists who were among the exiles from Spain in 1492 and who foregathered in the small Upper Galilean town of Safed. They made sixteenth-century Safed an unequaled center of Kabbalistic life and studies whose influence radiated into all parts of the Jewish Diaspora. Of the splendid galaxy of sixteenth-century Safed Kabbalists there are only two whose names are familiar today to nonscholarly practicing Jews, although few know that they were leading Kabbalists. One is that of Joseph Caro, to whom we have already referred as the author of the *Shulhan 'Arukh*. Caro was also a great Kabbalist who believed and maintained that a special spirit, whom he called *Maggid*, was in constant communication with him; he collected these angelic messages in a book titled *Maggid Mesharim* ("The Teller of Truth"), which is a kind of mystical diary covering some fifty years.[4]

The second Safed Kabbalist, Solomon Alkabez (1505–1584), is known as the author of the famous hymn, *L'kha Dodi* ("Come, My Beloved"), which is sung at Sabbath eve services in all synagogues. It is, in reality, a mystical hymn which was incorporated into the liturgy thanks to the Safed Kabbalists.[5] Alkabez was the author also of Kabbalistic commentaries on several Biblical books, and other works that brought him exceptional esteem.

However great Caro and Alkabez were in other fields of Jewish achievement, in the Kabbala they were overshadowed by Isaac Luria (b. Jerusalem, 1534; d. Safed, 1572) who, although born to German parents, was a product of the Sephardi Diaspora to such an extent that he must be considered an Ashkenazi in name only. After spending seven years in isolation on the banks of the Nile, the thirty-five-year-old Luria moved to Safed where, for the remaining three years of his life, he was the acknowledged mentor of the circle of Kabbalists. Like a true master, he himself wrote nothing; he only taught, spoke, and held discourses. His disciples took notes of his lectures and utterances, which were collected and edited by Hayim Vital (born at Safed, 1543; died in Damascus, 1620), Luria's favorite pupil. The relationship between Vital and Luria resembles to a remarkable extent that between Plato and Socrates. In both cases we have a master who leaves no writings behind and whose life's work is known only as reflected in the books of a disciple. In the cases of both Plato and Vital it is difficult to determine what is truly Socratic and Lurianic respectively, and what are the fruits of the disciples' minds hung on the trees of the masters.

The spread of Lurianic Kabbala, as transmitted by Vital and the other disciples and followers of the master, is much too complex a process to indicate here in even the barest outlines. Suffice it to say that, within a few decades after Luria's death, works attributed to him were published not only in Venice but also in Prague, Hanau, and other centers of Ashkenazi learning, not to mention the numerous Lurianic manuscripts that were circulated as precious and rare treasures.

Next to Luria the most important Kabbalist in sixteenth-century Safed was Rabbi Moses Cordovero (1522–1570). The scion of a family from Cordova, Cordovero expounded Kabbalistic theory in a large number of weighty tomes, many of which were published in the late sixteenth and early seventeenth centuries in Venice, Cracow, Lublin, Fürth, Prague, and other centers of Jewish culture, and some of which were even translated into Latin by the middle of the seventeenth century. Cordovero is considered the greatest theoretician of Jewish mysticism, who, a century before Spinoza and Malebranche, attained an insight into the relationship between God and the world which he summed up in the pithy statement: "The Deity (haEloah) is all reality, but not all reality is the Deity."[6]

In addition to these major masters, the Kabbalistic circle of sixteenth-century Safed included a considerable number of secondary luminaries, such as Moses Alshech, Elijah de Vidas, Joseph Hagiz, Elisha Galadoa, Moses Bassola, Joseph ibn Tabul, and others.[7]

The combined effect of the teachings and writings of these men—all Sephardim—was that the Kabbala of the Safed school rapidly spread into all parts of the contemporary Jewish world. If we stop to consider for a moment that the great codificatory works of the Sephardim never managed to gain acceptance by the Ashkenazim until the last one, Caro's *Shulhan 'Arukh,* had the good fortune of being provided with emendations by Moshe Isserles which introduced into its very body the Ashkenazi viewpoint, it will become readily apparent what extraordinary powers of attraction the Sephardi Kabbala of Safed must have had in order to break through the wall of Ashkenazi resistance to Sephardi doctrine. For the fact is that within less than a century after the death of Cordovero and Luria, Kabbalism had become as much part of Ashkenazi religious life as of Sephardi, and had developed into a truly popular religious movement in both these divisions of the Jewish people as well as in the third one, the Oriental Jews. Thus the stage was set for the birth and spread of the great pseudo-Messianic movement of Shabbatai Zevi that gripped the Jewish world in 1665 and that was the last great upheaval in the Diaspora triggered by Sephardi Jews.

Before leaving sixteenth-century Safed, I cannot resist indulging in a conjecture. In addition to the Kabbala, there were also other factors that prepared the ground for the Messianic hopes of the second half of the sixteenth century. Among these factors, historians often refer to the Chmielnicki massacres perpetrated between 1648 and 1658, which, together with the plague that broke out at the same time, claimed some half a million Jewish victims in Eastern Europe. It seems to me that one other factor should be added: the great prestige that the Sephardi Jews had in the Ashkenazi world in the period following the issuance of the *Shulḥan 'Arukh* and the Kabbala from sixteenth-century Safed. My conjecture is that had Shabbatai Zevi been an Ashkenazi, and had he appeared not in Smyrna, but in, say, Lvov or Warsaw, the Messianic movement he created would have been much weaker in the Ashkenazi world and would barely have touched the Sephardi and Oriental Jews.

Turkey

However, it was not only in Palestine that the Sephardi exiles from the Iberian Peninsula, as a result of their outstanding talent, vitality, and energy, became the leaders of older Jewish Diasporas. In Turkey, where Jews had lived probably since the days of Alexander the Great, individual Iberian Jews stood out even prior to the expulsion from Spain. After it the refugees from Spain and Portugal not only prospered in Turkey but also became, within a remarkably short time, the dominant element in the Jewish community.

Two distinct Jewish communities had been established at the time of the arrival of the Sephardi Jews. One was that of the Romaniots, the indigenous Jews of the former Byzantine Empire who spoke Greek and most of whom were subsequently absorbed into the Ladino-speaking Sephardi communities,[8] while some of their customs were, in turn, adopted by the Sephardim and incorporated into the *Shulḥan 'Arukh*.[9] The other was that of the Ashkenazim who had arrived shortly before from Germany, where they had been exposed to persecutions and expulsions, and who established Ashkenazi colonies in many Turkish cities and town, such as Constantinople, Adrianople, Nicopolis, Salonica, Sofia, Plevna, Philippopolis, and Vidin.[10]

The Sephardim, who arrived in considerable numbers, did

not, as a rule, join these existing communities but formed new ones of their own, frequently establishing several separate congregations according to the localities whence they had come. Soon there were no less than ten separate Sephardi congregations in Constantinople, eleven in Salonica (of which four were Portuguese), while in Adrianople there were eight Spanish and several Portuguese ones. In many cities (including Cairo, Jerusalem, and Salonica), the Sephardim before long came to outnumber the autochthonous Jews. The special skills of the Sephardim were noticed even by an outsider such as Nicolo Nicolai, court chamberlain to the king of France, who in 1551 wrote: ". . . one meets among them [the Jews of Turkey] many skilled artists and mechanics, expecially among the Marranos, who some years ago were driven out of Spain and Portugal. These . . . have taught the Turks to make implements of war. . . . [They have] also established a printing press . . . they know most languages, so that they are employed as interpreters."[11] They also became leaders in trade and commerce and were diplomatic agents and physicians.[12] A Sephardi Jew, Don Joseph Nasi, obtained the city of Tiberias from Suleiman the Magnificent and was created Duke of Naxos and of the Cyclades Islands by Selim II in 1566. Following the arrival of the Spanish exiles, Jewish literature flourished in Turkey, and most names on the roster of outstanding authors are those of Spanish Jews.

In the seventeenth century a decline set in. Nevertheless, the linguistic assimilation of the original Jewish inhabitants of the Turkish Empire to the Sephardi Jews continued, so that by the eighteenth century the great majority of the Jews in western Turkey and in the Balkans were Ladino-speaking.

The case of the Turkish Jews can be adduced as the best example for the thesis that the general cultural condition of the Jews in any given country is greatly influenced by the culture of the non-Jewish environment in that country. After the beginning of the wars with Russia in the eighteenth century, internal conditions in Turkey greatly deteriorated. Corruption was rife, and the ineffectual reform measures adopted by one sultan after another in the eighteenth and nineteenth centuries could not stem the process of disintegration. It would have been a miracle if the Jews of Turkey had remained unaffected by these conditions. They suffered from them directly: the Janissaries frequently started fires in the Jewish quarter of Constantinople for the purpose of robbing the stores while pretending to quench the flames; anti-Jewish measures were enacted; extortions were the order of the day; there was no recourse to law. The Jewish community sank into a state of wretched stupor; its houses were covered with filth, its ranks were decimated by epidemics, its intellectual life was stagnant. This was the general state of affairs until the Alliance Israélite Universelle, in the second half of the nineteenth century, began its two-pronged attack on the misery of the Turkish Jews: the organization of schools for children, and intervention with the authorities on behalf of the Jews.

North Africa

In Turkey the Sephardi Jews absorbed the indigenous Jewish communities (except the Kurdish Jews in eastern Anatolia); in the West they retained their separate identity down to the present. In North Africa, however, neither of these two situations obtained. What happened instead was that many of the *toshavim* (Hebrew for "residents"), as the autochthonous Jews were called, assimilated to the *m'gorashim* (Hebrew for "exiles"), especially in the coastal areas where most of the Sephardi newcomers settled, while in the hinterland, and, particularly in the Atlas Mountains of Morocco and in other mountainous areas to the east of it, the old-established Jewish communities retained their original physiognomy. The Sephardim, who began to arrive after the Spanish atrocities of 1391 and who, a century later, after the expulsion of 1492, came in much greater numbers, settled primarily in the coastal cities and also in cities farther inland.

In Tangiers, Tetuan, and Spanish Morocco in general, the Sephardi Jews preserved practically intact the entire cultural heritage they had brought along from Spain. Whatever native Jewish communities existed in this area were totally absorbed by them, linguistically as well as culturally. Considerable cul-

271

tural assimilation to the Sephardim also took place among the native Jews in the other cities of northern Morocco, such as the port cities of Arzile, Larache, Sale, Rabat, Safi, and the inland cities of the northern part of the country—Debdou, Fez, Meknes.[13] However, the Sephardim never penetrated the south, the real hinterland of the Barbary Coast, the Arab and Berber villages of the mountains and the desert fringes, so that in those parts the small Arabic and Berber-speaking Jewish village communities remained unaffected by them and retained their old languages.

The Sephardim not only actually surpassed the *toshavim* in education, intellectual achievement, and commerical ability, but did not hesitate to make them feel that they had been favored by the arrival of a superior element in their midst. Objectively seen, the Sephardi skill and experience in European commerce, their knowledge of arts and crafts, as well as their wealth, polish, and diplomatic ability contributed greatly to the rise and development of the Barbary states. In Morocco they soon achieved important court positions which resembled in many respects the positions they had held in Spain. From the early sixteenth century until the nineteenth, the Sephardim supplied the Moroccan court with a long line of ministers of state, counselors, representatives of the rulers in foreign courts, and the like.[14] In the field of Jewish learning, however, the Spanish newcomers did not excel. Although Fez, as well as Meknes and Rabat, again became centers of Jewish learning, their scholarly output was mediocre compared to that of the tenth and eleventh centuries.

The division of the Jews of Morocco into a native and a Sephardi group still held good in the twentieth century. Until the upheaval of 1948 the native Jews in the interior and mountain areas continued to live the same kind of life that they inherited from their ancestors of yore, whereas the Sephardi Jews, in the coastal cities and districts, retained their Ladino and constituted a more advanced and Europeanized community, more ready to absorb modern influences such as those offered by the schools of the Alliance Israélite Universelle after 1860.

Polygyny, practiced by the Sephardi Jews only in exceptional cases, and then only with the consent of the first wife, was more frequent among the Arabic- and Berber-speaking Jews. However, child marriage (with brides as young as six to eight years) was still quite common in both communities as late as the present century.[15]

Statistics as to the numerical strength of the two Jewish elements in Morocco are, of course, nonexistent, but we have estimates made by experts. According to one, the Sephardi element in Morocco comprises 36.8 percent of the total Jewish population, while the autochthonous groups comprise 30.5 percent Arabic-speaking and 6.95 percent Berber-speaking elements, plus 17.85 percent with Hebrew or Aramaic names (which is supposed to indicate their origin), and 7.9 percent unidentified.[16] According to another expert, the Jews of Sephardi extraction (including the Italians) make up only 17.2 percent of the Moroccan Diaspora, while the Arab-Berber Jews constitute 44.5 percent, and the Hebrew-Arameans 12.65 percent, leaving some 25 percent for others.[17]

A different development took place in Algeria. From the early fifteenth century, nearly all the Algerian Jewish communities were led by rabbis who had emigrated from Spain. After the 1492 exile, some ten thousand Sephardi Jews settled in Algeria. However, about the middle of the seventeenth century the division of Jews into "residents" and "exiles" disappeared. The vernacular of all Algerian Jews became, or remained, Arabic. This assimilation of the Sephardi Jews to the autochthonous Algerian Jews brought in its wake a decline in the educational and cultural attainments, as well as in the commercial and diplomatic activities of the former. It was this circumstance that enabled the so-called *Gorneyim* (Jews from Leghorn, Italy) to establish themselves in Algiers and other cities of the regency as leaders in commerce, bankers to the deys, intermediaries between the deys and the European powers and influential counselors, almost ranking as ministers. The subsequent periods in the history of the Algerian Jews form a chapter in the history of Oriental (or Middle Eastern) Jewry and, accordingly, were treated in Chapter XI.

As for Tunisia, very few of the Sephardi exiles settled there.

The country therefore soon became a satellite of neighboring Algeria in intellectual life, and of Morocco in religious matters. Only in the city of Tunis was there, side by side with the *Tunsi* community (that of the descendants of the early inhabitants) also a *Grana* community (as those who came from Granada were called) which included the descendants of all Spanish and Portuguese Jews, as well as those of the *Gorneyim,* who arrived here, too, in the seventeenth and eighteenth centuries. It was not until 1824 that the Tunisian authorities finally granted the *Grana* congregation independence from the *Tunsi* community.

The two communities remained separated as a result of the different traditions they followed: like the *toshavim* in the other Barbary states, the *Touansa* (Tunisians) were influenced by their long sojourn among Muslims; the *Grana,* by the Christian environment in which they had lived in Spain. To mention only one point on which they differed, women were comparatively emancipated among the *Grana,* who had also virtually abolished polygyny, while among the *Touansa* the position of women was more or less the same as it was with the Muslim majority of Tunisia. Rapprochement between the two groups began only in the 1860s under the influence of the schools of the Alliance Israélite Universelle; in 1899 the French decreed that all the Jews of the country must have one single Chief Rabbinate and a combined representation in the Community Council and the Government Council. A decree enacted in 1944 completed the unification of the *Grana* and the *Touansa.*[18]

Holland

In Holland, where the Spanish exiles arrived in 1593, their mercantile ability soon enabled them to occupy a prominent place not only in the development of the country's domestic and continental commerce but also in the establishment of Dutch power in the newly discovered Americas. In 1621 they participated in the establishment of the Dutch West India Company, and in 1642 about six hundred of them went to Brazil in response to the appeal of the Dutch settlers there for craftsmen of all kinds. In Amsterdam, many of them were physicians. The names of Rabbi Manasseh ben Israel (1604–1657), a polyhistor who wrote in numerous languages, was a friend of Rembrandt, and was instrumental in obtaining permission for the Jews to resettle in England; and of the philosophers Uriel Acosta (1590–1647) and Barukh Spinoza (1632–1677) are too well known to require more than mention. All three were Sephardi Jews: the first two were born in Portugal, the third in Amsterdam.

The beginning of the eighteenth century marked the beginning of the decline of the Sephardi Jews in Holland. Yet their disdain for the Ashkenazim (to whom they referred as *"Todescos"*) continued; they disapproved of marriages with Ashkenazi women, while among themselves they continued the practices of child marriage (both bride and groom were often less than twelve years old) and cousin marriage. The separate congregations of the Portuguese Jews continued in Amsterdam and The Hague into the twentieth century. By 1850 only 3,372 Sephardim were left in Holland; fifty years later their number had increased to 5,645. (In the same period the number of Ashkenazim increased from 59,238 to 98,343.)[19]

England

In 1655, as a result of the pleas of Manasseh ben Israel and of Oliver Cromwell's desire to attract trade to British shores, the Jews were readmitted to England, from where they had been expelled in 1290. Marranos posing officially as Spanish Christians had lived in England before 1655, but when England declared war against Spain in 1656 they had to avow their Judaism in order to avoid arrest as Spaniards and the confiscation of their goods. Such dilemmas did not beset the Sephardi merchants who settled in London in the second half of the seventeenth and the first half of the eighteenth century. They brought with them into England some five million pounds sterling, and one of them, Solomon de Medina, was knighted in the early 1700s. Most of them having come from Amsterdam, they founded in London communal institutions patterned after those they had maintained there, all centering around their great synagogue built in Bevis Marks in 1701. The Sephardi community of London included a considerable number of wealthy families, who rendered invaluable services in the expansion of British commerce. In 1753 a bill passed by Parliament allowing Jews to become naturalized citizens created such an uproar that it was repealed the following year, but not before widespread rioting had frightened many of the wealthiest and most cultured Jews (there were only Sephardim in this category) into conversion to Christianity. Early in the nineteenth century another wave of conversions further thinned the ranks of the London Sephardim, this time in reaction to the unbending and autocratic rule of the *"mahamad"* (i.e., *ma'amad,* presidium) of their congregation. It was thus in keeping with the "spirit of the time" as understood by these Sephardim that the English Sephardi author, Isaac Disraeli (1766-1848), had his son Benjamin baptised at the age when other Jewish boys celebrated their Bar Mitzva.

The decline of the British Sephardim was thrown into bolder relief by the simultaneous rise of the Ashkenazim. Nathan Mayer Rothschild (born in Frankfurt 1777; died 1836), the third son of the founder of the house of Rothschild, had been living in Manchester since 1798; in 1805 he moved to London where he soon became the central figure of the Jewish community. His sister Henrietta became the wife of Abraham Montefiore, brother of Sir Moses Montefiore; in 1840 his second son Anthony (later Sir Anthony de Rothschild, baronet) married Louisa, the daughter of Abraham and Henrietta Montefiore. Thus in the circle of the very rich, the old Sephardi prejudice against marrying Ashkenazi women suffered an early breakdown.

However, by the time these intercommunity marriages took place, the hegemony of the community was definitely passing from the hands of the Sephardim into those of the Ashkenazim. As early as the late eighteenth century the chief rabbis of the Ashkenazim had begun to vie in importance with the "hahamim" (i.e., *Hakhamim*) of the Sephardim. The shift in prestige was accompanied (and partly caused by) a shift in numbers. In 1883 there were only 3,500 Sephardim in London as against 43,500 Ashkenazim. Twenty years later, mainly as a result of the arrival of Ashkenazi Jews fleeing from the Russian pogroms (as well as of natural increase and migration from smaller provincial communities), the total number of Jews in London was estimated at 150,000, among whom the Sephardim were not more than 5,000.

The United States

The history of the Sephardim in the United States parallels that of their brethren in Western Europe. The first Jewish immigrants to come to what later became the United States were twenty-four Sephardim who arrived from Brazil in New Amsterdam (later New York) in July and September 1654. The very next year the directors of the Dutch West India Company instructed Peter Stuyvesant, the Dutch governor of New Netherlands, that the Jews "shall have permission to sail to and trade in New Netherlands, and to live and remain there." The first Jew to own land in the colony was a Dutch Jewish trader, Asser Levy, (died 1680), also known as van Swellem. In 1660 Levy and another Sephardi, Abraham de Lucena, received licenses as butchers. The family of the latter, as his name shows, came originally from the city of Lucena near Cordova, Spain. By 1706 the Spanish and Portuguese congregation of Shearith Israel had been established in New York. Another synagogue of some twenty families had been in existence at least since 1695. Until the Revolutionary War more Jews of Spanish and Portuguese extraction continued to arrive.

The Sephardi Jews who arrived in America were not only well-to-do, but had considerable experience in international trade, including transoceanic mercantile operations. They were, therefore, attracted to the larger and rapidly growing port cities of America, where they continued the vocations for which they were best prepared by their experience in international, intercolonial, and transoceanic trade as well as other forms of commerce. Before long they made satisfactory adjustment and became, if not exactly merchant princes, certainly people of substance and even wealth.

They were characteristically Sephardi also with regard to the posture they assumed on the question of Jewish piety and secular culture. Like their ancestors and contemporaries in other Diasporas, they were characterized by considerable general

277

education and a worldliness in their approach to secular matters. Unlike the Ashkenazim, but like the Sephardim elsewhere, they held that Jewish religious observance did not impose or even imply self-isolation from the cultural achievements of the non-Jewish world. On the other hand, again unlike the Ashkenazim and like the Sephardim elsewhere, they had relatively little Jewish culture by the end of the seventeenth century. Their Judaism expressed itself in, and was confined to, a strict pietism, a meticulous observance of Jewish religious law and custom, the latter incorporating a great amount of popular beliefs and practices commonly referred to as superstitions. An interesting later consequence of this attitude to secular and Jewish culture was that the religious reform which in the early nineteenth century penetrated the ranks of German Jews in America (or, more precisely, was brought along by German Jewish immigrants to America, where it subsequently spread among the East European Ashkenazi Jews as well) never gained any foothold among the Sephardim.

The decline that the Spanish-Portuguese Jews in the United States experienced around the middle of the nineteenth century was for the most part only of a relative nature. Sephardi immigration to the United States had come practically to an end by the eighteenth century. From 1654 to 1800 the total number of Jewish immigrants was about 1,000. Even if all of them were Sephardim, it is evident that such a small contingent was rapidly outnumbered by the German Jews, whose immigration increased in the mid nineteenth century. In that century, while the leadership of the community still rested firmly in Sephardi hands, the non-Sephardi, mainly German-Jewish, immigrants reduced the Sephardim to a small minority. By the mid nineteenth century "the aristocratic Sephardic families were in a process of disappearing and Sephardic youth was forced increasingly to marry Ashkenazim or face the prospect of intermarriage with Gentiles."[20] By the mid twentieth century, while they still maintained their old synagogues in New York, Philadelphia, and elsewhere, and still published a Ladino weekly, their decline had reached the stage where in most cases they were unable to find qualified rabbis of Sephardi extraction

278

so that most of their spiritual leaders had to be recruited from Ashkenazi ranks.

The Sephardi Attitude toward Ashkenazim and Oriental Jews

In each country (except in the New World) where the Sephardi Jews settled a Jewish community had been in existence for many generations prior to their arrival. In each they considered themselves an elite group and regarded their own language, culture, and traditions as higher in value and better in quality than those of the local Jewish groups. The indigenous Jewish communities were, in most cases, willing to adopt the same view. As a result of this prestige relationship, the Sephardi Jews retained their language everywhere, except in places where their numbers were too small (as, e.g., in Algeria), and considerable elements of the older Jewish communities assimilated to them both linguistically and culturally. (The language of the Sephardi Jews was discussed in some detail in Chapter VII, "The Languages of the Jews.")

A trait complementary to this exaggerated pride and self-esteem was the Sephardi derogation of both the Ashkenazim and the Oriental Jews. The Sephardim mocked at the customs of the Ashkenazim, regarded them as inferior to themselves, and tried to keep their distance by setting up, wherever possible, separate congregations and institutions.[21] This ethnocentric trait of haughtiness, which had existed among the Sephardi Jews prior to their expulsion from Spain,[22] surfaced more visibly after the exile when the Sephardim, for the first time in their history, had to live side by side with Ashkenazim in the same cities (e.g. in Turkey, Holland, and England). In Turkey their inclination to lord it over others led to the absorption of many non-Sephardi communities by the Sephardim. The same attitude was displayed in North Africa by the Sephardi immigrants from Spain and Majorca,[23] and led to the same results.

At first there was an unquestionable objective basis for the negative Sephardi attitude to the Ashkenazim: the Sephardim were a more cultured element, in both Jewish and secular matters,

279

than the Ashkenazim, whose *forte* in the Jewish field was largely confined to Talmudic learning, and who considered all interest in, or knowledge of, secular education as anathema. But even a century or a century-and-a-half after the exile, when the cultural élan of the Sephardim showed definite signs of decline and exhaustion, their pride remained undiminished. In fact, it seems that the fewer objective reasons they had to look down upon the Ashkenazim, the more emphatically they continued doing so, as if they felt constrained to compensate with patterns of elitistic behavior and attitudes for their waning cultural excellence.

In the second half of the eighteenth century, by which time the Sephardi Jews had been quiescent, as far as cultural creativity was concerned, for a hundred years, they still maintained their traditional pride and their disdain for the Ashkenazim. Thus Isaac de Pinto (1715–1787), the Sephardi economist, moralist, and Jewish apologist, wrote in his French treatise defending the Jews against Voltaire's attacks:

> M. Voltaire cannot be ignorant of the scrupulous exactness of the Portuguese and Spanish Jews not to intermix in marriage, alliance, or any other way with the Jews of other nations: He has been in Holland, and knows that they have separate synagogues, and that although they possess the same religion and the same articles of faith, yet their ceremonies have often no resemblance: The manners of the Portuguese Jews [Pinto himself was of Portuguese extraction] are also very different from those of the rest: the former have no beards nor anything peculiar in their dress. The rich among them vie with the other nations of Europe in refinement, elegance and show: and differ from them in worship only. [This was the theme that two generations later was to become a basic tenet of German Reform Judaism.] Their variance with their other brethren is at such a height that if a Portuguese Jew in England or Holland married a German Jewess, he would of course lose all his prerogatives, be no longer reckoned a member of their synagogue, forfeit all civil and ecclesiastical preferments, be absolutely divorced from the body of the nation, and not even buried with his Portuguese brethren.

And now comes the historical-mythical explanation of all this *noblesse:*

> They think in general that they are descended from the tribe of Juda, and they hold that the chief families of it were sent to Spain

280

at the time of the Babylonish captivity: This is the cause of those distinctions and of that elevation of mind which is observed among them, and which even their brethren of other nations seem to acknowledge.[24]

Pinto's reference to the penalties a Sephardi Jew would incur in Holland or England if he were to marry an Ashkenazi woman was based on fact. In 1766 the Sephardi congregation of London issued a decree forbidding such marriages. In 1772 a member asked permission from the synagogue committee to marry a *"Tudesca"* (i.e., German Jewish woman) but was refused. In the Sephardi synagogues of both London and Amsterdam, Ashkenazim, if they insisted on attending services, had to stay behind wooden barriers.[25]

In the United States, too, the first reaction among the Sephardim to their decline in numbers and importance relative to the Ashkenazim was to place greater emphasis on their own elitism. As late as 1830 to 1850, when the German Jews constituted the largest as well as the wealthiest group in American Jewry, the Sephardim of New York still managed to constitute "an exclusive coterie whose members mingled only among themselves and married within their own group."[26]

The Sephardi disdain for the Ashkenazim was due partly to the marked differences between the overt behavior patterns of the two groups. Conditioned by greatly disparate historical experiences, the general Sephardi deportment was one of dignity, while the Ashkenazi was one of subservient cringing; where the Sephardim paid scrupulous attention to dress, the Ashkenazim often walked about in dirty clothes; where the Sephardim were men of the world, used to associating freely with non-Jews whether the latter were their social equals or superiors, the Ashkenazim had shut themselves off from contact with the gentiles and approached them when they had to with a diffidence that verged on servility. This difference in the roles of the Sephardim and the Ashkenazim with regard to their respective non-Jewish environments was reflected in intra-Jewish relations as well: the Sephardim among themselves were polite, polished, and pleasant in their behavior, while the Ashkenazim were gruff, gross, and uncouth in their approach to one another.

As Rabbi Meyer Kayserling, an expert on Sephardim and himself an Ashkenazi, observed about 1900: "Even those among them [the Sephardim] whose station in life was low, as, for example, the carriers [meaning porters] of Salonica, or the sellers of 'pan de España' in the streets of Smyrna, maintained the old Spanish 'grandezza' in spite of their poverty."[27]

If the Sephardi Jews looked down upon the Ashkenazim, their opinion of the North African Jews was, if possible, even worse. Typical of this attitude was the opinion of the great Maimonides who, on his way from Spain to Egypt, sojourned for some time in various localities of the Barbary States and described the Jews he encountered there in a letter addressed to his son:

> Beware of the inhabitants of the West [i.e., the Maghrib, or northwest Africa], which is called az-Zirbi [i.e., the Island of Jerba, Tunisia], that is the places in the Barbary States, for they are dull and have a crude nature. And beware especially of the people who live between Tunis and Alexandria of Egypt, and those who live in the mountains of Barbary, because they are more ignorant than the rest of mankind, though they be very strong in their belief. God is my witness that they can be compared to the Karaites who deny the oral law. They evince no lucidity of spirit in their study of the Pentateuch, the Prophets, the Talmud, not even when they discuss the haggadot and the laws.

This is how Maimonides characterizes the scholarship of North African Jews, only a few decades after the time when in one single city in Morocco, Fez, such outstanding religio-legal luminaries as Dunash ibn Labrat (tenth century), Judah b. David Hayyuj (b. 950), Isaac Alfasi (1013–1103), were born or lived. One cannot help suspecting that it is Spanish haughtiness rather than measured scholarly judgment that speaks in these lines, especially if one remembers that Maimonides himself was a pupil of Joseph ibn Migash, who in turn was a pupil of Isaac Alfasi, and that Maimonides lavishly praised Alfasi's great work, the *Halakhot*, calling his rulings "unassailable."

Then Maimonides goes on to ridicule the North African Jewish customs and beliefs regarding women:

Some of their *dayyanim* [rabbinical judges] believe and behave with regard to menstruating women as do the Beni Meos, a Muslim tribe which inhabits the lands of the Ishmaelites: they do not look at all upon the menstruating woman, and turn their eyes neither to her figure nor to her garments. Nor do they speak to her; and they even forbid to tread on the ground touched by her feet. Nor do they eat the hind quarter of animals, and they practice many more such things about which there would be much to say.[28]

In his well-known letter to the Jews of Lunel, Maimonides paints another very dim picture of the level of learning in the Jewish communities in Muslim lands—northwest Africa, Palestine, Syria, Yemen, and India.

After the exile, the Sephardi Jews who arrived in North Africa in considerable numbers, topped their obvious cultural and intellectual superiority to the native Jews by an attitude of haughtiness that the latter found hard to put up with.[29] Friction was frequent over customs, manners, and mores. In Tunisia it led to a serious split, known as the "Schism of the *Grana*." The *Grana* (i.e., Granadans) looked upon the *Touansa* (Tunisians) with the familiar derision displayed everywhere by the Sephardim toward outsiders. They referred to the *Touansa* as "the Turks with the black cap and the violet turban," and the latter, in their impotent rage, finally put pressure on the Bey of Tunis to expel the *Grana,* whom they described as "false Jews" and "wearers of the perruque," whose religious practices and unbounded conceit were offensive to the dignity of the Jews living under the protection of Islam. The *Grana* were actually expelled from the city and founded a new town near what is now the village of Mélassine. Their energy and ability brought them continued prosperity, which only contributed to the bad blood between them and the *Touansa*. In 1733 the French consul at Tunis remarked: "They hate each other with a perfect hate." Finally, in 1741 the heads of the two communities worked out a *modus vivendi*.[30]

It is tempting to speculate, in conclusion, on the origin of these specific Sephardi traits of pride, self-esteem, *grandezza,* haughtiness. As indicated in the beginning of this chapter, the readiest explanation is that it was one of the characteristics the Spanish Jews had absorbed from their Christian and Arab environment in the Iberian Peninsula. Ample historical data are available to show that pride in descent, in nobility, and in purity of family line was a highly emotion-laden value among the Muslims and the Christians as well as among the Jews in Spain in the centuries prior to the expulsion.[31] As far as the Muslims are concerned, they undoubtedly brought along this trait from the east, where it had been their characteristic feature at least since the days of Mohammed.[32] The pride of the Spanish *hidalgo* (literally "son of something"), let alone that of the grandee, is too well known to need more than mention. It was, therefore, from both of the dominant population elements of Spain that the Spanish Jews could have absorbed the trait of haughtiness, for which, in fact, their own spiritual leaders reproached them even prior to the exile.[33]

The conclusion that Sephardi pride is a reflection of Christian Spanish pride in particular is strengthened by the consideration of another Sephardi trait, this time an institutional one, which also seems to be derived from a Spanish prototype. I refer to the extreme rigidity and authoritarianism of the *ma'amad,* as the presidium of a congregation was called among the Sephardim. The *ma'amad* consisted of a very small number of congregational leaders, such as the president and the rabbis, and its powers were practically absolute. It made authoritive decisions on all congregational affairs and communal questions, and, beyond that, it had the right to scrutinize the religious conduct of each individual who lived within the territory of the congregation, to punish him for trespassing against the law (as laid down by the *ma'amad*), and to prosecute and discipline him for suspicion of heresy. The cases of Uriel Acosta and Spinoza in Amsterdam come readily to mind as illustrations of the last point, while the general rigidity of the *ma'amad* that led to wholesale defections from Judaism in the England of the early nineteenth century has been referred to previously.

Now it is almost inevitable that one should recognize in these powers and conduct of the *ma'amad* a reflection of the powers and conduct of the Spanish Inquisition, in the shadow of which the Jews lived from the early thirteenth century and whose

threat hung over those who remained in Spain after 1492 as
Marranos, as well as over those who migrated to the New World.
In Spain and Portugal the Catholic church had the power,
through the "Holy Office" of the Inquisition, to impose rigid
outward conformity with the rules and regulations of Catholicism upon every member of the Church, whether born into it or
forced to convert to it. The Jews suffered more from the
Inquisition than any other population element in Iberia, but at
the same time they willy-nilly internalized the unyielding
Catholic attitude toward religion as such to so great an extent
that the unquestioning, obedient acceptance of religious doctrine and ritual became the cornerstone of their own religious
life and remained such well into the nineteenth century.

The peculiar psychological mechanism of adopting traits of a
hated and feared adversary is known from other examples found
among both Jews and other peoples. To mention only one, the
Jews of France, at the very height of their persecution by the
Catholic Church in that country, held several rabbinical synods
at which they enacted numerous regulations; these synods were
nothing other than a Jewish counterpart of the Catholic local
and national councils held in France in the eleventh to thirteenth centuries.[34]

It thus appears that the Sephardi Jews retained Spanish
influences in areas very different from language: in character, in
attitudes, in communal life. For about 150 years after the
expulsion, the momentum of the excellence which was theirs,
coupled with the typically Spanish trait of pride and the
typically Spanish inquisitorial severity in controlling congregational life, not only carried them forward in all the countries of
their new settlement but sufficed to elevate them everywhere
into positions of preeminence. Then the momentum was lost,
inertia became inertness, and Sephardi Jewry gradually ground
to a standstill. The cultural inactivity was paralleled by a decline
in numbers. Today the once great and unique Sephardi division
of the Jewish people is in the process of merging, both ethnically and biologically, into the Ashkenazi majority all over the
world, while in Israel it fuses partly with the Ashkenazim and
partly with the Oriental Jews. In another generation or two
Sephardi Jewry will be a thing of the past.

15 THE ASHKENAZI JEWS

For the last three centuries Ashkenazi Jewry was not only numerically predominant in the entire Jewish Diaspora but was also the only truly active and creative element in it. The last significant historic movement that originated in Sephardi circles was the Messianic upheaval created by Shabbatai Zevi, which was discussed in the foregoing chapter. Thereafter, all the significant Jewish religious or intellectual movements were initiated by the Ashkenazi Diaspora and remained largely limited to it: the Hasidic movement of Rabbi Israel Ba'al Shem Tov (c. 1700–1760) of Miedzyboz, Podolia; the movement of its opponents, the *Mitnagdim,* who rallied around great Talmudists such as Rabbi Elijah of Vilna (1720–1797); the Haskala (Jewish Enlightenment), triggered by Moses Mendelsohn (1729–1786) of Berlin, which within a few decades put an end to the Jewish cultural isolation in the midst of the European world and had other fateful consequences for Ashkenazi Jewry; the assimilationist trend which engulfed major parts of the Central and Western European Jewish communities and led to their social integration into their host countries; the Science of Judaism that combined Jewish and European learning for a scholarly investigation of all aspects of Jewish life and letters; the religious reform movement which was begun by German rabbis in the early nineteenth century and soon claimed the adherence of sizable segments of the Ashkenazi Diasporas in Central and Western Europe and in America; the *Hibbat Zion* (Love of Zion) movement that started in 1882 among the Jews in the Russian Pale of Settlement and spread from there to other Ashkenazi communities; and the political Zionism of Theodor Herzl (1860–1904) which rapidly built up a world organization and resulted in 1948 in the establishment of the State of Israel. All these were great historic developments for world Jewry; all were

287

initiated and led by Ashkenazi Jews; in all of them, with the exception of Zionism, the participants were almost exclusively Ashkenazi Jews. The two other divisions of the Jewish people stood on the sidelines; no longer part of the mainstream of Jewish life, they knew little or nothing of these great waves of change that shaped and reshaped Jewish history.

Nor did the non-Ashkenazi Jews participate to any considerable extent in the great migration that brought some three million Ashkenazi Jews from Central and Eastern Europe to the Americas between 1881 and 1945. Although the earliest Jewish settlers in the New World were Sephardi Jews, and although again in recent decades some Jews from the Middle East have come to both North and South America, in the period of mass immigration only Ashkenazi Jews had the energy and the initiative, or were exposed to sufficient pressure, to embark on the long and frightening voyage to the Western Hemisphere. On the other hand, the non-Ashkenazi Diaspora—with the exception of the Yugoslavian, Italian, and Greek Jews and some of the Dutch—escaped the worst horrors of the Nazi holocaust: of the six million Jews killed by the Germans and their satellite henchmen, some 5,872,000 were Ashkenazi Jews, and only 128,000 were non-Ashkenazim.[1]

Franco-German Scholarship

In spite of the early presence of Jews in the area which subsequently was to become the domain of the Ashkenazi Diaspora, it was not until the tenth century that these Jews developed into a historically significant group. Rabbenu ("Our Master") Gershom ben Judah (960–1040) was largely responsible for transplanting Jewish scholarship from the Provence, which was part of the Sephardi orbit, to the Rhineland, which was Ashkenazi territory, thereby making the Ashkenazi division culturally independent of the Sephardim.

Once this breakthrough was accomplished, Ashkenazi talent in religious studies developed with astounding rapidity. Gershom himself, taking a leaf out of the book of the French Christian world in whose midst he lived, convened a synod in

Mayence (ca. 1000) which passed the famous *takkanot* (improvements or ordinances) that, their intrinsic value apart, for the first time gave an official and formal expression to Ashkenazi religious usage, as distinct from Sephardi. Of Gershom's *takkanot*, the prohibition of polygyny and of divorce without the wife's consent raised the status of the Ashkenazi woman high above that of her Sephardi sister (let alone that of the Oriental Jewess). The Talmudic academy that he founded and headed in Mayence, although the first of its kind in the Ashkenazi Diaspora, achieved such fame that students flocked to it from many countries. With Rashi (Solomon ben Isaac; 1040–1106), who was born in the year in which Gershom died and whose masters had been Gershom's pupils, Ashkenazi religious scholarship reached its zenith. The school Rashi founded at Troyes was unequaled in the field of exegesis carried on by Rashi's grandsons and the other Tosafists. Troyes became, not only a great center of Jewish learning in Western Europe, but also one of the main fountainheads of Jewish scholarship in Eastern Europe. Within a single century French Ashkenazi Jewry had come to outshine all other divisions of the Jewish people in the vital field of Biblical and Talmudic commentary, without which these prime sources of Jewish religion would have been inaccessible to all those who considered their study a basic religious duty. In the twelfth and thirteenth centuries the French masters found their equals in the German Jewish haggadists, moralists, and mystics, of whom Rabbi Shimeon HaDarshan (c. 1150), R. Judah haHasid of Ratisbon (c. 1200), R. Eleazar of Worms (c. 1200), and R. Meir of Rothenburg (c. 1250) left behind the most impressive literary monuments.

The Khazars

While the Franco-German schools thus forged ahead, Eastern European Jewry still lagged behind. Although Jews lived in what is today Rumania and southern Russia since the early centuries of the common era (and, according to tradition, for many centuries earlier), the first significant historic movement in which they were instrumental was the conversion, about 740, of the Khazars, a semi-nomadic Turkic people whose country, Khazaria, was bounded by the Caucasus in the south, the Black Sea in the west, the River Don and roughly the fiftieth parallel in the north, and the Ural River in the east. The Khazar ruler, the Khaqan, at first, accepted a modified Judaism; then in about 800, he fully accepted Rabbinic Judaism. For more than two centuries Judaism was the religion of the ruling class while other religions, notably Islam, but also Christianity, were extensively practiced among the people. After Khazaria's power was broken by the Russians in 965, Khazar groups survived for another three centuries, and then completely disappeared from the stage of history.[2]

The Rise of Polish Jewry

In contrast to the Spanish Jews who, as we saw, divided their attention and talents between the Jewish religious field and the secular world of their Christian or Muslim environment, the Ashkenazi Jews were cut off from participation in public life and withdrew entirely into their own religious and traditional world. It is indeed nothing short of remarkable to what extent the Ashkenazi Jews managed to isolate themselves from the surrounding gentile society and culture, and to build an entire intellectual world of their own which had nothing in common with its Christian surroundings except on the lowest level of popular beliefs and practices.

Such a complex phenomenon as cultural self-isolation usually has not one but several motivations; but one of them undoubtedly was the great hostility evinced by the host peoples. During the Crusades the Jewish communities in the Franco-German area were repeatedly the victims of large-scale massacres. Entire communities, such as those of Treves, Speyer, Worms, Mayence, and Cologne, were slain. These atrocities were followed by accusations of ritual murder, of poisoning wells (at the time of the Black Death, 1348-49), and of treason (in connection with the Mongol inroads), which in turn led to more killings, burnings, and expulsions. No comparable large-scale Jewish massacres were ever perpetrated in Spain, certainly not by the

290

Muslims, and not even by the Christians. These events resulted in the great Jewish migration from West-Central Europe to the Slavic lands, where the refugees from the West encountered the remnants from the East, mingled with them, and, within a short time, culturally absorbed them.

The same series of traumatic events precipitated an equally great psychological movement involving Jewish withdrawal from the gentile environment, concentration on inner-Jewish interests, and fostering of traditional Jewish values to the point of total absorption in them. When the external world was hostile, cruel, and often deadly, the only available security was the psychological one to be found in self-isolation in the ghetto, with Tora study as the core and meaning and purpose of life. This new form of Jewish life, which emerged in the thirteenth century in Eastern Europe, was carried back in subsequent centuries to Central and Western Europe, and some elements of it were transplanted in the late nineteenth century to America. Thus it came about that the atmosphere and the mentality of Eastern European big-city ghetto and *shtetl* life became diffused over most of the Diaspora and became identified, in the eyes of both Jews and gentiles, with the essence of Jewish life in general.

However, to go back to the thirteenth century, the rulers of Poland were not slow to recognize the advantages that would accrue to their country—a rather underdeveloped agricultural land at the time—from a settlement of Jews who were known for their commercial and financial skills. It was primarily this economic self-interest that prompted the Polish kings in the thirteenth and fourteenth centuries to issue charters of privileges to the Jews, thus affording them protection against both the jealousy of the Christian merchants (who were mostly German) and the anti-Semitism of the Church.

It did not take long for the Jews to establish themselves in the economy of Poland, although the economic basis of their existence remained a limited one throughout. But it took almost three centuries before they attained that minimal standard of prosperity which was necessary for the emergence of some individuals who could devote themselves to intellectual endeavors and achieve distinction in them. When that level was finally reached, the only intellectual pursuit engaged in was the *halakha*—that is, the study of the Talmud from the religio-legal point of view.

It was thus not until the sixteenth century that there appeared in Poland the first great Talmudic-halakhic scholars, whose work resulted in a definite shift of Ashkenazi religio-intellectual hegemony from the Franco-German to the Slavic area. Foremost among the sixteenth-century rabbis who were outstanding in laying the foundations of that quality which secured the undisputed first place in the world for the Eastern European schools of Tora study were R. Shalom Shakhna (1500–1558) of Lublin, R. Solomon Luria (1510–1573) of Posen, and R. Moshe Isserles (1520–1572) of Cracow. The last named we have met already, so that we know that it was by means of his emendations to the *Shulhan 'Arukh* that this final religio-legal code of the Sephardim gained acceptance among the Ashkenazim as well, thereby producing an overall unification of Jewish ritual with the preservation of no more than two subvarieties—the Sephardi and the Ashkenazi.

The Kahal

The rise of Polish Ashkenazi Jewry coincided with the rise of Sephardi predominance in North Africa, Turkey, and Western Europe. But while the latter was a short-lived phenomenon that soon showed signs of exhaustion, the Jews in Poland and the contiguous countries of Eastern Europe remained the undisputed leaders of world Jewry in all areas of religious life for the next three centuries. A considerable share of this development must be attributed to the powerful community organization known as the *Kahal* that was created by Eastern European Jewry.

We shall recall that, beginning with the tenth century, French Jewry had its rabbinical synods for the purpose of settling religio-legal issues. Those early French Jewish synods were the example followed by sixteenth-century Polish Jews in establishing their own provincial or countrywide councils. But while the

French gatherings were *ad hoc* affairs, called together at the initiative of individual rabbis at indefinite intervals, the Polish councils developed into permanent organizations that met regularly and functioned as a quasi-governmental body expressive of a large measure of internal Jewish autonomy.

The most important of these Eastern European Jewish community organizations was the "Council of Four Lands"—i.e., Great Poland (capital: Posen), Little Poland (capital: Cracow), Polish Russia (Podolia, and Galicia with its capital Lemberg-Lwow), and Volhynia (capital: Ostrag or Kremenetz). From the mid-sixteenth to the mid-eighteenth century this *Va'ad Arba' Aratzot,* as it was termed in Hebrew, was the central body of Jewish autonomy in Poland, a veritable religio-political parliament, that met regularly twice a year, issued decisions and decrees, tried civil and criminal cases, imposed penalties, and kept records. Its important legislative, administrative, juridical, and spiritual-cultural functions came to an end in 1764, when the Polish Diet ordered Jewish general congresses to be discontinued.[3]

Eastern European Talmudism

Of great significance were the religious developments in Eastern European Jewry in the two centuries during which the *Va'ad* functioned as its effective government. For one thing, the Yeshivot or Talmudic academies multiplied to the point where most of the male Jewish population was learned in Rabbinics, which meant that, in addition to their Yiddish vernacular, they knew Hebrew and Aramaic, and were adept at dealing with dialectic problems (the so-called *pilpul*). As Salo W. Baron remarked, "for a long time almost all Jewish youths received a type of education roughly similar to that of the Christian clergy."[4]

However, Eastern European Jewry not only was a literate, educated, and intellectual element in the midst of a largely illiterate and culturally deprived general population; it also had higher moral standards that found expression in such forms as mutual aid institutions, charity, a low incidence of criminality, and a markedly better position for its women. The inevitable concomitant of these differences was a Jewish opposition or even hostility to secular learning, associated as the latter was in the eyes of the Jews with a gentile ethos whose manifestations were repugnant to them. This attitude contributed to the self-isolation of the Jews from the affairs and interests of the gentile environment. In sharp contrast to the Sephardi Jews, who in their heyday were among the leading statesmen, diplomatists, philosophers, scientists, mathematicians, astronomers, navigators, physicians, etc., of Spain, North Africa, and Egypt, the Eastern European Jews (with a very few notable exceptions) considered interest in all realms of non-Jewish intellectual endeavor as *un-Jewish* and therefore prohibited. Even the reading of books other than the Bible, the Talmud, the codes, and the Midrashim was strictly forbidden, and has remained so to this day in those circles in which the Eastern European Yeshiva tradition survives. Woe to the Yeshiva student who was caught reading Maimonides' great work of Jewish religious philosophy, *The Guide of the Perplexed* (which was available in a Hebrew translation prepared by Samuel ibn Tibbon from the Arabic original about 1190), although the *Mishne Tora,* the code of religious law written by the same Maimonides, was part of the usual Yeshiva curriculum.

In this atmosphere of concentration on Talmudic learning it was a rare Jew indeed who found in himself the audicity to break out of the "four cubits of the *halakha*" and engage in secular studies or pursuits. Yet we know of a Viennese Jewish physician named Jacob who settled in Posen after the expulsion of the Jews from Vienna in 1670, became the physician of the Posen Jewish community, sent his son to study medicine in Padua (where he himself had studied), and was succeeded by the latter. A grammarian, Isaac ben Samuel Halevi, a philosopher, Solomon Ashkenazi, and a mathematician, Elijah of Pinczow, were among the few other Jews in seventeenth-century Poland known to have engaged in non-halakhic intellectual pursuits. A few others, such as Mordecai Jaffe (1530–1612), author of *L'vush* ("Garment"), a law code that, had it not been for the *Shulhan 'Arukh,* would have been accepted as authoritative by Ashkenazi Jewry, were versed in secular sciences but resorted to them only for the purpose of utilizing them for their halakhic studies.

Times of Troubles

The seventeenth century was a time of unusual troubles even for trouble-tried Eastern European Jewry. From the early sixteenth century on the Kabbala had become entrenched in the world of Polish rabbinism. The greatest Polish rabbinical scholars, such as Solomon Luria, Moshe Isserles, and Mordecai Jaffe studied it and were influenced by it. By the seventeenth century the study of the Lurianic Kabbala was considered an organic part of rabbinical training. While thus practically all the Polish rabbis became Kabbalists, and many of them wrote Kabbalistic works, the latter were, by and large, mediocre, with the possible exception of the writings of the Shabbatian Jonathan Eybeschutz (1690–1764) and his opponent Jacob Emden (1697–1776), both rabbis of Altona, Germany.

The popularity of the Kabbala was one of the two main factors that predisposed Eastern European Jewry for becoming caught up in the pseudo-Messianic movement of Shabbatai Zevi. The other was the Cossacks' uprising that culminated in the large-scale persecution, torture, and massacre of the Jews under Bogdan Chmielnicki and other Cossack and Haidamak leaders in the decade of 1648 to 1658. The whole of Eastern Europe, including White Russia, Lithuania, the Ukraine, Poland, and Galicia, was buffeted by relentless waves of violence. More than three hundred Jewish communities were massacred and sacked, and more than half a million Jews perished, either by the sword or by the plague that simultaneously decimated the entire area. In Polish Ukraine, Volhynia, and Podolia only one tenth of the Jewish population remained; the other nine tenths either perished or sought refuge by emigrating to countries in which the Jews stood a somewhat better chance to survive, such as Lithuania, Poland proper, and Western Europe. A few years later the news about the Messiah of Smyrna reached the still smoldering ruins of the Eastern European Diaspora.

According to an old Jewish tradition, the advent of the Messiah was to be preceded by the "war of Gog and Magog" in which untold numbers of Jews were to perish. The claim of Shabbatai Zevi that he was the long-awaited Messiah led the Eastern European Jews, suffused as they were with Kabbalistic thinking, to interpret the Cossack massacres as the suffering that it was believed the Jewish people would have to experience at the onset of the Messianic age. On the other hand, the appearance of Shabbatai Zevi following the "wars of Gog and Magog" was considered an indication that the Messianic era had dawned and that he himself actually was the long-expected Son of David.

The short period of Shabbatian enthusiasm was followed by the bitter humiliation and disillusionment of many, and by the refusal of some to give up their faith in him. Among the latter there were those who continued to worship him as the "hidden Messiah," and handed down this belief to disciples as late as the eighteenth century. They formed numerous sects whose doctrines and practices placed them at varying distances from orthodox Judaism. In 1759 the adherents of one of these sects, founded by Jacob Frank (born in Podolia about 1726; died in Offenbach, Germany, 1791), took the fateful step of group conversion to Christianity, duplicating thereby the group conversion to Islam of Shabbatai Zevi's adherents in Turkey in 1666.

Hasidism

While these minor Shabbatian or semi-Shabbatian sects disturbed the unity of orthodox rabbinical Judaism in Eastern Europe, it remained for another outgrowth of Kabbalistic mysticism to cause a serious disruption threatening to lead to a schism the like of which Judaism had never before experienced in the course of its long history. This new religious development, which, incidentally, was the only major original contribution of Eastern European Ashkenazi Jewry to the historical transformations of the Jewish faith, was Hasidism.

Hasidism grew out of the Kabbalistic movement and doctrine.

But while the Kabbala conquered major parts of all the three divisions of the Jewish people, Hasidism never gained a foothold outside the Eastern European half of the Ashkenazi world.

Within that Diaspora, however, Hasidism completely supplanted Kabbalism; there remained no Kabbalists who were not Hasidim, so that Kabbalism and Hasidism became synonymous. Among the Central and Western European Jews there were neither Kabbalists nor Hasidim, except for those who migrated from Eastern Europe and settled in the West. As to America, it was not until the rise of Nazism that Hasidic Jews came to this continent in sufficient numbers to establish congregations of their own. Among the Sephardi and Oriental Jews, Kabbala in its pure form, primarily Lurianic Kabbala, continued to be popular; Hasidism either never reached them or, at any rate, never touched them. While Hasidism thus remained essentially a phenomenon of the Slavonic Diaspora, its emergence and rapid spread in Eastern Europe is one of the most remarkable chapters in Jewish history.

In the seventeenth and early eighteenth centuries there were in Eastern Europe numerous rabbis as well as other, semi-learned Jews who catered to the susceptibilities of their more ignorant co-religionists by supplying them with amulets and talismans, administering popular medication, exorcising demons, invoking spirits, and the like. The decline in Talmudic learning, the belief in the so-called "practical Kabbala," the trauma of the mid seventeenth-century massacres and other horrors, and the despair following the Shabbatian debacle—all this contributed to the proliferation of these magic practitioners. The generic name by which they were referred to was *Ba'al Shem*, "Master of the Name" (i.e., of God), because they were believed to perform their magic miracles with the help of divine names over which they had acquired mastery.[5]

While the center of Ba'al-Shemism was in Eastern Europe, where *Ba'ale Shem* (plural of *Ba'al Shem*) continued to function and flourish down to the twentieth century, several of these miracle men lived and worked in the West: in Vienna, in Germany, and even in Worms (e.g., Gedalia Ba'al Shem, who died between 1622 and 1624). However, in the West they never managed to achieve anything approximating the popularity they enjoyed in the East.

It was as such a Ba'al Shem that the founder of Hasidism, Rabbi Israel Ba'al Shem Tov ("Master of the Good Name" or "Good Master of the Name," 1700–1760), usually referred to by the initials of his name, Besht, began his career. It was not until 1740, when he was forty years old, that the Besht began to expound his new teachings in Miedzyboz, Podolia. Like a true religious founder, he himself wrote nothing; it was his disciples who memorized, wrote down, and published his sayings, stories, and other teachings, as had been the case with Isaac Luria two centuries earlier. Also, and again like in the case of other true religious founders, the key to the phenomenal spread of his doctrine, Hasidism, all over the Eastern European Diaspora must be sought primarily in the personality of the Besht. As Solomon Schechter put it, "To the Chassidim Baalshem . . . was the incarnation of a theory and his whole life the revelation of a system."[6]

While without the Kabbala there could have been no Hasidism, it is significant that the Besht was opposed, not only to Shabbatianism, but also to Lurianic Kabbala which emphasized asceticism and mortification of the spirit. In contrast, he stressed the importance of serving God with joy, of loving Him and surrendering oneself to Him with enthusiasm (Hebrew, *Hitlahavut*). His key concept was *d'vekut,* "cleaving," a state one achieves when one gives up the consciousness of separate existence and joins oneself to the eternal being of God. In this pantheistic-mystical concept of God and the universe, in which we recognize a certain similarity with Buddhist teachings, great importance is attached to the ideal man who, as the Besht expressed it, "is to be a revelation himself, clearly to recognize himself as a manifestation of God." This man is the *Tzaddik* (the "saintly" or "pious one") who forms a connecting link between creator and creation. (Mary, we are reminded, was considered in some Catholic schools of thought to be the neck, the mediatrix, connecting between the head, God, and the body, the Church.) It was this centrality of the *Tzaddik* in Hasidic doctrine that soon led to the breakup of the movement into numerous subsects, each centered around a miracle-working saintly rabbi, called *Tzaddik*. In the nineteenth century, Hasidism degenerated into Tzaddikism with competing dynasties of *Tzaddik*-saints, ensconced in their luxurious "courts," and with all the overtones of saint-worship as known from the Jewish and Muslim Middle East.

The Mitnagdim

No sooner did Hasidism begin its conquest of the Eastern European Diaspora than opposition to it arose, especially in the north, in Lithuania and its vicinity, inhabited by a Jewry that was more hardheaded, more rational, more logical, sharper, colder, and tougher than the Jews of the south, of Poland, Galicia, the Carpathians. Before long, Eastern European Jewry was split into two hostile camps, that of the Hasidim, and that of their opponents, the *Mitnagdim*. The complaints of the Mitnagdim against the Hasidim were many: the Hasidim played down the importance of Tora study, which was the lifeblood of Ashkenazi Jewry; by negating the value of Talmudic study they also negated, or were suspected of negating, the importance of observing all the minutiae of the Law for which painstaking study was a prerequisite. They deviated from old-established custom by importing the "Sephardi" prayer book of Isaac Luria and following its *nusah* in their services. They attributed superhuman powers to their *Tzaddikim,* unheard of in Ashkenazi Judaism since the close of the Talmudic period. They emphasized serving God with joy—often helped along by inbibing strong spirits—a most regrettable approximation of the ugly, and to the Jews often frightening, gentile custom of drunkenness. All this made the Hasidim so repugnant to the Mitnagdim that, especially in the north, the latter felt constrained to take firm action.

In 1772 the *Kahal* (council) of Vilna, with the approval of Elijah ben Solomon, known as the "Gaon of Vilna" (1720–1797), arrested the local Hasidic leaders and excommunicated the adherents of the sect. A few years later (1781) the Council of Zelva (Grodno governorate) ordered the faithful to expel the

Hasidim from every Jewish community, to regard them as members of another faith, to have no intercourse with them, not to intermarry with them, nor bury their dead. However, even this was not considered enough, and, still before the end of the century, the Mitnagdim resorted to the un-Jewish measure of denouncing the Hasidim to the Russian government as dangerous agitators and teachers of heresy. Some arrests were made, but, by and large, the Russians found no fault with the Hasidim, who thus came to no harm.

By the early nineteenth century the Mitnagdim ceased their useless struggle against the Hasidim; the two groups, often organized in two separate congregations in the same township, learned to live side by side, and even began to intermarry. At this time about half of the Jewish population of Eastern Europe (Russia, Poland, Galicia, Hungary, and Rumania) were Hasidim, the other half Mitnagdim.

The Haskala

This twofold division of the East European Ashkenazim soon gave way to a threefold one. The new movement that, from the early nineteenth century, began to make inroads into the ranks of both Hasidim and Mitnagdim, was that of the Haskala, the Jewish Enlightenment which we discussed earlier in a different context. The Haskala began in Central Europe in the late eighteenth century and, in general terms, it advocated the abandonment of Jewish cultural isolationism in favor of the acquisition of the knowledge, manners, and aspirations of contemporary Europe, and primarily those of the German lands. In Germany itself a large proportion of the early *Maskilim* ("enlighteners") became, within one generation, assimilationist, and in many instances converted to Christianity.

When the Haskala first penetrated Eastern Europe, both the Hasidim and the Mitnagdim sensed the danger it represented, and both engaged in a struggle against it. While one cannot say that the Hasidim and Mitnagdim joined forces against the Maskilim, it is certainly true that the fight against the Haskala made the Hasidim and the Mitnagdim practically cease their struggle against each other and diverted all their attention to the new common enemy. For a while it seemed as if the Haskala could make no headway in the face of the opposition it encountered. But by the middle of the nineteenth century it had become clear to all that the Maskilim had managed to penetrate the strongholds of both Mitnagdic conservatism and studiousness and Hasidic enthusiasm and Tzaddikism, and that there were now, not two, but three categories of Jews in Eastern Europe who had to learn to live with one another, if not peacefully, at least without active infighting.

The Science of Judaism

Following the rise of the Haskala, the center of Jewish creativity again shifted from Eastern to Central Europe, dominated by German culture. It was here that, in the wake of the Enlightenment, the next two important Jewish religious and intellectual developments took place: the births of the *Wissenschaft des Judentums* ("Science of Judaism") and of the Jewish religious Reform movement.

For centuries Jewish learning in all parts of the Diaspora had been centered on *halakha*—i.e., the study of the Law, for the double purpose of being able to obey all its minutiae and to apply it to changing conditions in new eras and new countries. Even Kabbalism never broke away from the study of the Talmud and *halakha* as the central concern in Jewish life. Especially for the Eastern European Jews the study of the Kabbala was merely an added facet of traditional halakhic studies as manifested by the fact that the same rabbinic authors who wrote halakhic and codificatory works also wrote Kabbalistic treatises, and that Kabbala, in the two centuries preceding the emergence of Hasidism, was part and parcel of rabbinic studies.

With the rise of Hasidism there emerged a definitely new attitude toward Talmudic learning. Not that Hasidism had taught that Talmudic study was not a high value in itself; despite the accusations of the *Mitnagdim,* the Hasidim never took this position. What they did teach, however, was that simple Jews, who had to work hard in order to earn a living and therefore were unable to spare the many hours daily necessary to achieve a proficiency in Talmudic study, were not, because of this, relegated to a mean existence as *"am-ratzim"* (i.e., ignoramuses), than which there was no greater disgrace in the eyes of the *Mitnagdim.* On the contrary, such an uneducated Jew, with the guidance of his *Tzaddik,* could reach an emotional attachment to God, a *d'vekut,* that was dearer to God than the greatest Talmudic erudition. While Hasidism unquestionably made a breach in the bastion of Talmudic learning, it never dreamt of derogating the value of halakhic studies as such, and certainly never envisaged the possibility of substituting for it a new type of study patterned after the sciences in vogue in the gentile world.

Ever since the canonization of the Biblical books and down to the Haskala, all the literary production that was significant for the continued existence of the Jewish people was either exegetic (as exemplified by the work of Rashi, the Tosafists, and others), or codificatory (concluding with the *Shulhan 'Arukh*), or, in a combination of these two trends, annotatory (e.g., explanatory or emendatory notes appended to the *Shulhan 'Arukh*). Throughout those centuries Tora study, in its essence, was a continuing and concentrated effort at ascertaining God's will as understood by the authoritative religious leaders of all ages, and adapting it to the actual circumstances. In its most typical manifestation, that of the Polish Yeshiva of the sixteenth to nineteenth centuries, this study was so all-absorbing and all-demanding that it prevented intellectual curiosity from as much as glancing in any other direction. It is against this background that the true significance of the new departure represented by the Science of Judaism must be evaluated.

The very idea that the many works in the rich storehouse of Jewish literature can and should be studied from an objective, nonreligious, scholarly viewpoint, that they can be scrutinized in order to learn about the development of Jewish religion, philosophy, history, liturgy, and poetry, was nothing short of revolutionary. Just such a modern scientific study of the life and works of the Jewish people was made possible by the Jewish Enlightenment. Among the comparatively large number of young Jewish intellectuals who had mastered German and

302

familiarized themselves with the attainments of modern German scholarship and literature, there were several who were stimulated to apply the same scientific methods to Jewish studies. This is how the Science of Judaism was born.

Its founder was Leopold Zunz (1794–1886), a German Maskil, one of the earliest to receive both a Jewish and a secular education, who as a youth wrote Hebrew poetry, and after graduating from high school took up mathematical, philological, Biblical, and Semitic studies at Berlin University. In 1819 he was one of the founders of the Society for the Culture and Science of the Jews, and in 1822 launched the *Zeitschrift für die Wissenschaft des Judenthums (Journal for the Science of Judaism).* Ten years later he published his first major book, the *Gottesdienstliche Vorträge der Juden (Synagogal Lectures of the Jews),* which remained the most important Jewish study of the nineteenth century. The present context allows us neither to enumerate all the works of Zunz nor to list the other important early exponents of the Science of Judaism. Soon the new discipline spread to the east and to the west, and by the time Zunz died Jewish scholars in all parts of the Ashkenazi Diaspora were busily engaged in applying modern methods of historical and literary research to all areas of Jewish studies, or devising new approaches as required by the unique aspects of the life and history of the global Jewish dispersion.

The Reform Movement

The Reform movement in Jewish religion emerged in Germany simultaneously with the Science of Judaism. It began as an effort by enlightened German Jews with the relatively limited aim of improving and embellishing the Jewish synagogue service by an elimination of the many *piyyutim* (liturgical poems), the introduction of order and dignity, and the preaching of the sermons in German rather than in Yiddish. The budding Science of Judaism and the advent of young rabbis with both Jewish and secular academic educations before long contributed to the desire to introduce improvements into the contents and substance of the services as well.

Then the hope that the Jews would soon be granted emancipation and full equality led to the revision, or rather elimination, of certain traditional Jewish doctrines and tenets, such as the concept of exile, the expectation of the Messiah, the hope for the return to Zion and the restoration of the sacrificial service in the Temple, and the like. In the extreme form that Reform assumed in several newly organized congregations, it did away with the wearing of hats in the synagogues, introduced organs and women's choirs, changed the Sabbath morning service to Sunday morning gatherings, eliminated most of the Hebrew prayers, substituting "modernized" German prayers in their place, eliminated the traditional Jewish doctrine of the chosenness of Israel, and changed the name of the premises in which the services were held from synagogue to "temple." On the positive side, it emphasized morality and spiritual reliance on God, and accorded a central place to the "Jewish mission" doctrine according to which the God-given mission of Judaism was to live in dispersion in order to teach the nations of the world belief in the One God.

As far as individual Jewish conduct was concerned, Reform Judaism summarily discarded all the "practical" commandments (except circumcision) and abolished such appurtenances of worship as the *tallit* (prayer shawl) and the *t'fillin* (phylacteries). In general, it gave Jewish religion a distinctly gentile tinge. As its critics pointed out, Reform Judaism taught that Jews differed from gentiles in nothing but their religion, and that Reform Judaism differed from Christianity in nothing but its view of Jesus, whom the Christians considered the son of God and Reform Jews considered a Jewish prophet.

The first Reform temple was established in 1810 in Westphalia, which shortly before had come under French occupation. In 1815 a private Reform temple was founded in Berlin, in 1818 the Hamburg Temple was dedicated. In the ensuing years Reform spread to other German cities, and in the 1840s and 1850s, with the arrival of a wave of German Jewish immigrants in America, Reform was transplanted into the New World.

The reaction of the traditional Jews was what one would have expected. They tried to utilize all the means at their disposal to block Reform. As the Eastern European *Mitnagdim* had done two generations earlier when they appealed to the Russian government denouncing the Hasidim, so now the opponents of Reform appealed to the German government to prohibit Reform worship. For a while they succeeded in stopping the spread of the movement, but by about 1850 Reform temples had been established in many German cities, in Austria, Hungary, France, and Denmark, as well as in England and America.

The extent and degree of reforms introduced into their services by the various Reform congregations varied greatly and changed with time. In the United States, the only country in the world where at present a considerable proportion of the Jews are members of Reform congregations, a limited, but nevertheless distinct, return to certain traditional forms could be witnessed in the last two decades. Still, Reform Judaism differs from Orthodox and Conservative Judaism on many issues of doctrine and principle, and it represents a new departure in Jewish religious development, as did Kabbalism and Hasidism in previous centuries.

Assimilation

A few words must be said here of assimilation, another of those historic processes which the Ashkenazi Diaspora underwent in the nineteenth century. In general, Jewish historians give a largely negative evaluation to assimilation. They characterize it as a movement that "consciously strove (and still strives) for the elimination of the national, cultural, and ethnic characteristics of the Jews as a people" and that was "aimed at making Jews identical in everything except religion with the ruling majority group" in every country of the Diaspora.[7]

While one cannot deny the truth in these assessments of assimilation, one will do well not to lose sight of the historical context in which assimilation appeared, nor of the positive values it contained. As to the historical context, we must remember that nineteenth-century Jewish assimilation to German and other European (and American) cultures was but the last example of a long series of assimilationist trends that had emerged each time the Jews moved into the orbit of a culture they considered attractive. All the Jewish languages, beginning with Biblical Hebrew itself, were the products of assimilation (see Chapter VII, "The Languages of the Jews"). Many of the specific ethnic characteristics of each Jewish Diaspora were the products of assimilation. Without assimilation some of the greatest works produced by Jewish creativity in the last two thousand years could not have been written: we would have no Philo, no Josephus, no *Guide of the Perplexed,* and in all probability not even the *Zohar.* We certainly would have no Hebrew grammar, no Jewish historiography, no Jewish Biblical studies and archaeology, no Jewish elucidation of the development of Jewish religion, not to mention the by no means negligible contribution made by Jews to general literature, poetry, science, and many other fields of artistic, intellectual, scholarly, economic, and political endeavor. Without assimilation there would have been no Marx, no Freud, no Einstein, no Bergson.

Moreover, assimilation was an inevitable consequence of Enlightenment and emancipation—inevitable in that, once the Jews learned European languages and got acquainted with European culture, the historical circumstances allowed them no choice but to participate and take a share in their cultural environment. The same process had occurred at least twice before in the Jewish past: in Hellenistic times and in the Arab-Spanish Golden Age. Especially the second of these two assimilations is instructive, not only because it is nearer in time, but because it showed most clearly that it was possible for a Jewish Diaspora to live and excel in two worlds simultaneously—their own and that of the non-Jewish majority among whom they dwelt. The Spanish Jews were enlightened and assimilated (i.e., were full carriers of the Arab culture of the Iberian Peninsula) and they were emancipated (in the particular Muslim-Arab sense of the word), and yet continued faithful to their own religio-national culture.

Similarly, in the nineteenth century it seemed possible that the turn of the Ashkenazi Diaspora had finally come to achieve a positive and fruitful adjustment between Judaism and Western culture. The idea, in principle, was praiseworthy. Many, in fact, succeeded in striking a balance between the demands of the two worlds by making a selection of as many of the traits contained in each of the two cultural storehouses as suited them and as they found compatible with each other. Some thought they could reject everything the gentile cultural environment had to offer, and live a totally and exclusively Jewish traditional life. This, of course, proved an illusion. (Let us mention here in parentheses that it would be a fascinating anthropological exercise to subject such a group—e.g., the Satmarer Hasidim of Williamsburg—to a detailed cultural analysis; we could predict that such an analysis would find that they had adopted a large number of non-Jewish traits and that, therefore, they are far from being free of the taint of assimilation.) Others took the opposite position and turned their backs on Judaism. In these cases the opposite phenomenon could be observed: even a Jew who totally dissociated himself from Judaism by converting to another religion, and, beyond that, made a conscious effort to divest himself of the slightest residual survival of his Jewish past, nevertheless soon found that in the eyes of everybody who knew him he had remained a Jew, even if a converted one.

It certainly cannot be denied that one of the consequences of assimilation was to make it possible, and relatively easy, for a larger proportion of Jews to leave the fold and for their children or grandchildren to grow up as gentiles. Apostasy and flight from the beleaguered camp always occurred; now assimilation has made it both easier and more frequent. But to blame the Jewish Enlightenment and the emancipation for this is unwarranted. That assimilation today poses a greater threat to Jewish survival in the Diaspora than ever before cannot be denied. Fortunately, Ashkenazi Jewry, against which this threat was and is primarily directed, was still vital enough in the late nineteenth century to counter it with a totally new movement that inscribed Jewish national survival on its banner. This movement was political Zionism.

Zionism

All the Ashkenazi historical movements that we have discussed so far had one thing in common: they originated in the Ashkenazi Diaspora, spread within the Ashkenazi Diaspora, and remained largely confined to the Ashkenazi Diaspora. Hasidism

307

remained a distinctly Eastern European movement. Haskala had a wider diffusion, but barely touched the Sephardi Diaspora for which, in any case, it was not a significant innovation since the Sephardim had never cut themselves off from the secular culture of their environment as had the Ashkenazim. Assimilation, although not unknown in Sephardi history, never assumed in it the dimensions of a mass movement as it did in the Ashkenazi Diaspora from the nineteenth century on. The only non-Ashkenazi Jewish community that followed the Ashkenazi lead into various fields of the Science of Judaism was the Italian. Reform remained on the whole a Central and Western European movement; it was brought by German Jews to America where only Ashkenazi Jews joined it. With Zionism, however, the case was different: although it began as a distinctly Ashkenazi movement, before long it awakened the interest of the Sephardi and Oriental Jews as well and gained adherents also among them.

What I mean by terming Zionism a distinctly Ashkenazi movement is that without the specific Ashkenazi background, Ashkenazi historical developments, and Ashkenazi experiences that preceded it, political Zionism could neither have been conceived nor have won for its aims an increasing proportion of the Ashkenazi Diaspora. This is not to say that Zionism had no deep historic roots common to all the three Jewish divisions. The longing for a Messianic redemption and a return to Zion, together with the deeply embedded religious belief in the ultimate realization of this two-thousand-year-old dream were shared by all Jewish Diasporas (with the sole exception, in Herzl's day, of the Reform Jews in Western Europe and America). Without this longing and belief, a political scheme to build a national home for the Jewish people in Palestine would have found no echo among the Jewish masses. But given this psychological, historical, and religious readiness, the Zionist movement could still not have emerged had as much as a single one of the Ashkenazi developments of the preceding hundred years remained unrealized.

Without the Haskala, a man of outstanding talent such as Theodor Herzl (1860–1904) would have become a great rabbinical leader; he could never have studied in a secular high school, and at a university; would have spoken Yiddish only and would never have mastered the languages in which he was fluent— Hungarian, German, French, English; would never have had a chance to obtain a legal education, and beyond it a familiarity with the political thought of Europe, with the ideas of European nationalism, with problems of economy, with the intricacies and finesses of international diplomacy. Without being himself a product of assimilation, he would never have acquired that polish and charm which, coupled with his innate personal magnetism, were primary prerequisites for any man, let alone a young middle-class Jewish intellectual, to be received and listened to by the monarchs and masters of the great powers of his day. And, of course, neither Enlightenment nor assimilation would have been of much use had not those same powers just a few years previously granted emancipation to their Jewish subjects, which made them, officially at least, citizens equal before the law and which enabled some of them to occupy seats in parliaments and other national and local representative bodies.

The disciples of Herzl, his early followers and helpers, the growing numbers of the Zionist membership, all of them had to be preconditioned to a greater or lesser extent by the same events and processes that enabled him to become the founder and leader of an international Jewish political movement, the first of its kind in all Jewish history. Had Enlightenment and religious Reform not weakened the hold of orthodoxy over them, they would have rejected Herzl and his program, as the most tradition-bound elements in the Ashkenazi Diaspora actually did, and continued to do until the establishment of the State of Israel, and some even thereafter. Had they not been assimilated, at least to some extent, they simply would not have grasped the meaning of political organization, diplomatic action, and parliamentary procedure. Had the Science of Judaism not imparted to them as least some inkling of what historical process meant in relation to Jewish fate they would have been unable to understand the historical significance of the new movement. On the other hand, had Reform Judaism made greater headway, had it been able to persuade the bulk of the Ashkenazi Diaspora to accept its view of the Jewish religion, history, and mission, this would have rendered Herzl's call an echoless cry in a wilderness of indifference.

But all these "ifs" were not present. The Ashkenazi Diaspora, and it alone of the three major divisions of the Jewish people, was ready for Zionism. Although the response came slowly and hesitatingly at first, come it did, and the movement grew to embrace larger and larger segments of Ashkenazi Jewry, until it was strong enough to reach out to the other two divisions as well. That Zionism did extend an urgent invitation to Sephardi and Oriental Jews to join it was in keeping with the Herzlian idea of Zionism as a political movement of the Jewish people as a whole and of the Herzlian conception of national unity extending to all Jews irrespective of their ethnic backgrounds.

In this respect, as in numerous others, Herzlian Zionism differed significantly from its forerunner, the Hibbat Zion ("Love of Zion") movement, which had begun among Russian and Rumanian Jews and which remained confined throughout the fifteen years of its existence to small circles within a few Ashkenazi communities.

When Herzl organized his political Zionist movement in 1896, he quite naturally propagated his idea initially among those Jewish Diasporas with which he was personally acquainted: Austria, Hungary, Germany, France, England. The majority of the participants of the First Zionist Congress convened by Herzl in Basle in 1897 had come from Russia (63 participants), Germany (42), Austria (27), Switzerland (23), Galicia (19), France (12), England (11), and other Ashkenazi Diasporas. Nevertheless there were also a few Sephardim present: a lawyer, Premiado Romano from Philippopolis, Bulgaria; a journalist, Jacques Bahar, and his wife from Paris; a student, Moise Padua, from Montpellier; another student, Abraham Shalom Yahuda, from Jerusalem; and a physician, Dr. David Alcalay, and his wife from Belgrade.[8]

For many years after the first Zionist Congress, non-Ashkenazi participation in the movement remained extremely limited. The same was the situation with respect to actual immigration to Palestine: from 1882 to 1939 some 93 percent of all immigrants were Ashkenazi Jews, while the Sephardi and

Oriental Jews constituted only about 7 percent.[9] It almost looked as if the return to Zion and the building of a national home for the Jews in Palestine would remain largely an Ashkenazi affair.

Then came the Nazi genocide that reduced the number of Ashkenazi Jews in Europe by close to six million. Most of those who survived were in Soviet Russia, from where emigration was prohibited. The five million American Jews, although willing to come to the aid of the Zionist endeavor with money and political support (and both were desperately needed), were on the whole reluctant to leave their established positions in the United States for the hardships and spiritual satisfactions of a pioneering life in the Jewish national home. In England and France the situation was similar. This left a few hundred thousand survivors in displaced persons camps, and a million and a half Sephardi and Oriental Jews, as potential immigrants to Palestine. Consequently, when the State of Israel was established three years after the end of World War II, about two thirds of the immigrants who thereupon began to converge on Israel were Sephardi and Oriental Jews. Thus, as a result of the Zionist endeavor initiated by Ashkenazi Jews more than half a century earlier, major parts—sometimes whole communities—of the Sephardi and Oriental Jewish Diasporas were ingathered in the new Jewish State, reversing for the first time in two millennia the historical trend of Jewish dispersion.

In the following chapters we shall consider in some detail the five largest Ashkenazi Diasporas which, among them, account for more than 90 percent of all Ashkenazi Jews living outside the State of Israel: the Jewish communities of France, England, Soviet Russia, the United States and Argentina. It would be desirable, but within the context of a single volume obviously impracticable, to give similar consideration to all the other Diasporas that make up the Ashkenazi division of the Jewish people. The number of Ashkenazi (or primarily Ashkenazi) Diasporas is at present about 60.

16 THE ASHKENAZI JEWS: FRANCE

Early History

Historians assume that Jews first entered France not loo long after the conquest of Gaul by Julius Caesar (58–51 BCE). The earliest documents attesting to their presence, however, date only from the fourth century CE. Throughout its entire history the French Jewish community was always small; it is estimated that until the eighteenth century it never numbered more than a few thousands, and in the nineteenth a few tens of thousands at the utmost.

Beginning with the early Middle Ages, French Jewry comprised two distinct population elements—a northern, Ashkenazi, and a southern, Sephardi. Cultural excellence in French Jewry moved up from the south to the north, and by the high Middle Ages it produced some of the most outstanding Jewish scholars of all times. Among them were the greatest commentators of the Bible and the Talmud, Hebrew grammarians, codifiers of religious law, compilers of Hebrew dictionaries, translators from Arabic into Hebrew, mathematicians, astronomers, and philosophers.

Their rich historical background and the awareness of their great cultural attainments combined to infuse French Jewry with an elitistic attitude in relation to the Central and Eastern European Jews who began to arrive in France in larger numbers in the nineteenth century. While the French Jews escaped the extremes of haughtiness that often characterized the Sephardim in their contacts with Ashkenazim and Oriental Jews, their deportment toward those Jews who came from countries to the east of France was typically the same as the attitude of the German Jews to co-religionists who lived to the east of their country and whom they condescendingly termed *Ostjuden.*

As far as their experiences with France herself were concerned, the French Jews suffered neither less nor more persecution, discrimination, and oppression than did the Jews in other Christian countries. They were alternatingly tolerated, protected as agents ("court Jews") and physicians to princes and bishops, subjected to restrictions, forced to convert to Christianity, expelled (as in 1182, 1306, and 1394), allowed to return, exploited, granted privileges, compelled to wear the Jew-badge, attacked and massacred (as during the Crusades), accused of ritual murder and of poisoning the wells, and burned at the stake. At times their holy books were burned. And even when not in danger of life or limb, not infrequently they had to suffer cruel humiliation, as in Toulouse in the ninth to the eleventh centuries, when it was customary for the count of the city to slap the face of the head of the Jewish community as part of the annual Good Friday celebrations.

The seventeenth century saw, in general, an improvement in the position of French Jews, so that the Marranos of southern France felt encouraged to return openly to their ancestral faith. But not until 1784 was the head tax removed from the Jews of Alsace, where more than half of the forty thousand French Jews lived at the time.

The French Revolution (1789) was accompanied by at least one anti-Semitic demonstration that occurred in Alsace. In 1791 equal rights of citizenship were granted to those French Jews who were ready to take the oath of citizenship. Napoleon convened a Jewish Assembly of notables in 1806, and a "Grand Sanhedrin" in 1807, and in 1808 he decreed that all French Jews must assume last names—a law that was preceded by a similar one in Austria-Hungary by some two decades. It was not until 1818 that the law of equal rights for Jews came into force in all France, and only in 1831 was Jewish religion recognized as equal before the law with other religions. The "Jewish oath," the last remnant of Jewish civil inequality, was removed in 1846.

Contributions to French Culture

Once all the legal disabilities had been lifted from the shoulders

314

of the French Jews, many of them threw themselves with extraordinary energy into the mainstream of French life, and, within an unparalleled short period, they rose to the top ranks in French literature, journalism, the arts, the sciences, the legal profession, the army, and all other fields of intellectual, economic, and business endeavors. Great Jewish actresses, such as the tragedienne Rachel (1820–1858) and Sarah Bernhardt (1845–1923), as well as actors were among the most celebrated stars of the Paris stage, and assured success to plays written by Jewish playwrights. Jewish composers of serious and light opera, concert, and other types of music were acclaimed. Before the nineteenth century drew to a close, a Jew, Henri Bergson (1859–1941), was recognized as the foremost French philosopher, and another, Emile Durkheim (1838–1915), as the most outstanding French sociologist. Marcel Proust (1871–1922), considered by many the greatest figure in modern French literature, was the son of a Jewish mother. The name of Adolphe Crémieux (1796–1880), a highly respected political leader, has been mentioned earlier several times. Jewish financiers such as Baron Maurice de Hirsch (1831–1896) and Baron Edmond de Rothschild (1845–1934) made important contributions to the development of the French economy. And even in painting and sculpture, fields from which the Jews had been barred by their own traditional religious restrictions, French Jewish talent suddenly burst into bloom. No wonder that, faced with such a record of achievement, French Jewry felt that it was *arrivé* in every sense of the word, that it had become part and parcel of French life, and that its talented sons and daughters were among the foremost carriers, representatives, and advancers of the great, unique, and precious French culture.

Anti-Semitism and Immigration

The reaction on the part of non-Jewish France was not long in coming. To see the Jews, who only a few short years before had not even been full-fledged citizens of the Republic, competing with them in all, and outdoing them in several, fields of achievement which were traditionally their pride, was too much for many Frenchmen to take placidly. As in the other countries where similar processes had taken place (Germany, Austria, and Hungary come most readily to mind), anti-Semitism stirred in the heart of many a French patriot. The last decade of the nineteenth century witnessed the agitations of Edouard Drumont, Viau, and others, and saw the Dreyfus Affair, which was celebrated by the crowds on the streets of Paris with cries of *"Mort aux Juifs."* To what extent French anti-Semitism was influenced by the rise of anti-Semitism in Germany after 1880 is a moot question. But the fact remains that anti-Semitic books, pamphlets, and newspapers made their appearance in France beginning with the mid 1880s, and a National Anti-Semitic League of France was founded. The Dreyfus trial ended with the Jewish captain's conviction, and despite Emile Zola's spirited *J'accuse,* which was published in 1898, it was not until 1906 that Dreyfus was finally exonerated. Especially the royalist and clerical circles and the army provided fertile soil for the seed of anti-Semitism, while, on the other hand, the republicans used the Dreyfus case as a catalyst in their struggle against these reactionary forces.

In the meantime the number of Jews in France increased, temporary fluctuations notwithstanding. Due to the efforts of Adolphe Crémieux, the Jewish Minister of Justice in the French regime of national security, French citizenship was given to 40,000 Algerian Jews in 1870. This was followed within one year by a decrease of the number of French Jews by 30,000 when France had to cede Alsace-Lorraine to Germany. Thus after the Peace of Frankfurt (1871), the number of French Jews (including the Algerian Jews) was about 90,000. The Russian pogroms of 1903 to 1905 were followed by a sizable influx of Russian and other Eastern European Jews to France, so that by 1910 the number of Jews in France and Algeria reached 200,000.

The patriotic deportment of French Jewry in World War I is illustrated by many examples. No less than six thousand of them gave their lives for the country, to which many of them or their parents had immigrated only a few years previously. In the interwar period Jewish immigration to France continued and increased. First they came from Eastern Europe, many to study in

316

the famous French universities; then, after the rise of Hitler in 1933, many more came from Germany. No sooner had these arrived and settled down than an old historic experience of the Jewish Diaspora repeated itself: the increase in the number of Jews brought about an increase in anti-Semitism. Following unrest at the universities, restrictions against the Jewish students were put into effect, and soon Paris was once again the scene of anti-Semitic demonstrations (1935). A year later, the immigration of aliens (mostly Jews) was made subject to controls, and just before the outbreak of World War II it was severely curtailed. Nevertheless, some 150,000 Jews managed to enter France in the two interwar decades, either legally or illegally, and all succeeded in finding livelihoods, mostly in artisanship and small trade. Nor did the measures designed to reduce the influx of foreign Jews into France affect the position of the French Jews themselves, whose participation, and not infrequently leadership, in many aspects of French economic, cultural, and political life continued.

French-Jewish Scholarship

As in other countries in which the Jewish community found itself in a friendly environment, so in France as soon as the Jews had acquired the tools of the local variety of European civilization, they began to utilize them for the enrichment of their own traditional culture. In neighboring Germany this trend found its most significant expression in the emergence of the *Wissenschaft des Judentums,* the scholarly investigation of Jewish religion, history, philosophy, and traditions. In France the same endeavor led to the launching of several scholarly journals in which Jewish *savants* could discuss such subjects in the French language and thereby demonstrate their ability to apply the methods and approaches of French scholarship to the varied fields of Jewish research. The *Archives Israélites* was founded in 1840, to be followed in 1844 by *L'Univers Israélite,* and in 1880 by *La Revue des Etudes Juives* which to this day is the leading French Jewish scholarly publication.

The Alliance Israélite Universelle ───────────────

Even before Crémieux's efforts for Algerian Jewry, the idea that the well-established French Jewish community has a moral and humanitarian obligation to help its less fortunate brethren in other countries, and especially in Eastern Europe and in Muslim lands, expressed itself in the foundation of the Alliance Israélite Universelle (1860), the first, and for many years the most important, organization of its kind. In Eastern Europe the main activity of the Alliance consisted in facilitating and organizing the emigration of Jews from those lands of Jewish plight to countries in which the prevailing liberal atmosphere promised them a life of freedom and dignity. In the Muslim countries of the Middle East and North Africa the Alliance established an impressive network of schools, which greatly improved the life and lot of the local Jewish communities by raising them above the generally low educational level of the Muslim majority. This activity of the Alliance continues to this day in those countries in which there still is a Jewish community, notably in Morocco, Tunisia, Lebanon, Syria, and Iran, as well as in Israel. (In 1969–70 the Alliance schools in these countries still had a total of 19,570 pupils.[1])

Assimilation ────────────────────────────────

It is a remarkable fact that a Jewish community which for over one hundred years could sustain an unflagging effort to impart a Jewish and French education to Jewish children in the Muslim world should have neglected the Jewish educational needs of its own young generation. To speculate on the causes of this neglect would be intriguing but futile. The fact is that the children of both the established French-Jewish sector and the newly arrived immigrants from still largely tradition-bound Eastern Europe received in France no Jewish education to speak of, and that, consequently, the assimilation of the Jews to the French culture and way of life was rapid and almost total.

In this respect the fact that in the two interwar decades France was the center of numerous large international Jewish organiza-

318

tions active in the political field and in social work made little difference. Paris was the seat of the *Comité des Délégations Juives,* originally set up to represent Jewish interests at the Paris Peace Conference of 1919, but subsequently given a permanent character. The American Jewish Joint Distribution Committee, the largest aid organization ever created and maintained by the Jewish people, established its European headquarters in Paris, as did the ORT, OSE, HICEM, and other Jewish welfare organizations.

Thus France, and in particular Paris, developed into the hub of a huge, multipronged effort organized by that part of the Jewish people which had the ability to give and to help, for the benefit of that part which was in need of such help in the areas of education, civil rights, economic support, medical aid, and so on. French Jewry took a creditable part in this large-scale philanthropic work. Yet while all this was going on in France, the majority of French Jews knew little of it and remained almost completely unaffected by it. They lived their lives, pursued their economic interests, enjoyed their civil liberties, played their roles in various French cultural endeavors, and assimilated away cheerfully. Then came World War II, and soon thereafter the fall of France and the catastrophe.

World War II

It has been pointed out by historians of the holocaust that while the actual physical destruction of French Jewry by the Nazis and their French followers was not as extensive as that of other Jewish Diasporas located to the east of France, psychologically the blow suffered by the French Jews was more devastating because it fell without any advance warning or preparation. In Eastern Europe anti-Semitic agitation and excesses had been the order of the day for decades prior to the irruption of the Nazi war machine. In Central Europe, where the Jews had enjoyed a liberal breathing spell prior to World War I, the interwar period brought back anti-Semitic measures in a more and more intensive form in one country after another, beginning with the so-called White Terror in Hungary in 1919, and followed by the

Nuremberg Laws introduced in Germany soon after Hitler took power. These events and developments psychologically prepared the Jewish Diasporas in Eastern and Central Europe for the increasingly heavier blows that followed, just as they prepared the gentile populations of those countries to countenance, and even to support, more and more extreme measures taken against the Jews, until the "final solution" of mass extermination could be carried out with scarcely a voice raised in protest.

French Jewry did not have the advantage of being gradually inured in this manner to the horrors of Nazism. Until the fall of France in 1940, French Jews seemed to believe with deep conviction that anti-Semitism in their country was long dead and buried, that they were considered by their gentile fellow citizens as Frenchmen differing from them only in religious persuasion, and that they actually were part and parcel of the French people destined to share with them whatever triumphs and tragedies fate had in store for France.

The German occupation of a major part of France suddenly shattered these beliefs and proved them to be largely illusory. In France the Germans decreed the same anti-Jewish measures they introduced in other countries that fell to their armed onslaught. In every country these anti-Jewish decrees brought to the surface the true feelings of the local gentile population toward the Jews. In countries like Poland, Hungary, Rumania, long simmering anti-Semitic tendencies burst into the open, and the local populace, and in particular whatever armed formation they were allowed to retain under the Nazi rule, vied with the Nazis, the Gestapo, and the SS in hunting down and exposing Jews in hiding and in contributing their share to the "Endlö-sung." In other countries, such as Italy, Denmark, and the Netherlands, where the local population by and large refused to cooperate with the German occupation authorities, many Jews were saved, including refugees who were able to reach these countries from Eastern and Central Europe.

France did not fall in the first category, but neither did it belong to the second. No virulent anti-Jewish sentiment surfaced, and most Frenchmen did not go out of their way to ferret out Jews who had gone into hiding following the German occupation. Whether this reticence was due to their feelings of solidarity with their persecuted Jewish fellow citizens or to their overriding hatred of the Germans is a moot question, the answer to which would be academic in any case. On the other hand— and here was the factor that created a traumatic experience for the French Jews—the gentile French, by and large, were unwilling to face the risks to life and property that active aid to the Jews would have meant under the circumstances and that their neighbors to the north did not hesitate to undertake. Not being actively hindered by the French population in hunting down and rounding up the Jews, the German authorities, and to a certain extent the Vichy French government as well, were able to apprehend and send to their death more than 100,000 Jews from France, or more than one out of every three French Jews: Those who survived were, for the most part, destitute, broken in spirit, disillusioned, and, to a considerable extent, alienated from gentile France.

The picture of French Jewry during World War II would not be complete without mentioning the part French Jews played in the Resistance. They had their own resistance organization, the *Organisation Juive de Combat,* which was active throughout the period of German occupation.

Reconstruction and the North African Immigration ———

Following the liberation of France in 1944, the reconstruction of Jewish life in France proceeded with astonishing speed. General de Gaulle and his Free French government, which during the war had its seat in London, declared the anti-Jewish laws of the German authorities and of the Vichy French government null and void. The return of those French Jews who survived concentration camps in Eastern Europe began immediately, followed by thousands who came from Displaced Persons Camps in Germany and Austria, and later by Jewish refugees from Eastern Europe, especially Poland and Hungary. A few years later, when all North African territories of France achieved independence, tens of thousands of Jews came from Morocco and Tunisia. The years 1961–62 saw the arrival of some 120,000 Algerian Jews who, since the famous Crémieux Decree of 1870, had been French citizens, and therefore could make the move from Algeria to France by right and not by sufferance. Since most of the Algerian Jews had been educated in French schools, they knew French and were sufficiently imbued with French culture to find adjustment in metropolitan France relatively easy—much easier than it was for the Eastern European Jews. As a result of these immigrations the number of Jews in France passed the half-million mark in 1963—a greater number than had ever before lived in France (see Table VIII).

TABLE VIII.

THE JEWISH POPULATION OF FRANCE

Year	Number of Jews	Percentage in the Total Population
1851	73,975*	0.2
1900	80,000	0.25
1914	100,000	0.25
1933	240,000	0.57
1939	300,000	0.6
1945	180,000	0.4
1950	235,000	0.6
1955	300,000	0.7
1961	350,000	0.8
1963	500,000	1.1
1966	520,000	1.08
1968	535,000	1.07

Sources: Arye Tartakower, *Shivte Yisrael* (Tel Aviv, 1966), II, 198; *American Jewish Year Book* (individual editions for years listed).
*Census. All the other figures are estimates.

Apart from its increased numbers, the French Jewish population in the 1960s differed from that of the earlier periods in one important respect. In the past, most of the Jews, both the established population and the newly arriving immigrants, tended to concentrate in Paris. The most recent immigrants (and especially those who came from North Africa) settled frequently in the *Midi*, the south of France, whose climate and landscape reminded them of the North Africa they had left behind. As a result of this immigration, sizable Jewish communities sprang up in Marseille, Nice, Toulouse, Leon, and other cities of southern France. On the other hand, the immigrants from Eastern Europe brought about a marked increase in the rise of the Jewish communities in northeastern France, and especially in Alsace-Lorraine. These special circumstances make France an exception in the Jewish Diaspora with reference to the change in rural-urban distribution. While there is no Jewish trend in France to settle in rural areas, there has been a development of Jewish communities in middle-sized French cities; in other Diasporas the typical trend has been in the direction of concentration in the two or three largest cities in the country, with a corresponding decrease of the Jewish population in the middle-sized cities, and its eventual total disappearance from them.

Integration

Whenever a new wave of Jewish immigrants arrived in France, most of its members were forced by the pressure of economic circumstances to seek their livelihoods as small tradesmen, artisans, or shopkeepers, and for a number of years barely managed to eke out a living in these all but lucrative fields. During this period there was a marked gap between the newcomers and the old-established and economically much better-off sectors of French Jewry. The newcomers spoke Yiddish (except the North Africans), were more observant in matters of religion, and were the carriers of a strong Jewish consciousness. The established French Jews spoke French, were largely indifferent to religious issues, and had successfully assimilated to French culture. The two groups had very little in common, contact between them was minimal, except that the newcomers could always count on financial aid from the former.

The group with which the newcomers had direct contact was the French gentile small tradesmen, artisans, and shopkeepers, who considered these new arrivals to be intruders and competitors. Inasmuch as anti-Semitism nearly always has an economic component, this competitive situation was conducive to the burgeoning of anti-Jewish feelings in the French lower middle class.

However, the immigrant Jews in France had brought along with them one trait which has characterized Jewish immigrants in all the countries that admitted them: the strong will to economic advancement. Consequently, many of the newly ar- rived Jews in France soon began to rise to higher economic levels. This had a number of significant consequences: first, it removed them from direct competition with the French small tradesmen, artisans, and shopkeepers, and enabled them to occupy positions on the higher levels on which neither contact nor competition was as immediate. Secondly, it enabled them to follow the path well beaten by those who preceded them toward assimilating to French culture, and thus gradually to become "French Jews" in contradistinction to immigrant Jews of varied origins.

One characteristic expression of the cultural entrenchment of the Jews in those countries of immigration in which they enjoy civil liberties is the tendency of the young Jewish generation to gravitate to academic professions. The first manifestation of this tendency is their high percentage among university students, high, that is, in proportion to the relative numbers of the Jewish community in the total population. We shall see (in Chapters XVII, XIX and XX) that this phenomenon can be observed in England, the United States and Argentina. And even in Soviet Russia, as far as the authorities permit, the same tendency manifests itself (see Chapter XVIII). As to France, no general estimate of the percentage of Jewish students in the total number of students is available, but such information could be obtained for the University of Paris. In the four faculties the percentage of Jewish students in 1964 was as follows: the Sorbonne, 6 percent; law, 5 percent; sciences, 5 percent, medi- cine, 9 percent. The overall average in the four faculties was 6.25 percent,[2] at a time when the total number of Jews in the country was about 1 percent.

Again: Assimilation

France, which in the Middle Ages was the locale of one of the greatest Jewish scholarly and intellectual flowerings (Rashi, the Tosafists, for example; cf. Chapter XV), has, since she spearheaded the emancipation of the Jews, become for them something like the siren in Heine's *"King Harald Harfagar":* her irresistible song has again and again lured them into her arms, making them forget their own history, traditions, values, and even religion. In the late nineteenth and early twentieth centuries French Jewry, numbering some forty thousand (not counting the Algerian Jews), seemed doomed to extinction. Had it not been for successive waves of new Jewish immigrants, French Jewry, in all probability, would have gradually melted away in the early part of the present century.

In the pre-World War I decade came the relatively large-scale Jewish immigration from Russia and Rumania, more than replacing in number those whom the French Diaspora had lost through assimilation. These immigrants transplanted into France much of their Eastern European *shtetl* life, with all its social, cultural, religious, and other aspects.[3] However, by the 1920s these newcomers, too, had largely succumbed to the French cultural allure. A similar process was repeated after the arrival of Jewish immigration from Poland, some of whose members I met in Paris in 1939 by which time they were well on the way to becoming thoroughly Frenchified.

After the trauma of the Nazi and Vichy period, the lure of French culture again asserted itself. It almost seemed as if the survivors had resolved to hasten the process of their assimilation in order to become, as rapidly as possible, indistinguishable from the general French population. Then, precisely at the time when this group had almost succeeded in following in the footsteps of its predecessors, a totally unforeseen development took place: the arrival of some 230,000 North African Jews in the 1954–63 decade.[4]

The Effects of the North African Immigration

These Oriental Jews, who today constitute about half of the Jewish population of France, not only replenished the waning numbers of the French Diaspora but, since most of them were destitute, spurred the established French-Jewish community to a great organizational and philanthropic effort. Curiously enough, while the assimilated French Jews ostensibly responded to the plight of their unfortunate North African brethren (a response in keeping with the hundred-year-old tradition of the Alliance Israélite Universelle), in effect, by doing so they infused a new meaning into their own Jewishness, and created new frameworks for a Jewish life in France in which they as well as the newcomers were enabled to participate.

Another effect of the arrival of the North African Jews in France was that it introduced into the country a population element characterized by a very high birth rate. As a result of this factor, the French Diaspora in its totality has become the one Jewish community with a relatively high natural increase in the entire Western world, and constitutes a sharp contrast to the neighboring West European Diasporas in which births have fallen behind deaths.

As far as occupational structure is concerned, here too the North Africans have introduced a new dimension. The old-time elements of French Jewry are mostly employees, members of the professions and middle-class petit bourgeoisie. The Eastern Europeans who had arrived prior to World War II were originally mostly workmen and small artisans (including fur and leather workers, etc.); their children, however, have largely approximated the occupations of the indigenous French Jews, which, of course, is indicative of a considerable upward mobility. As to the North Africans, they comprised intellectuals, bourgeoisie, middle-level civil servants (such as postmen, clerks, even policemen and prison guards), a strong proportion of proletariat, such as industrial workers, and also people with skills of no use in the French economy.[5]

However, the French socio-economic environment enabled these latest newcomers as well to embark on a course of upward social mobility. While statistical studies to substantiate this directly are not available, the rise of the North Africans in the socio-economic scale is clearly reflected in the rapid increase in intercommunity marriages between them and members of the indigenous French and the Eastern European Jewish groups. According to the Paris Consistory rolls, of all French Jews who got married in 1945, only 3 percent wed a North African Jew; in 1962 this was 42 percent. Of all Eastern European Jews who got married in 1955, only 5 percent wed a North African Jew; in 1962, 32 percent. Of all North African Jews who got married in 1962, 44 percent wed a non-North African spouse.[6]

These rapid increases in intercommunity marriage between the Oriental and Ashkenazi Jews in France (which can be explained only on the basis of an equally rapid rise in the socio-economic status of the former) are the more remarkable since they are not paralleled in Israel. In Israel, too, in the 1960s about half of the Jewish population was of Ashkenazi and the other half of Sephardi-Oriental Jewish extraction. And yet, although most members of both groups had been living in the country since 1952 (that is, several years longer than the North African Jews in France), the intermarriage rate between them has been rising only slowly and in 1965 had reached only 15 percent.[7]

What is more, linguistic assimilation to French proceeded apace. A survey carried out in 1963 among the North African immigrants who had settled in France in 1958–59 showed that within this short four or five year period 32 percent of the manual wage earners, 20 percent of the independent workers, and 16 percent of the white collar workers had abandoned Arabic in favor of French as their home language. Similarly, more than 50 percent of the interviewed immigrants stated that they were less religiously observant in France than they had been in North Africa. Three times as many of the immigrants "kept quiet about the fact that they were Jewish" in France than did in North Africa.[8] All these are signs of an assimilatory tendency which indicates that despite their very different background, the North African half of the present-day French Diaspora will, in all likelihood, follow the older element down the assimilationist path.

Of course, unexpected happenings can always intervene and stop or even reverse this tendency. One such event was the Israeli crisis of May and the Six-Day War of June 1967, which evoked in French Jewry a reaction whose depth, intensity, and unanimity surprised both Jews and non-Jews. All of French

Jewry, including those who had remained Jews in name only, keeping their religion only because in the generally a-religious atmosphere of the country they would have found it ridiculous to undergo a formal ceremony of conversion to Catholicism, was gripped by a sense of great solidarity with Israel, a feeling of identification with it, and a resurgence of the seemingly long-forgotten awareness of the community of fate between Israel and the scattered members of the Diaspora. In May 1967 a *Comité de Coordination des Organisations Juives en France* was created, headed by Guy de Rothschild, and an emergency campaign, *Fonds de Solidarité avec Israel,* raised $12 million within a few weeks, contributed by seventy thousand donors.[9]

Outlook

Yet withal, the future of the French Diaspora is in doubt. A race is on between the Jewish educational, cultural, and organizational efforts on the one hand, and the persistent lure of French culture and French life on the other. In theory one can, of course, conceive of a French Jew being a part of French life to the same extent as any non-Jewish Frenchman, and at the same time continuing a "good" Jew, conscious of his Jewish past, familiar with his Jewish heritage, concerned about Israel and world Jewry, participating in one way or another in the life of the Jewish community, and observant of at least a modicum of Jewish religion. In theory, yes. In practice, it appears that this feat of maintaining a dual cultural allegiance is considerably more difficult of achievement in France than in any other cultural milieu, be it Italian, British, Latin American, or even American. Perhaps the specific esthetic, emotional, refined, or, if you will "feminine," quality of French culture has something to do with it. Other cultures, too, have, of course, their attraction to which many Jews succumb. But none, or so it seems to this observer, has the irresistible Circean allurement that characterizes the French. This is why the chance that the Jewish organizational and educational efforts will win the race for Jewish group survival seems so much slighter in France than in other countries of the Western world.

This unique attraction of French culture was felt by the Jews not only in France herself, but also overseas. In it, undoubtedly, lies at least part of the explanation of the success of the Alliance schools at inculcating French culture into their pupils in the Muslim countries. In Libya, the Jews were exposed, in addition to French culture, also to Italian; in Egypt—also to English. Yet in both countries French remained the overriding cultural orientation of the educated Jews. For this reason it seems likely that the large masses of North African Jewish immigrants in France will continue to assimilate to French culture more rapidly and more thoroughly than they will absorb Jewish traditional, cultural, and religious values in the expanding Jewish school network.

Among the first signs of the internalization of French cultural influence is the spread among the Jews of the belief that anti-Semitism cannot reemerge in France. This belief was found to increase with length of residence in the country. A poll conducted in 1967 showed that among immigrant Jews 62 percent believed that anti-Semitism might return in France; among native-born French Jews, whose parents were immigrants, only 39 percent held the same belief; and among Jews whose parents, too, had been born in France—only 32 percent.[10] In many another country, including the United States, a question as to the possible resurgence of anti-Semitism would have been meaningless in a poll, for the simple reason that anti-Semitism, in one form or another, is, and is known to be, part of the actual social scene and not merely a future possibility. However, quite apart from this question, the very fact that two-thirds of the French-born Jews believed in 1967 that anti-Semitism could not return in France indicates to what extent French Jewry accepted as actual reality the liberal tenets of the great idealistic French slogans. Such a substitution of belief in an ideal for observation and evaluation of reality is a typical example of the effect cultural conditioning can have on individual judgment.

There was some irony in the fact that even before the results of this poll could be published, the president of the French Republic made (on November 27, 1967) anti-Jewish and anti-

Israel pronouncements that were, in effect, a resounding refutation of the belief that "it can't happen again" expressed by two-thirds of the French-born Jews who responded to the poll.

President de Gaulle's anti-Semitic remarks came as a shock to French Jewry, as did the embargo on arms to Israel imposed by him in 1968. Protest meetings were called,[11] personal efforts were made by prominent French Jews as well as gentiles to have the embargo repealed, but to no effect. The embargo continued in force even after Georges Pompidou replaced De Gaulle as president of France, and the deterioration of the relationship between France and Israel caused many French Jews considerable anguish.

17 THE ASHKENAZI JEWS: ENGLAND

Early History: Eleventh to Eighteenth Centuries ———

From the scanty historical evidence available it appears that Jews were first brought to England from Rouen by William the Conqueror (r. 1066–1087). His son Henry I (r. 1100–1135) granted the London Jews certain commercial privileges. Under Henry's successor, King Stephen (r. 1135–1154), England had the doubtful distinction of becoming, in 1144, the country in which the first recorded blood accusation against Jews took place, although Stephen prevented outbursts against the Jews. Under Henry II (r. 1154–1189) Jews were found in many English cities and had an important share in financing the king and occasionally even his opponents. The favorable position English Jews enjoyed at this time is indicated by, among other things, the visit in 1158 of the famous Spanish-Jewish scholar and poet Abraham ibn Ezra, and by the arrival in 1182 of Jews expelled from France.

The opulence of the Jews increased the disaffection of the populace toward the "enemies of Christ," and during the coronation festivities of Richard I (r. 1189–1199) the mob violently attacked the Old Jewry quarter in London. Numerous attacks on Jews including massacres at Lynn, Stamford, Bury St. Edmunds, and other places, occurred during Richard's absence on a Crusade.

Throughout this period, as well as under King John (r. 1199–1216), the Jews were constantly squeezed financially, in many cases so ruthlessly that despite all their financial ingenuity they were unable to defray the royal impositions. To this was added the Jew-badge, introduced in 1218 during the reign of Henry III, in the form of an oblong white patch measuring about six by twelve inches. During the Barons' war the Jews of several towns were looted and either the records of indebtedness in their possession destroyed, or all indebtedness to them was simply declared null and void by the feudal lords in whose domains they dwelled.

In 1255 eighteen Jews were executed in London in connection with a ritual murder charge; in 1271 the Jews were denied all freehold tenure; and in 1275 Edward I (r. 1274–1307) forbade Jews to lend on "usury," thereby denying them the only means of livelihood available to them. Forced to resort to illegal transactions, many Jews were apprehended, and in 1278 no less than 293 of them were executed in London.

Having been rendered useless for the Crown by being made unable to earn and hence to be taxed, the Jews became expendable altogether as far as the Crown was concerned. Consequently, in 1290 all the Jews—some sixteen thousand all told—were expelled from England. Some of them sought refuge in Flanders, while most of them went back to France, whence their ancestors had come two centuries earlier and whose language they never gave up throughout their stay in England.

Although the edict of expulsion was officially voided only in 1655, some Jews, posing as Lombard traders, returned in the fourteenth century. Others, at various periods, were given permission to visit England, and at the time of the Spanish expulsion (1492) a considerable number of Jews actually settled in the country. In 1542 many of them were arrested on suspicion of being Jews. In the middle of the seventeenth century more Marranos (posing as Catholic Spaniards) settled in London, formed a secret congregation, and engaged in international and trans-Atlantic trade. Finally, in 1655, in keeping with the typical British combination of commercialism and religiosity, Oliver Cromwell (1599–1658), Lord Protector of England, readmitted the Jews into the realm. In doing so he was motivated by both a mercantilistic policy, which made him desirous of attracting the rich Amsterdam Jews and their international trade to London, and the puritanical spirit of which the belief in a mystical Messianism was an integral part. It was upon this belief that the Dutch Jewish leader Manasseh ben Israel (1604–1657) played when he argued that the Messiah could appear only after the Jews were scattered in all countries of the world: England, therefore, by admitting the Jews, could help usher in the Messianic age.

Although Cromwell's legal experts determined that there was nothing in the laws of England to prevent the settling of Jews in the country, the Jews were still considered foreigners, suffered from all the disabilities of alien status, and their position was precarious. Nevertheless, the number and financial strength of the London Jews increased, and in the course of the eighteenth century the chief Jewish financiers of northwestern Europe, all Sephardim, were well represented in the London Jewish community.

The trials and tribulations of the Sephardi Jews in eighteenth- and nineteenth-century England were discussed in Chapter XIV, so that here we can proceed to a survey of the numerical growth of Anglo-Jewry and related developments from the nineteenth century on.

Immigration, Growth, and Decline

The story of Jewish immigration to England during and after the seventeenth century parallels in many respects that of Jewish settlement in America. Both movements began practically simultaneously: to America in 1654, to England in 1655. The first immigrants to both countries were Dutch Sephardi Jews. Although the first Jews to arrive in New Amsterdam came from Brazil, the first Jews who began to resettle in England came from old Amsterdam. In both countries the number of Jewish immigrants during that first, or Sephardi, period was quite small. Both England and the United States received a larger immigration of German Jews in the eighty years between 1800 and 1880; in both countries the Sephardi Jews were consequently reduced to a minority position, but managed to retain their social superiority and prestige. Then, from 1881 on, still larger contingents of Jewish immigrants from Eastern Europe began to stream into both countries, spurred by the same events in Russia: the pogroms. Thus around 1900 in both countries there was a threefold division of the Jewish community: a small Sephardi group, a German Jewish group several times the size of the former, and an Eastern European Jewish group several

333

times the size of the German Jewish group. The difference between the two countries was that American Jewry as a whole was by 1900 roughly ten to twelve times as numerous as British Jewry, a ratio that, by and large, has been maintained down to the present time.

In absolute figures, around 1800 there were about 20,000 Jews in all England; by 1880 this number had grown to 60,000. By 1900, as a result of large-scale Russian Jewish immigration, the number had increased to about 160,000 (including about 11,000 in Scotland and Ireland). Before World War I it had grown to a quarter of a million and by 1950 to 450,000. Since 1950 there has been no further increase and in the 1960s the size of the community declined by an average of 800 persons annually.[1] (See Table IX.) This was due primarily to the disappearance of natural increase, a phenomenon found in other Western European Diasporas as well. As to immigration, whatever of it still continued after 1950 has been more than counterbalanced by emigration.

TABLE IX

THE ESTIMATED JEWISH POPULATION IN GREAT BRITAIN, 1690–1970

Year	Number	Year	Number
1690	350-400	1880	60,000
1734	6,000	1890	100,000
1753	8,000	1900	160,000
1800	20,000	1910	242,000
1830	27,000	1920	297,000
1845	35,000	1930	333,000
1849	40,000	1940	385,000
1851	35,000	1950	450,000
1853	25,000	1960	450,000
		1970	410,000

Sources: V. D. Lipman, *Social History of the Jews in England, 1850–1950* (London, 1954); H. Neustatter, in Maurice Freedman, ed., *A Minority in Britain* (London, 1955); *The Jewish Yearbook* (London); *American Jewish Year Book*

The Jews and British Culture ─────────────

The movement to grant equal rights to members of religions other than the Church of England began in the early nineteenth century. The Roman Catholics in England were freed from all civil disabilities in 1829; the Jews—after a parliamentary struggle of thirty years—in 1860. Complete equality to both Roman Catholics and Jews was not granted until 1890. By that time a few individual Jews had taken a prominent part in British parliamentary life for several decades. In 1858 Baron Lionel Nathan de Rothschild became the first Jewish member of Parliament, and from 1885 on several Jews were raised to the peerage and were seated in the House of Lords (Lord Nathaniel Meyer Rothschild, Lord Pirbright, Lord Wandsworth). Several Jews became members of governments. Some made important contributions to the financial and economic development of England. Baron Lionel Nathan de Rothschild provided the funds for Disraeli's purchase of the Suez Canal shares; his son, Lord Nathaniel Meyer Rothschild, became a governor of the Bank of England and was a member of the Royal Commission on Alien Immigration (1902) which heard a testimony by Theodor Herzl. Italian-born Sir Moses Montefiore (1784–1885), having made his fortune as a broker (among his clients was Lord Rothschild), went on to an important career in public service.

A few more names could be added to this brief list, but the fact remains that the Jewish participation in British life was, for a long time, limited to a few areas, such as politics,[2] finance, pugilism (a Sephardi accomplishment), and colonial development, to which were added later—i.e., in the twentieth century—the organization of mass production and distribution of consumer goods.[3]

It is in the last mentioned area that, as most thoughtful observers of the Anglo-Jewish arena agree, British Jews have made their greatest contribution to the life of the country. In personal interviews in London with individuals active in various public Jewish fields I was told again and again about the greatness and excellence of the Marks and Spencer chain stores, built into a multi-billion dollar merchandising empire by two Jews, Simon

335

(later Lord) Marks, and Israel (later Lord) Sieff. M. & S., it is generally agreed, brought high quality merchandise at low prices within reach of everybody in England: their customers include members of the royal family and the nobility, as well as the lowest wage earners such as shopgirls or transportation workers. Equally important, they take excellent care of their own employes, having pioneered in providing them with benefits that exceed by far all other welfare and social security schemes available in the country. M. & S. has done more, it is felt, to eliminate the external signs of class differences in England than any other British institution, or law, for that matter. As Chaim Bermant put it:

> M. & S. have become a by-word for value. It has brought the quality and service associated with Knightsbridge within the range of every man, and has virtually caused a social revolution. One could tell the classes apart before the war by a glance at the womenfolk. Today all classes are dressed and well dressed by Marks & Spencer. If one was to name the biggest single Jewish contribution to British life, it would probably be summed up in these two words—Marks & Spencer.[4]

While my own personal observations in the summer of 1970 were at variance with the generalizations that one could no longer tell apart the British classes by their clothing (Savile Row still seemed to do a thriving business), and that all classes were well dressed, I have no basis for disagreeing with the last sentence of the foregoing quotation, which appears to express the consensus of those who take a watchful interest in the British scene. But this emphatic and positive assertion leads me to question what it means with respect to the larger issue of Jewish participation in British culture. For if it is true that Marks and Spencer is "the biggest single Jewish contribution to British life," it seems to follow that in areas outside mass merchandising Anglo-Jewry can only claim smaller contributions, that its share in British science, literature, arts, and other fields does not measure up—in the judgment of the Jewish observers themselves—to the significance of Marks and Spencer's unique emporium.

336

What, in fact, is the situation as to the Jewish contribution in Britain to those areas of culture which in general parlance are usually understood by this term? Earlier in this book (Chapter IX) we touched upon the anomalous absence of British-bred Jews among the sixty British Nobel Prize winners (anomalous, that is, in comparison with the other leading Nobel Prize winning countries, with their high percentage of Jewish laureates) and attributed it to the fact that the small and newly acculturated Anglo-Jewish community expended its best energies on those fields of activity which were the primary concerns in the British national culture and in which no Nobel Prizes are awarded. The secondary talents which, thereafter, Anglo-Jewry could send into such fields as literature and the sciences were not sufficient to secure Nobel Prizes side by side with the greatest British literary masters, researchers in physics, chemistry, and medicine, and workers for world peace. In fact, as far as literature is concerned, the only significant Anglo-Jewish names one can recall are those of Benjamin Disraeli, later Lord Beaconfield (1804–1881), who inherited his literary talent from his father, but whose most significant contribution, of course, lay not at all in literature but in the field of politics, and Israel Zangwill (1864–1926), a definitely minor luminary in the galaxy of great English novelists. Nor has the situation changed appreciably in recent times. True, the number of Jews contributing to British letters has greatly increased and they are numerically overrepresented (that is, in relation to their percentage in the general population), especially among the avant-garde dramatists, modern poets, novelists, and critics. Nevertheless, in analyzing the Anglo-Jewish literary scene, Chaim Bermant comes to the conclusion that it is "not outstanding," and that "it has rarely taken a distinctly Jewish form."[5]

In the arts, Joseph Jacobs' succinct dictum, made around 1900—that "the list of Jewish names is somewhat scanty"[6]—still seems to hold good. While most of the large art galleries in London are owned by Jews, there are few Jewish artists; and even among those few who have achieved some name, there are barely two or three in whose work Jewish influences play any part. In music the situation is similar.

337

In the sciences, while no British Jew has reached the pinnacle of a Nobel Prize, Anglo-Jewish participation is most intensive. Membership in the Royal Society can be taken as an indication. The Royal Society elects a strictly limited number of fellows every year, solely on the basis of scientific merit. From 1848 to 1900, only 0.8 percent of the fellows elected were Jewish; in 1901, 1 percent of the fellows were Jews; in 1920—2 percent; in 1940—3.7 percent; and in 1948—5 percent. In 1968, of the total of 713 Fellows of the Royal Society, 39, or 5.5 percent, were Jewish. Since Jews still constituted less than 1 percent of the total population of Great Britain in 1968, their proportion in the Royal Society was more than five-and-one-half times as high as in the country's population.

The proportion of Jews among university students in Great Britain indicates that in the future as well the high Jewish representation in the Royal Society—that is, among the country's top ranking scientists—may be maintained. In 1949–50, of 85,000 full-time students in England 3,000, or 3.53 percent, were Jewish.[7] According to a later survey, in 1954–55 Jewish students made up 2.8 percent of the total number of full-time university students in Britain; in 1962 the total number of Jewish students was over 3,500.[8] Since the birth rate of the Jews (11.6 in 1945–49) was considerably lower than the birth rate for the general population (18.6 in the same period), it follows that the number of Jewish college-age youth, too, was lower in proportion to the total number of Anglo-Jewry than was the case among the general population. If so, the percentage of Jewish youths attending college in relation to the total number of college-age Jewish youths can be estimated at being five times as high as the percentage of youths attending college relative to the total number of college-age youth in the general population.

In British public life also the Jewish participation exceeds several times that of the Jewish proportion of the population. In 1968, of the 630 members of parliament, 40, or 6.4 percent, were Jewish; so were 10, or about 3.5 percent, of the approximately 280 Privy Councillors. In the same year, twelve peers, eleven life peers, eleven baronets, and sixty-three knights were Jewish.[9]

This is as good a place as any to point out that the one major causative factor making for statistically ascertainable differences between the Jews and the general population in the economic, cultural, and many other fields is the greater concentration of Jews in the urban middle class. Since Chapter VI dealt with this phenomenon in a general way, it only remains to state here that it is in the urban middle-class character of British Jewry that many of the specific features discussed in this section are anchored. This includes Jewish participation, out of all proportion to the size of the community, in politics, officialdom, commerce, industry, science, arts, and literature. In the same circumstances lies the explanation of several additional features, frequently pointed out as distinguishing British Jewry as against the general population of the country—e.g., the fact that while in the nation as a whole only 34 percent of the households had refrigerators in 1965, no less than 99 percent of Jewish households which responded to the *Jewish Chronicle*'s Readership Survey boasted of this major appliance.[10] These, and similar percentage differences in homes equipped with central heating, ownership of a car, the use of a garden, frequency and length of vacations, frequency of theater attendance, and the like, merely go to show that the readership of the *Jewish Chronicle* surveyed was comprised almost entirely of urban middle-class Jewish families, while the general British population consists only partially of a comparable urban middle class. That the relatively new Anglo-Jewish community did achieve such a status with such rapidity was, to a great extent, due to two factors. The first of these was the urban middle-class status and mentality brought along by the Jewish immigrants from Eastern Europe; the second, the strenuous and successful efforts made by the older element in Anglo-Jewry to bring about the speedy Anglicization of the younger.

Anglicization

The process of Anglicization of immigrant Jews in England proceeded more rapidly than the Americanization of their brethren in the United States. In America, the sheer bulk of immigration, the settlement of the immigrants in purely Jewish neighborhoods, the possibility of obtaining jobs in Jewish-owned, Jewish-run, and Jewish-manned industries and businesses favored the retention for a longer time of the language and culture the Jews had brought along from the old country. Conditions in England made for more rapid changes. Immediately upon their arrival, the children of the immigrants began attending the nondenominational, free, and compulsory elementary schools in which they not only learned to speak English but also acquired, as the Reverend S. Levy observed as early as 1911, "English habits of thought and character," a process of Anglicization which has "inevitably a retroactive effect upon the parents in the home."[11]

This process of institutionalized educational Anglicization proceeded with such speed in the case of the Jewish immigrants' children that it evoked special praise from British school board officers and headmasters. Nobody in those days doubted that the British values were absolute and that their inculcation into the children, whether native-born or immigrant, was the highest and most important task of the school system. (Today, in America, this would be decried as an "imposition of middle-class values" or a similar cultural violation. Accordingly, it was the greatest accolade when a headmaster said:

> Jewish boys soon become Anglicized and cease to be foreigners ... The lads have become thoroughly English. They have acquired our language. They take a keen and intelligent interest in all that concerns the welfare of our country. . . . They enter heartily into English games [i.e., sports]. . . . I am firmly convinced that the Jewish lads who pass through our schools will grow up to be intelligent, industrious, temperate and law-abiding citizens and, I think, will add to the wealth and stability of the British Empire.[12]

The Anglicization of the adult immigrants also proceeded apace. There were special English classes for them, and the Jews themselves organized clubs for adults as well as for boys and girls, in which they learned English and practiced English sports such as cricket, football, and swimming. In the Jews' Free School the children acquired "English notions of cleanliness" so that there was a "marked change in their appearance and habits. They enter the school Russians and Poles and emerge from it almost indistinguishable from English children."[13]

340

In contrast to the Jewish friendly and fraternal societies in America, which were the bastions of Yiddish, their counterparts in England insisted on the English language and British manners:

> One of the chief benefits it [the friendly society] confers is that it is a means of anglicizing the foreign Jews. . . . It is in these societies that the foreigner learns order and discipline, respect for the chair and the mode of conducting public business. The proceedings are always in English. It is only seldom, if he has something of special importance to say, that a foreigner is permitted to address a meeting in Yiddish.[14]

Comparable to the friendly societies in this respect, the Federation of Synagogues was specifically set up, under the aegis of the older families, to Anglicize the newcomers.

While one cannot help feeling a certain nostalgic envy for a state of mind in which value hierarchies were so clearly demarkated, it is quite clear that this unquestioning acceptance of the superiority of British values implied a tacit, or not so tacit, derogation of the traditional Jewish values brought along to England by the Jewish immigrants. What the processes of Anglicization, wholeheartedly embraced by the majority of the Jewish leadership as well as the rank and file, amounted to was a radical transculturation: the substitution of the "better" British variety for the "inferior" Eastern European Jewish equivalents in all fields of culture. The line was drawn only at the Jewish religion, which was officially considered as sacrosanct and hence untouchable, except for small modifications in the forms of communal worship in order to bring it more in line with what was considered dignified behavior in Britain. The result was the emergence of a quite specific type of Jewry, one whose Judaism was largely reduced to the maintenance of an officially orthodox religious organization, the United Synagogue (as well as a few smaller ones) without being accompanied by any vital expression of Jewishness in the social and cultural fields. As several observers of the Anglo-Jewish scene have emphasized, only the Zionist movement, with its adult and youth organizations, has added a note of vitality.[15]

A strong indication of the widespread Anglicization is supplied by the changes and developments in Jewish occupations.

It has been observed that the occupational structure of Anglo-Jewry evinces a progressive diversification. This process initially was facilitated by the policies of the communal authorities in fostering apprenticeships; subsequently it was also favored by "the removal of the barriers of religious restrictions and popular prejudice" and "the relaxation by the Jews themselves of religious observances which had previously been an impediment to many types of employment."[16]

As in other countries, the general tendency for the Jews in England has been to move out of the small trades and small manufacturing (most typically tailoring, the boot, shoe, and slipper trade, and cabinet making) in which they had concentrated until World War I, into other trades and the professions. In the 1960s the main Jewish trades were clothing and tailoring (20 percent of all gainfully occupied males); drapery, textiles, and the fashion trade (7–8 percent); furniture (also 7–8 percent). No less than 22 percent of the gainfully employed males were engaged in professional pursuits (as against 5 percent in the general population). Of this total, nearly 30 percent were in medicine and dentistry, and about 10 percent each in accountancy, chemistry, engineering, and law. It was also found that the Jews tended to work as self-employed or as owners of small businesses to a much greater extent than the national average (15 percent as against 6 percent).[17]

As a result of their rapid and successful Anglicization, and the unswerving concentration of their energies "on two objects: to develop the industry with which they were associated and to raise themselves in the social scale,"[18] the Jews within a relatively short time "surpassed the general population in reaching upper and middle-class standards, i.e. proportionately to their numbers more of them will be found in the higher income groups."[19]

All this amounts to, in the words of one observer, "the progressive adaptation or assimilation of Anglo-Jewry to life in the general community,"[20] or, as another student of modern Anglo-Jewry put it:

> although there persists a minority community with distinctive religious and cultural values, and with the social distance from

the host society largely maintained, its members have proved in the economic field to have the very qualifications that are essential for successful living in the urban milieu of industrial society.[21]

Jewish Education

Because of the nature of the data it is difficult to gain a clear picture as to the situation in Jewish education in Great Britain. However, it appears that in 1968 a total of 35,844 (or 35,880) Jewish children of elementary and high-school age received some kind of Jewish education (Yeshiva, day school, part-time classes, and so forth). The overwhelming majority of the pupils were under thirteen years of age, and about two thirds of them were boys, one third girls. Since the number of Jewish children in England between the ages of five and fifteen, and thus subject to compulsory schooling, is estimated at 52,000, it appears that about 69 percent of them received in 1968 at least some Jewish education, while 31 percent received none at all.[22]

However, a considerable percentage of the children who did receive Jewish education got it in an extremely rudimentary form which was far from sufficient to provide them with a lasting basis for Jewish identification. Also, the percentage of children receiving even this minimal amount of Jewish education has been steadily declining over the years. In London (where 280,000 of the country's 410,000 Jews lived in 1968) in 1911 more than 70 percent of the Jewish school-age children attended Hebrew classes; in 1923—64 percent; in 1935—50 percent; in 1953—40 percent.[23]

From 1960 to 1964 the number of pupils at provincial and London Board centers fell by 15 per cent. On the other hand, the attendance at the 49 Jewish day schools in the United Kingdom rose from 4,400 in 1954 to 7,054 in 1959, to 8,900 in 1963 to 10,000 in 1965. Four-fifths of these were under the age of eleven and in primary schools. By May 1969 there were 11,236 children in Jewish day schools, of whom 8,204 studied in primary, and 3,032 in secondary, schools. However, the children attending Jewish day schools still represented only 15 percent of the Jewish school-age population in Britain; another 20 percent attended regular supplementary classes; 30 percent attended only a few hours per week; the remaining 35 percent received no Jewish education at all.[24]

Anglo-Jewish Culture?

A few words have to be said in conclusion about the achievements of Anglo-Jewry in Jewish culture and scholarship. Its contribution to these home grounds has been judged insignificant by historians and sociologists observing the Anglo-Jewish scene since the early twentieth century. In the early 1900s the eminent Anglo-Jewish historian, Joseph Jacobs, put it with characteristic British understatement: "The favorable conditions of the English Jews have not hitherto resulted in any remarkable display of Jewish talent. English Jews have contributed nothing of any consequence to rabbinic scholarship or even to halakic or exegetic learning. . . . "[25] It is doubtful whether this situation has changed to any marked degree since the writing of the above lines. Sixty years after Jacobs, another Anglo-Jewish historian, Cecil Roth, made what amounts to essentially the same judgment: "Throughout its history, Anglo-Jewry has had as it were a satellite existence, at least so far as its spiritual and intellectual life was concerned. . . . Whether it can be self-dependent in the future is now one of our great problems."[26]

And contemporary Israeli sociologist Arye Tartakower sums it all up succinctly: "No substantial Jewish culture has developed on British soil."[27]

18 THE ASHKENAZI JEWS: SOVIET RUSSIA

The Union of Soviet Socialist Republics is a multi-storied political structure, comprising union republics, autonomous republics, and autonomous regions. In each of these units one nationality is predominant. While all the Soviet republics are under the strictest control of Moscow, they enjoy a certain formal autonomy, as well as the freedon of preserving and fostering their national culture, including their language. Such national, cultural, and linguistic autonomy has formally been granted also to the Jews of Soviet Russia, who in 1967 numbered more than 1 percent of the total population of the USSR, or about 2,500,000. In fact, however, the Jews are not allowed to enjoy any of these national rights.[1]

The reason advanced by the Soviets for this "special" treatment of the Jews is that the latter do not constitute a territorial nationality, but are dispersed in all parts of the Soviet Union. As early as 1926, Soviet chairman Michael I. Kalinin said:

> The Jewish people is confronted by a great problem—the maintenance of its own nationality, and for this it is necessary to transform a substantial portion of the Jewish population into a compact, settled rural population numbering at least some hundreds of thousands. It is only in such conditions that the Jewish masses will be able to hope for their future existence as a nationality.[2]

The Birobidzhan Experiment

Two years later the Soviets began to settle Jews in Birobidzhan, a region in the farthest corner of the Soviet Far East, bordering on Manchuria, some three hundred miles west of the Sea of Japan. From 1928 to 1933 inclusive, 19,635 Jews actually arrived in Birobidzhan; during the same period 11,450 again left the area, so that in 1934, when Birobidzhan was declared a Jewish Autonomous Region, there were in the area 8,185 Jews, constituting about 20 percent of the total population of the region. Faced with such poor results, the Soviet authorities resorted to active "recruiting" of settlers, which brought the region's Jewish population to 20,000 by 1937. In that year there were eighteen Jewish collective farms in the region; conditions continued to be extremely difficult, and, consequently, whatever Jewish cultural life developed, remained rudimentary. There were a few Yiddish schools (all of which ceased functioning during World War II), a small Yiddish paper, the *Birobidzhan Stern* (circulation 1,000), was published,[3] and there was a Yiddish theater; this was about all.

During World War II the Jewish population of Birobidzhan diminished and Jewish cultural life practically disappeared. After the war, in 1946–48, another 10,000 Jews arrived, mostly in organized echelons. After 1948 the Soviet government's interest in settling Jews in Birobidzhan abated, the number of Jews in the region gradually declined as a result of outfiltration, and according to the January 1959 Soviet census, there remained only 14,269 Jews in the region, constituting 8.8 percent of its total population.[4]

Irrespective of the failure to transform the Jews into a "compact, settled, rural population," as envisaged by Kalinin, the Soviets continued to discriminate against the Jews. This treatment caught the Jews in a vise by applying two opposite pressures: on the one hand, it made it almost impossible for them to preserve their language, culture, traditions, and religion; on the other, by identifying every person born to a Jewish father as Jewish in the passport which every Soviet citizen must carry at all times, it made it impossible for them to assimilate completely and "pass" into the Russian majority. Thus the typical, Russian Jew of the younger generation grew up knowing nothing or next to nothing of his Jewish background, but nevertheless bearing the full onus of being a Jew. Soviet policy does not enable the Jews to live as a nationality, but neither does it allow them to die as a nationality. As Jews, Soviet Jewry is thus forced to live in limbo, to continue to exist as a zombie nation.

Religious Life ───────────────────────────────

It is well known that the Soviets do much to combat all religious faiths except their own special brand of Marxism. Since antireligious propaganda is one of the hallmarks of the Communist value system, no religion has a comfortable position in Russia. But even within this generally antireligious atmosphere Judaism is subjected to special discriminatory measures. There is one church for every 2,000 and one priest for every 1,143 Russian Orthodox in Russia; one parish and pastor for every 500 Baptists; and so on for other religious denominations. But there is only one synagogue and rabbi for every 33,000 Jews.[5] Many synagogues have been forcibly closed down and the buildings confiscated by the Russian authorities.

While these figures give the general outline of the picture, the colors can be filled in with a few details. Other religions are allowed to have their central organizations, publish religious material, manufacture religious appurtenances used in worship, maintain organizational relations with fellow believers in other countries, and so forth. In the case of the Jews all this is forbidden: they are not allowed to have a countrywide rabbinical or other religious organization, to publish religious books, calendars, or the Hebrew Bible, to study Hebrew, to manufacture prayer shawls, phylacteries, and mezuzahs, or to have contact with Jewish religious organizations or institutions outside Russia.[6]

In 1962 Rabbi Judah Leib Levin of Moscow called, or, more precisely, was forced to call, on the members of the Jewish religious community not to accept presents (i.e., prayer books, prayer shawls, and the like) from Jewish visitors from abroad. After no Jewish prayer books had been printed since the early 1920s, permission finally was granted in 1968 to Rabbi Levin to print ten thousand copies of a new Hebrew prayer book, or one copy for every 250 Jews in Russia.[7]

Other manifestations of religious harassment are the closing down of Jewish cemeteries in numerous cities, the prohibition of the baking of matzot, and the publication of anti-Jewish literature in which Jewish religion is described as a cluster of superstitions based on religious intolerance and reactionary ideas.[8]

Clearly, it is the policy of the Soviet Government "to isolate the Jews inside the Soviet Union from their brethren by kinship and by faith, beyond the borders of Russia, and to smother the Jewish spirit within them."[9]

Anti-Semitism

While the official Soviet position is to deny the existence of anti-Semitism in Russia, anti-Jewish sentiments and policies find their expression in numerous areas in addition to the purely religious discrimination touched upon above. In their franker moments, Soviet political and intellectual leaders admit the existence of anti-Semitism, although they try to explain it away as mere survival from the pre-Soviet period.[10]

One area in which Soviet anti-Semitism clearly manifests itself is that of civil service. Jews are systematically excluded from responsible civil service positions, or their number is sharply limited in such jobs. This policy is carried out despite the Jewish concentration in urban areas where most of the administrative offices are located, and despite the Jewish predilection for working with the head rather than the hands—both phenomena as pronounced in the USSR as in the USA. Keeping in mind that in the 1960s Soviet Jewry constituted a little more than 1 percent of the total population, and that most of the Jews were an urban element, the following figures are significant: The number of Jews among the deputies of the Soviet of the Union was reduced from 5.6 percent in 1937 to 0.8 percent in 1946, and to 0.3 percent in 1950. The number of Jews in the Soviet of Nationalities decreased from 2.6 percent in 1937 to 0.5 percent in 1950. Thereafter, the number of Jewish deputies in both houses continued to dwindle into minuscule proportion—ranging from one half to one quarter of one percent. A similar elimination of Jews from the elitist Central Committee of the Communist Party took place between 1939 and 1961. In 1939 no less than 10.9 percent of its members were Jews; by 1952 this was reduced to 3 percent, by 1956 to 2, and by 1961 to 0.3[11]

In 1964, among the 1,443 members of the Supreme Council of Nationalities and the Council of Unions there were five Jews, or a little more than one third of one percent. Of the close to 2 million members of the municipal and central soviets, there were 7,647 Jews, or 0.38 percent.[12]

While the limitation of Jewish participation in politics and the higher administrative echelons is merely a statistical matter, the anti-Semitic tenor of the press has been outspoken and often brutal. In newspapers the synagogues have been frequently described as places in which Jews conclude all sorts of dirty deals; even echoes of the age-old blood libel could be heard on the pages of at least one provincial paper; and, to cap it all, in 1963 a book entitled *Judaism Without Embellishment* was published under the auspices of the Ukrainian Academy of Science, containing the vilest *Stürmer*-like calumnies.[13]

Yet another manifestation of Soviet anti-Semitism took the form of exposing so-called "economic" crimes in what amounted to show trials. Although the individuals put on trial for such crimes as speculation in foreign currency and gold, bribery, appropriation of state property, and the like, included non-Jews as well, the proportion of accused Jews was extremely high— e.g., in one of these trials in Moscow in 1962 there were nineteen Jews among the fifty accused; at another, in Moscow in 1964, of the ten accused sentenced to death, seven were Jews; according to incomplete data, from July 1, 1961, to July 1, 1963, 140 defendants were sentenced to death, of whom 80 were Jews. Hundreds of other Jews received various other severe punishments. These trials evoked strong protests in the Western world, and by 1966 reports of such economic trials became less and less frequent.[14]

Occupational Structure

It is a most remarkable testimony to the cultural resilience and intellectual powers of the Soviet Diaspora that despite the prevalence of discrimination and anti-Semitism, the Russian Jews were able to achieve an occupational structure that, considering the overall features of a Communist economy, does not differ markedly from the occupational structure of other Jewries in the Western world. The first characteristic of this structure is concentration in academic professions, which also means concentration in urban areas.

In 1959, the year of the last census, Jews constituted 1.09 percent of the population of Soviet Russia (2,268,000 in absolute figures). In Moscow they constituted 4.7 percent; in Lenigrad 5.1 percent. In the same year, 9.9 percent of all Soviet scientific workers were Jews (30,600 persons). By 1965 their number increased to 53,000, but this increase was slower than that of the total number of Soviet scientific workers, so that by that year only 7.9 percent of the latter were Jews. However, this percentage still represented about eight times the proportion of Jews in the general population. In the early 1960s, 14.7 percent of all doctors were Jews, as were 10.4 percent of all lawyers, 8.5 percent of all writers and journalists, and 7 percent of all artists, including actors, sculptors, and musicians. About 10 percent of the members of the Academy of Sciences as well as of the winners of the Lenin Prize in science were Jews.[15] In 1963, of the 128,000 persons who had a doctor's or a candidate's degree, 7,680, or exactly 6 percent, were Jews. In 1966, of the nineteen scientists who received the Lenin Prize, five, or 26.3 percent, were Jews, as were 29, or 14.3 percent, of the 203 persons who got state prizes in 1967. Although Jews encountered special difficulties in admission to universities, nevertheless in l963–64 no less than 82,600, or 2.5 percent of all students (total number 3,260,700), were Jews. The absolute number of Jewish students was on the increase (in 1960 they had numbered 77,117), but their relative number decreased.[16]

Among teachers in institutions of higher learning, according to the 1939 census 7,000 were Jews; the 1959 census gives no information about the professional composition of the Jewish population, but an unsigned article in the volume *Soviet Jewry 1917–1967* estimates that by that year the number of Jewish college and university teachers must have reached 30,000.[17]

It is thus evident that the number of Jewish academic workers is on the decrease in relation to the total number of such workers in the USSR, as is the number of Jewish students relative to the total number of students in the Union (in 1935: 13 percent; in 1960: 3.2 percent; in 1963–64: 2.5 percent). However, from the internal Jewish point of view, the trend of intellectualization continues. In 1956, 24,600 Jews were scientific workers, or about 1 percent of all Soviet Jews. By 1965 their number had increased to 53,000, or 2.5 percent. In 1960, 290,700 Jews with university education (or about 13 percent of all Jews) worked as technical specialists.

The 77,177 Jewish students enrolled in that year in universities represented about 3.5 percent of the total number of Jews in the USSR. It thus appears that the percentage of professional workers in the Jewish population of the Soviet Union remained on the increase in the 1960s. In the same period, of the total non-Jewish population of the Soviet Union only about 1 percent attended institutions of higher education. The fact that, proportionately, three and one half times as many Jews as non-Jews were enrolled in universities indicates that the Jewish tendency of gravitating toward academic professions was still very much alive in the 1960s in the Russian Jewish Diaspora.[18]

Cultural Life

"During the last years of Stalin's life," Leon Shapiro has written, "Jewish culture was totally destroyed in the Soviet Union. Jewish theaters and publishing houses were liquidated, Jewish periodicals were shut down. The same fate befell Jewish books, which vanished without a trace from bookshops and even libraries."[19] In view of this, it is most remarkable that in the 1959 census there were still 405,936 Jews, or about 18 percent of all Soviet Jewry, who gave Yiddish as their national language, and that according to a Parisian Jewish Communist newspaper editor, Gershon Koenig of the *Neie Presse,* who visited Moscow in 1965, the "Russian Jews have retained their national physiognomy, independently of whether they talk Russian or Yiddish."[20] Faced with the reality of this stubborn survival of a Jewish "physiognomy," the Soviet press admitted late in 1966 that "the so-called territorial principle is inadequate to explain such a complex and peculiar phenomenon as national self-consciousness, and that in this question what must also be taken into account are factors of a cultural and historical character."[21]

Nevertheless, little or nothing was done to remedy the objective conditions of perpetuating Jewish culture. In 1966 there were no Yiddish schools at all in the Soviet Union, including Birobidzhan. In the twenty years from 1948 to 1968 only twenty books in Yiddish came out in the Soviet Union, including three reprints of old Yiddish classics by Peretz, Mendele, and Sholem Aleichem (all three published in 1959 by the State Publishing House in Moscow). However, 282 books by ninety Yiddish authors were published in Russian, Ukrainian, Kirgiz, and other translations. A Yiddish periodical, *Sovietish Heimland* [Soviet Homeland], has appeared since 1961, faithfully representing the official Soviet line with regard to the Jews. Almost all of the estimated one hundred Yiddish writers who lived in the Soviet Union in the late 1960s, and most of whom were born after 1911 and were thus products of the Communist era, worked simultaneously as journalists or translators into Russian, or had some other nonwriting occupation, such as those of teachers in Russian schools, physicians, accountants, engineers.[22]

In the theater the situation was even worse. In 1962 there were 495 professional theaters in Russian, Ukrainian, and other languages; none in Yiddish. However, several amateur little theaters in Yiddish did function in various cities, performing plays, musicals, concerts, reviews, variety acts; they were attended by an audience of hundreds of thousands every year, including many who did not understand Yiddish. In art, there were several painters, graphic artists, and illustrators who produced pictures with Jewish themes.[23]

For several decades Jewish youth in the Soviet Union had received no Jewish education. The great majority today knows neither Yiddish nor Hebrew, is familiar neither with Jewish religion nor with Jewish history. Yet on Yom Kippur, in the 1960s, year after year thousands and tens of thousands of Jewish youth would fill the synagogues of Moscow and the other cities in which such Jewish houses of worship still existed, and on Simhat Tora they would clog the streets in front of the synagogues singing Jewish songs and dancing late into the night to the accompaniment of hundreds of guitars. In describing this remarkable phenomenon, Leon Shapiro asks: "How . . . could it happen that in spite of the atheistic training, in spite of the prevailing mood of the public, this tug toward the age-old

Jewish way of life has been preserved even in the youngest generation of Russian Jewry?" And, unable to find a satisfactory explanation for this remarkable phenomenon, he says: "We . . . can only register these amazing facts testifying to the creative forces that have been thrusting themselves to the surface and that, under free conditions, will exert an influence on the cultural formation of Russian Jewry in [a] post-revolutionary Russian society."[24]

While Jewish cultural life of Soviet Jewry was thus moribund, the participation of Jews in Soviet cultural activities evinces an intensity that is out of all proportion to the numerical strength of the Jewish community in the USSR. This is especially appararent in music. After a detailed review of the role of Jews in the musical life of the Soviet Union, Gershon Swet reaches the conclusion that "It may be said without exaggeration that in the domain of performance the Jewish virtuosos of the Soviet Union occupy a pre-eminent position." As to the Jewish composers, they "have contributed an interesting page to the history of musical creation in Russia during the Soviet period." In musical education, "the Gnessin Institute occupies an outstanding place, as do many Jewish writers and researchers." All this makes "the Jewish contribution to Russian musical culture during the Soviet period . . . extremely significant."[25]

Outlook

There is thus a clearly discernible trend indicating the position the Jews of the Soviet Union will, in all likelihood, hold within the occupational structure of the country. Politics, government, and higher officialdom will increasingly become tabooed territories for them. On the other hand, more and more Jews will be concentrated in the arts, the sciences (including various technical fields), and an increasing proportion of the young generation will acquire a higher education. The typical Jewish Diaspora tendency to live by the work of the brain rather than by that of the brawn will thus increasingly assert itself, despite the exclusion of Jews from certain occupations.

The extent to which this trend will actually be realized will, of course, depend on the rulers of the Soviet Union. They can, should they so wish, bar all Jews from higher education and thereby put an end to the Jewish concentration in the arts and sciences within one generation, just as they have eliminated in the past two decades practically all the Jews from politics and government. However, it is not likely that they will resort to such measures. The Soviets are stark realists, bent on advancing their country in all areas that contribute to its power and prestige in the world. In this endeavor, they know, Jewish brainpower can make important contributions in the future as it did in the past. Therefore, it stands to reason that the resources of higher education will continue to be made available for the fullest realization of the Jewish scientific, intellectual, and artistic potential.

The danger for the Jewish Diaspora in the Soviet Union threatens from a different quarter. The Soviet Union is unmistakably intent on reducing and ultimately eliminating the Jewishness of its Jewish ethnic groups. The Soviet leadership seem to feel that Jewish talent will continue to be transmitted in the genes without the encumbrance of Jewish tradition, religion, and other aspects of the Jewish heritage, which predispose the Jews to take an undue interest—undue from the Russian point of view—in Israel and the fate of other Jewish Diasporas. Like an expert cattle raiser who breeds for meat or for milk, so the Soviets, by imposing particular political, social, and cultural limitations on the Jews, seem to be intent on breeding them for talent to the exclusion of other Jewish ethnic traits. Their aim manifestly is a de-Judaized future Jewish generation whose Jewish identity will be nothing more than a label in the passport, a name, and a dim historic memory, like that of the fervently religious Catholic Chuetas on the island of Majorca.

Nor do the Soviets have to resort to the violence of the Spanish Inquisition that resulted in the Majorcan Chueta group.[26] They have much more refined but no less effective methods at their disposal for achieving the same purpose. They try to obliterate, by various devices and pressures, all traces of the Jewish past, whether in their own country or in the world at large. In Soviet textbooks for secondary schools, in discussing Nazi death camps, no mention is made of the Jews whom the Germans annihiliated; in listing nations newly established since World

War II, Israel is not mentioned; in discussing recent French history, the Dreyfus case is not referred to; in describing Czarist Russia as a "prison house of nations," the pogroms and persecutions of the Jews are omitted. Equally characteristic is the elimination of the 117-page article that discussed Jewish history and culture in the first (1932) edition of the *Great Soviet Encyclopaedia,* and its replacement by a mere two pages in its second (1952) edition.[27]

All this is unmistakably intended to make the Jews a "non-people" in the eyes of Soviet Jews and gentiles alike. By, so to speak, cutting the Jewish ground from under the feet of Russian Jewry, the Soviets try to make it strike roots in the soil of Russia alone. We cannot know how successful this policy would be were it accompanied by a sincere and wholehearted willingness to accept those Jews who have thus been deprived of their Jewish background as full and complete Russians. Under the actual circumstances—in which forcible obliteration of all Jewishness is coupled with a mechanical-bureaucratic rubber-stamping of the Jews as Jews and continued discrimination against them—it has been largely a failure.

The Jewish reaction to these measures shows a remarkable similarity to what has been happening to the new Jewish physiognomy in the United States: in America the voluntary abandonment of Jewish religious forms and the spontaneously developed ignorance of Jewish background, tradition, and history are yet accompanied by a persistence of Jewish identification. In the Soviet Union the abandonment of Jewish religious forms under compulsion and the government-imposed ignorance of Jewish background, tradition, and history are also accompanied by a persistence of Jewish identification. Mass demonstrations of Jewishness on certain Jewish holidays are one way in which this identification manifests itself; attendance of Yiddish amateur theatrical performances, even by those ignorant of the language, is another. To these have been added in the most recent years, and especially since 1969, open and quite daring requests addressed to the Soviet authorities for exit permits to go to Israel, based on an argument which implies a summary rejection of fifty years of forcible Russification: "I am a Jew and only in Israel can I live a full Jewish life."[28]

355

Immigration

Every voluntary migration is the result of a combination of two types of factors: those that push the people to leave the country in which they live, and those that pull them to the country they choose to go to. During the heyday of Jewish migration from Eastern Europe to America the Diasporas from which most of the Jewish immigrants had come were not yet threatened with genocide. The very word had yet to be coined. The "push" to emigrate was supplied, not by a desperate last-minute effort to escape imminent death, but by such factors as dissatisfaction with miserable living conditions; the anti-Semitism of both the governments and the people (how "mild" this Jew-hatred was became evident only when the German *Endlosung* was initiated after the outbreak of World War II); the occasional local pogroms (how small-scale indeed these were in comparison with the Nazi holocaust!); and the general unpleasantness of Jewish life in the Eastern European small towns and big cities alike. The "pull" was not a Jewish-national ideology like the one that from 1882 on motivated the Eastern European Zionist *'aliyot* to Palestine, nor a quasi-Messianic upheaval that contributed to the immigration of many Middle Eastern and North African Jews to Israel immediately after the Jewish State attained independence. It was rather the more down-to-earth attraction exerted by a country which was a true democracy, in which there was no anti-Semitism to speak of (certainly not in comparison with Eastern Europe), in which one could make a living, and, more than that, one had a fair chance to "make it," and in which one could live among people of one's own kind who were found in increasing numbers in New York and the other big cities.

While the "push" factors made for large-scale Jewish emigra-

357

tion from Eastern Europe without giving it a specific direction or goal, it was due to the strong "pull" factors emanating from the United States that the overwhelming majority of the emigrants preferred America to any other country. The result was that of the 17.3 per thousand of all Russian Jews who emigrated during 1899–1914, 13 went to the United States, as against only 2.6 who went to other overseas countries, and 1.7 who emigrated to other European countries. The Jewish emigrants from Austria-Hungary and Rumania showed a similar preference for the United States.[1] Never before in the long history of Jewish migrations have the Jews who left their old homeland, for any reason, shown such an overwhelming preference for one single country of immigration, with the exception of post-independence Israel.

The earliest, Sephardi, phase of Jewish immigration into America was discussed in Chapter XIV, "The Sephardi Jews," which also touched upon the relationship between the Sephardim and the Ashkenazim in the United States down to the nineteenth century. While the Sephardim had the primacy in establishing a Jewish bridgehead in the Western hemisphere in general and in what was to become the United States in particular, one must be aware of two factors in order to view this achievement in the proper perspective. First, that throughout the 150 years of the so-called Sephardi phase of Jewish immigration the number of immigrants was exceedingly small, so that in 1818 the Jewish population of the United States was no more than three thousand. Second, that even this very limited immigration comprised not only Sephardim but also Ashkenazim, as attested, for instance, by the presence of Haym Salomon (1740–1785), a Polish Jew who placed the fortune he made as a broker in New York at the disposal of the Revolutionary cause, or of the Gratz family in Pennsylvania whose members were businessmen and civic leaders before the American Revolution, and others. Nevertheless, the Sephardim remained the dominant element in American Jewry both numerically and in prestige until 1840, when the total number of Jews in the United States was about fifteen thousand. From 1840 on, the Sephardim were reduced to a smaller and smaller percentage within the growing

358

Jewish population, until, by 1970, they constituted less than one half of 1 percent of American Jewry.

The second phase of Jewish immigration to America that began in the early nineteenth century came from Germany, and brought about 200,000 German Jews into the country before the century was over. Most of the early German Jewish immigrants were peddlers, small traders, wage workers, and others belonging to the lowest levels of the petit bourgeoisie. They were poor, but most of them were no longer strictly Orthodox, and, arriving as they did at a time when the conquest of the West was well under way, they managed to participate in it and contribute their share to it. In contrast to the Sephardi Jews who spoke Ladino, a language foreign to the countries (Holland, England) in which they had lived for many generations, the German Jews spoke German—that is, they had assimilated linguistically to the country in which they had lived. Having only recently gone through a process of switching languages (when, with the onset of the Enlightenment and assimilation, they gave up Yiddish for German), they found it relatively easy, once they settled in America, to replace it with English. This was undoubtedly a factor in the rapid advancement of the German Jewish immigrants from poverty to middle-class respectability, and, from the middle of the nineteenth century on, in a growing proportion, into the ranks of the well-to-do.

At the very time when this process of economic advancement got under way, the third wave of Jewish immigrants, that of the Eastern European Jews, began to reach the American shore. This immigration, which started in relatively modest numbers in the middle of the nineteenth century but reached huge dimensions beginning with the 1880s, brought to the United States a Jewish element whose majority had no choice but to become laborers in factories and workshops (most typically in the garment industry), which in those years experienced their great expansion in New York and other cities. The German Jews could now mete out the same treatment to these Eastern European Jews they had received from the Sephardim upon their arrival, although, at the same time, they also participated in the setting up of important charitable organizations to help the

359

needy newcomers. For a short while, until the further decline of the Sephardim and the rise of the Eastern European Jews, there was thus in America a three-storied structure of Jewish prestige hierarchy: the Sephardim on top, the Germans in the middle, and the Eastern Europeans at the bottom. As one would expect, this structure had the shape of a population pyramid: the higher the layer, the smaller its numbers.

By the time the large-scale Eastern European immigration began, that of the Sephardim had dwindled to almost nothing. In the thirty years from 1881 to 1910 the total number of Jewish immigrants to the United States was 1,562,800. During this period only 5,276 Jews immigrated from Turkey, all of them between 1899 and 1910.[2] Presumably most of the Jewish immigrants who had come from Turkey, which at the time included Syria, Palestine, and part of Greece,were Sephardi Jews. Even so, the percentage of Sephardi Jews among the immigrants in those thirty years was only one-third of 1 percent.

The remarkable thing about Jewish immigration into the United States was not so much its large size as its permanent character. Within fifty years, from 1882 to 1923, about 2,200,000 Jews came to America. Following the introduction of immigration quotas in 1924, the flow of immigration was reduced but did not stop; nor did it stop during World War I, the depression years, World War II, or following the establishment of Israel (see Chapter V, Table III). All in all, in the hundred years from 1870 to 1970 close to 3 million Jews immigrated into the United States—making this immigration by far the largest population movement in in the history of the Jewish people.

As to the permanence of the Jewish immigration, this was expressed in the fact that, in contrast to the non-Jewish immigrants, a high proportion of whom subsequently again left the United States, reemigration among the Jews was insignificant. In the thirty years from 1908 to 1937 only 5 percent of the Jewish immigrants reemigrated as against 34.6 percent of all immigrants.[3] The explanation of this significant difference is obvious: whatever difficulties the Jewish immigrants encountered in the United States, such as economic hardships, discrimination, depression, for them America was still a much better place to be in than the old countries they had left behind in Europe; for the non-Jewish immigrants, on the other hand, difficulties in the new country made the old one appear attractive enough to motivate them to return. To these factors was added in the World War I years the feeling many non-Jewish immigrants had that they must return to help their old country win the war. (In 1915–20 the general reemigration amounted to 56.6 per cent of the immigration.) The Jews, however, "felt far more obligated to the United States during the war than to their old countries";[4] consequently, only 4.3 percent of them reemigrated in 1915–20.

TABLE X

ESTIMATED NUMBER OF JEWS IN THE UNITED STATES, 1654–1970

Year	Number	Percent in Total Population
1654	24	
1790	2,500	
1818	3,000	
1826	6,000	
1830	10,000	
1840	15,000	
1850	50,000	0.2
1877	230,000	0.5
1887	400,000	0.7
1897	938,000	1.3
1907	1,777,000	2.0
1917	3,389,000	3.2
1927	4,228,000	3.6
1937	4,771,000	3.7
1947	5,000,000	3.5
1957	5,200,000	3.1
1967	5,800,000	2.9
1970	6,000,000	2.8

Sources: H. S. Linfield, *Statistics of Jews and Jewish Organizations* (New York, 1939), p. 23; Nathan Goldberg, "The Jewish Population in the United States," Encyclopedic Handbooks, *The Jewish People: Past and Present* (New York, 1948), II,25; *American Jewish Year Book.*

The extraordinary influx of Jewish immigrants resulted not only in a phenomenal growth of the Jewish community in America (see Table X) but also in making it the largest Diaspora that ever existed. More than that: not even in their own country have the Hebrews ever attained such numbers. In the dispersion, although in prerevolutionary Russia there were between 5 and 7 million Jews,[5] they lived in several greatly disparate socio-cultural environments (Russia, the Caucasus, the Ukraine, White Russia, Poland, Lithuania, Bessarabia, Bukhara, Khiva, etc.), which circumstance was reflected in their fragmentation into numerous disjointed Jewries, often with strong antagonisms among them. American Jewry, on the other hand, while it comprises a large number of sectors and trends, is not broken up into geographical parts, and in fact as well as in consciousness constitutes one community.

The next largest Jewish community after the American was the Polish. But even at its zenith, in 1939, Polish Jewry numbered only an estimated 3,300,000. Russian Jewry, the third largest in size, numbered at the same time about 2,825,000 and has since shrunk to about 2,500,000.[6] In 1968 Israel's Jewish population, after two decades of phenomenal growth, to which both the ingathering of the exiles and the high rate of natural increase of the Oriental Jews have contributed, had reached 2,383,000, a figure that still falls short of the number of the Jews in Greater New York alone.

Education: Jewish

More remarkable than its mere numerical growth is the phenomenal educational record of American Jewry. A considerable percentage of the immigrant Jews were illiterate (26 percent of those who came from 1899 to 1910);[7] others could read and write in Yiddish only; few of them had any secular education to speak of; almost none had ever come near a university. And yet their actual depressed educational state did not diminish their age-old tradition of putting a higher value on education than on almost anything else in life. As soon as they could afford it, and actually often even before they could afford it, they began to educate their children, even if this required the greatest sacrifices. One to two generations later, the picture has changed so radically that it had become a matter of course for all Jewish children to graduate from high school, and that a Jewish high school graduate who did not go on to college had become an exception. And, at the same time, increasing attention was being paid to the Jewish education of the children as well.

All minority groups in the United States are well aware of singular importance education has in the perpetuation of traditional values, although not all of them have been able to muster the energy and resources required for the setting up an extensive network of schools of their own. The largest nonpublic, parochial school system is that of the Catholic church, which has devoted a disproportionately large part of its total income in the country to Catholic education from elementary schools up to and including universities.

The American Jewish community, too, knows only too well that its entire future depends to a large extent on its educational effort. Consequently, each constituent sector of American Jewry has organized, and maintains, an extensive school network of its own. There are Orthodox, Conservative, Reform, Inter-Congregational, Communal-Noncongregational and Yiddish schools, which in 1968 had a total enrollment of 446,648 pupils. There are Jewish nurseries, kindergartens, elementary schools, and high schools. Among those Jewish children who attended Jewish schools, about one third went to a Jewish school one day a week; considerably smaller numbers studied two, three, four, or five afternoons weekly; a very few (approximately 15,000) studied in Jewish day schools. Of all the Jewish children aged eight to twelve years (443,079 children) 69.8 percent (or 308,833 children) were enrolled in one or another of the above types of Jewish elementary schools. It is interesting to note that the larger the Jewish community (i.e., the larger the city in which the Jewish group in question dwelt), the lower the percentage of Jewish children attending Jewish schools. In communities with fewer than 100 Jews, 99.4 per cent of the Jewish children were sent to Jewish schools; while in the largest cities, in communities with more than 150,000 Jews, only 61.3 percent of the Jewish children were sent to Jewish schools.[8]

These figures support the frequently voiced opinion that

the pressure of the non-Jewish environment is a significant contributing factor making for Jewish identification. The smaller the town and the smaller the Jewish community in it, the more the Jews feel they must conform in their religious behavior to the gentile pattern; and since in surburbia the general American expectation is that parents will belong to a religious organization and train their children in their religion, enrollment of the children in one type of Jewish school or another becomes virtually mandatory. Whatever the motivations and the variations as between small town and big city, it is no mean achievement to have on the average seven out of every ten Jewish children aged eight to twelve enrolled in a Jewish school. The available data do not make it clear whether this seven-out-of-ten figure means that seven out of every ten Jewish children attend Jewish schools for four full years, and the remaining three do not attend at all; or that all ten of them attend Jewish school but for an average of a little less than three years only. In all probability the actual situation is somewhere between these two extremes. In any case, the fact remains that the great majority of Jewish children growing up at present in the United States do receive at least a rudimentary Jewish education. It is in this fact that the primary guarantee of the survival of American Jewry lies.

Education: General

While the effort to expand Jewish education continues unabated, no one can deny that Jewish education is considered by most American Jews as a luxury in comparison to the bread-and-butter offerings of secular higher education. The American people in general subscribe to the view that higher education is the key to most of the good things life has in store for the young generation; consequently, the relative number of college and university students in America is much higher than in any other country. In 1966 (the latest year for which at the time of writing figures were available), 3.24 percent of the total American population was enrolled in colleges and universities as against 1.76 percent in Soviet Russia, 1.49 percent in Israel, 1.04 percent in France, 0.76 percent in Ireland, 0.71 percent in West Germany, 0.66 percent in Italy, 0.63 percent in Syria and 0.60 percent in Egypt.[9]

The age-old Jewish predilection for educational attainment reasserts itself in every Diaspora in connection with college and university attendance. Whatever the percentage of the general college population in a country, that of the Jewish students in relation to the total numbers of the Jewish community in the country is always higher, often considerably higher, unless, of course, Jews are kept from entering institutions of higher learning by laws or unwritten understandings. In the United States, when 3.24 percent of the total American population was enrolled in colleges and universities, the corresponding percentage for the Jewish community was 5.60, or 72.84 percent higher.[10] By 1970, between 325,000 and 350,000, or almost all American Jewish young men and women in the college-age group, actually attended a college or university.[11] At least as far as formal educational attainments are concerned, the American Jewish youth of today is undoubtedly the best educated group in the world.

Studies made in several cities also show that invariably the Jewish population contains a higher percentage of college graduates than the general population. This is clearly shown in Table XII, which compares the Jewish with the total population of eleven American cities, accounting, among them, for 63.5 percent of the American Jewish community at the time (1950–52). If, instead of comparing the Jewish with the *total* population, the data would compare the Jewish with the *non-Jewish* population in the cities studied, the results would have indicated even greater percentage differences.

Occupational Structure

It is a foregone conclusion that a group whose members over a period of several decades go to college in much greater proportion than is the case in the population in general will have an occupational structure that will differ from that of the majority in a manner determined by the higher percentage of college

365

TABLE XI

PERCENTAGE OF THOSE WHO ATTENDED COLLEGE, GRADUATED FROM COLLEGE, AND ATTENDED POST-GRADUATE SCHOOLS

Year	City	Jews	Total Population	Number of Jews
1952	New York City[a]	18.9	4.0	2,294,000
1950	Los Angeles[b]	29.0	20.9	323,000
1950	Newark, N.J.	19.6	7.6[a]	56,800
1950	Atlanta	26.3	15.8	10,217
1950	New Orleans[c]	19.2	7.5	9,100
1950	Trenton	18.1	4.9	8,500
1950	Camden	21.3	5.3	6,517
1950	Indianapolis	33.9	15.7[d]	6,268
1950	Gary	38.8	10.7[e]	2,500
1950	Port Chester	23.8	13.5[b]	2,235
1950	Miami	28.5	22.3	40,000
				2,759,137

[a]Age 5 and over.
[b]Age 15 and over. Unless otherwise indicated, based on age 25 and over.
[c]Age 6 and over
[d]Age 20 and over
[e]Does not give age limit.
Sources: Ben B. Seligman with Aaron Antonowitsky, "Some Aspects of Jewish Demography," and Ben B. Seligman, "The Jewish Population of New York City: 1952," both in Marshall Sklare, ed., *The Jews: Social Patterns of an American Group* (Glencoe, Ill., 1958), pp. 51, 84–85, 95, 106.

graduates in its midst. It comes therefore as no surprise that American Jews tend to specialize in managerial, proprietorial, commercial, professional, artistic, and literary occupations to a higher degree than gentiles. On the other hand, relatively fewer among the Jews engage in clerical work, skilled, semi-skilled, and unskilled labor, and in service occupations. Hand in hand with these differences go the following: American Jews tend more than gentiles to achieve higher incomes, to live in the biggest cities of the country and their suburbs, to marry later, divorce less frequently, have fewer children, and live somewhat longer. (Also, they attend religious services less frequently—but the subject of religion will be discussed later.)

No overall study of the occupational structure of American Jewry being available, the foregoing generalizations can be substantiated only by reference to a few local samples. For instance, in Ohio in 1936 there was one doctor per every 756 of the general population, as against one Jewish doctor per every 231 of the state's Jewish population. In the general population one out of every 1,603 was a dentist; among the Jews one in 469. In the general population one of 682 was a lawyer; among the Jews one in 147. On the other hand, there were fewer teachers, engineers, and architects among the Jews than in the general population.[12]

Similarly, in several cities studied it was found that a higher percentage of the Jews than of the total white population was in the "professional and semi-professional" category. In some cities the difference was small (as, e.g., in Indianapolis, where 12.4 percent of the Jewish and 9.4 percent of the total white male population was in this category in 1950); in others, considerable (as, e.g., in Camden, where the corresponding percentages were 18.8 and 5.5 respectively). A no less marked difference existed in the "proprietors, managers, officials" category, in which, incidentally, in each of the cities studied, at least twice as many Jews were found in the professional and semi-professional category. Putting the two categories together, we find that in a typical American city some 50 to 70 percent of all gainfully employed Jews were in the professional, semi-professional, proprietorial, managerial, and official category, while of the general population only 15 to 25 percent were in the same categories.[13] Or to quote Seligman, "the proportion of the Jewish male labor force engaged in all professional and semi-professional occupations was almost two and one-half times the proportion found in the total white male labor force."[14]

Another interesting observation is the marked tendency among the Jewish professionals to concentrate in medicine and dentistry (24 to 39 percent of the total Jewish professionals in eight cities studied), law (14–26 percent), and teaching (including rabbis and cantors, 13–19 percent).

In New York City, where some two-fifths of the entire American Jewish community live, and where they constitute about one fourth of the city's total population, they comprised over 45 percent in the proprietor and managerial category and 33 percent of the professional and semi-professional categories. They constituted only 6.2 percent of the services categories and 19.1 percent of the craftsmen, operative, and labor categories. Over two thirds of employed Jews were in nonmanual occupations compared to only one half of the employed white non-Jews.[15]

Not only is the proportion of professionals higher among Jews than non-Jews, but it is also rising. In 1935–45 the percentage of professionals among the gainfully employed Jews in ten communities studied was 11. In fourteen communities studied in 1948–53, it was 15. The latter percentage is almost twice as high as that of professionals in the total American population, which in 1950 was 8.[16]

The occupational categories mentioned yield, as a rule, higher incomes than other occupations (mainly clerical, sales, craftsmen, foremen, skilled and semi-skilled workers, service workers, and unskilled workers). Consequently, the average income level of the Jewish population is higher than that of the general population. In a study based on a very small sample of families (87 Jewish, 901 white Catholic, 1076 white Protestant, and 330 Negro Protestant) in Detroit (1951–55) it was found, for example, that the median income of the Jewish family heads was $6,200, as against $4,800 for the white Protestants, $4,650 for the white Catholics, and $3,400 for the Negro Protestants. The same

368

study found that 40 percent of the Jewish, 21 percent of the white Protestant, 14 percent of the white Catholic, and 1 percent of the Negro Protestant family heads had an income of $7,000 or more.[17]

In New York City 12 percent of the Jewish households had, in 1951, incomes of more than $10,000, as compared with 5 percent of the non-Jewish households; and 29 percent of the Jewish households had less than $4,000 income, as compared to 49 percent of the non-Jewish households.[18]

Upon closer inspection, a further fact emerges: in every locality, and within every profession, Jewish college graduates tended to have higher incomes than the non-Jewish.[19] Analyzing the probable causes of this phenomenon, Nathan Glazer conjectures that the Jewish immigrants to America, although "they had been forced out of their age-old pursuits and proletarianized" in Czarist Russia and, in general, in Eastern Europe, brought along with them the tradition and memory of their fathers and grandfathers who were, typically, merchants and scholars. And thus, even while the Jewish immigrants had to make a living in sweatshops and engage in other types of hard larbor, they immediately turned "their minds to ways and means of improving themselves that were quite beyond the imagination of their fellow workers." The same background, the same historical experience, predisposed the Jewish immigrants and their children to maintain a pattern of foresight and sobriety, and motivated them to accept "today's restraints for the rewards of tomorrow." When the children of these immigrants were enabled to go to college—to do which was their greatest ambition—they studied harder, when they entered a business or a profession, they worked harder, just as their fathers had done before them.[20]

Linguistic Assimilation

Students of American Jewry have often pointed out the tendency of Jewish immigrants in America to give up their language (which in most cases was Yiddish) and assimilate linguistically to the English vernacular of the country. To this we may add that in the English-speaking environment of America the children of immigrants often develop an antagonism to the old language spoken by their parents in the home, want to forget their mother tongue, rapidly succeed in doing so, and within an incredibly short time after their arrival actually know no other language but English.

This is not a specifically Jewish phenomenon. Non-Jewish immigrants have the same experience with their children. A few years ago a non-Jewish Hungarian friend of mine, who is professor of Turkish at a metropolitan university, told me about his experience with his children. He had married in Hungary, where his two sons were born; the boys had begun to go to school in Hungary when he accepted an invitation to the University of Ankara. In Turkey the boys went to a Turkish school and quickly enough learned Turkish; but the parents continued to talk to them in Hungarian, so that the boys not only did not forget their mother tongue, but broadened their knowledge of it as the years passed. Then my friend was invited to a university in the United States and came here with his family. The children were sent to a local school, but again the parents were resolved to retain Hungarian as the home medium. Within a few months the boys were able to get along in class with their rapidly increasing knowledge of English. Soon thereafter, when their parents addressed them in Hungarian, they began to answer in English, and very soon, despite their resolve, the parents had to admit that they were beaten at their language game. Whether a year later the boys still knew how to speak Hungarian could not be ascertained because the only language they used was English.

Evidently, English in America had a much more powerful impact on these Hungarian boys than Turkish had in Turkey. This has, in all probability, something to do, not so much with any difference between the two languages themselves, as with the much more aggressive, intrusive, and penetrating nature of American culture of which English is the vehicle. It was the powerful attraction of American culture that made the English language the only tongue the boys wanted to use and to know, while in Turkey the Turkish culture that was offered to them through the medium of the Turkish language obviously did not have the same magnetic force.

Much the same has been the experience of German, Italian, Polish, and other immigrants. Their children, brought at a young age to America, quickly forgot their mother tongue; the younger siblings, born in the United States after the immigration of the parents, never learned it despite all the efforts of the latter.

Almost, but not quite, the same thing happened to Yiddish. This Jewish language, to which the Jews had remained faithful for centuries in Slavic and other foreign linguistic environments, held its own a little longer than the other immigrants' languages. But its decline, too, came soon enough. Most of the children of Yiddish-speaking immigrants, associating the Yiddish language with the outlandish, old-fashioned ways of their parents, came to consider it a quaint and primitive tongue in which it was not possible to express complex or refined ideas. It was, they felt, a folksy, homey language, to which one resorted when wishing to use a vulgarism or to indicate, when in the company of other Jews, that one was an insider, that one belonged. In brief, the typical second generation Jew in America still understood Yiddish but his ability to speak it had become rudimentary. In the third generation, even the passive knowledge of the language disappeared.

This process of linguistic assimilation got underway soon after the arrival of the immigrants, and especially as soon as job situations took them away from all-Jewish environments such as New York's Lower East Side. Aiding in the process was the system of compulsory education of the children which meant English as the language of tuition. In the early 1920s came the radio, bringing the English language right into the homes, and thus contributing to the replacement of Yiddish by English as the family colloquial. By the 1930s most American Jews no longer spoke Yiddish; by the 1940s, the younger generation no longer understood it either. The gradual decline of the Yiddish press is an index of the passing of the last Yiddish speakers of whom, by the 1980s, only a few Methuselahs will remain.

As far as language is concerned, therefore, American Jewry

371

has assimilated to English in much the same manner as, but with a somewhat slower speed than, the other immigrant groups.

The Attitude to Religion

In studying the acculturative processes among American Jews, it is most instructive to observe how much Jewish religious customs have lost of their traditional Jewish character and to what extent they have been recast into a quasi-American mold. This transformation does not necessarily mean an adoption of Christian coloration—although that, too, happens quite frequently—but it almost invariably takes place in reaction or as an adjustment to the American mores, whether the latter have a Christian or a secular basis.

Professor Abraham G. Duker, who discussed these phenomena with great insight, observed that "the primary culture of the overwhelming majority" of American Jews by the 1950s had become American culture, consisting of an "amalgam mainly of Anglo-Saxon, Protestant, and democratic-secular ingredients, under the growing impact of Catholic influences."[21]

That American culture should be the main determinant in all areas of the *secular* cultural life of American Jews is so self-evident that it needs no elaboration. Jews have, in fact, become a ranking group among both the producers and consumers of American culture in each and every field; in some areas, such as art, music, literature, and science, their participation is conspicuous. What does call for comment, because it is a phenomenon one would not ordinarily expect, is the marked influence American culture has had on the *religious* aspect of American Jewish life. Religion is, after all, the most specifically Jewish of all aspects of Jewish culture; American influence in this area, therefore, is the most eloquent indication of the depth to which American influences have penetrated into the fabric of Jewish life. Moreover, since in the religious area American influence is always Christian influence, all changes that can be observed in American Jewish religious life in the direction of Americanization represent, at one and the same time, also steps in the direction of Christianization.

Before adducing concrete examples of this process, let us first state in general terms that the very attitude to their religion manifested by second and third generation American Jews is a reflection of Christian American influence. It has been pointed out by many students of American Jewish life that the establishment of Jewish congregations, especially in suburbia, the membership in them, the weekly attendance at synagogue services, the enrolling of children in the synagogue-affiliated religious school, and many more manifestations of Jewish institutionalized religious life are but the translation into Judaism of the corresponding features found in Christian America. Were it not for the fact that to participate in this manner in the religious life of a congregation is considered good American form, the membership of the Jewish congregations all over the country would never have reached its present dimensions. This is not to say, of course, that this consideration is the only motivation for congregational membership and all that it involves, but it is a powerful contributing factor.

Most second and third generation American Jews are not willing to undergo formal conversion to one of the many Christian denominations that make up the Christian majority of America; such a step they would consider an act of disloyalty to their Jewish religion, traditions, history. Also, while conversion is sought and encouraged by most denominations, it is considered a laudable act only by the faith *to* which one converts; the faith *out* of which one converts considers it apostasy, betrayal, and a sin. In addition, the secular American attitude to conversion is, by and large, negative: one is supposed to remain, however loose the ties, within the religious community into which one was born. All this gives conversion a slightly un-American tinge: proper people just don't do it. The American ethos has been sufficiently internalized by most American Jews to make them cringe at the idea of conversion, quite apart from their residual but traditional Jewish abhorrence of apostasy.

What many American Jews would prefer is to have no institutionalized Jewish religious affiliation whatsoever. In the anonymity of big city life many, in fact, find it possible to avoid becoming members of a Jewish congregation, although even there it is a rare Jew who can manage to remain outside the entire complex network of Jewish organizations. In suburbia or small towns, the general American expectation that all good Americans not only have a religion but are members of a religious organization makes it well-nigh impossible for a Jewish family to remain unaffiliated with a synagogue.

In this manner, and somewhat paradoxically, it is precisely the urge many Jews feel to follow the American pattern that contributes in no small measure to the preservation of American Judaism.

Religious Forms

It goes without saying that where the emulation of American Christian patterns is an important contributing factor to the establishment and maintenance of Jewish congregations and synagogues, the forms taken by congregational activities and the synagogue services also exhibit considerable similarities to their Christian counterparts. This is expressed in many ways.

Take the very frequency of synagogue attendance. In traditional Judaism a religious man would go twice daily to the synagogue: to participate in the morning *(shaharit)* prayers and in the afternoon-evening *(minha-ma'ariv)* prayers. In American Jewry, even within the small minority that still goes to the synagogue regularly, most men attend services only once a week at the utmost, usually the late Friday evening prayers. Such attendance at services once a week at a fixed hour all year round can be attributed to Christian American influence. In traditional Judaism the Friday evening services were (and are) held at varying times, always about half an hour or so before sunset so as to actually usher in with prayers the Sabbath which begins at sunset. Similarly, non-Jewish influence can be seen in the attendance of women at these (and other synagogue) services. Traditional Jewish religion does not require women to go to synagogue at all, nor, for that matter, does it require women to recite any prayers apart from a few specifically for women. In America, under the influence of the Christian environment, one often finds that at services in Reform or Conservative syna-

374

gogues more women than men are present. In numerous Reform and Conservative synagogues women are called up to the reading of the Torah and stand up to recite the *Kaddish:* both customs are foreign to Jewish tradition, but have become accepted in emulation of the greater role played by women in Christian churches (where, e.g., it is mostly women who light candles in memory of the dead).

This question apart, new religious customs, mostly again under Christian influence, have been added: "the invocation at public gatherings, the rabbinical robe, the type of hymns, the sermon, and the posture at prayer."[22]

On the other hand, a number of old Jewish religious customs have completely or practically disappeared from American Jewish life: the ritual bath *(mikve),* the premarital agreement *(t'na'im),* the celebration after the birth of a male child *(ben zakhar),* the observance of not mixing wool and flax in one's clothes *(sha'atnez),* the wearing of the small tallit *(tzitzit* or *arba' kanfot),* the fasting by first-born men on the eve of Passover *(tzom b'khorim),* the posting of a written or printed text in the room in which a woman lies after childbirth *(shir hama'alot),* the sale of *hametz* before Passover, the symbolic casting of bread crumbs into water on the afternoon of the first day of New Year *(tashlikh).*[23]

There may be different individual causes for the decline in the observance of each of these customs; but one cannot help wondering whether the fact that they all seem outlandish in the context of modern American life has something to do with it, as well as another fact—namely, that they have no counterpart, not even anything vaguely similar to them, in the world of Christian American religion. This suspicion becomes strengthened when one considers the increase in importance of those Jewish religious customs which do have a Christian equivalent, or, more precisely, those Jewish religious customs which can be and are considered by the Jews as the Jewish equivalents of widely observed Christian religious customs.

The Bar Mitzva and Bat Mitzva celebrations come to mind as an example. In traditional Judaism Bar Mitzva, the onset of the adulthood of a boy from the religious point of view, at the age of thirteen, was marked by calling him up to the reading of the Tora in the synagogue. No further festivity or celebration took place. The Bat Mitzva (the celebration of reaching adulthood by a girl) simply did not exist. What was of great importance in traditional Judaism in the early life of the male child was the *mila,* his circumcision, on the eighth day after his birth, in the synagogue, on which day the father used to treat the congregation to as sumptuous a feast as he could afford. But since circumcision has no equivalent celebration among non-Jewish Americans (although most of them do have their sons circumcised for hygienic reasons), among most Jews the *mila* is no longer an occasion for a celebration but is performed by a doctor without any religious observance.

The Bar Mitzva, on the other hand, has developed into a major event, a catered affair, because it corresponds to the Christian confirmation. And since Christian Americans celebrate the confirmation of girls as well as boys, it was inevitable that also among American Jews an equivalent celebration should be introduced, in the form of the Bat Mitzva, although it is totally devoid of any traditional Jewish basis.

The extent to which the Bar Mitzva and Bat Mitzva celebrations have ben secularized, formalized, commercialized, and, indeed, vulgarized can be gauged, among other things, from the way these "affairs" are treated in the tabloid press. Take the February 13, 1969, issue of the *New York Post* as an example. That issue carried caterers' display advertisements for a "Fabulous Kosher Bar Mitzvah Package," offering for "$10.50 per person complete" a full ten course dinner preceded by "an ultra deluxe hot smorgasbord" including such temptingly *"Trefa"*-sounding dishes as Cantonese Chow Mein, Barbecued Ribs, Beef Stroganoff, Chicken Cacciatore, and the like. In the same issue, several articles instructed the parents how to go about arranging a Bar Mitzva, beginning with a full year in advance, when the "date should be chosen and size of Bar Mitzvah settled. Engage space, caterer and musicians." Then, 6 months ahead of the event,

> prepare guest list; 4 months—select an engraver and place your order for invitations; 3 months—begin to address invitations,

start seating plan and place cards. Purchase gifts for the rabbi, cantor or teacher and temple. 2 months—select a florist and place your order. Go over family wardrobes for the Bar Mitzvah. Reserve rooms for guests from out-of-town (for which you are not expected to pay). 1 month—mail invitations and arrange for a photographer to cover the event. 3 weeks—go over orders with the caterer and florist, and order a birthday cake if it is needed. Polish silver to be used at the Bar Mitzvah and put in plastic bags until the occasion. 2 weeks—confirm hotel reservations . . . 2 days— make sure the seating plan is completed . . . 1 day—check the final arrangements for the reception or luncheon. The day—relax and enjoy.

Well, not quite yet. Because on another page we read that it is desirable to have a "receiving line," which, if in the synagogue, should observe the following order: "president of the congregation, rabbi, cantor, the Bar Mitzvah boy, hostess and host. But, if the receiving line is at home or in a catering hall, the order is: hostess, host, Bar Mitzvah boy, rabbi and cantor. The grandparents are welcome to join the receiving line, if they wish." On yet another page, the parents of the Bas [i.e., Bat] Mitzvah girl are told how to phrase the invitations for that occasion. All comments are superfluous.

One of the most striking examples of the development of new Jewish religious or quasi-religious observances under the influence and in emulation of a Christian celebration is American Jewish practice with respect to Hanukka. Hanukka is a post-Biblical feast, celebrated since Talmudic times only, in memory of the Maccabean victory and the cleansing of the Temple, in the course of which a minor miracle is said to have taken place: the only undefiled cruse of consecrated oil that could be found burned for eight full days, while the Levites prepared new oil for the Eternal Light. It has always been a minor, insignificant holiday; in fact, it is the only annual feast, apart from Purim, on which it is *not* forbidden to work. In traditional Jewish homes throughout the ages it used to be celebrated by a simple and brief ritual of lighting one candle on the first day, then two on the second, and so on until the full row of eight candles were lit on the eighth and last day; each time a brief benediction was said by the master of the house, after which the family sang the

Ma'oz Tzur, a rather primitive poem of thanksgiving (written in the thirteenth century), in which the Syrian enemy of the Maccabees is referred to as "the barking foe"—fortunately few people understood the words or cared about them, and the melody to which they were put, taken from an old German folk song, was pleasant enough.

Apart from this brief rite, followed by a game of tops (*dreidel*) by the children, and the addition of the "Hallel" to the usual weekday morning prayer in the synagogue, the eight days of Hanukka were in no way differentiated from ordinary weekdays and working days. Everybody went about his normal occupation as usual. The great traditional Jewish children's festival has always been Purim, not Hanukka.

On Purim children wearing masks and fancy costumes would go from house to house and get presents, they would perform traditional plays about King Ahasuerus and Queen Esther, pious Mordecai and evil Haman, and even in the synagogue they would enjoy otherwise unheard of liberties, making deafening noise with rattles, stamping their feet, whistling and shouting whenever the name of Haman was read in the Book of Esther. Of all this practically nothing has survived in the American Jewish Diaspora, with the exception of the most Orthodox congregations. Why this demise of Purim and its replacement by Hanukka as the children's celebration, although traditionally Hanukka was not at all a children's holiday?

The answer lies, of course, in the fact that Purim occurs in February or March, at a time of the year when there is no Christian holiday for which it could serve as a Jewish counterpart, while Hanukka falls within two or three weeks of Christmas and thus is eminently suited to serve as the Jewish "answer" to it. Christian children get their Christmas tree; Jewish children their Hanukka Menora; both get lavish presents. Christmas has been transformed from a solemn religious festival to a day of delight for children, and, correspondingly, Hanukka assumed the same character.[24] The aping of Christmas has been carried to such lengths that not only has the *dreidel* practically disappeared, but in many Jewish homes the Hanukka Menora, too, has been discarded for what is rather ambiguously termed the "Hanukka bush," and Santa Claus, the mythical dispenser of Christmas presents, has been duplicated by "Uncle Max the Hanukka Man" who distributes gifts to the Jewish children.[25] These efforts at building a Christmaslike, and at the same time Jewish, image of Hanukka are undertaken by parents who are Jewishly conscious and conscientious; those who are not, simply have Christmas trees for their children, since, as the argument goes, Christmas is, after all, an American national holiday and not a Christian religious one.

Many more examples of the subtle and not so subtle penetration of Christian American features into Jewish religious life could be adduced. But the point has been sufficiently made and there is no need to belabor it. What requires stressing is that all this does not necessarily spell the demise or decline of Jewish religion. Throughout Jewish history features from the non-Jewish environment managed to become accepted into Judaism, and with time were endowed with a Jewish meaning and value, often of high intensity, while their foreign origin was completely forgotten. Among them are the Sabbath, circumcision, animal sacrifices, libations, the covering of the head, the Hasidic garb, the stories of Creation and of the great flood. By the same token, the Christian American elements, whose penetration into American Jewish life is today decried by religious leaders and sensitive laymen, can become part and parcel of Jewish religion, endowed with Jewish value and meaning, and thus represent but a new development in the old chain of tradition. Judaism has always stood for development, for the adaptation of the old laws to new conditions of life, even if this adaptation had to amount to a complete reinterpretation, or even to a reversal of the intent of the original law. As long as Judaism is able to change with the times, to admit and incorporate new elements or features, it is alive and it can look to a future. If it becomes rigid, if it rejects change, it runs the risk of fossilization, as happened to the Samaritans and the Karaites.

The Organizational Network

In no other country in the world have the Jews set up and

maintained such a complex network of organizations as in the United States. Not only is the number of organizations and institutions enormous (there are several thousands of them), but they fall into so many types that it is extremely difficult to present them in logical categories. In an attempt at such a presentation made almost three decades ago, Abraham G. Duker grouped them under religious institutions, cultural agencies (including educational), social and recreational establishments (including *landsmanshaften,* fraternal orders, and community centers), philanthropic and welfare agencies, agencies for overseas relief and reconstruction, and for the building of Palestine.[26]

Every year the *American Jewish Year Book* contains a list of national Jewish organizations in the United States, extending over twenty-eight pages, and enumerating (in the 1969) edition more than three hundred organizations. These are listed under categories according to functions: community relations, cultural, overseas aid, religious and educational, social and mutual benefit, social welfare, Zionist and pro-Israel. The list is not complete. Since it lists only *national* bodies, it contains no reference to the thousands of local organizations. Let us consider what this profusion of organizations means for the average individual American Jew.

The average American Jew will, in all probability, belong and pay dues to a religious congregation that, in turn, is affiliated with one of the three large national Jewish religious organizations—the Reform Union of American Hebrew Congregations, the Conservative United Synagogue of America, the Orthodox Union of Orthodox Jewish Congregations of America—or with one of the other smaller associations of Jewish congregations. These national bodies, in turn, have established, and are members of, an overall Jewish religious representative body of Orthodox, Conservative, and Reform Judaism in the United States, called the Synagogue Council of America.

In addition to his religious interest, the average American Jew, if he is of the older generation, may retain sufficient sentimental attachment, not actually to the place from where he came, but to its *memory,* to join with the others who came from the same place, in a mutual benefit society called *landsmanshaft* (from the

German *Landsmannschaft)*. Some, but not all, of these *lands-manshaften* are federated into countrywide organizations which comprise all groups hailing from one country, such as the American Federation of Polish Jews, United Rumanian Jews of America, United Galician Jews of America, United Hungarian Jews of America, and so forth.

Apart from, or in place of, membership in such an origin group, our average American Jew, especially if he is of the younger generation, may be a member in a fraternal order. These fraternal orders were established as the Jewish counterparts of the numerous American fraternal orders, such as the Masons, the Elks, the Knights of Pythias, the Shriners, which, too, attracted a large number of Jews. The Jewish orders have either a general Jewish service orientation, such as the B'nai B'rith, which is by far the largest of them (1970 global membership approximately 500,000, of which about 450,000 are in the United States), the Brith Abraham, Brith Sholom, Free Sons of Israel, Progressive Order of the West, and numerous others; or are labor- and socialist-oriented, such as the Workmen's Circle, the International Jewish Labor Bund, and the Jewish Socialist Verband of America; or else Zionist-oriented, such as the Bnai Zion-The American Fraternal Zionist Organization, and the Farband-Labor Zionist Order; or based on Sephardi descent, such as the Central Sephardic Jewish Community of America, the Sephardic Jewish Brotherhood of America, and the American branch of the World Sephardi Federation. At least one, the Mu Sigma Fraternity, is a Greek-letter (!) brotherhood; while the Jewish Chautauqua Society took its name from the American adult educational movement, which in turn derived its name from that of the town in which it was founded, and which is located on the shore of the lake of the same name, meaning in the original Seneca Indian language "one has taken out fish there." The founders of the Jewish society undoubtedly felt that if the Indian name was good enough for the Anglo-Saxon society, it was good enough for its Jewish counterpart.

But, to get back to our average American Jew, synagogue affiliation and membership in a *landsmanshaft* or a fraternal order are far from summing up his organizational life. He may be a member of one of the several Zionist organizations, or of a group supporting this or the other Jewish cultural, educational, or charitable institution in America, Israel, or elsewhere. In addition, he almost certainly contributes his annual share to the United Jewish Appeal, through his membership in a local group of one of the many divisions comprised in this giant fund raising organization, the largest not only in the Jewish world but in the entire United States.

The multiplicity of this organizational network means that the average American Jew participates in one way or another in American Jewish communal life even if he is not a member of a congregation and has no interest in the religious aspect of Judaism. In fact, not to participate in any of them requires almost as much of an open declaration of breaking off all relations with the Jews as would be involved in a formal conversion to another faith. A few do it; the great majority remains within the fold and undertakes neither step that would remove him from the Jewish community.

The sum total of American Jewish organizational life, as Israeli sociologist Arye Tartakower put it (in my literal translation),

> amounts to a unique picture of public initiative, undoubtedly one of the greatest in the social world of today. The achievements of American Jewry in this field are half-legendary in character: it is as if some mysterious power dwelt in the soul of hundreds of thousands that pushes them forward toward a broadening of the Jewish content, and at times also toward its deepening.[27]

Identification

Unquestionably, a most important index of the quality of Jewish life in America is the light in which American Jews see themselves and the way they feel about their Jewishness. All other manifestations of Jewish group life, such as the religious and educational institutions, the social and charitable organizations, the Zionist and pro-Israel federations, the fraternal orders, and other associations, whatever their specific character or purpose, can and will, when all the chips are down, continue to exist and function only as long as the Jews of America feel committed to Jewish group survival. Such a commitment, in turn, hinges upon the personal identification of the individual Jew with the Jewish community. Therefore, a consideration of the committedness—that is, of the identification of American Jews with Jewry and Judaism—is imperative at this juncture.

Identification with the community of Israel has always been one of the greatest values of traditional Judaism. To be termed an *ohev Yisrael,* a "lover of Israel," was the greatest praise; in the Passover Haggada the evil one among the traditional four sons is characterized as the one who dissociates himself from the community of Israel. Great wisdom of the ages lies at the root of this discernment: the teachers and sages of Judaism knew only too well that the gravest danger that can threaten the continued existence of the Jewish people was not the hatred and enmity of the gentiles—*that* the Jews have long learned how to weather—but the severance of the ties that bind the individual Jew to his people. He who repudiates his people, is the real *rasha',* evil one, because by removing himself from the community he undermines the very existence of the Jewish people.

When looking at American Jewry from this point of view, there can be no doubt that it constitutes a new departure in Jewish historical development. In the large Jewish Diasporas of Eastern Europe and even of Western Europe up to World War II there was nothing even remotely comparable to the high percentage of "un-Jewish" Jews abounding especially in the big cities of America. The absence of Jewish identification, however, does not necessarily mean alienation. Alienation is the painful realization by the individual that he does not belong to the society that physically surrounds him, and that he is estranged from it. The Jewish nonidentification is nothing as definite or acute as this. It is rather a neutral, passive, amorphous state of mind in which one feels nothing definite toward that human group which is called the Jews, not even the pain of alienation from it.

It is, of course, quite impossible to guess what proportion of the estimated six million Jews in America in 1971 belongs to this category. But students of the American Jewish scene gain the impression that their number in recent years has tended to decrease. In fact, some sociologists have pointed to the remarkable fact that Jewish identification and affiliation are on the rise despite the weakening of Jewish cultural expression.

At its most rudimentary level this Jewish identification is expressed in nothing more than a vague feeling of being more at ease in the company of Jews than in that of gentiles, and in a consequent preference, expressed in practice, for Jewish over non-Jewish social relationships.[28] That this feeling at ease has nothing to do with religion can be concluded from the fact that it does not extend to gentiles who had converted to Judaism. However, neither must the reason for this in-group attunement be sought in some mysterious racial affinity, but rather in the residual influence of the culturally transmitted Jewish historical experience: even when a Jew knows next to nothing of the past, the traditions, and the religion of his people, there still remains this vague but potent aftereffect of the Jewish ethos on the Jewish personality, not unlike the lingering echo of an old, forgotten melody.

A part of this vague feeling of relatedness filters through into the Jewish self-stereotype which revolves around the pivot of differences between Jews and gentiles. Whether or not such differences can be objectively established is beside the point. What is significant is that in the view of many Jews they do exist; that many Jews think Jews are more interested in "high brow" cultural activities, have a greater social consciousness, are more sympathetic to the problems of others than is the case with the gentiles.[29] Needless to say, all this amounts to a conviction that the Jews are not only different from, but somehow "better" than, the gentiles, a conviction in which we recognize the direct lineal descendant of the much more pronounced ethnocentric self-stereotype of Jewish superiority that for centuries was one of the main psychological life-preservers helping the Jewish Diasporas maintain themselves in the ghettos of Christian Europe as well as in the *mellah*s and *hara*s of Muslim lands.

On a more articulate level there is the phenomenon of third generation rebound. The Jewish immigrant in America, in his strong desire to see his children take their places in American society, stressed their American education to the almost total neglect of their Jewish education. When these children grew up they nevertheless retained enough Jewish identification to be appalled by the prospect that their children may know absolutely nothing about Judaism and grow up to become non-Jews. The specter of total assimilation motivated the second generation to provide at least a modicum of Jewish education to its children. To this very day, these semi-assimilated second generation parents feel they must make their children aware of their ethnic identity, and, being ignorant themselves, the only way they can achieve this purpose is by sending their children to Sunday school.[30] The third generation, on its part, evinces a greater interest in the world of its grandparents than did the second generation, and, as a result of these factors, in many cases the grandchildren of immigrants receive a better Jewish education than their parents. As Bezalel Sherman, quoting the thesis of Marcus L. Hansen, put it: "the grandchildren of the immigrants want to remember that which the children want to forget. . . . Only among [American Jews] do the grandchildren manifest a greater desire to be part of the community than the children of the immigrants. This is a fact which is subject to statistical substantiation."[31]

In addition, the Nazi genocide and, following it, the establishment of the State of Israel also contributed importantly to the rise in Jewish identification, whether or not the latter finds its expression in affiliation with Jewish organizations.

What all this boils down to in final analysis is this: the average second or third generation American Jew wants to, and largely is able to, assimilate to the gentiles by whom he wishes to be accepted. This assimilation extends into all areas of Jewish culture and personal behavior, including the forms in which the continued adherence to Jewish religion manifests itself. It is an intense, far-reaching, and all-pervading, but by no means total assimilation. Most American Jews retain, and want to retain, a certain minimum of Jewishness, a core that they are loath to give up. Most apparent is this Jewish minimalism in their religious observance: reshaped after the forms of the Christian majority religion, reduced to a barest minimum, this Jewish religious observance is yet strong enough not only to hold the present generation, but also to make it consider it a matter of utmost importance that their children, too, should remain within the fold. The only conclusion one can reach from observing the great efforts and sacrifices Jewish parents insist on making in order to ensure that their own minimalistic Jewish pattern be continued by their children is that this vestigial Judaism, neatly packaged in a quasi-Christian wrapping, is yet a matter of very grave concern for present-day American Jews.

On the surface of it this is highly paradoxical. Take, for example, the well-to-do Midwestern surburban Jewish community of Lakeville (not the real name) which in 1960 was intensively studied by a team of sociologists. Of the 8,000 Jews of Lakeville (in a total population of 25,000), the overwhelming majority (95 percent) did not observe dietary laws, did not observe the Sabbath (99 percent), did not go to the synagogue even once a week (94 percent). Forty-one percent did not attend services even on the High Holy Days.[32] One can assume that their familiarity with Jewish history, religion, and culture was equally minimal. They were not even able to articulate their concept of "good Jew" in Jewish, as against general ethical, terms.

And yet this same group of religiously indifferent and ignorant Jews felt it important that a Jew should "freely and proudly acknowledge his identity." No less than 95 percent of those among them who had children enrolled them in Jewish Sunday or Hebrew school, and, what is even more significant, 91 percent of those parents who themselves had not had any Jewish schooling did likewise. To be able to do so, the parents had to become members of one of the five synagogues in Lakeville, which they did, during, and frequently even after, the period of Jewish school attendance of their children (66 percent of all Jews in Lakeville).[33]

These data seem to point to a strong persistence of Jewish identification, despite the almost total rejection of (or indifference to) all Jewish ritual and observance, and the widespread ignorance of Judaism. This vestigial, almost visceral, Jewish identification found expression in ways other than the desire

386

that the children should remain Jewish. It came through in "vague but powerful feelings about . . . their kinship with Jews abroad" and especially the State of Israel. No less than 90 percent of the respondents in Lakeville stated that they would "feel a sense of loss (65 percent a very deep sense of loss) if Israel were destroyed," most of them (70 percent) because of "feelings of Jewish identity." The community as a whole translated this identification into action by raising, during the crisis of the Six-Day War of June 1967, "unprecedented amounts of money through improvised drives as well as through the regional Jewish welfare fund."[34]

This Jewish attachment to Israel is, it appears, the only typically Jewish manifestation of identity that is *not* a Jewish equivalent or counterpart of a gentile phenomenon. Other expressions of Jewish identification are clearly gentile-inspired. The most outstanding among them is the proliferation of Jewish organizations that are either of a purely social and recreational nature, or have formal charitable, welfare, cultural, communal, and social-service purposes while in practice also subserving sociability functions and providing diversion. Typical of the first category is the Jewish country club organized by Jews who found themselves "excluded from the posh gentile clubs" and set up as "a social institution consciously patterned after the gentiles' style of life." To the second category belong the ORT (Organization for Rehabilitation through Training), Hadassah, the National Council of Jewish Women, the B'nai B'rith. Some 71 percent of the Jews in Lakeville belonged to one or more of these organizations. This situation closely duplicated the one obtaining among the gentiles, most of whom belonged to a variety of social, humanitarian, and philanthropic groups, health and welfare groups, service clubs such as the Kiwanis and Rotary, various neighborhood associations, the League of Women Voters, and so on. Some of these volunteer organizations had both Jews and gentiles as members; others were "more or less restricted to gentiles," while "some clubs were blatantly discriminatory."[35]

In view of this situation (which is duplicated on various scales all over the country), it is clear that the proliferation of Jewish organizations is due to the Jewish wish to emulate the gentiles on the social-organizational level coupled with the refusal of some of the gentile clubs and groups to admit Jews. And as for the finding that relatively more Jews than gentiles belong to organizations not affiliated with church or synagogue, it can be seen simply as yet another confirmation of the old adage that the Jews behave like the gentiles, only more so. But it also can be considered an expression of the Jewish need to associate with Jews, the wish to preserve a link to the Jewish community even among those who have become indifferent to religion; in this sense, it is the last surviving manifestation of Jewish identity. As long as this feeling of identity exists in a group it is unquestionably an *ethnic group.* American Jewry, therefore, is to this day one of the ethnic groups of the global Jewish Diaspora.

THE ASHKENAZI JEWS: ARGENTINA

Of all the Latin American Diasporas, that of Argentina occupies a special place. This on four counts. First of all, numerically: more Jews live in Argentina (500,000 in 1968) than in all the other twenty-three countries of Central America, South America, and the West Indies together (272,250). Secondly, historically: the Argentine Diaspora is the oldest in all Latin America. Thirdly, because of a particular circumstance: Argentina is the only country in Latin America in which a relatively large-scale project of Jewish agricultural colonization was carried out. Fourthly, and most importantly: no other Diaspora exists in the modern Jewish world which was able to organize a unified, central representative and executive body to serve the social, cultural, and political purposes of the Jewish community as effectively as was done by Argentine Jewry.

History and Composition

The first Jews to set foot on what subsequently was to become the Republic of Argentina were Marranos who arrived in the sixteenth century. Soon thereafter the Inquisition began to persecute them in this part of the world as well (its first victim was Diego de Padilla, in 1579). In 1636 the local inquisitorial office reported that in Tucumán (an inland city in the north of the country) there was "an innumerable multitude of Jews." With time these early immigrants lost all contact with Judaism but their descendants can be found among the old Creole families.

In modern times the first Jewish immigrants began to arrive after the liberation of Argentina from Spanish rule in 1816. More came in the middle of the century. Among these, the earliest arrivals were German, French and British Jews; somewhat later

389

came Sephardim from the Balkans and Turkey and Oriental Jews from North Africa. In 1870, when France lost Alsace-Lorraine to Germany, some Alsatian Jews arrived.[1]

All this was immigration on a very small scale, and until 1889 the total number of Jews in Argentina remained under a thousand. In that year, a group of fifty Jewish families arrived from South Russia, and soon thereafter began the agricultural settlement work, organized by Baron de Hirsch and his Jewish Colonization Association (ICA; see next section of this chapter). By 1895 there were 12,000 Jews in the country; by 1900—18,000; by 1910—76,000; by 1920—131,000; by 1930—230,000; by 1940—307,000; by 1950—420,000; and in 1969—500,000.[2]

Since at present there is practically no immigration into Argentina, and the natural increase of the Jews, a highly urbanized population, is extremely small, it can be expected that their number will remain unchanged, since whatever natural increase they will evince will be counterbalanced by the continuing moderate emigration to Israel (approximately one thousand annually).

About 75 to 80 percent of the Argentine Jews are concentrated in Buenos Aires. Smaller communities exist in numerous provincial cities. Some 15,000 live in the old agricultural settlements of ICA and the neighboring small towns which are connected with, and dependent on, them.[3]

These small, and in many cases isolated, provincial Jewish groups face the usual problems of such a situation: inability to provide adequate Jewish education to the children, lack of Jewish peer groups of sufficient size to enable young men and girls to find Jewish dates and mates, and the like.

All three divisions of the Jewish people are represented in the Argentine Diaspora. The Ashkenazi group is the largest, comprising about 445,000. The Oriental Jewish group numbers about 40,000, most of whom derive from Syria, Morocco, and other Arab countries. The Sephardi group is the smallest, some 15,000 strong, hailing mainly from Greece and Turkey.

Among the Sephardim and the Oriental Jews, public initiative is, in general, weaker than is the case in the Ashkenazi division. However, the Zionist movement succeeded in winning many adherents among them, and especially the establishment of the State of Israel strengthened their Jewish identification and brought about an increasing cooperation between them and the Ashkenazim.[4]

In the Ashkenazi group the great majority is of Russian, Polish, and Bessarabian origin (some 375,000). This is the most active, most Jewishly-conscious, and most public-minded element, which sets the tone and is the moving spirit of Argentine Jewry. They were joined by the Central European group (some 40,000), most of them refugees from Hitler who experienced a kind of Jewish awakening, expressed in participation in the affairs of the community, in developing a Jewish intellectual life of their own, and in establishing their own Jewish organizations.[5]

Agricultural Settlements

In 1888, under the sponsorship of the Alliance Israélite Universelle, a group of 8 to 10 Jews arrived from Russia and settled in what is today known as the Grupo Monigotes of the Moisesville Colony in the province of Santa Fé. A year later they were joined by a larger group of 50 settlers who, probably influenced by the first pioneers, came on their own initiative, and settled in what later became known as *Grupo y Estacion Palacios* (Palacios Group and Station), so called after the owner of the land, Dr. Pedro Palacios. The farms were unsuccessful, but the settlers held out, and when Dr. William Loewenthal, passing through the area, saw their plight, he asked Baron Maurice de Hirsch (1831-1896), the well-known Jewish financier, railway magnate and philanthropist, to help them. This appeal was an important contributing cause in Hirsch's decision to found the Jewish Colonization Association (ICA), which he incorporated in England in 1891. In the same year, ICA bought from Dr. Palacios the land on which the 50 Jewish families had settled, and began to lend them its support. Within a short time ICA purchased a total of 617,500 hectares (or 1,525,842 acres) of land in various parts of Argentina and proceeded to set up villages on it. By 1900 some 20 villages were founded. One of the latest to be founded was settled in the 1930s by German Jewish refugees. The population of the villages reached a maximum of 30,000 just prior to World War I; thereafter it began to decline, until today no more than 15,000 are left in them, and of these not more than 10,000 live in the villages proper, the rest residing in the neighboring small towns.

Although in absolute figures the ICA settlement effort yielded only small results, its importance must not be belittled. It was the work of a private company with limited means and without powers of coercion, and yet its results, both in absolute numbers and in the relative numbers of those settlers who stayed on, compare more than favorably with the Birobidzhan settlement effort of the powerful Soviet state, which did not have to spend money on buying land, and which had diverse methods of suasion at its disposal. Apart from this, despite the enormous difficulties encountered by Russian small-town Jews in trying to become peasant cultivators in South America, more than half of the original settlers remained on their farms and struggled along for years until they managed to establish themselves. Of those who left, a very small minority went back to Europe; most moved to Buenos Aires where they engaged, and became successful, in various business enterprises.

In fact, these Jewish settlers, who were strangers to both Argentina and agriculture, not only mastered the innumerable problems facing them, but introduced important innovations into Argentine agriculture in general. Apart from demonstrating that intensive cultivation and especially dairy farming were feasible, the Jewish settlers set up (from 1900 on) large agricultural cooperatives that took charge of both the marketing of produce and purchasing for the farmers. They branched out into other fields of cooperation, setting up cooperative dairies, as well as credit and insurance, road building and construction cooperatives, or, rather, commercial consortia. In 1925, after an unsuccessful early effort, all these cooperatives were organized into a single institution, the so-called *Fraternidad Agraria,* which remains to this day one of the most important economic factors in the life of those Argentine Jews who live in the colonies. It publishes a monthly in Yiddish and Spanish, *El*

Colono Cooperator, and the volume of its business in 1961 amounted to 37 million Argentine Pesos. By 1968-69, however, the volume fell to about one million Pesos. Just as the methods of cultivation introduced by the Jews served as an example in the country as a whole, so too did the cooperative organization. Both still play a major role in Argentine economy. In the Jewish villages there is no trace of the illiteracy that still exists in many Argentine villages; in fact, with regard to schools, libraries, cultural centers, and the like, the Argentine Jewish "colonies" resemble Israeli villages more than Argentine ones.

However, as far as the Jewishness of the young farmer generation is concerned, there is much to be desired. Their Jewish education is neglected, their Jewish identification is minimal, and many of them (being much better educated than the average Argentine farmer) feel greatly attracted to the city and leave the farm in search of a more pleasurable life. Many, in fact, have made good in the city and even managed to acquire higher education and enter the professions, while retaining their pride in their farmer origin.[6]

The Jewish Role in the Argentine Economy

As to the achievements of Argentine Jews in economic fields in general, Israeli sociologist Arye Tartakower observes: "The new ways they opened up in the country's economy, and the stormy tempo of their activities and attainments resemble in many respects the achievements of the Jewish community of the United States." They introduced new methods into commerce, industry, and credit organization, which represented an important contribution to the country. Especially in the retail trade, as itinerant peddlers, the Jews fulfilled a truly pioneering task in this semi-developed country in which this kind of work was, in many cases, quite risky; by making the semi-primitive farmers acquainted with new types of merchandise, they created new demands, and thus, in a sense, played a civilizing role.

With time these Jewish peddlers made considerable progress. After several years of lugging around the merchandise on their backs, the peddlers could finally afford to buy horses and carts, and, still later, automobiles. Then they opened storehouses in the city and merely showed samples to their customers, sending the merchandise later. They founded cooperative warehouses from which each merchant could draw. They also founded credit cooperatives to finance the itinerant peddlers, the small craftsmen, and anybody who needed funds to build up a business for himself. Several of these originally modest financial institutions developed in the interwar period into important banks. In addition, numerous other branches of industry were literally created by the Jews—e.g., the textile, clothing, furniture, and shoe industries.

Side by side with this important share in the industrial development of Argentina, the Jews played a no less significant role in the Argentine professions as physicians, lawyers, engineers, scientists, scholars, writers, and artists.[7]

Communal Organization

One of the most important characteristics and most significant achievements of Argentine Jewry is its communal organization. In Chapter XV we discussed briefly the powerful *Kahal* organization that existed in Poland from the sixteenth to eighteenth centuries. The same type of strong, cohesive community organization was set up by the Eastern European Jews in Argentina.

As it was in Poland, the *kehilla* in Buenos Aires is a voluntary organization, but its powers are wide and its activities extend into many areas. On foundations laid in the nineteenth century, the Buenos Aires *kehilla* was formally organized in the 1920s, when it was called *Asociacion Mutual Israelita Argentina, Communidad de Buenos Aires* (AMIA). The purposes subserved by the *kehilla* are many: social assistance was one of the first; to it were added Jewish education, youth programs, welfare, health, religious affairs, (the Rabbinate functions as a branch of AMIA), 'aliya to Israel, and the distribution of Jewish books. Within a few years, education in a national Jewish spirit became the central concern in the activities of the *kehilla*, on which it spent in 1968 23.8 percent of its entire budget. The number of its members grew steadily, and by the late 1960s a large proportion of the Ashkenazi Jews of Buenos Aires were enrolled in it. Its budget in 1968 was $3,468,400. The Sephardi Jews have their own parallel *kehilla* organizations.

Here again, as in the case of agriculture, commerce, and the cooperative movement, the Argentine Jews were true pioneers. This type of *kehilla* organization had not existed in the Jewish Diaspora since its demise in Poland in the eighteenth century. After it proved viable in Argentina, it was emulated in other countries.

The AMIA is the major member of the *Federacion de Comunidades Israelitas,* also known in Hebrew as *Va'ad HaKehillot,* which has some 145 affiliates and is the largest Jewish communal body in Latin America.[8]

Anti-Semitism and the DAIA

It is a tragic circumstance that precisely in Argentina, where the Jews have shown such initiative in economic, organizational, and cultural life, and have made such an important contribution to the country as a whole, they should be faced with manifestations and outbursts of anti-Semitism. While the traces of Spanish inquisitorial Jew-hatred have long disappeared, the new anti-Semitism is fed by racist, Hitlerist and fascist theories, as well as by the so-called "nationalist" ideologies, and, especially in recent years, by Arab propaganda. Faced with recurrent manifestations of anti-Semitism, the Argentine Diaspora set up in 1935 a defense organization of its own in the form of the *Delegación de Asociaciones Israelitas Argentinas* (DAIA), which soon developed into the central political representative body of Argentine Jewry.[9] In 1970 it had 145 affiliated institutions in Greater Buenos Aires, and fifty branches in the interior. When, as occasionally happened, the Argentine authorities were not responsive to the demands of the DAIA to stem the wave of anti-Semitic outrages, the Jews were forced to resort to direct action. A memorable instance occurred on June 28, 1962, when, in the face of increasing organized anti-Semitic attacks, the Jews of Buenos Aires declared a general twelve-hour work stoppage

395

by all Jewish storekeepers, factory workers, professionals, and students. In the window of every closed store was the sign, "Closed as a protest against Nazi aggression in Argentina." The effect of this strike was felt throughout the country.[10] DAIA is also engaged in developing contacts with the gentile world and enlightening public opinion through the publication and distribution of books, booklets, articles and the results of research. It also sponsors a Center of Social Studies which issues the magazine *Indice.* DAIA is affiliated with the World Jewish Congress and is a member of the World Conference of Jewish Organizations.

Deculturation

Despite the strong Jewish consciousness that characterizes the Argentine Diaspora, its survival is threatened by the Jewish deculturation of the young generation. The Yiddish language is no longer known to most of the young Jews; their Jewish education and knowledge have been shrinking rapidly. In addition, Argentine Jewry, even the older generation, has been nonreligious and secularistically oriented, which means that the young generation has neither culture nor religion on which to base a Jewish identification.[11] The interest of the young generation is increasingly concentrated on participation in the general Spanish-Argentine culture of the country—all phenomena well known from many other Diasporas as well. That this process has been going on for some time in Argentina is apparent, among other things, from the frequent occurrence of Jewish names among the top ranking scholars, writers, and artists of the country.[12]

Social contact between Jews and gentiles of the middle class (which is numerically the most important one) is a common-place phenomenon in both the capital and the interior. It can be observed daily in all areas of life and activity: in the schools, universities, business industry, sports, literature, arts, music, etc.[13]

The familiar phenomenon of higher concentration in university studies among the Jews than among the general population is the case in Argentina as well. Only about 1 percent of Argentina's total population attended universities in 1967, whereas in the Jewish community no less than 3.4 percent, or 17,000 in absolute figures, were university students in that year.[14] This figure represents a truly remarkable record which becomes apparent when one compares it with the Jewish university attendance in Great Britain. In that country in the same year the total number of Jews was roughly the same as in Argentina, and yet only somewhat more than 3,500 Jewish students were enrolled in the universities.

However, university attendance in the case of many Jewish students spells estrangement from Judaism and Jewish values—a phenomenon also encountered in many other countries. Of the 17,000 Argentine Jewish students, only 1,400, or 8 percent, were active in Jewish institutions (as against almost 50 percent of the Jewish students in England). Taking the ten-to-twenty-five-year age group as a whole (an estimated total of 90,000), only 8,000 of them (or 8.8 percent) were members of organizations having specific Jewish content.[15]

Jewish Education and Culture

Argentine Jewry awakened at a relatively late date to the necessity of establishing a network of Jewish schools for its children. Although Jewish schools had existed in Argentina since the very beginnings of the community, as recently as 1941 there were in Buenos Aires only forty-nine Jewish schools, with eighty-nine teachers and 2,447 pupils. Since then the Jewish educational network was gradually expanded: it had an enrollment of 7,116 in 1947, 9,151 in 1953, and 7,271 in 1961.[16] In 1967, 15,644 children were enrolled in Jewish schools in Buenos Aires, and some 4,400 in the provinces, or a total of over 20,000 in the whole country.[17]

Almost all Jewish elementary schools (six grades; total enrollment in 1967: 8,900) operate either as day schools (2,450 pupils), or on a five-afternoons-a-week basis (6,130 pupils) with about fifteen weekly hours of instruction. That is to say, as far as intensity is concerned, the Jewish education received by the pupils in these schools greatly surpasses that received by most children enrolled in Jewish supplementary schools in the United States. Most of the Argentine Jewish schools are on the elementary level; there are, however, also kindergartens (5,069 pupils), high schools (1,535 students), two teachers' seminaries, two rabbinical schools, one school of higher Jewish education, and several Yeshivot.

Since the six-to-eleven-year age group (the age group of the elementary school population) can be taken to constitute about 10 percent of the total Jewish population,[18] it can be assumed that there were in 1967 about 48,000 children in the Argentine Jewish school-age population. Of them 11,687, or 24.3 percent, attended Jewish schools. This percentage is considerably lower than the corresponding figure in the United States, where close to 70 percent of all Jewish children were enrolled in a Jewish school in 1968 (see Chapter XIX).

Argentine Jewry maintains several social and cultural institutions in addition to purely educational ones. The *Sociedad Hebraica Argentina* (20,000 members) is the largest Jewish sports and cultural center in Argentina; it publishes a journal, *Davar,* and sponsors a library, a theater, the *Instituto de Estudios Superiores Judíos* (Institute of Higher Jewish Studies), and, jointly with the Jewish Agency and the *Consejo Juvenil Judeo-Argentina* (Jewish Youth Council), conducts a School of Institutional Leadership. The AMIA sponsors annual book fairs, had a weekly television program, and maintains a dormitory for Jewish students from the interior. In 1969 it inaugurated the House of Jewish Culture, in which are located the Jewish Teachers Seminary, the School for Kindergarten Teachers, and other institutions.

There is also an *Asociacion pro Cultura Judia* (Jewish Culture Congress) which publishes important Jewish books in Yiddish translation and promotes Yiddish language as part of Jewish culture. The *Instituto Judeo Argentino de Cultura e Informacion* publishes the Spanish Jewish bi-monthly *Comentario,* while the Latin American office of the American Jewish Committee publishes pamphlets, a yearbook, and film strips, and organizes lectures (all in Spanish).[19] The Jewish sports clubs, such as Hacoaj (Hakoah), attract large numbers of young people.

The Zionist Hope

In view of the widespread apathy among the young Jewish generation of Argentina with regard to Jewish religion and culture, many leaders of the community felt that the only hope of restoring or strengthening Jewish consciousness lay in Zionism and an identification with Israel. Even prior to the Six-Day War of 1967 Zionism and its various movements and organizations played an extremely important role in Argentine Jewish life. The largest Zionist organization was the Argentine affiliate of the Women's International Zionist Organization (WIZO), which in 1967–68 had thirty-one thousand members in 370 centers throughout the country. By 1969–70 its membership had increased to thirty-five thousand. The Zionist Organization of Argentina fulfils a centralizing and coordinating function in Zionist ranks, conducts programs for the dissemination of Zionism, and publishes (since 1968) the monthly *Raices*. All other major Zionist parties had branches in Argentina; they sponsored all types of cultural, social, and welfare programs. From the creation of the State of Israel in 1948 to 1966 (inclusive), fifteen thousand Argentine Jews made their 'aliya.[20] In fact, already in 1962 it was observed that

> Zionism and the State of Israel were the strongest unifying forces in the Argentine Jewish community. Just as most Jewish schools were sponsored by Zionist parties, and were therefore Zionist-oriented, so it was in almost all organized Jewish life. . . . Zionism was the main bulwark against assimilationism. It appeared to offer the only kind of Jewish identification attractive to young idealistic intellectuals.[21]

Five Jewish communities in five widely separated parts of the world do not fit into the threefold scheme of the Oriental, Sephardi, and Ashkenazi divisions, whose major constituent Diasporas were discussed in the foregoing chapters. They are the Italian, the Greek, the Caucasian, the Indian, and the Ethiopian Jewish communities. None of them belongs to the Oriental division because none of them lived or lives in Asia or Africa under Muslim rule. Likewise, they are not Sephardim because their ancestors did not come from Spain and they did not speak Ladino; and they are not Ashkenazim, because they do not hail from German lands, nor have they ever adopted Yiddish as their vernacular.

The five are exceptional for another reason too. The Diasporas comprised in each of the three main divisions have certain common factors in their history and culture—the Yiddish of the Ashkenazim, the Ladino of the Sephardim, the Muslim environment of the Oriental Jews. The five communities we are now about to discuss have no such common factor. One of them, the Italian, is and has been throughout its long and well documented history a most sophisticated and culturally productive community in both the Jewish and the secular Italian areas; the second, the Greek, was, after a history of seventeen or eighteen centuries, almost wholly submerged by the post-1492 influx of Sephardim; the third, that of the Caucasus, is composed of several different language-groups with barely a trace of post-Biblical Jewish religio-cultural developments; the fourth, the Indian, while it leads a totally Jewish life, has been fragmented into castes in a typical Indian manner; the fifth, the Ethiopian, is quite definitely marginal to Judaism. This being the case, there is no methodological justification for treating these five Diaspo-

401

ras under a joint heading; they are presented herewith, one after the other, simply as five greatly disparate communities, none of which fits into the scheme of the threefold division of the Jewish people.

The Jews of Italy

When the legions of Rome captured Jerusalem and put an end to the Second Jewish Commonwealth (70 CE), there was in Italy an established Jewish community whose origins antedated the Maccabean period (second century BCE). From that time to the present there has been an Italian Diaspora, always small in numbers, often prominent in intellectual achievement, mostly living in safety, rarely persecuted, and almost never pogromized. Italy, moreover, is the only country in Europe in which the Jews, in the course of a history spanning more than two millennia, never experienced a countrywide expulsion. When, as occasionally happened, the Jews were forced to leave one city, they were, as a rule, hospitably received in others. Despite papal, and more rarely ducal, anti-Jewish measures, the relationship between the Jews and the Italian population in general was friendly, and it was this feature that set apart the position of the Jews in Italy from their situation in other countries of Europe.

Related to this feature is another remarkable phenomenon that was specifically Italian. In this country, the seat of the papacy, the Church was less able to translate its anti-Jewish decrees into a reality of everyday life than in any other country of the Christian world. At a time when the Inquisition persecuted the Jews in other countries most cruelly, the Jews of Rome—the fountainhead of inquisitorial power—and of the rest of Italy continued to live in relative tranquility. Nor did the Protestant persecutions of the Jews following the Reformation have any counterpart in Italy, which remained a Catholic country.

These favorable circumstances (about which more will be said later) turned Italy in the Middle Ages into a place of refuge for Jews who fled or were expelled from other countries. Ashkenazi Jews from German lands began to arrive in the late thirteenth and fourteenth centuries, with their influx reaching its peak about 1400; settling in northern Italy, they soon became thoroughly Italianized. (A German-Jewish immigrant by the name of Ettlingen, for instance, became the ancestor of the famous Ottolenghi family.) Sephardi Jews from Spain came after 1391, and mostly after the 1492 expulsion, to the duchies of Ferrara and Tuscany, to Rome (some nine thousand of them), and to the Kingdom of Naples. Oriental Jews from North Africa settled in Sicily, and in the late sixteenth century, Jews from Turkey and Palestine settled in the Venetian Republic and in Leghorn.[1]

While the heads of the various Italian states and principalities willingly admitted Jews from other lands, the relationship between the indigenous Italian Jews and the newcomers was not always a harmonious one. Thus Leon de Modena (1571–1648), the Italian rabbi and poet, about whom we shall hear more later, stated with typical Italian hyperbole: "The Ashkenazim, Sephardim and Italian Jews hate one another and are alien to one another in the same way as Christians, Turks and Jews, as if each Jewry possessed a different Tora."[2]

For a while the Italian, German (Ashkenazi), and Spanish (Sephardi) Jews, popularly referred to as the *tre nazioni* ("three nations"), preserved their separate characteristics. After the end of the Renaissance, however, this tripartite division of the Jews gradually disappeared, and all the Jews in Italy, whatever their provenance, assumed an Italian character.[3] Once Italian replaced the languages brought along by the Ashkenazi, Sephardi, and Oriental Jewish immigrants, the original distinctions disappeared; all the Jews living in the country became Italian Jews, and as such contributed to the emergence of a distinct Italian Jewish culture.

This culture began to emerge as early as the tenth century when Shabbatai Donnolo (913–982) wrote his medical and astrological books in southern Italy. From the twelfth century on Italian Jewry produced a long list of poets, exegetes, Talmudic authorities, authors of lexicons, dictionaries, writers of responsa, and translators, many of whom combined Jewish scholarly work with the practice of medicine or other secular accomplishments, and at least one of whom was a woman, Paola (d. ca. 1285), a member of the illustrious Roman Anau or dei Mansi family. Special mention must be made of an early and outstanding poet and author of Biblical studies, Immanuel *HaRomi* (of Rome) (ca. 1270–1330), who wrote elegant, witty, and satirical poetry, some of it lascivious and erotic, in both Hebrew and Italian, and was a friend of Dante, whom he imitated in his Hebrew poem "Hell and Paradise."

These pre-Renaissance stirrings among the Jews of Italy, however, were minor and relatively sporadic phenomena compared with the irruption of Jewish talent into all fields of creativity during the High Renaissance itself. In the fifteenth and sixteenth centuries, apart from and in addition to outstanding achievements in all areas of Jewish scholarship, Italian Jews were prominently active in writing—in Italian—poetry and drama, travelogues, books on grammar, astronomy, philosophy, and history. They were professors at various Italian universities, translators, painters, graphic artists, illuminators of manuscripts, gold and silversmiths, musicians. They were also leading bankers and merchants, printers, and, of course, physicians (including some who served as the personal physicians of popes and princes). This was truly the golden age for Italian Jews, a period in which they were as much part of the Italian cultural scene as their co-religionists had been in Spain a few centuries earlier.

When confronted with such a galaxy of talent it is difficult indeed to select a few names that can serve as illustrations. The first that comes to mind is that of Judah Abravanel, better known as Leo Hebraeus (died in Venice, 1535) a physician, philosopher, astronomer, and poet, who wrote, among other works, an Italian treatise titled *Dialoghi di Amore* which became so popular that within twenty years it went through five editions and was translated three times into Spanish, twice into French, and once into Latin. Also other Jewish authors became well known to the Italian public, and not a few of the outstanding Jewish scholars had among their disciples Christian Italians some of whom attained considerable mastery of Hebrew.

Parallel with these secular activities, and often pursued by the same individuals, Jewish studies also flourished. The Italian rabbis engaged in Talmudic and Kabbalistic studies, and made important contributions to *halakha* and ritual.

404

In the second half of the sixteenth century the position of the Jews deteriorated in several parts of Italy. In 1555 they were confined to ghettos in the papal states. In 1559 no less than twelve thousand Hebrew books were burned in Cremona; only the *Zohar* was spared because the princes of the Church believed it contained the mysteries of Christianity, and because the introduction to it had been printed only a year earlier with the sanction of the Inquisition. Under Pope Pius V (r. 1566–72) the Jews suffered much, especially when he expelled them from all the papal states, except Rome and Ancona. Most of the thousand exiled families found refuge in Turkey.

Life in the ghettos from the late sixteenth century on brought about a diminution of the Jewish intellectual activity. Scholarship became confined to the rabbis, who concentrated on the Talmud and Jewish ritual. A few outstanding scholars among them continued to foster secular studies as well, and it was they who made the first attempts to treat Jewish fields of learning from a general scholarly point of view, thus becoming the forerunners of the Science of Judaism that emerged, full-fledged, in Germany more than a century later. Leon de Modena and Simone Luzzatto (1583–1663) were unquestionably the most prominent exponents of this new trend.

Leon de Modena, a rabbi in Venice, was so famous as a preacher that his addresses in Italian attracted large audiences, including Christian priests and noblemen. He was also an inveterate and unlucky gambler. He wrote fine Italian and Latin poetry, compiled an Italian-Hebrew dictionary, and authored collections of sermons in Hebrew, an aggadic index, a booklet on *materia medica,* and other works. All these and many more of his writings were printed in Venice while he was still alive.[4] Simone Luzzatto, in addition to his Hebrew responsa and other religious studies, wrote two Italian books, one in defense of the Jews *(Discurso circa il stato de gl'hebrei,* Venice, 1638) and the other a religious-philosophical treatise (Venice, 1651).

Italian prose and poetry were written in this period by numerous Jews, including two women, Deborah Ascarelli and Sara Copia-Sullam. A Jewish mathematician, Joseph Solomon Delmedigo, was a disciple of Galileo. Some Jewish authors wrote Italian treatises in defense of the Jews; others wrote

405

Kabbalistic works; still others compiled great rabbinic encyclopedias or translated parts of the Bible into Italian.

Throughout the seventeenth and eighteenth centuries the position of the Jews depended to a great extent on the attitude of the popes, and since most popes ruled only a few years, there were frequent and radical ups and downs in the situation of the Jews in the papal states. In the ducal dominions, on the other hand, they found more equitable conditions in most periods, and their lives ran a more even course. The list of outstanding individuals among them is a long and illustrious one even in this unfavorable period of their history. Jewish scholars and poets divided their creative talents between the Jewish fields to which they made their contributions in Hebrew, and the secular areas which they cultivated in Latin and Italian. Having always been part of the mainstream of Italian cultural development, the Jews of Italy have never been in a position in which acquiring the culture of their non-Jewish environment would have required a daring, revolutionary, anti-orthodox movement, as was represented by the Haskala among the Central and Eastern European Jews. The wide range of Jewish religious and cultural attitudes that emerged in Central and Eastern Europe in the nineteenth century as a result of the Enlightenment, emancipation, Reform, and the Science of Judaism, had been part and parcel of Italian Jewish life since the Middle Ages. On the one hand, there were Jews in Italy who preserved a totally conservative, tradition-bound existence down to the present time—e.g., the inhabitants of the Roman Ghetto;[5] on the other, there were the medieval and Renaissance Italian Jewish poets, dramatists, artists, painters, musicians, scientists, statesmen whose achievements are integral parts of the cultural history of Italy. From the mid nineteenth century on Jews were ministers of Italian states well in advance of the emancipation of the Jews, and after the unification of Italy, by the turn of the century, one Jew (a Luzzatti) became prime minister, another (an Ottolenghi) served as minister of war, and other Jews were ministers of finance.

In these conditions, emancipation, which came to the Jews of the various Italian states at different times and was completed in 1870, did not have the same revolutionary impact on Jewish life as it had in other European countries. It resulted, of course, in an overall improvement in their position, but since written laws and rules never had as strong a hold on everyday life in Italy as they had, say, in Germany, even prior to emancipation the Italian Jews did not suffer as much from their legal disabilities.

The generally liberal attitude toward the Jews continued in Italy even following World War I, when Central and Eastern Europe witnessed an upsurge of anti-Semitism. Many Jewish students, excluded by the *numerus clausus* from Hungarian, Polish, and other universities, were enabled to study in Italy. The anti-Jewish laws of 1938, which deprived the Jews of civil rights, remained largely on paper. True, the laws called for the dismissal of the Jews from public offices and their exclusion from schools and the professions. But since the Italian population as a whole was not anti-Semitic, the anti-Jewish measures were not generally carried out. Non-Italian (i.e., foreign) Jews were put in concentration camps in which, however, they were treated leniently. Psychologically the Italian Jews received comfort from the knowledge that the laws were promulgated by the Italian government more as a gesture to satisfy its Nazi German ally than as an expression of its own feelings about the Jews.

Nevertheless, emigration and the severance of ties with the Jewish communities reduced the number of Italian Jews from 45,000 in 1932 to 35,000 in 1939. After the outbreak of World War II, the humane attitude of the Italian population, officialdom, and army to the Jews became common knowledge in the German-occupied areas of Europe, and many Jews fled from them into Italy, and Italian-occupied France, Yugoslavia and Greece, often with the help of the Italian authorities.[6]

Ironically, it was precisely the surrender of Italy to the Allied forces, late in 1943, that brought about the most tragic chapter in the two-thousand-year-old history of Italian Jews. Southern Italy had been occupied by the Allies when, in response to the surrender, the German forces took most of Italy, including Rome, and immediately put into effect their policy of *Endlösung*. The economic destruction they wrought cannot even be mentioned in one breath with the genocide: more than eight thousand Jews were sent to extermination camps in Eastern Europe; of these on a handful survived. In German-occupied Italy itself several thousands of Jews escaped by converting to Christianity, or with the help of Italians who hid them, or due to the efforts of partisans, among whom, incidentally, there were numerous Jews. Some five thousand Jews managed to flee abroad. About a year-and-a-half later, in the middle 1945, the Allies occupied all of Italy, and the Fascist rule came to an end. At that time the total number of Jews in Italy was estimated at 29,000.[7]

A quarter of century after the war the general impression the Italian Diaspora gives is one of a community in a period of rapid numerical decline that, unless reversed, will lead to its disappearance within another few decades. Already in 1931–35 the Jews in Italy evinced an annual decrease of 5.28 per thousand, at a time when the general Italian population showed a natural increase of 1 percent annually. In recent years, as against every seventy marriages in which both bride and groom were Jewish, there were thirty in which one of the two was Christian.[8]

Italian Jewry has manifested most typically the general Jewish tendency of the last hundred years of concentrating in the largest cities of the country: of the 35,000 Jews who lived in Italy in the late 1960s, more than two thirds dwelt in Rome and Milan. Also, with regard to occupational structure the Italian Jews are typically urban and middle class: by 1931, 70 percent of them were either merchants (34.3 percent), white collar workers (25.2 percent), or professionals (10.8 percent). The civil and economic status of the Italian Jews continues satisfactory; anti-Semitism does not exist, and they can live as happily in Italy as any other element of the population.

As against these factors, which, for all their positive value, pave the way to assimilation, one can point out the establishment of a network of Jewish schools (after World War II) which, by the mid 1960s, provided education for half of all the Italian Jewish children, from kindergarten to high school, and comprised teachers and rabbinical seminaries as well. These schools, together with the Zionist-oriented youth organizations and the work of the *Unione delle comunità israelitiche italiane*

TABLE XII

Number of Jews in Italy, 1901–1969

Year	Number
1901	42,963
1911	46,448
1931	46,080
1938	58,412[a]
1939	46,908[b]
1945	55,417[c]
1956	27,705
1964	29,184
1965	33,144[d]
1966	35,000[e]
1967	35,000
1968	34,277[f]
1969	30,000[g]

[a] "Persons of the Hebrew race," according to the Fascist government's Census of the Race. The figure included persons of Jewish descent.
[b] Actual Jewish population.
[c] Total of 29,117 Italian Jews plus 26,300 refugee Jews in Italy.
[d] Total of 30,644 Jews who were affiliated with the Jewish communities of Italy plus 2,500 Jews who had no contact whatsoever with the Jewish community.
[e] American Jewish Year Book, based on questionnaire.
[f] As a result of the Six-Day War of 1967, some 3,300 Libyan Jews migrated to Italy.
[g] American Jewish Year Book, 1970, p. 539, based on questionnaire. However, on p. 436 the number is given as 34,000.

Sources: Sergio della Pergola, "L'Indagina Statistica Sugli Ebrei in Italia," La Rassegna Mensile di Israel (Roma, October 1968), pp 570–81; American Jewish Year Book, 1967, 1968, 1969, 1970; Lunario Ebraico 5729 [1968–69] (Milano, 1968).

ion of Italian Jewish Communities, approved by government decree of October 30, 1930),[9] are today the backbone of Jewish life in Italy.

The Greek Jews

The Jews of Greece occupy a special position in the worldwide Jewish Diaspora. They do not belong to any of the three major divisions of the Jewish people, although the Sephardi influence has been strong among them since 1492. Still, despite the large number of Ladino-speaking Sephardim who settled in the country and soon became the dominant Jewish element in it, some Jewish communities retained their old Judeo-Greek vernacular down to the very end, which came when the country was occupied by the Nazis in World War II and most of its Jews were killed.

Jews lived in Greece since before the end of the Second Jewish commonwealth. As they did in Alexandria in Hellenistic time, in Greece, too, they adopted Greek as their language. Hellenization, both linguistically and culturally, was the first example of large-scale Jewish assimilation to a foreign culture; as with subsequent assimilatory waves it resulted in the production by the Jews of important religious, literary, and historical works written in Greek, especially in the first and second centuries CE. The philosopher Philo of Alexandria (ca. 20 BCE – 50 CE) and the historian Josephus Flavius (ca. 37 – 103 CE) are too well known to require more than mention. They were preceded by other, less known, authors, such as Aristobulos of Alexandria (second century BCE), a peripatetic philosopher, of whose works only fragments remain;[10] Ezekielus, the Alexandrian tragedian (second century BCE) who dramatized Biblical episodes in Greek hexameters; [11] and, of course, the anonymous Alexandrian Jewish translators of the Bible into Greek who produced the so-called Septuagint in the third and second centuries BCE.

Following this early outpouring of Jewish creativity in Greek, we hear little of Greek-speaking Jews for several centuries, except for occasional restrictive measures issued by the Byzantine emperors, such as Theodosius (fifth century), and Justinian sixth century). The records also tell of synagogues being attacked and converted into churches, of Jewish legal and civil rights impaired, and of Jews persecuted in many different ways. Especially in the eighth century did the Byzantine hand oppress the Jews most heavily. It was partly due to these difficulties that Jews moved farther and farther away from Greece and settled, among other places, on the northern shores of the Black Sea, along the Danube, and in Slavic lands still farther north. In the ninth century, the position of the Jews showed improvement, or at least they were better off economically. Some of them were quite prosperous; many engaged in the silk industry, planting mulberry trees, rearing silkworms, and weaving silk. The two Jewish travelers, Benjamin of Tudela and Petahia of Regensburg, both of whom visited Greece about 1170, report that a very large number of Jews lived in the country, that they were well off, and that many of them counted as the best silk weavers and dyers.

As happened in other Diasporas, a solid economic base made the development of Jewish scholarship possible. Greek Jewish authors were active from the fourteenth century on, among them several with the surname *HaY'vani*—i.e., "the Greek"; and Talmudic studies had an important place in the life of the community. After the Spanish exile, many Sephardi Jews settled in the Ottoman Empire, which by that time controlled most of Greece, and their numbers and prestige caused many Greek-speaking Jews to become Sephardized. Nevertheless, Greek-speaking communities maintained themselves in several towns down to the twentieth century. About 1900 their numbers were estimated as follows: Ioannina and Preveza in Epirus, 4,000; Xanthe (Zante), 175; Arta, 300; Khalkis (Chalcis), on the island of Euboea, 200; or a total of fewer than 5,000. In addition, in the same period there were also Greek synagogues or congregations in Corfu, Constantinople, Salonica, and Adrianople, although the majority of the Jews in these places had by that time adopted Ladino, with the exception of Corfu (total Jewish population in 1900 approximately 5,000), where the immigration of Apulian Jews (expelled from Southern Italy in 1540) resulted in the Apulian dialect of Italian becoming dominant.

However, the importance of Greece in Jewish history lay not

411

in these small remnants of ancient Greek-speaking Jewish communities, but in the cultural and economic flowering experienced in Greece by the Sephardi exiles who arrived there in considerable numbers after their expulsion from Spain in 1492. Especially Salonica developed into a large Jewish center, with a prosperous, learned, Ladino-speaking community, which comprised an extraordinarily worldly and pleasure- and luxury-loving element. In fact, the rabbis of the community found it necessary to forbid women to wear any gold or silver jewelry, to curb nocturnal wedding processions, to stop the employment of male musicians at solemnities, and to prohibit games of hazard and the dancing together of men and women.[12]

After a period of decline in the seventeenth and eighteenth centuries, the position of the Jews in Salonica improved again in the nineteenth, in the middle of which they numbered about 80,000, constituting one of the largest Jewish communities at the time, and some two thirds of all inhabitants of the city. After the Greeks gained control over Salonica in 1913, the Jews encountered economic difficulties and had to put up with certain discriminatory measures. These factors led to the emigration of a large number of Jews, so that by 1930 there were only 70,000 and in 1940 only 56,000 Jews left in Thessalonike, as the city was officially called from 1937. During the same period, however, the cultural life of the community did not suffer: the school network of the Alliance Israélite Universelle and other organizations provided education to most Jewish children, there were Jewish newspapers and libraries, and the younger generation increasingly learned to speak both Greek (the language of the country) and French (which they were taught in the Alliance schools) in addition to Ladino.

In 1920 the number of all Jews in Greece was estimated at 110,000; in 1930 at 120,000. Thereafter many left the country, so that when the Germans, Bulgarians, and Italians occupied Greece in April 1941 the total number of Jews in the country was about 80,000. Three and a half years later, when the Germans began to evacuate Greece (September 1944), only 10,000 to 15,000 Jews were still alive. All the rest had been deported to extermination camps (about 63,000), or were killed in Greece itself. From the city of Thessalonike alone 46,000 were deported and killed. Only a few hundred Greek Jews managed to escape and to reach Palestine or Egypt.

After the end of the war, and the return of some camp survivors, about five thousand Jews continued to live in the capital, Athens; some two thousand in Thessalonike, and a few dozens in several other towns. Since in the meantime Greeks had, in most cases, occupied the residences or taken possession of the businesses of the Jews, they were not at all welcomed upon their return. This situation contributed greatly to the moral discouragement of the Jewish remnant in postwar Greece and the emotional inertia which had to be overcome before any measure of individual and communal life could be reconstituted. Most of the survivors felt that emigration held more hope for them than continued residence in Greece. Several thousand actually left, most of them for the United States and Latin America (where Ladino could serve as a basis for easily mastering the closely related Spanish of these countries). Some 2,500 had gone to Palestine prior to the establishment of Israel, and another 2,500 thereafter. By the mid 1960s not more than 6,000 Jews had remained in Greece, and the emigration continues to this day. Those who did remain have almost completely given up their old Ladino vernacular for modern Greek. The rate of intermarriage is on the increase (intermarriage in Greece is possible only after one of the couple first converts to the religion of the other); the Jewish education still available to the young generation is minimal. It can thus be foreseen that the days of the ancient Greek Jewish community are numbered.

The Jews of the Caucasus

The Caucasus is bounded in the north by European Russia, in the west by the Black Sea, in the south by Turkey and Iran, and in the east by the Caspian Sea. Its division into eighteen major administrative regions reflects the cultural diversity of the population, whose component elements were enabled by the isolated mountain valleys of the area to retain their languages and cultures: there are no less than thirty major nationalities in the Caucasus in a total population of about 12 million.

This ethnic heterogeneity of the environment facilitated the

413

survival of several disparate groups among the Jews as well: the Georgian (Gurgian or Gruzinian), Lesghian, and Osete Jews differ greatly from one another and even more from the so-called Mountain Jews of Daghestan, which lies on the western shore of the Caspian Sea to the north of Azerbaijan. Since it is obviously impossible within the present framework to discuss each of these Jewish groups in any detail, we shall have to be satisfied with a very few remarks about them.

The history of the Caucasian Jews begins with the oft-encountered mythical claim to descent from the lost ten tribes of Israel. It seems likely that the origin of these Jewish communities goes back to migrants who, at various times, moved north from Azerbaijan and the contiguous Persian and Kurdish areas in which there had been old Jewish settlements. The fact that in several parts of Caucasia the Jews have retained a Persian dialect as their vernacular points to a Persian-speaking area as their place of origin. The earliest reliable historical reference to them is found in the writings of Arab and Persian historians of the eighth century CE, from whom one learns that at that time a large number of Jews lived in the Caucasus. Thereafter, scattered references, often separated by centuries, attest to their continued presence down to the present time. Many popular beliefs and customs of these Jewish groups, some of which seem to go back to pre-Mishnaic times, while others are reflections of the non-Jewish environment of the Caucasus,[13] also point to an early settlement of the Jews in the region.

According to the Russian census of 1897, the total number of the Jews in the Caucasus was about 58,471, of whom the Jews of Daghestan comprised 9,850, those of Baku 11,650, and those of Tiflis 8,504. The others were distributed among seven other governorates, territories, and provinces.

Just prior to World War I the number of Daghestani Jews was estimated at 26,000, of whom about 6,000 lived in the city of Derbent and 10,000 in Kuba (in the Baku province). The rest were scattered in numerous auls or villages (there were several exclusively Jewish villages), where they practiced agriculture. Many of them lived in large extended families, familiar to all students of the Middle East, except that the Caucasian Jewish extended family seems to have comprised a much larger number of individuals than was usual in the Middle East.[14]

The Jews of Daghestan speak Judeo-Tati, an Iranian dialect; those of Georgia use a slightly archaic Georgian tongue similar to that spoken by their Christian neighbors, which belongs to the southwest Caucasian group of languages. While many of the North Caucasian Jews engaged in agriculture, the Jews of Georgia (often referred to as Ebraeli) were mostly concentrated in the towns and were mostly merchants. The latter suffered much after the Communist takeover, and many emigrated to Constantinople. Their emigration to Palestine began as early as the middle of the nineteenth century. By 1863 they had an organized community in Jerusalem—the first Oriental Jewish community established in the Holy City after that of the North African Jews or Mughrabim (1844). After World War I more came, and their estimated number in Palestine grew to 1,700.[15] By 1883 the Daghestani Jews also had their separate community organization in Jerusalem, and in 1912 yet another organization of Jews from the Caucasus, that of the Hararim (i.e., "mountaineers") was established in the Holy City. As a result of emigration, conversion, and other factors, the number of Jews in the Caucasus declined, and the 1926 Soviet census registered only 21,105. However, the Soviet census of 1959 again lists 51,582 Jews in the Georgian SSR, including 3,332 in the Abkhazian, 1,723 in the South Osetian, and 1,617 in the Adjar Autonomous Socialist Soviet Republics. In addition, there were 40,204 Jews in the neighboring Azerbaijanian SSR.[16]

The Jews of India

India, the classic country of the caste system, has become the home of three Jewish groups whose rigid castelike patterns of behavior in relation to one another reflect the influence of the environment. Two of the three groups, the Bene Israel of Bombay and the Jews of Cochin, are old, indigenous communities. The third, that of the Baghdadi Jews, is new. The total number of the three groups together was about 26,000 according to the 1951 census.

The largest group is that of the Bene Israel, who claim descent from the Ten Tribes of Israel: hence their name which means Children of Israel. The many often contradictory, legends current among the Bene Israel about their origin and arrival in India contain little that could be extracted as a historical kernel. Only one thing is sure: the Bene Israel must have been living in India at least since the early Middle Ages, and had dwelt for several centuries in the Konkan area on the west coast of India not far from Bombay. During those centuries they were totally cut off from other Jewish communities, and this isolation is one of two possible explanations of the state of their Jewish religious knowledge and observance, which at the time were most rudimentary. The other explanation is that they had come to India at such an early stage of Jewish history that all they had brought along with them was the Bible (we shall again hear of a similar theory in connection with the Falashas of Ethiopia), and that, in the course of the long centuries of their isolation they forgot most of the Biblical teachings as well, just as they forgot Hebrew altogether and adopted Marathi, the local Indian vernacular. What they did retain were the observance of the Sabbath and some of the holidays, the Sh'ma' prayer, circumcision, and dietary laws.[17]

This state of ignorance continued until the appearance among the Bene Israel of a veritable culture hero by the name of Juda Rahabi, who imparted Jewish learning to three young men, Thiratkar, Shapurkar, and Rajpurkar. The three disciples assumed the office of kaji, and passed on their Jewish knowlege to the community. Traditions differ as to the time in which this happened; some place it in the twelfth, others in the fifteenth, and still others in the seventeenth or eighteenth centuries. However, even in the middle of the nineteenth century, when the Jewish traveler Jacob Sapir Halevi visited the Bene Israel, he found that they did not observe many of the basic Jewish religious laws.[18]

In the course of the eighteenth century most of the Bene Israel moved from the villages in the Konkan territory into the city of Bombay, and subsequently worked as carpenters, enlisted in the army, and engaged in clerical occupations. Soon their religious life became intensified, they built synagogues, published Jewish periodicals, and translated books of Jewish interest into Marathi. The Bible, translated into Marathi by Christian missionaries, became for the Bene Israel the most important source book for Jewish religion, available for the first time in the language they all spoke and understood.[19]

Yet this recent superimposition of Judaism on the Bene Israel could not alter the traits they had absorbed from the environment in the course of many centuries. One of the most characteristic of these was the division of the community into two castes: the Gora, or White, and the Kala, or Black, Bene Israel. The Gora, of course, were not really white, and, in fact, there were many among them who were darker in skin color than most Kala. But they maintained that even the darkest were "pure" descendants—that is, in both the male and female line—of the original even couples who, according to the Bene Israel origin myth, landed after a shipwreck on the Konkan coast in the distant past. "Poverty and the excessive heat of India greatly affected the fair complexion of our ancestors," was the explanation they gave to Miss Strizower.[20] The Kala, on the other hand, are held to be descendants of Bene Israel men and native women. Until some years ago the two groups observed a strict caste-like separation: they neither intermarried nor ate together, nor was a Kala allowed to touch any of the kitchen utensils used by the Gora. When worshiping in the same synagogue, the Kala were given sanctified wine (which was distributed after the Sabbath and holiday services) only after the Gora had received theirs. All attempts at "passing" by the Kala (even by wealthy and influential members) were resisted and frustrated by the Gora. By the 1950s the differences were no longer so pronounced, and occasional intermarriages even took place between the two groups. While the total number of the Bene Israel at the time was fourteen thousand, of whom twelve thousand lived in Bombay, the numbers of the Gora and the Kala could not be ascertained.[21]

Hand in hand with the crumbling of the barriers between the White and Black Bene Israel went the breakup of the extended family which could not withstand the pressures of modern big city living. Polygyny, too, had almost completely disappeared. Some of the functions of the family have been taken over by informal friendship groups and formally organized clubs. New occupations and professions had been engaged in, removing individuals from the community framework. At the same time a certain religious differentiation set in, and, in addition to the old Bene Israel synagogues (the first of which was built in 1796), a liberal congregation was formed among them.

The relationship between the Bene Israel and the Baghdadi Jews, who began to arrive in Bombay early in the nineteenth century, was smooth in the beginning. The Bene Israel received the newcomers hospitably, opened their synagogues to them, and since among the Bene Israel there were no *kohanim* (traditional descendants of Aaron), they were glad to have Baghdadi *kohanim* perform the priestly functions for them—e.g., the priestly blessing on holidays, and the ritual of the redemption of the first-born son. Soon, however, the Baghdadi Jews began to put a distance between themselves and the Bene Israel. They established their own synagogue and school (with English as language of tuition), and while they did employ some Bene Israel (e.g., as headmaster and teachers in their school), and some 16 percent of the children in the Baghdadi Jewish school have been Bene Israel, there has been little contact between the two groups.

In the 1950s there were 11,500 Bene Israel and 1,900 Baghdadi Jews in Bombay, yet no more than one or two cases of intermarriage between the two communities are on record. The most serious grievance of the Bene Israel was the haughty attitude of the Baghdadi Jews, who maintained that the Bene Israel were "not pure Hebrews."[22]

The same problem was encountered by the roughly five thousand Bene Israel who settled in Israel after the establishment of the state. The Rabbinate in Israel could not be sure that the Bene Israel in former generations observed the Jewish laws pertaining to marriage and divorce, and therefore, in some cases Israeli rabbis refused to perform marriages between members of the Bene Israel and other Jewish communities. Occasionally it was demanded of them that they undergo a formal conversion ritual before they could marry a non-Bene Israel. This created great embitterment among the Bene Israel, who staged mass demonstrations and hunger strikes. Finally, in 1964, a special session of the Knesset (Israel's parliament) was convened to deal with the problem. The Rabbinate was forced to alter its policy, and thus the matter seemed to have been settled.

In connection with this controversy one interesting fact could be observed. Back in 1951 some of the Bene Israel found life too difficult in Israel and the attitude of some Israelis too discriminatory. They demanded to be sent back to India, and several dozen families were actually repatriated. In 1954 most of these returnees, finding the situation in India also not to their liking, again returned to Israel. As against this, in the early 1960s, when the marriage problem of the Bene Israel burst into the open, none of them demanded to be, or actually was, sent back to India. It would seem that in the ten or twelve years that had elapsed since their settlement in Israel, they had become sufficiently "Israelized" to fight out their problems in Israel without having recourse to escape back to India, which they had left with so much hope for a new and better life in the new Jewish State.

Some 650 miles south of Bombay, near the southern tip of India on the Malabar (west) coast, lies the province of Cochin with its capital city of the same name. At some period in the distant past a group of Jews came to this area and settled in Cranganore, about twenty miles north of Cochin. The date of their arrival is unknown. Even the myths of the Cochin Jews themselves differ on it greatly, one placing it into the days of King Solomon, another in the period of the Assyrian exile of Israel, a third in the time of the Babylonian exile of Judah. Scholarly opinion is similarly divided; however, the range of scholarly hypotheses spans, not the tenth to the sixth centuries BCE, but the second to the eleventh centuries CE. In any case, Benjamin of Tudela reports about 1167 that there were a hundred Black Jews (according to a variant reading "several thousand") on the Malabar coast, who, he says, "are good men, observers of the law, and possess the Torah of Moses, the Prophets, and some little knowlege of the Talmud and the Halakha."[23]

The Jews of Cochin have preserved to the present day a

document engraved on copper which was for centuries their charter for the possession of the township of Anjuvannam near Cranganore as their principality. The Copper Plates were given by the Raja of Malabar to a certain Joseph Rabban, endowing him and his descendants in perpetuity with princely privileges, which included a palanquin, a parasol, a drum, a trumpet, a garland, and the less personal but more lucrative prerogatives of collecting taxes. Apart from the problems presented by the exact interpretation of the text of the Plates, the vexing thing about them is that they cannot be dated with certainty; they are variously attributed to the fourth, fifth, eighth, and eleventh centuries.[24]

While the date of the beginning of the Jewish principality of Anjuvannam thus remains in doubt, its end can be fixed with greater certainty. In the late fifteenth and early sixteenth centuries internal dissension and external pressures on the part of the Portuguese forced the Jews to abandon the Cranganore region and seek refuge farther to the south, in the territory controlled by the Raja of Cochin. Here the number of the Jews, augmented by exiles from Spain and Portugal, increased so rapidly and so greatly that the Portuguese historian De Barros (1496–1570) refers to the Raja of Cochin as "King of the Jews."

In 1565 the Raja gave the Jews a strip of land next to his own palace in the city of Cochin, and in 1568 he permitted them to build a synagogue not thirty yards from his own private temple. Some of the Jews entered into the service of the Raja, and constituted a brigade in his forces.

In 1560 an office of the Inquisition was set up by the Portuguese in Goa (halfway between Bombay and Cochin), and its activities resulted in more and more Jews seeking and obtaining the protection of the Raja of Cochin. A hundred years later, as a parting present, the Portuguese burnt the Cochin synagogue (1663).

The establishment of Dutch rule in the same year brought a tolerant regime to the coastal area. The Dutch employed Cochin Jews as commercial agents and enabled the Cochin community to establish contact with their co-religionists in the Netherlands as well as in New Amsterdam (later New York). In 1668 the

Cochin Jews rebuilt their synagogue. The Dutch occupation brought some Dutch Jews to Cochin, and in 1686 the Jews of Amsterdam sent a research expedition to study the conditions of Cochin Jewry. The report of this expedition, prepared by Moses Pereira de Paiva, was printed the following year in Amsterdam under the title *Noticias dos Judeos de Cochin,* and it shows that by the late seventeenth century there were in Cochin Jewish families from Cranganore, Castile, Algiers, Jerusalem, Safed, Damascus, Aleppo, Baghdad, Persia, and even Germany.[25]

It was inevitable that in a country in which the caste system dominated the social order the descendants of Jews of such diverse origins should develop castes of their own. By the early sixteenth century these divisions had been solidly entrenched in the life of the Jews of Cochin. The two castes that had developed in those days continue to constitute the two major divisions of the community down to the present time. One was that of the White Jews, named *m'yuhasim* (i.e., those of pure lineage). These were the Jews who claimed pure Jewish descent both patrilineally and matrilineally, irrespective of their countries of origin. Around 1520, when Rabbi David ben Solomon ibn Abi Zimra (c. 1479–1589), the great rabbinical authority of Cairo, wrote his responsum to the Jews of Cochin concerning the question of the permissibility of intermarriage between *m'yuhasim* and other Jews, the former numbered one hundred families. De Paiva's report mentioned above lists twenty-five households of White Jews, which is either an incomplete figure or indicates a great decrease in the number of White Jews in the 166 years from 1520 to 1686.

The second group, called Black Jews, was, and has remained, much larger than that of the White Jews. Their seven congregations comprise 86 percent of all Cochin Jews. Concerning their origin there are different theories, of which the most plausible is the one that considers them the descendants of natives of the area who many centuries ago converted to Judaism. The Black Jews themselves, however, maintain that they are the pure descendants of Jewish immigrants, like the White Jews, and that "their skin color is but the result of many centuries of exposure to the tropical sun."[26] By the early seventeenth century they had

421

a synagogue in Cochin; about 1850 they numbered two thousand and had "two or three synagogues."[27] About 1900 they had two synagogues, and by the mid twentieth century four in Cochin itself, as well as several more in the villages of its environs. Prior to the onset of their emigration to Israel, the Black Jews numbered some 2,400, representing about 95 percent of all the Jews of Cochin.

The third Jewish group is that of the *m'shuhrarim* or "liberated ones." As their name indicates, these are the descendants of the converted and manumitted slaves of both the White and the Black Jews, as well as the offspring of White and Black Jewish men and their slave concubines. The *m'shuhrarim,* accordingly, fall into two subgroups: those of the White Jews and those of the Black. Regretably, no information is available as to the relationship between the two. It is, however, known that the Black Jews used to treat their *m'shuhrarim* more liberally and with more consideration than did the White Jews.

The strenuous efforts of the Liberated Ones to improve their position in the community led to some concessions in their seating in the synagogue and their participation in the service, but social intercourse among the three castes remained minimal. When a White Jewish girl married a *m'shuhrar* (they went to Bombay to get married), the incident shook the White community. Residential segregation also continues: the White Jews live in the upper part of Jew Town (as the Jewish street in Cochin is called), the Black Jews in its lower part. Virtually all White Jews speak English in addition to Malayalam, but only a few Black Jews do. The White Jews are more liberal in their religious services, the Black Jews more conservative. For example, in the early 1930s the White Jews gave up ceremonial scourging the day before Yom Kippur, while the Black Jews have retained this painful rite. The 1931 census of Cochin counted 1,600 Black Jews organized in seven congregations. The number of White Jews in the same year was 144; that of the *m'shuhrarim,* about thirty. However, by that time many Cochin Jews had moved to Bombay.[28]

In 1954–55 there was a strong movement among the Jews of Cochin to emigrate to the Jewish State. By 1968 there were no less than three thousand Jews from Cochin in Israel. Together with the five thousand Bene Israel and the five thousand Baghdadi Jews who had also left India for Israel, the great majority of the three major Jewish communities of India (a total of thirteen thousand) had been ingathered in the Jewish State.

By 1964 only three hundred Jews remained in the Cochin area, of whom eighty were left in Cochin proper, 120 in Ernakulam, sixty-five in Parur, and thirty in Chenamangalam. The only reason that these last remnants of the community had not joined the majority in Israel was that from 1962 on the Indian government no longer allowed emigrants to take their assets with them. Thus, rather than go to Israel penniless, the three hundred Black and White Jews wait in Cochin until such time as the government relaxes its rule.[29] In 1968 the regulations were still in effect, and consequently there were still forty or fifty White Jews—the well-to-do element—in Cochin.[30]

The Falashas of Ethiopia

In the hills of Ethiopia there are scattered villages inhabited by a tribe that calls itself Falasha. The name means "exiled," and it was given to the Falashas either by the native population to indicate that they were foreign immigrants, or by the Falashas themselves, whose tradition has it that they are the descendants of exiles from Jerusalem. The Falashas of the villages in the Gondar region (in northern Ethiopia), however, do not use this name but call themselves *beta Israel* ("House of Israel"), or *Israel,* or *kayla* (a Cushitic term).[31]

The Falashas, whose total number in 1970 was estimated at 23,000,[32] claim that they are the descendants of Jews who came from the Land of Israel to Ethiopia with Menelik I, the (legendary) son of King Solomon and the Queen of Sheba (see 1 Kings 10:1–13), or the "Queen of the South." Others claim an even earlier origin. At the time of the Exodus from Egypt, they say, some of the Children of Israel migrated to the south and reached Ethiopia. Yet others are satisfied with placing their beginnings in the days of the first or of the second Exile. Most scholars, however, hold that the Falashas are descendants of a segment of

423

the indigenous Agau population that converted to Judaism, under the influence of Jewish missionaries from either Egypt or Yemen. No educated guess can be ventured as to the time of this event. The fact that physically no appreciable difference exists between the Falashas and the other Ethiopians supports the conversion theory. Interestingly, the Falashas themselves claim that no such difference exists.[33] Both Falasha men and women dress like the other Ethiopians, but the Falasha women wear their hair cut short, while the Amhara women wear it long.[34]

Legends apart, the first historical mention of the Jews of Ethiopia is found in the writings of Benjamin of Tudela, that peerless traveler and reporter of the Jewish communities who, from 1166 to 1171, visited numerous Jewish Diasporas.[35] He speaks about the Jews of "India" who had cities and castles on mountains and fought Christians. Since mountain strongholds are not an Indian feature and since the name India was often given to Ethiopia in the Middle Ages, it is generally assumed that this piece of intelligence refers to the Jews of Ethiopia.[36]

Tudela's reference to fights between the Ethiopian Jews and Christians is fully borne out by the Ethiopian chronicles which recount frequent wars between the adherents of the two religions from the fourteenth century on. The Falashas succeeded (with some interruptions) in retaining their independence, made an alliance with the Muslims who invaded northern Ethiopia in 1536, and were defeated by the powerful Ethiopian King Serşe Dengel Melek Seged (1563–1597). Fight for Falasha independence continued until the seventeenth century, when their leader Gedeon was defeated and their independence irrevocably lost. The Falashas were expelled from Semyen where they had lived for many centuries, became dispersed all over the country, and many adopted Christianity. To this day they are scattered in all parts of the country, although their main concentration is in northern Ethiopia, in the regions north of Lake Tana.[37]

The Falashas once spoke a language of Cushite origin, and in part of Begemder they still seem to speak Agau dialects such as Quarenya. However, the great majority of the Falashas have long since given up these old Cushitic tongues and they now speak Amharic (the Semitic national language of Ethiopia) in the central regions of the country, and Tigrinya (another important Semitic language of Ethiopia) in the north. The language of ancient Falasha literature is Geez, or Old Ethiopic, a South Semitic language closely related to South Arabic. By the end of the seventh century the Old Testament had been translated into Geez (from the Greek of the Septuagint), and subsequent centuries saw the writing of several other religious books, such as the Commandments of the Sabbath, the Book of Abba Elijah, The Book of Angels, and others, all of which form today the sacred literature of the Falashas. The Falashas knew nothing of the post-Biblical Jewish literature, such as the Talmud and the Midrash, except a few apocryphal books (e.g., Baruch, the Testament of Abraham, the Death of Moses, the Apocalypse of Ezra). They knew no Hebrew at all, except a very few words that occur in their prayers or in the Bible *(Adonay, gadol, Saba'ot, El Shaday, Elohe, Torah, goyim).* Recently a few Falashas have begun to study in Jewish institutions in the United States and Israel and attempts have been made to teach some Hebrew in their local schools.[38]

Most of the Falashas live in villages scattered all over Ethiopia, many of them around the city of Gondar. There are purely Falasha villages, and others inhabited by both Falashas and other Ethiopians, in which case the Falashas live in a separate compact quarter, usually apart from the others.[39] In appearance and location there is no difference between Falasha and Ethiopian villages: both are situated near a river, because water is essential for men and cattle and, in the case of the Falashas, because their religion bids them to perform frequent ablutions. The huts have the same circular shape, but the Falasha villages have, in addition to the huts normally inhabited by the families, also a hut serving as the synagogue, and two others at some distance from the village—one in which the menstruating women spend seven days in isolation, and the second, to which a woman retires on the eighth day after the birth of a boy (after he is circumcised) and in which she remains for thirty-two days. If she gives birth to a girl, she remains for fourteen days in the "hut of blood" and then goes to the hut of childbed for sixty-six days. This in accordance with the Biblical rule specified in Leviticus 12:25.

Most Falashas are agriculturists, practicing plough culture

with one or two oxen, and sowing barley, wheat, or millet. A part of their crops goes to the landowner for rent. In the dry season (October to June) they also engage in crafts, some working as smiths, others as weavers. Pottery is a women's occupation. The product of their labors is sold in the nearest city.

Whatever the historic origin of the Falashas, they are at present a marginal Jewish community. Their religion is based only on the Bible; they observe the Biblical commandments, often in a manner quite different from that of rabbinic Judaism; they are not familiar with post-Biblical Jewish literature (except for the few apocryphal books mentioned above), and thus are unaware of the developments that have taken place in Judaism in later periods. On the other hand, their religion has absorbed a certain amount of non-Jewish influence from the native African, Christian, and Muslim religions, among whose practicioners they have lived for many centuries.

Contact between Falashas and world Jewry is minimal. Some Jewish scholars have visited and studied them in the last four or five decades, and a very few Falashas have gone to Israel and America to study. The number of Falashas who settled in Israel amounts to a few dozen. The life of the rest of them in Ethiopia continues largely unchanged.

22 THE DIASPORA AND ISRAEL

The relationship of the Diaspora to the Land, and since 1948 the State, of Israel, and the significance of Israel for the Diaspora are issues that have gone to the very core of Jewish existence for the last two thousand years. A full discussion of these matters would necessitate its own large book. However, the extent to which the concept Eretz Yisrael ("Land of Israel") and its symbols, Zion, and Jerusalem, have pervaded Diaspora life has been illustrated in many of the foregoing chapters. One point that remains to be dealt with, however briefly, is the transformation of the role played by Zion as the sustenance of Diaspora Jewry. In contemplating the radical change that took place in this role in the late nineteenth century, and of the circumstances in Jewish life that brought it about, one is led to think of the old Talmudic saying: "The Holy One, blessed be He, provides the remedy before the malady."

The Messianic Zion

From the destruction of the Second Jewish Commonwealth until the Jewish Enlightenment, that is for more than seventeen centuries, the Land of Israel remained the Holy Land for the Jews, their spiritual homeland and religious center. It also was a country whose sacred history, coupled with its remoteness and inaccessibility, turned it into an ideal place quite divorced from reality, a land of dreams and visions, the Navel of the Earth, a land flowing with the milk and the honey of the spirit, a place partaking of the character of a lost paradise of piety. Throughout those long centuries very little was known to the simple, believing Jews, scattered in their Diaspora communities, about the actual conditions in Palestine, and thus no realistic and prosaic facts intruded into the picture, nurtured by a faith-filled

427

tradition, of the Holy Land of the Fathers that was lovingly referred to as *Eretz Tz'vi,* "the land of the deer" (that is, of beauty), *Eretz Hemda,* "the land of charm," and many more such love-inspired epithets.

In this religio-romantic view Eretz Yisrael represented both the desire and the destiny of the Jewish people. It was the land the return to which was to be accomplished by a great divine miracle, the coming of King Messiah, around whose advent— expected and prayed for day by day—popular lore wove the richest wreath of myths that any people ever projected into an indeterminate but imminent future. I have studied mythologies for close to forty years now, but have yet to come across a myth that in sustaining power approximated even remotely this unique Jewish myth of Messianic redemption, return to the Holy Land, and reestablishment of the throne of David.

However, since myths are living things, they must share the fate of all living, which is to decline and die. The myth of the Messiah died as far as the great majority of the Jewish people was concerned when the Enlightenment and assimilation brought about a modernization and rationalization of the synagogue. By the end of the nineteenth century, for most of the Jews in the Western world the Messiah was dead because his eventual advent was no longer believed in. The death of the Messiah myth signified also the demise of the religio-romantic belief in a return to the Land of Israel, in a divinely decreed end of the Exile, and, in fact, in the very existence of the Exile itself. Once this state was reached, the entire traditional structure of Judaism, like a wheel whose hub has been torn out, began to crumble. Notwithstanding the sincere but futile efforts of Jewish religious Reform to substitute the mission theory for the Messianic ideal, a Judaism deprived of its traditional core lost the magic power which had kept its far-straying flock together. Assimilation, religious indifference, inobtrusive sneaking away and passing into the gentile majority made increasing inroads into the ranks of the ancient people. The very existence of the Diaspora seemed to be threatened.

The National Zion

But, "the Holy One, blessed be He, provides the remedy before the malady." In this case it happened just in the nick of time. A moment before assimilation, which had begun in Western Europe, reached the Jewish masses of the east of the continent, the idea of *Hibbat Zion,* the Love of Zion, sprang up among them. The *Hoveve Zion,* or Lovers of Zion, as the followers of this movement were called, believed and taught that it was the duty of the Jews to return to the Land of Israel and to engage in the cultivation of its soil. It was this *Hibbat Zion* movement that prepared the ground for Theodor Herzl's political Zionism which followed it some fifteen years later. Each of the two movements in turn served as the remedy that was ready for use when the epidemic of assimilationism struck the Jewish body politic. Consequently, at a time when the belief in a Messianic return to Zion could no longer fire the Jewish imagination, Zion assumed a new meaning, a new significance in the form of Zionism. Borrowing one of the most powerful myths from the arsenal of the new European mythology, Zionism firmly implanted nationalism into the midst of the tottering Jewish existence. The remedy worked: it was both curative and prophylactic. A Jewry no longer capable of believing in a Messianic Zion was saved from going under for quite possibly the last time by the idea of Zion as the national home of the Jewish people.

Transformation is a favorite theme in many mythologies. It is, moreover, one of the most reliable signs of life attesting to the vitality of a myth. From a historical perspective we now recognize that the mythical sustaining role Israel played in the life of the Diaspora has not yet come to an end. The Messiah myth has not died: it merely transformed itself into a new myth form, one that can work on, motivate, and sustain a modern, overurbanized, and widely scattered Jewish community. Zion the religio-romantic ideal has been replaced by Israel the State as the new hub of the Jewish Diaspora.

For half a century, from the First Zionist Congress to the

429

establishment of Israel, an increasing proportion of Diaspora Jewry placed its best talents and energies in the service of the realization of the Basle Program: the establishment in Palestine of a publicly recognized and secured national home for the Jewish people. In doing so, Diaspora Jewry formally evoked and avowed a new Zion-ideal to replace the old one, even before the latter completely disappeared. Almost miraculously, the new eschatology proved no less powerful than the old: practical and political work for Zion proved as potent a sustenance as was the adherence to, and the daily emotional and faith-filled reaffirmation of, the old myth of a Messianic Zion. In the process, Diaspora Jewry as a whole increasingly assumed a new physiognomy: that of a people geographically scattered all over the world, but united in spirit and in purpose, working for its national renaissance in the ancient land of its fathers.

Once the State of Israel was reestablished, a new and most remarkable phenomenon began to manifest itself in the Jewish world: an unexpected strengthening of the old emotional ties that had run from the Diaspora to Israel and from one Diaspora community to another. As is the case in individual families, manifestations of brotherhood, identification and readiness to sacrifice surfaced primarily in times of stress and danger. Whenever Israel was threatened, the Diaspora solidly closed ranks behind it. Whenever any Diaspora community faced danger, Israel and the other Diasporas did what they could to help.

A paradoxical and almost tragic situation developed in consequence of the emotional interdependence between the Diaspora and Israel. Any adversity that threatened Israel had the incidental effect of augmenting the chances of the Diaspora's survival. The mechanism through which this was achieved was set in motion by the age-old sense of Jewish community of fate which persisted wherever Jewish identification had not yet completely disappeared. We have seen above (Chapter XIX, on the Jews in the United States) that the feeling of Jewish identification remained as the last vestige of Jewish ethnicity, even when and where all other factors or components of Judaism, such as religion, traditions, and knowledge of history, were gone. The embers of this sense of Jewish identification, of the community of fate that unites all part of the Jewish people, are fanned to a new flame whenever the winds of enmity rise from across the borders of the small Jewish State.

What will happen once Israel dwells secure in its land? Will the Diaspora gradually disappear? Or will the cultural influences emanating from the Jewish State be powerful enough to provide new sustenance for it? At this fateful moment in Israel's history one can only wish that a day will come soon when this question is no longer hypothetical, but an actuality to be faced!

1. THE EMERGENCE OF THE DIASPORA

[1] Exodus 3:8, and again in v. 17.
[2] Genesis 11:31.
[3] Genesis 12:1.
[4] Exodus 3:6.
[5] Genesis 12:1.
[6] Cf. Exodus 6:16,18,20.
[7] Deuteronomy 34:1.
[8] First time: Genesis 12:7.
[9] First time: Exodus 3:8.
[10] Genesis 15:7,13.
[11] Deuteronomy 5:15; 15:15; 16:12; 24:18,22.
[12] Exodus 22:20; 23:9.
[13] Deuteronomy 10:19.
[14] Exodus 23:9.
[15] Deuteronomy 23:8.
[16] Deuteronomy 23:4,9.
[17] Exodus 7:16,26; 8:16,24; 9:1,13; 10:3, 8,11,24; 12:31.
[18] 2 Kings 17:6.
[19] Cf. 2 Kings 25:12; Jeremiah 39:10; 52:16.
[20] Deuteronomy 17:16; cf. Hosea 11:5.
[21] Jeremiah 42-43.
[22] Jeremiah 44. As to the worship of the Queen of Heaven, see R. Patai, *The Hebrew Goddess* (New York, 1967), pp. 64, 97-98.
[23] Jeremiah 42:10-12.
[24] Moritz Güdemann, *Geschichte des Erziehungswesens und der Cultur der Juden in Frankreich und Deutschland* (Vienna, 1880), pp. 114, 273-76.

2. EXILE AND DIASPORA

[1] Judges 5:12.
[2] Ezra 2:1; Nehemiah 7:6.
[3] Genesis 11:4.
[4] Ezekiel 28:25.
[5] Deuteronomy 4:27.
[6] Deuteronomy 30:2-3.
[7] Cf. 2 Kings 15:29; 16:9; 17:26-28,33; 18:11; 24:14-16; 25:11,21; Jeremiah 13:19; 22:12; 24:1; 27:20; 29:1; 39:4; 40:1,7; 43:3; 52:15,27-28,30; Amos 1:6; Esther 2:6; Ezra 2:1; Nehemiah 7:6; 1 Chronicles 5:6,26; 8:6-7; 9:1; 2 Chronicles 36:20.
[8] The three mentions in Jeremiah 29:4, 7,14 occur in a letter Jeremiah sent to his exiled brethren in Babylon. His purpose was to emphasize that it was God's will rather than Nebuchadnezzar's victory that lay at the roots of the exile. In the introduction to the same epistle the people are described as "all the people whom Nebuchadnezzar exiled from Jerusalem to Babylon" (Jeremiah 29:1). This, therefore, was the generally accepted view: Nebuchadnezzar, king of Babylon, defeated Judah and took the people into exile. To counter this with his own theocentric view, Jeremiah puts into God's mouth the words: "Thus saith the Lord of hosts, the God of Israel to all the exiles whom I caused to be exiled [*higleti*] from Jerusalem to Babylon [v.4]. . . . And seek the peace of the city whither I have caused you to be exiled [v.7]. . . and I will bring you back unto the place whence I caused you to be exiled [v. 14]."

Similarly Ezekiel emphasized that it will become known among the nations that "I am the Lord their [i.e., Israel's] God, in that I caused them to be exiled [*b'hagloti*] among the nations and have gathered them unto their own land . . ."(Ezekiel 39:28).

The same motivation makes Amos say "Therefore I will cause you to be exiled [*v'higleti*] beyond Damascus, saith He whose name is the Lord God of Hosts" (Amos 5:27).

In Lamentations 4:22 the prophet promises God's mercy to the Daughter of Zion: "He will no more cause you to be exiled [*l'haglotekh*]. . . ."

433

And finally, in 1 Chronicles 5:40 we find a brief historical note which is in accordance with the general pervasive piety and God-centered view of the author of this book: "And Jehozadak went [i.e., into captivity] when the Lord caused Judah and Jerusalem to be exiled [*b'haglot*] by the hand of Nebuchadnezzar."

It would appear, therefore, that in each of these five passages the authors had a definite theological-didactic purpose for stating that it was God who caused or would cause the people of Israel to be exiled. The paucity of these formulations contrasts with the frequent references both to the exile as the result of the armed defeat of Israel and to the dispersion (Diaspora) of Israel as having been brought about by direct divine action.

Similarly, and for the same theological-didactic reason, one Biblical author refers to God's having exiled other peoples before Israel, thereby enabling Israel to settle in Canaan; cf. 2 Kings 17:11.

9 Deuteronomy 4:27; 28:64; 30:2; Isaiah 24:1; Jeremiah 9:15; 30:11; Ezekiel 11:16–17; 12:15; 20:23,34,41; 22:15; 28:25; 34:12; 36:19; Nehemiah 1:8.
10 Cf. quotations in Eliezer Ben-Yehuda's *Thesaurus*, s.vv.
11 B. Sanhedrin 11b.
12 *Galuyot*, B. Yom Tov (Betza) 4b; J. Ta'anit 63d, mid.
13 B. Ta'anit 22b.
14 *B'ne haGola*, B. 'Avoda Zara 306.
15 B. Menahot 110a.
16 Exodus Rabba 15:6, ed. Mirkin pp. 166–67.
17 B. Megilla 17b; B. Pesahim 88a; B. Zebahim 116a; etc. The 18 benedictions in which that phrase occurs date from the days of Rabban Gamaliel in Jabne, following the destruction of the Temple; cf. B. Megilla 17b.
18 B. Sanhedrin 11b.
19 Cf. Ben-Yehuda, *Thesaurus*, s.v. "gal-ut."
20 B. Sanhedrin 98a.
21 B. Sanhedrin 97b.
22 B. Sukka 52b.
23 Pesikta diRav Kahana, ed. Buber, 112a-b.
24 B. Ketubot 111a.
25 *Sepher Mitzvot Gadol*, Mitzvot 'Ase 73, Venice 1547 (reprint: Jerusalem, 1961), p. 152c bot.
26 Isaac Aboab, *Menorat HaMaor*, par. 310, chapter 9, and par. 309, chapter 8, p. 409 of the Livorno edition, reprinted in Jerusalem, 1958.
27 Eleazar Azkari, *Sepher Haredim*, Introduction (Jerusalem, 1966), p. 18b top.
28 B. Ketubot 110b–111a.
29 B. Ketubot 111a.

3. DIASPORA IN MODERN JEWISH THOUGHT

1 *The Israelite* 1:20 (1854), as quoted by David Philipson, *The Reform Movement in Judaism* (New York, 1907), p. 478.
2 *The Asmonean* x:85 (1854), as quoted in Philipson, *op. cit.*, p. 476.
3 Philipson, *op. cit.*, p. 561.
4 *Ibid.*, pp. 440–41.
5 As quoted, *ibid.*, pp. 483–84.
6 *Protokolle der Rabbiner Conferenz abgehalten zu Philadelphia*, 1869 (New York, 1870), pp. 86–87, as quoted in Philipson, *op. cit.*, p. 489.
7 Philipson, *op. cit.*, p. 492.
8 *Ibid.*, p. 536.
9 *Ibid.*, p. 467.
10 *Ibid.*, p. 556.
11 Cf. pp. 97, 114, 126, 130.
12 See also p. 324, where the English version asks God to enable Israel to be the messenger of peace "unto the peoples of the earth"—a passage which has no basis in the original Hebrew; and p. 325, where the words "and all the nations" are added in the English translation of the Hebrew prayer, which merely ask God to bless "Thy people Israel." The original conclusion of the prayer, "Blessed art Thou, O Lord, who blessest Thy people Israel with peace," has been emended to read in Hebrew "Blessed art Thou, O Lord, who makest the peace" (my literal translation from the Hebrew). Also see p. 327 where an English prayer describes "the synagogue" as "Israel's sublime gift to the world," etc.

[13] Cf. s.v. "Central-Verein deutscher Staatsbürger jüdischen Glaubens," in *Jüdisches Lexikon* (Berlin, 1927), Vol. I; *Encyclopaedia Jüdaica* (Berlin, 1930), Vol. V; *Lexikon des Judentums* (Gutersloh, 1967).

[14] This, and all subsequent quotations describing the aims of the American Jewish organizations mentioned are taken from the *American Jewish Year Book 1968* (New York, 1968).

[15] Cf. Moses Sopher, *T'shuvot* (Responsa) Yore De'a 138; as quoted by S. H. Weingarten, *HaHatam Sopher V'-Talmidav* (Jerusalem, 1944), pp. 50–51.

4. THE JEWISH "RACE"

[1] R. Patai, *Golden River to Golden Road: Society, Culture and Change in the Middle East,* 3rd ed. (Philadelphia, 1969), p. 352.

[2] These theories were effectively exposed and disposed of by Karl Saller in *Die Rassenlehre des Nationalsozialismus in Wissenschaft und Propaganda* (Darmstadt, 1961), and in Karl Thieme, ed., *Judenfeindschaft* (Frankfurt a. M. and Hamburg, 1963), pp. 180–208, 298–99.

[3] The following discussion is based on an extensive study by the present author, scheduled to appear in *Rassengeschichte der Menschheit,* ed. by Karl Saller, which is being published in a series of volumes since 1968 by R. Oldenbourg Verlag, München und Wien.

[4] Cf. Ignacz Zollschan, *Das Rassenproblem,* 4th ed. (Wien und Berlin, 1920), pp. 45–46, 55. My translation from the German original.

[5] Cf. Carleton S. Coon, "Have the Jews a Racial Identity?" in I. Graber and S. G. Britt, eds., *Jews in a Gentile World* (New York, 1942), pp. 30–33, 35, 37.

[6] Cf. Arthur Ruppin, *Soziologie der Juden* (Berlin, 1930–31), I, 29–36.

[7] Cf. Jan Czekanowsky, "Die anthropologische Struktur von Europa im Lichte polnischer Untersuchungsergebnisse," *Anthropologischer Anzeiger* XVI (1939), as reprinted in English translation in Earl W. Count,

ed., *This Is Race* (New York, 1950), pp. 600–1.

[8] Cf. Alfred Kroeber, *Anthropology* (New York, 1948), p. 144.

[9] Cf. Ashley Montague, *Statement on Race* (New York, 1951), pp. 63–64.

[10] Ezekiel 16:3, 45.

[11] *Entziklopedia Mikrait,* s.v. "Emori."

[12] Deuteronomy 26:5.

[13] Genesis 25:20.

[14] Genesis 28:5; 31:20.

[15] Genesis 34.

[16] Pirke Rabbi Eliezer ch. 38, etc,; cf. Robert Graves and Raphael Patai, *Hebrew Myths: The Book of Genesis* (New York, 1964), p. 237.

[17] Sources in Graves and Patai, *op. cit.,* pp. 236–77.

[18] Genesis 38:2.

[19] Genesis 38:29–30.

[20] Genesis 46:8–26.

[21] Genesis 41:45.

[22] Genesis 41:50–52.

[23] Exodus 2:21; Numbers 12:1.

[24] Numbers 25:6–8,14–15.

[25] Leviticus 24:10.

[26] Deuteronomy 23:9.

[27] Deuteronomy 21:10–13.

[28] 2 Samuel 11:2ff.

[29] 2 Samuel 11:11.

[30] 1 Samuel 26:6.

[31] 1 Kings 11:1.

[32] 1 Kings 9:20; 2 Chronicles 8:7.

[33] 2 Samuel 8:2,14.

[34] 2 Samuel 8:18.

[35] Ruth 1:4,22.

[36] Ruth 4:17–22.

[37] 2 Chronicles 24:26.

[38] Nehemiah 13:23.

[39] Nehemiah 13:28.

[40] Nehemiah 13:16.

[41] Nehemiah 13:3; cf. 9:2.

[42] Ezra 10:2,18–44.

[43] Ezra 10:19,44.

[44] Cf. Mishna Kiddushin 3:12, B. Kiddushin 68b.

[45] Cf. footnote 3 above.

[46] More of them can be found in the study referred to in footnote 3.

[47] Cf. Rudolf Virchow's report in *Verhandlungen der Berliner Gesellschaft für Anthropologie und Urgeschichte* (1876), pp. 16–18, and his "Gesamtbericht" in *Archiv für Anthropologie* (1886), XVI, 275–475; Maurice Fish-

berg, *The Jews* (London and New York, 1911), pp. 62–65.

5. DEMOGRAPHY
[1] Cf. Arthur Ruppin, *Soziologie der Juden* (Berlin, 1931), I, 80–81.
[2] E.g., Egypt had a population of 2,-460,000 in 1800, 14,500,000 in 1930, and 30,000,000 in 1966; cf. R. Patai, *Golden River to Golden Road: Society, Culture and Change in the Middle East*, 3rd ed. (Philadelphia, 1969), p. 14.
[3] Liebman Hersch, "Jewish Population Trends in Europe," in Jewish Encyclopaedic Handbooks, *The Jewish People: Past and Present* (New York, 1948), II, 10–11.
[4] Cf. H. S. Halevi, "The Demography of Jewish Communities in Eastern Europe, "*The Jewish Journal of Sociology* (June 1960), pp. 104–8.
[5] Cf. Hersch, *op. cit.*, p. 23.
[6] Cf. Roberto Bachi, "The Demographic Development of Italian Jewry from the 17th Century, " *The Jewish Journal of Sociology* (December 1962), p. 189; Sergio della Pergola, "L'Indagina Statistica sugli Ebrei in Italia," *La Rassegna Mensile di Israel* (Rome, October 1968), p. 576.
[7] Cf. "Dutch Jewry: A Demographic Analysis," *The Jewish Journal of Sociology* (June 1962), p. 51.
[8] Cf. Nathan Goldberg, "The Jewish Population in the United States" and "The Jewish Population in Canada," in *The Jewish People: Past and Present*, pp. 26, 36.
[9] Cf. Jacob Lestschinsky, *HaT'futza HaY'hudit* (Jerusalem, 1960), pp. 204–6.
[10] Cf. Alvin Chenkin, "Jewish Population in the United States, 1966," *American Jewish Year Book 1967* (New York, 1967), p. 231.
[11] Hersch, *op. cit.*, pp. 8–9; Nathan Goldberg, "Population Trends Among American Jews," *Jewish Affairs* (New York, April 1948), II, 3–23.
[12] *Statistical Abstract of Israel 1968*, p. 71.
[13] André Chouraqui, *Les Juifs d'Afrique du Nord* (Paris, 1952), pp. 335, 357.

[14] Hersch, *op. cit.*, p. 45.

6. URBANIZATION
[1] Arthur Ruppin, *Soziologie der Juden* (Berlin, 1931), I, 250ff.
[2] *Ibid.*, I, 422.
[3] *Ibid.*, I, 357.
[4] *Ibid.*, I, 108–9.
[5] *Ibid.*, I, 110; Andrè Chouraqui, *La Condition juridique de l'Israelite Marocaine* (Paris, 1950), p. 32.
[6] Ruppin, *op. cit.*, I, 94, 121–22.
[7] *American Jewish Year Book 1966* (New York, 1966), pp. 361, 381; *1967*, pp. 374, 396, 400, 404, 408, 411.
[8] R. Patai, *Golden River to Golden Road: Society, Culture and Change in the Middle East*, 3rd ed. (Philadelphia, 1969), pp. 13–15.
[9] Cf. for Kurdistan, Erich Brauer, *Y'hude Kurdistan*, ed. R. Patai (Jerusalem, 1948), pp. 170ff.; for Iran: *American Jewish Year Book 1951*, p. 410 (in 120 towns and villages); for Yemen: Erich Brauer, *Ethnologie der Jemenitischen Juden* (Heidelberg, 1934); Shlomo D. Goitein, "Portrait of a Yemenite Weavers' Village," *Jewish Social Studies*, XVII, 3–26; for the Aden Protectorate:Count Carlo Landberg, *Arabica*, V, Index, s.v. Juifs; D. van der Meulen, *Aden to the Hadhramaut* (London, 1947), pp. 33, 37, 40, 47; for Saudi Arabia: H. St. John B. Philby, *Arabian Highlands* (Ithaca, N.Y., 1952), pp. 387, 389–90; for Oman: Bertram Thomas, *Alarms and Excursions in Arabia* (London, 1931), p. 170; for Libya: Cohen Marducheo, *Gli Ebrei in Libia, usi e costumi* (Rome, 1927); Bernard Newman, *Mediterranean Background* (London, 1949), p. 137 (troglodytes in Garian-Tigrinna); for Tunisia: *American Jewish Year Book 1951*, p. 431 (0.4 percent engaged in agriculture); B. Newman, *op. cit.*, p. 98 (Island of Djerba); for Tunisia and Algeria:Peter Moeschlin, "Im Afrikanischen Frankreich," *Atlantis* (May 1950), pp. 181–88; for Algeria: R. V. C. Bodley, *Wind in the Sahara* (New York, 1944), pp. 111, 194ff. (in the oases of Algerian Sahara); *American Jewish Year Book 1951*,

pp. 432ff.; for Morocco: *American Jewish Year Book 1951*, pp. 426ff; Rom Landau, *Moroccan Journal* (London, 1952), p. 63 (in Midelt and Rish); *Universal Jewish Encyclopaedia*, s.v. Morocco (on the Berber or Mountain Jews); on North Africa in general: M. Eisenbeth, *Les Juifs de l'Afrique du Nord* (Alger, 1936), p. 59; Jean Despois, *L'Afrique du Nord* (Paris, 1949), p. 197 (1.51 percent rural proprietors and agricultural laborers); for the Caucasus: Joseph Baron de Baye, *Les Juifs des montagnes et les Juifs georgiens* (Paris, 1902).

[10] Ruppin, *op. cit.*, I, 103–4.

[11] Cecil Roth, in Julius Gould and Shaul Esh, *Jewish Life in Modern Britain* (London, 1964), p. 108.

[12] *American Jewish Year Book 1967*, pp. 4–5.

[13] Georg Levitte's study in the volume *Aspects of French Jewry* (London, 1969), p. 12, n. 2.

[14] Arye Tartakower, *Shivte Yisrael* (Tel Aviv, 1966), II, 231.

[15] *American Jewish Year Book 1967*, p. 321.

[16] Tartakower, *op. cit.*, II, 243–45; *American Jewish Year Book 1967*, p. 327.

[17] *American Jewish Year Book 1966*, p. 338; Tartakower, *op. cit.*, II, 218–19.

[18] Cecil Roth, *loc. cit.*, p. 108.

[19] *American Jewish Year Book 1967*, p. 303.

[20] Cecil Roth, *loc. cit.*, p. 109.

[21] *American Jewish Year Book 1929*, pp. 118–19.

[22] Calculated on the basis of data in the *American Jewish Year Book 1967*, pp. 235, 237–41.

7. THE LANGUAGES OF THE JEWS

[1] See Chapter XXI.

[2] B. Sota 49b; B. Baba Kama 83a.

[3] Cf. B. Sota 49b; B. Baba Kama 83a, in the name of Rabbi Yose, a fourth-century Babylonian Amora.

[4] Cf. Nahum Slouschz, *Judéo-Hellenes et Judéo-Berbères* (Paris, 1909).

[5] This is the explanation given me in 1945 by the late Farajullah Nasrullayof, head of the Meshhed community in Jerusalem.

[6] Cf. Wilhelm Bacher, "Jüdisch-Persisches aus Buchara," *Zeitschrift der deutschen morgenländischen Gesellschaft* 55 and 56; and "Türkische Lehnwörter und unbekannte Vokabeln im persischen Dialekte der Juden Bucharas," *Keleti Szemle* (Budapest, 1902), vol. 3.

[7] Cf. S. D. Goitein, *Jews and Arabs* (New York, 1955 and 1964), p. 134; see also Abraham S. Halkin, "Judeo-Arabic Literature," in Louis Finkelstein, ed., *The Jews: Their History, Culture, Religion* (Philadelphia, 1949), III, 784–816.

[8] Cf. Michael Molcho, "Hebrew Words in Ladino" (in Hebrew), *Edoth ("Communities"): A Quarterly for Folklore and Ethnology* (Jerusalem, April-July 1948), III, 77–88.

[9] Cf. Moshe Attias, "The Bed-Time Shema in Ladino," *Edoth ("Communities"): A Quarterly for Folklore and Ethnology* (Jerusalem 1946-47), II, 211–17 (in Hebrew), and p. 310 (English summary).

[10] Yudel Mark, "The Yiddish Language: Its Cultural Impact," *American Jewish Historical Quarterly* LIX:2 (December, 1969), pp. 201–02.

[11] *Ibid.*, p. 202.

[12] The above summary is based on Mark, *op. cit.*, pp. 202–03.

[13] We must add here that Rashi's commentaries contain thousands of French words, transliterated in Hebrew characters, which he used to explain (actually, to translate) difficult Hebrew and Aramaic words. This French vocabulary of Rashi's is an important source for the study of early medieval French; cf. Arsene Darmesteter and D. S. Blondheim, *Les gloses Françaises dans les commentaires talmudiques de Raschi*, 2 vols. (Paris, 1929–37). Judeo-French poems written in the Middle Ages in Hebrew characters were published among others by D. S. Blondheim, *Poémes judéo-français du Moyen Age* (Paris, 1927).

[14] Cf. Moritz Güdemann, *Geschichte des Erziehungswesens und der Cultur der Juden in Frankreich und Deutschland* (Vienna, 1880), pp. 114, 273-76.

[15] Simon Federbusch, *HaLashon Ha' 'Ivrit B'Yisrael Uva'Amim* (Jerusalem, 1967).

8. FOLK CULTURE

[1] Cf. Y. Baba Metzia 7, 1; 11b mid.
[2] Cf. Jacob Z. Lauterbach, "The Naming of Children," *Year Book of the Central Conference of American Rabbis* (Cincinnati, 1932), p. 335; H. J. Zimmels, *Ashkenazim and Sephardim* (London, 1958), p. 165.
[3] Cf. B. Baba Bathra 60b.
[4] Cf. sources in Zimmels, *op. cit.,* pp. 255–56.
[5] *Ibid.,* pp. 180–81.
[6] *Ibid.,* p. 180.
[7] *Ibid.,* pp. 92, 181, 338.
[8] *Ibid.,* p. 183
[9] *Ibid.*
[10] *Ibid.,* p. 184.
[11] Cf. Edward William Lane, *The Manners and Customs of the Modern Egyptians,* 5th ed. (London, 1871), I, 297; Everyman's Library ed. (London and New York, no date), p. 241.
[12] Zimmels, *op. cit.,* p. 247.
[13] R. Moses ben Nahman, *Responsa,* no. 283; cf. also R. Solomon ben Adret, *Responsa,* I, no. 413; as quoted by Zimmels, *op. cit.,* p. 247.
[14] Exodus 20:3.
[15] Nahmanides, Commentary to Exodus 20:3.
[16] In the Babylonian Talmud, Hagiga 16a.
[17] Nahmanides, Commentary to Leviticus 17:7.
[18] Nahmanides, Commentary to Numbers 14:9.
[19] Cf. Abudarham, *T'fillot shel Sukkot* (Amsterdam, 1726), p. 111a (he opposes the custom); Isserles, on *Tur Bet Yoseph Orah Hayim,* cap. 664, no. 2; Moritz Güdemann, *Geschichte des Erziehungswesens und der Cultur der abendländischen Juden* (Vienna, 1880–88), I, 206; Joshua Trachtenberg, *Jewish Magic and Superstition* (New York, 1939), p. 215 (the last two on the custom in Germany); and, most recently, Israel Weinstock, "HaAdam V'Tzilo," in Shaul Yisr'eli, ed., *Shana B'Shana* (Jerusalem, 1962), pp. 252–74.

[20] Cf. Tobias HaKohen, *Ma'ase Tovia,* 11 (Jesnitz, 1721, p. 86c), as quoted by Zimmels, *op. cit.,* p. 249.
[21] Cf. Trachtenberg, *op. cit.,* pp. 41ff., 172; Zimmels, *op. cit.,* p. 164, and sources there.
[22] Cf. R. Patai, *The Hebrew Goddess* (New York, 1967) p. 224ff.
[23] Cf. R. Patai, *Sex and Family in the Bible and the Middle East* (New York, 1959), pp. 188ff.
[24] Cf. Abraham G. Duker, "Notes on the Culture of American Jewry," *The Jewish Journal of Sociology,* II, No. 1 (June 1960), 98–99.
[25] In discussing this trend, Seymour Leventman remarks:". . . in a society placing such great emphasis on appearance and style, it is possible to play a non-Jewish role without actually assimilating." Cf. Seymour Leventman, "From Shtetl to Suburb," in Peter I. Rose, ed., *The Ghetto and Beyond* (New York, 1969), p. 51.
[26] Cf. R. Patai, "Indulco and Mumia," *Journal of American Folklore,* LXXVII (January-March 1964), 7–11.
[27] *Ibid.,* p. 8.
[28] Cf. Edward Westermarck, *Ritual and Belief in Morocco* (London, 1926), I, 72, 195, and literature on p. 196, n. 2; A. Ben-Ya'akov, "'Id al-Ziyara b'Baghdad," in R. Patai and J. J. Rivlin, eds., *Edoth ("Communities"): A Quarterly for Folklore and Ethnology* (Jerusalem, 1945), I, 37–40 (in Hebrew).
[29] L. Voinot, *Pélérinages judeo-musulmans au Maroc* (Paris, 1948).
[30] André Chouraqui, *Les Juifs d'Afrique du Nord* (Paris, 1952), pp. 293–94.
[31] *Ibid.,* pp. 294–95.
[32] Esther 3:8.
[33] A. Berliner, *Geschichte de Juden in Rom,* II (2), 107; as quoted by Israel Abrahams, *Jewish Life in the Middle Ages* (New York, 1958), p. 410.
[34] Fritz I. Baer, "HaM'gama HaDatit V'haHevratit Shel Sepher Hasidim," in *Zion,* III (1938), 1–50; Gershom G. Scholem, *Major Trends in Jewish Mysticism* (New York, 1941), pp. 83, 97f.
[35] Patai, *The Hebrew Goddess,* pp. 164–85.

9. ETHNICITY AND EXCELLENCE

[1] The above defintion largely follows that of Charles F. Marden and Gladys Meyer, *Minorities in American Society* (New York, 1968), pp. 24 and 406.

[2] Cf. H. J. Zimmels, *Ashkenazim and Sephardim* (London, 1958), pp. 6, 168, 275 n. 2

[3] Cf. *Encyclopaedia Judaica* (Berlin, 1934), X, 110.

[4] Leviticus 20:23.

[5] Cf. *Shulhan 'Arukh Yore De'a,* 178, 1.

[6] Alfred Rubens, *A History of Jewish Costume* (New York, 1967), pp. 125–28.

[7] In Dagobert D. Runes, ed., *The Hebrew Impact on Western Civilization* (New York, 1951), pp. 214–15, 212, 219.

[8] A fairly complete picture of the Jews in British politics and colonial affairs is given by Hugo Bieber in Runes, *op. cit.,* pp. 129–34.

10. THE ORIENTAL JEWS

[1] Cf. Reuben Levy, *The Social Structure of Islam* (Cambridge, 1957), p. 310.

[2] *Ibid.,* p. 66. The last phrase in single quotation marks is from the Koran 9:29.

[3] Cf. André Chouraqui, *Between East and West: A History of the Jews in North Africa* (Philadelphia, 1968), p. 55.

[4] Cf. Levy, *op. cit.,* p. 273.

[5] Cf. J. C. Hurewitz, "The Minorities in the Political Process," in Sydney N. Fisher, ed., *Social Forces in the Middle East* (Ithaca, N.Y., 1955), p. 214.

[6] Koran 9:29.

[7] Levy, *op. cit.,* p. 273.

[8] Cf. R. Patai, *Golden River to Golden Road: Society, Culture and Change in the Middle East,* 3rd ed. (Philadelphia, 1969), pp. 33ff., 322ff.

[9] Cf. Hurewitz, *loc. cit.,* p. 219.

[10] Cf. Patai, *op. cit.,* p. 491.

[11] Lloyd Cabot Briggs and Norina Lami Guède, *No More For Ever: A Saharan Jewish Town* (Cambridge, Mass., 1964), p. 59.

[12] Briggs and Guède, *op. cit.,* p. 66, report that in the Saharan town of Ghardaia, "a woman could always get a divorce if she really wanted to, no matter how strongly her husband . . . might object. . . . In fact, a majority of the divorces in the mellah were initiated by discontented wives." Whether it was the husband or the wife who started the action, the rabbi tried to bring about a reconciliation, but, if he saw that this was impossible, "he summoned the couple to appear together before him, read them the marriage contract specifying what and how much must be given to the divorced woman, and then declared the marriage dissolved." If this account is correct, it is surprising that in a Jewish community a marriage, entered into by writing a *ketubba,* should be dissolved by oral declaration of a rabbi, instead of the written *get* ("bill of divorcement") given by the husband to his wife and signed by two witnesses, as is done in the entire Jewish world. It is, of course, equally surprising that a divorce should become effective without the express consent of the husband. I strongly suspect that the authors did not ascertain the correct details.

[13] Cf. Patai, *op. cit.,* pp. 115ff, 437ff. The traditional Jewish explanation of this blessing is that the male Jew thanks God for not having created him a woman because women are not required by religion to fulfil the positive commandments that are tied to certain time periods; he is happy and grateful for being a man who, by fulfilling these commandments, performs acts that please God. Nevertheless, the fact remains that, whatever the reason, man is considered superior to woman.

[14] H. J. Zimmels, *Ashkenazim and Sephardim* (London, 1958), p. 254.

[15] *Ibid.,* pp. 63, 169.

[16] Briggs and Guède, *op. cit.,* p. 46.

[17] Patai, *op. cit.,* pp. 116–27.

[18] Briggs and Guède, *op. cit.,* p. 64.

[19] Patai, *op. cit.,* p. 441; cf. also pp. 439–44.

[20] Oral information from the late Rabbi David Prato, Chief Rabbi of Rome and Alexandria; cf. also Briggs and Guède, *op. cit.,* p. 26.

[21] B. Baba Bathra 141a.

439

[22] Patai, *op. cit.*, pp. 97–98.

[23] Briggs and Guède, *op. cit.*, p. 28.

[24] Patai, *op. cit.*, p. 474, where Koran 4:38 should be corrected to read Koran 4:34.

[25] B. Baba Metzia 59a.

[26] Maimonides, *Mishne Tora*, Nashim 15:19.

[27] E.g. in Morocco 23.24 percent of the school-age girls as against 54.32 percent of the school-age boys actually attended school in 1965; in Yemen 0.74 percent of the girls and 12.49 percent of the boys; in the United Arab Republic 44.36 percent of the girls and 64.73 percent of the boys; etc. Cf. Patai, *op. cit.*, p. 491, table 8, which contains educational statistics for all Middle Eastern countries.

[28] Oral communication from Saadia Cherniak, Director of the American Friends of the Alliance Israélite Universelle in New York.

11. ORIENTAL JEWS: NORTH AFRICA

[1] H. Z. Hirschberg, *Toldot HaY'hudim B'Afrika HaTz'fonit* (History of the Jews in North Africa) (Jerusalem, 1965), I, 7.

[2] André Chouraqui, *Les Juifs d'Afrique du Nord* (Paris, 1952), pp. 33–34: the relevant passages of Ibn Khaldun are quoted in Hirschberg, *op. cit.*, I, 63.

[3] Hirschberg, *op. cit.* I, 23–25.

[4] R. Patai, *Golden River to Golden Road: Society, Culture and Change in the Middle East*, 3rd ed. (Philadelphia, 1969), p. 236.

[5] Chouraqui, *op. cit.*, pp.47–49; Hirschberg, *op. cit.*, I, 61–67, 110ff., 233–34.

[6] Hirschberg, *op cit.*, I, 26 (Introduction), 71–72, 77, 226–32, 234–55.

[7] *Jewish Encyclopedia*, s.v. Fez; Hirschberg, *op cit.*, I, 260–64, 281–82, 288–90, 291–305; II, 216, 220ff.

[8] Hirschberg, *op. cit.*, I, 260, 328; II, 83.

[9] André Chouraqui, *Between East and West: A History of the Jews in North Africa* (Philadephia, 1968), p. 107.

[10] The above summary of the role of the Kabbala in the Maghrib is based on *ibid.*, pp. 107–11.

[11] *Ibid.*, appendix V; Chouraqui, *Les Juifs d'Afrique du Nord*, p. 328.

[12] Chouraqui, *Les Juifs*, pp. 333, 335; *Between East and West*, pp. 231–32, 238–42.

[13] Chouraqui, *Between East and West*, p. 136.

[14] Maurice Eisenbeth, *Le Judaisme nord-africain: Etudes demographiques sur l'Israelites du department de Constantine* (Paris, 1931), pp. 40–43; Chouraqui, *Between East and West*, p. 103; Hirschberg, *op. cit.*, II, 29–30.

[15] Lloyd Cabot Briggs, *Tribes of the Sahara* (Cambridge, Mass., 1960), pp. 91–92.

[16] Patai, *op. cit.*, pp. 177–250.

[17] Briggs, *op. cit.*, p. 80; Lloyd Cabot Briggs and Norina Lami Guède, *No More For Ever: A Saharan Jewish Town* (Cambridge, Mass., 1964), pp. 10, 20–21, 44–45, 59–60.

[18] Georg Gerster, *Sahara: Desert of Destiny* (New York, 1961), p. 111.

[19] Briggs, *op. cit.*, pp. 92, 104–5.

[20] R. V. C. Bodley, *Wind in the Sahara* (New York, 1944), pp. 194–95.

[21] Hirschberg, *op. cit.*, II, 196, 201.

[22] Bernard Newman, *Mediterranean Background* (London, 1949), p. 137; cf. also Nahum Slouschz, "Troglodyte Jews" (in Hebrew) in the anthology *Yahadut Luv* (Tel Aviv, 1960), pp. 39–40.

[23] Hirschberg, *op. cit.*, II, 313; Chouraqui, *Between East and West*, pp. 137–38. On the origin of these rules of clothing, the so-called *"ghiyar,"* imposed on the Jews from the ninth century on, cf. Hirschberg, *op. cit.*, I, 146–50.

[24] Arye Tartakower, *Shivte Yisrael* (Tel Aviv, 1969), III, 186.

[25] Hirschberg, *op. cit.*, II, 162–64.

[26] Tartakower, *op. cit.*, III, 179–81; cf. also Robert Attal, "Tunisian Jewry in the Last Twenty Years," *The Jewish Journal of Sociology* (June 1960), pp. 4–15.

[27] Chouraqui, *Between East and West*, p. 119.

[28] *Ibid.*, pp. 352–53.

[29] Tartakower, *op. cit.*, III, 168.

[30] *Ibid.*, III, 169.

[31] Hirschberg, *op. cit.*, II, 185ff.

[32] *Ibid.*, II, 200–201.

[33] Cf. Hirschberg, *op. cit.*, II, 204–6; Tartakower, *op. cit.*, III, 218–22.

[34] Patai, *op. cit.,* pp. 364–85.

[35] R. Patai, *Israel Between East and West,* 2nd ed. (Westport, Conn., 1970), pp. 294ff., 306ff., 371ff.

12. THE ORIENTAL JEWS: EGYPT AND SOUTHWEST ASIA

[1] R. Patai, *Golden River to Golden Road: Society, Culture and Change in the Middle East,* 3rd ed. (Philadelphia, 1969), pp. 62–72 and map opposite p. 62.

[2] R. Patai, *Israel Between East and West,* 2nd ed. (Westport, Conn., 1970), pp. 82–83.

[3] For a general characterization of Egypt as a cultural area, and of the other culture areas of the Middle East, cf. Patai, *Golden River to Golden Road,* pp. 65–72.

[4] Israel Joseph Benjamin (Benjamin II), *Eight Years in Asia and Africa* (Hanover, 1859), pp. 230, 233.

[5] Bension Taragan, *Lés Communautés Israélites d'Alexandrie* (Alexandria, 1932), pp. 41–42, 85, 87, 101, 103.

[6] *Ibid.,* pp. 124–50.

[7] Arye Tartakower, *Shivte Yisrael* (Tel Aviv, 1969), III, 211.

[8] Joseph B. Schechtman, *On the Wings of Eagles* (New York-London, 1961), p. 185.

[9] *Ibid.,* pp. 187–89.

[10] *The New York Times,* October 20, 1968, p. 24.

[11] Schechtman, *op. cit.,* pp. 401–5; Tartakower, *op. cit.,* III, 211–12. From 1948 to 1960 a total of 35,887 Jews from Egypt settled in Israel (private communication from Mr. Z. Rabi, director, Demograpic Section, Central Bureau of Statistics, Government of Israel, Jerusalem.

[12] *Encyclopedia of Islam,* new edition, s.v. Dhu Nuwas.

[13] Charles M. Doughty, *Travels in Arabia Deserts,* 3rd ed. (New York, 1937), I, 435; II, 146, and index s.v. *Yahud.*

[14] *Ibid.,* I, 331, 594, 600.

[15] H. St.J. B. Philby, *The Heart of Arabia* (London, 1922), I, 268; II, 225, 229; and *Arabian Highlands* (Ithaca, N.Y., 1952), pp. 277, 280, 387.

[16] Philby, *Arabian Highlands,* pp. 277–78.

[17] *Ibid.,* pp. 279–80; *The Heart of Arabia,* II, 229.

[18] Philby, *The Heart of Arabia,* II, 350–51.

[19] Richard H. Sanger, *The Arabian Peninsula* (Ithaca, N.Y., 1954), p. 217.

[20] D. van der Meulen, *Aden to the Hadhramaut* (London, 1947), p. 33.

[21] *Ibid.,* pp. 37, 40–42, 47.

[22] Schechtman, *op. cit.,* pp. 82–83.

[23] Tuvia Ashkenazi, "The Jews of Hadhramaut" (in Hebrew), *Edoth ("Communities"): A Quarterly for Folklore and Ethnology* (Jerusalem, 1946–47), II, 58–71.

[24] Schechtman, *op. cit.,* p. 86.

[25] Bertram Thomas, *Alarms and Excursions in Arabia* (London, 1931), p. 170.

[26] *The Jewish Encyclopedia,* s.v. Aden.

[27] Erich Brauer, "The Yemenite Jewish Woman," in *The Jewish Review* (London, 1933), IV, 36; and *Ethnologie der Jemenitischen Juden* (Heidelberg, 1934), pp. 203 ff.

[28] Patai, *Israel Between East and West,* pp. 198–99; Joseph Kafih, *Halikhot Teman* (Jerusalem, 1961), pp. 228–44.

[29] Patai, *Israel Between East and West,* pp. 185, 191, 194. According to figures supplied to me by Mr. Z. Rabi, director, Demographic Section, Central Bureau of Statistics, Jerusalem, the number of Yemenite Jews who immigrated to Israel from 1952 to 1960 was 738. This seems to indicate that very few Jews could have been left in Yemen.

[30] Josephus Flavius, *Wars of the Jews,* 2:20:2; 7:8:7.

[31] Benjamin, *op. cit.,* p. 40.

[32] *Ibid.,* p. 46.

[33] Abraham Elmaleh (Almaliah), *Ha-Y'hudim B'Damesek* (Jerusalem, ca. 1910), as quoted by Tartakower, *op. cit.,* III, 235, notes 29 and 30.

[34] Schechtman, *op. cit.,* pp. 151–52.

[35] *Ibid.,* p. 152.

[36] Tartakower, *op. cit.,* III, 226–27.

[37] Schechtman, *op. cit.,* p. 181; cf. also Tartakower, *op. cit.,* III, 230–31. The total number of Syrian and Lebanese Jews who immigrated to Israel from 1948 to 1960 was 5,940 (Mr. Z. Rabi).

[38] Schechtman, *op. cit.,* p. 218.

[39] *Ibid.,* pp. 229–30.

[40] Tartakower, *op. cit.*, III, 260–62.

[41] All historians agree that the Gaonic period came to an end in 1038. As to its beginning, opinions vary: the dates suggested are 540, 589, 657; cf. Abraham Ben-Ya'akov, *Y'hude Bavel* (Jerusalem, 1965), p. 10.

[42] The above summary of the history of the Jews in Iraq is largely based on Ben-Ya'akov, *op. cit.*

[43] Great Britain, Foreign Office, *Treaty Series No. 17* (1925), p. 4.

[44] Ben-Ya'akov, *op. cit.*, p. 238.

[45] A. H. Hourani, *Minorities in the Arab World* (London, 1947), p. 104.

[46] Erich Brauer, *Y'hude Kurdistan* (Jerusalem, 1948), pp. 40–41, 44–45.

[47] *Ibid.*, pp. 47–48.

[48] Benjamin, *op. cit.*, pp. 54–58, 62, 66, 70, 77, 79, 86, 93.

[49] Abraham Ben-Ya'akov, *K'hillot Y'hude Kurdistan* (Jerusalem, 1961); cf. also Yitzhak Ben Zvi, *Ukhlusenu BaAretz* (Jerusalem, 1929), I, 67.

13. THE ORIENTAL JEWS: THE IRANIAN-SPEAKING DIASPORAS

[1] Thomas Wright, ed., *Early Travels in Palestine* (London, 1848), pp. 109–10.

[2] Cf. the admirable detailed article on the subject by Wilhelm Bacher, in *The Jewish Encyclopedia*, s.v. Judaeo-Persian Literature.

[3] R. Patai, *Historical Traditions and Mortuary Customs of the Jews of Meshhed* (in Hebrew, with English summary) (Jerusalem, 1945), pp. 36–38, 56–57; Patai, "A Popular 'Life of Nadir,'" *Edoth, ("Communities"): A Quarterly for Folklore and Ethnology* III, no. 3–4 (1948), 1–16 (in Hebrew), and i-xx (in English).

[4] Israel Joseph Benjamin (Benjamin II), *Eight Years in Asia and Africa* (Hanover, 1859), p. 184.

[5] R. Patai, "The Chuetas of Majorca," *Midstream*, VIII, no. 2, (Spring 1962), 59–68.

[6] Joseph B. Schechtman, *On the Wings of Eagles* (New York-London, 1961), pp. 236–37, 243–47; Arye Tartakower, *Shivte Yisrael* (Tel Aviv, 1966), II, 249–50.

[7] R. Patai, *Golden River to Golden Road: Society, Culture and Change in the Middle East,* 3rd ed. (Philadelphia, 1969), p. 491, Table 8.

[8] Cf. sources in Schechtman, *op. cit.,* pp. 241–42.

[9] Patai, *Golden River,* p. 225; cf. also S. S. HaAfghani, "Tribes in Pushtunistan" (in Hebrew), *B'Terem* (Tel Aviv, 1952), no. 1, pp. 41–43 ("B'ne Israel").

[10] Erich Brauer, "The Jews of Afghanistan," *Jewish Social Studies* (April 1942), pp. 121–38; cf. also Tartakower, *op. cit.*, III, 265.

[11] Sason Siman-Tov, "The Cry of the Afghan Jews" (in Hebrew; a letter to the Editor), *HaAretz,* Tel Aviv, February 7, 1950.

[12] Tartakower, *op. cit.*, III, 263.

[13] *American Jewish Year Book 1967* (New York, 1967), p. 464.

[14] Yitzhak Ben Zvi, *The Exiled and the Redeemed* (Philadelphia, 1957), p. 99.

[15] *The Jewish Encyclopedia,* s.v. Bokhara.

[16] Ben Zvi, *op. cit.*, pp. 86–87.

[17] *Op. cit.*, pp. 88–98.

[18] Leon Shapiro, "Russian Jewry after Stalin," in Gregor Aronson, Jacob Frumkin, Alexis Goldenweiser, and Joseph Lewitan, eds., *Russian Jewry 1917–1967* (New York, 1969), p. 446.

14. THE SEPHARDI JEWS

[1] *The Jewish Encyclopedia,* s.v. Spain.

[2] Gershom Scholem, *Shabtai Zvi V'haT'nu'a HaShabtait BIme Hayav,* 2 vols. (Tel Aviv, 1957).

[3] Gershom Scholem, *Major Trends in Jewish Mysticism* (New York, 1941), p. 156.

[4] Zvi Werblowsky, *Joseph Karo: Lawyer and Mystic* (London, 1962).

[5] R. Patai, *The Hebrew Goddess* (New York, 1967), pp. 261–63.

[6] Scholem, *Major Trends,* pp. 252–53.

[7] Scholem, in *Zion,* (Jan. 1940), 133–60; Solomon Schechter, *Studies in Judaism,* 2nd Series (Philadelphia, 1908), pp. 202–306.

[8] Sh'lomo Rosanes, *Divre Y'me Yisrael B'Togarma* (Husiatyn, 1907), I, 9.

[9] H. J. Zimmels, *Ashkenazim and Sephardim* (London, 1958), p. 51.

[10] *Ibid.*, p. 41.

[11] Nicolo Nicolaì, *Viaggio nella Turchia* (Venice, 1580), pp. 142–43; as quoted in *The Jewish Encyclopedia*, s.v. Turkey.

[12] Zimmels, *op. cit.*, pp. 44–45.

[13] André Chouraqui, *Between East and West: A History of the Jews in North Africa* (Philadelphia, 1968), pp. 91–92.

[14] *The Jewish Encyclopedia*, s.v. Morocco.

[15] Budgett Meakin, in *The Jewish Encyclopedia*, s.v. Morocco.

[16] Abraham I. Laredo, *Bereberes y Hebreos en Marruecos* (Madrid, 1954), p. 212.

[17] André Chouraqui, *La Condition Juridique de l'Israelite Marocain* (Paris, 1950), p. 31, quoting Maurice Eisenbeth, *Les Juifs d'Afrique du Nord, Demographie et onomastique* (Algiers, 1936), pp. 71–72.

[18] Chouraqui, *Between East and West*, pp. 94–95.

[19] *The Jewish Encyclopedia*, s.v. Netherlands.

[20] C. Bezalel Sherman, *The Jew within American Society* (Detroit, 1961), p. 65.

[21] Shim'on Bernfeld, Introduction to David Messer Leon's *K'vod Hakhamim* (Berlin, 1899), pp. ixff.; Mair José Benardete, *Hispanic Culture and Character of the Sephardic Jews* (New York, 1953), pp. 64ff.; as quoted by Zimmels, *op. cit.*, p. 60.

[22] Abraham Saba, *Tz'ror HaMor*, on *Pikkude* and *BeHar* (Venice, 1567), pp. 89c, 104; as quoted by Zimmels, *op. cit.*, pp. 279, 281, and additional sources there, p. 281, n. 1.

[23] Zimmels, *op. cit.*, p. 43, and sources there in notes 4 and 5.

[24] Isaac de Pinto, *Apologie pour la Nation Juive, ou Réflexions Critiques* (Amsterdam, 1762); as translated by Philip Lefanu, *Letters of Certain Jews to Monsieur Voltaire Containing an Apology for their own People and for the Old Testament* (Philadelphia, 1795), p. 22; as quoted by Zimmels, *op. cit.*, pp. 61–62.

[25] Sources in Zimmels, *op. cit.*, p. 62, n. 1.

[26] Hyman B. Grinstein, *The Rise of the Jewish Community of New York* (Philadelphia, 1945), p. 169.

[27] *The Jewish Encyclopedia*, s.v. Sephardim.

[28] H. Z. Hirschberg, *Toldot HaY'hudim B'Afrika HaTz'fonit* (Jerusalem, 1965), I, 123. Hirschberg points out the striking similarity between these customs described and decried by Maimonides and those of the Berber inhabitants of the Island of Jerba in the same period as described by al-Idrisi.

[29] Cf. *ibid.*, I, 150–51.

[30] Chouraqui, *Between East and West*, pp. 92–93.

[31] Zimmels, *op. cit.*, pp. 3, 62, 279ff.

[32] R. Patai, *Golden River to Golden Road: Society, Culture and Change in the Middle East*, 3rd ed. (Philadelphia, 1969), pp. 19, 79, 179.

[33] See footnote 22, above.

[34] Louis Finkelstein, *Jewish Self-Government in the Middle Ages* (New York, 1924); L. Rabinowitz, "France in the Thirteenth Century," in H. Loewe, ed., *Judaism and Christianity*, II, (London, 1937; reprinted New York, 1969), 217.

15. THE ASHKENAZI JEWS

[1] See Chapter V, "Demography," and especially Table I.

[2] Cf. D. M. Dunlop, *The History of the Jewish Khazars* (New York, 1967).

[3] Cf. Israel Halperin, *Pinkas Va'ad Arba' Aratzot* (Jerusalem, 1945).

[4] Cf. Salo W. Baron, s.v. Jewish History and Society, in *Encyclopedia Americana* (1958 edition), XVI, 79.

[5] For the Talmudic sources of this belief and practice, cf. R. Patai, *Man and Temple in Ancient Jewish Myth and Ritual*, 2nd ed. (New York, 1967), pp. 172ff.

[6] Cf. *Studies in Judaism* (London, 1896), p. 5.

[7] Uriah Zevi Engelman, s.v. Jewish History and Society, in *Encyclopedia Americana* (1959 edition), XVI, 90.

[8] Cf. Haiyim Orlan, "The Participants in the First Zionist Congress," in R. Patai, ed., *Herzl Year Book*, vol VI, (New York, 1964–65), pp. 133ff.

[9] Cf. R. Patai, *Israel Between East and West*, 2nd ed., (Westport, Conn., 1970), p. 74.

16. THE ASHKENAZI JEWS: FRANCE

[1] *Les Cahiers de l'Alliance Israélite Universelle* (Paris, December 1969), p. 9.

[2] Personal communication from Mr. Zachariah Shuster, European Director, American Jewish Committee, Paris.

[3] Georg Levitte, "A Changing Community," in *Aspects of French Jewry* (London, 1969), p. 15.

[4] Levitte, *op. cit.*, p. 11.

[5] *Ibid.*, p. 13.

[6] *Ibid.*, p. 16.

[7] R. Patai, *Israel Between East and West*, 2nd ed. (Westport, Conn., 1970), note to p. 103.

[8] Josiane Bijaoui-Rosenfeld, "Some Aspects of the Integration of North African Jews," in *Aspects of French Jewry*, pp. 131, 133, 138.

[9] J. G. Robinson, "F. S. J. U. La Politique du Don en France," *L'Arche*, No. 128 (Paris, October-November 1967), p. 17.

[10] J. G. Robinson, "Israel et les Juifs de France," *L'Arche*, No. 142 (Paris, December 1968-January 1969), p. 41.

[11] See *The New York Times*, January 11, 1969, p. 3.

17. THE ASHKENAZI JEWS: ENGLAND

[1] "Some Evidence on Anglo-Jewish Birth-Rate," *Working Paper no. 11* of the Statistical and Research Unit of the Board of Deputies of British Jews, January 1970.

[2] In 1967, 6 percent of the members of parliament were Jews (as against less than 1 percent of the total population).

[3] Cf. Vivian D. Lipman, "Trends in Anglo-Jewish Occupations," *The Jewish Journal of Sociology*, II, No. 2, (November 1960), 211.

[4] Chaim Bermant, *Troubled Eden: An Anatomy of British Jewry* (London, 1969), p. 145.

[5] *Ibid.*, p. 169.

[6] *The Jewish Encyclopedia*, s.v. England, p. 174.

[7] Hannah Neustatter, "Demographic and Other Statistical Aspects of Anglo-Jewry," in Maurice Freedman, ed., *A Minority in Britain* (London, 1955), pp. 131–32; cf. pp. 82–83.

[8] Raymond V. Baron, "I.U.J.F. Survey, 1954–5," *The Jewish Academy* (London, 1955–56), p. 9; Julius Gould and Shaul Esh, eds., *Jewish Life in Modern Britain* (London, 1964), pp. 90–91.

[9] Sources: general British handbooks and *The Jewish Year Book 1968* (London, 1968).

[10] *Jewish Chronicle* Readership Survey, February 1966, as quoted by Bermant, *op. cit.*, p. 258.

[11] As quoted by V. D. Lipman, *Social History of the Jews of England* (London, 1954), p. 144.

[12] *Ibid.*, p. 145.

[13] *Ibid.*, p. 147.

[14] *Ibid.*, p. 148.

[15] Beatrice Barwell and J. S. Roth, in Gould and Esh, *op. cit.*, pp. 22, 24.

[16] Lipman, "Trends in Anglo-Jewish Occupations," *loc. cit.*, p. 216.

[17] *Ibid.*, p. 213; Neustatter, *op. cit.*, pp. 126–27.

[18] Paul H. Emden, *Jews of Britain* (London, 1943), p. 475.

[19] Ernest Krausz, "Occupations and Social Advancement in Anglo-Jewry," *The Jewish Journal of Sociology*, IV, No. 1 (June 1962), 85–86.

[20] Lipman, "Trends in Anglo-Jewish Occupations," *loc. cit.*, p. 216.

[21] Krausz, *op. cit.*, p. 89.

[22] Azriel Eisenberg, ed., *World Census on Jewish Education 5728–1968* (New York, 1968), pp. 88–94.

[23] *American Jewish Year Book 1954* (New York, 1954), p. 17.

[24] *American Jewish Year Book 1966*, (New York, 1966), p. 312; *Jewish Chronicle*, September 19, 1969.

[25] Cf. *The Jewish Encyclopedia*, s.v. England, pp. 173–74.

[26] Cf. Cecil Roth, "The Anglo-Jewish Community in the Context of World Jewry," in Gould and Esh, *op. cit.*, pp. 103–4.

[27] Arye Tartakower, *Shivte Yisrael* (Tel Aviv, 1965), I, 123. My translation from the Hebrew.

18. THE ASHKENAZI JEWS: SOVIET RUSSIA

[1] Cf. Leon Shapiro, "Russian Jewry After Stalin," in Gregor Aronson, Jacob Frumkin, Alexis Goldenweiser, Joseph Levitan, eds., *Russian Jewry 1917–1967* (New York, 1969).

[2] Quoted from Solomon Schwarz, "Birobidzhan: An Experiment in Jewish Colonization," in Aronson *et al., op. cit.,* p. 344.

[3] However, by 1967 the paper's circulation had increased to 12,000 and copies of it could be procured in West Russian cities; cf. Shapiro, *loc. cit.,* p. 493.

[4] *Ibid.,* pp. 342–95.

[5] Recalculated on the basis of data contained in Gershon Swet, "Jewish Religion in Soviet Russia," in Aronson *et al., op. cit.,* pp. 219–20. According to Shapiro, *loc. cit.,* p. 455, there was in 1965 one synagogue for every 25,000 Jews.

[6] Swet, *loc. cit.,* pp. 218–21; Shapiro, *loc. cit.,* pp. 451, 458.

[7] Shapiro, *loc. cit.,* pp. 458–59.

[8] *Ibid.,* pp. 460–64.

[9] M. Decker, in *Foreign Affairs,* 1963, quoted in Swet, *loc. cit.,* p. 221.

[10] Shapiro, *loc. cit.,* pp. 466–67.

[11] Erich Goldhagen, ed., *Ethnic Minorities in the Soviet Union* (New York, 1968), pp. 338–39.

[12] Shapiro, *loc. cit.,* p. 468.

[13] *Ibid.,* pp. 474–79.

[14] *Ibid.,* pp. 481–84.

[15] Goldhagen, *op. cit.,* pp. 33–34, 318, 335, 339–40.

[16] Shapiro, *loc. cit.,* pp. 469–72.

[17] Aronson *et. al., op. cit.,* p. 329.

[18] Goldhagen, *op. cit.,* p. 335.

[19] Shapiro, *loc. cit.,* p. 484.

[20] Quoted, *ibid.,* p. 487.

[21] *Ibid.,* p. 488.

[22] *Ibid.,* pp. 489–95.

[23] *Ibid.,* pp. 495–99.

[24] *Ibid.,* p. 465.

[25] Swet, *loc. cit.,* p. 282.

[26] R. Patai, "The Chuetas of Majorca," *Midstream,* VIII, No. 2 (Spring 1962), 59–68.

[27] William Korey and Ina Schlesinger, *Jews as Non-Persons: A Study of Soviet History Textbooks in Elementary and Secondary Schools* (Washington, D.C., n.d. [1970]), p. 10.

[28] Joseph B. Schechtman, "New Stirrings in Soviet Jewry," *Midstream,* XV, No. 10 (December 1969), 3–14.

19. THE ASHKENAZI JEWS: THE UNITED STATES

[1] L. Hersch, "Jewish Migrations," in Jewish Encyclopedic Handbooks, *The Jewish People: Past and Present* (New York, 1946), I, 40.

[2] Samuel Joseph, *Jewish Immigration to the United States from 1881 to 1910* (New York, 1914), p. 93.

[3] C. Bezalel Sherman, *The Jew Within American Society* (Detroit, 1961), p. 61.

[4] *Ibid.*

[5] 5,189,401 according to the 1897 census, and 6,946,000 in 1913 according to *American Jewish Year Book 1917–18.*

[6] Arthur Ruppin, "The Jewish Population of the World," *The Jewish People: Past and Present* (New York, 1946) I, 350.

[7] Joseph, *op. cit.,* pp. 146ff., 192.

[8] All the data in this paragraph are based on Azriel Eisenberg, ed., *World Census on Jewish Education 5728–1968* (New York, 1968).

[9] Percentages calculated on the basis of population figures and figures of student enrollment contained in the United Nations *Statistical Yearbook 1968* and *Demographic Yearbook 1967.*

[10] I am indebted for this figure to my friend Alfred Jospe of the Hillel Foundation, Washington, D.C.

[11] According to a study conducted by B'nai B'rith in 1969.

[12] Sherman, *op. cit.,* p. 180.

[13] Ben B. Seligman, "Some Aspects of Jewish Demography," in Marshall Sklare, ed., *The Jews: Social Patterns of an American Group* (Glencoe, Ill., 1958), pp. 76–77.

[14] Seligman, *loc. cit.,* p. 80.

[15] *Ibid.,* p. 104, quoting Henry Cohen, *Jewish Population Trends in New York*

City (mimeographed), Federation of Jewish Philanthropies of New York, 1956.

[16] Nathan Glazer, "The American Jew and the Attainment of Middle Class Rank," in Sklare, ed., op. cit., p. 139.

[17] David Goldberg and Harry Sharp, "Some Characteristics of Detroit Area Jewish and Non-Jewish Adults," in Sklare, ed., op. cit., pp. 112–13.

[18] Glazer, loc. cit., p. 141.

[19] Ibid., pp. 141–42, quoting Ernest Havemann and Patricia Salter West, They Went To College (New York, 1952), pp. 187–89.

[20] Glazer, loc. cit., pp. 142–44.

[21] Abraham G. Duker, "Notes on the Culture of American Jewry," The Jewish Journal of Sociology, II, No. 1 (June 1960), 98–101.

[22] Ibid., pp. 99–100.

[23] Ibid.

[24] Herbert J. Gans, "Park Forest: Birth of a Jewish Community," Commentary (April 1951), pp. 330–39.

[25] Duker, op. cit., p. 100.

[26] Abraham G. Duker, "Structure of the Jewish Community," in Oscar I. Janowsky, ed., The American Jew: A Composite Portrait (New York, 1942), pp. 134–60.

[27] Arye Tartakower, Shivte Yisrael (Tel Aviv, 1965), I, 80.

[28] Cf. for instance Marshall Sklare, Joseph Greenblum and Benjamin B. Ringer, Not Quite at Home (New York, 1969), p. 83.

[29] Gans, op. cit., p. 337.

[30] Ibid., p. 333.

[31] Sherman, op. cit., pp. 207–8.

[32] Sklare, Greenblum, and Ringer, op. cit., pp. 12–13, 16.

[33] Ibid., pp. 38–39, 45ff.

[34] Ibid., pp. 30–32.

[35] Ibid., pp. 2, 6, 35, 68, 70.

20. THE ASHKENAZI JEWS: ARGENTINA

[1] Encyclopaedia Judaica, Eschkol, s.v. Argentinien. Enciclopedia Judaica Castellana, s.v. Argentina.

[2] Encyclopaedia Judaica, Eschkol, s.v. Argentinien; Enciclopedia Judaica Castellana, s.v. Argentina; American Jewish Year Book 1969 (New York, 1969), pp. 296–97.

[3] American Jewish Year Book 1969, loc. cit., Arye Tartakower, Shivte Yisrael (Tel Aviv, 1969), III, 39.

[4] American Jewish Year Book 1966 and 1969; Tartakower, op. cit., III, 39–40.

[5] Tartakower, op. cit., III, 39–40.

[6] Ibid., III, 43–46.

[7] Ibid., III, 46–49.

[8] American Jewish Year Book 1967 and 1969; Tartakower, op. cit., III, 49, 51.

[9] American Jewish Year Book 1966, p. 287; Tartakower, op. cit., III 53.

[10] American Jewish Year Book 1963, p. 282.

[11] American Jewish Year Book 1966, pp. 286; Tartakower, op. cit., III, 55–56.

[12] José Liebermann, Los Judios en la Argentina (Buenos Aires, 1966), pp. 67–146; as cited by Tartakower, op. cit., III, 57, 140, 143.

[13] I am indebted for this information to Miss Flora Toff and Mrs. Naomi F. Meyer of Buenos Aires.

[14] United Nations Statistical Year Book 1968; American Jewish Year Book 1967, p. 276.

[15] American Jewish Year Book 1967, p. 276.

[16] American Jewish Year Book 1954, p. 384; 1962, p. 475.

[17] Azriel Eisenberg, ed., World Census on Jewish Education (New York, 1968), pp. 66–67.

[18] In the general Argentine population the six-to-eleven age group constitutes 12 percent of the total (cf. United Nations Demographic Year Book, population table). The birthrate of the Jews is lower than that of the general population; hence the six-to-eleven Jewish age group can be estimated at 10 percent of the total Jewish population.

[19] American Jewish Year Book 1966 and 1967.

[20] American Jewish Year Book 1967, pp. 278–80.

21 Naomi Meyer in *American Jewish Year Book 1963*, pp. 278–79.

21. FIVE EXCEPTIONAL COMMUNITIES

1 Moses A. Shulvas, "The Jewish Population in Renaissance Italy," *Jewish Social Studies* (January 1951), pp. 3–24.

2 *B'hinat haKabbala*, ed. Isaac S. Reggio (Goricia, 1852), p. 42.

3 Shulvas, *op. cit.*, pp. 11, 13.

4 Ellis Rivkin, *Leon de Modena and the Kol Sakhal* (Cincinnati, 1952), pp. 40ff. Rivkin argues that the *Kol Sakhal*, attributed to Leon, could not have been written by him; cf. pp. 118ff.

5 Stephen P. Dunn, "An Outsider Visits the Roman Ghetto," *Commentary* (February 1958), pp. 130–40; and "The Roman Jewish Community," *Jewish Journal of Sociology* (November 1960), pp. 185–201.

6 Ayre Tartakower, *Shivte Yisrael* (Tel Aviv, 1966), II, 216–17.

7 *Ibid.*, II, 218–19.

8 *Ibid.*

9 Cf. the pamphlet *Communità Israelitiche e Unione delle Communita Israelitiche Italiane: Disposizioni legislative* (Roma, 1960).

10 Emil Schürer, *Geschichte des jüdischen Volkes im Zeitalter Jesu Christi*, 4th ed. (Leipzig, 1909), III, 512–22.

11 *Ibid.* III, 500–503.

12 *The Jewish Encyclopedia*, s.v. Salonica.

13 R. Patai, *Adam V'Adama* (Jerusalem, 1943), II, 216f.; and "Dancing on Yom Kippur among the Jews of the Caucasus and Tripolitania" (in Hebrew), *Edoth*, ("Communities"): *A Quarterly for Folklore and Ethnology*, I, No. 1, (Jerusalem, 1945), 55; *The Jewish Encyclopedia*, s.v. Caucasus, esp. p. 630.

14 J. J. Ichiloff, *Sovietskaya Etnografya* (1950), I; as summarized by Yitzhak Ben Zvi, *The Exiled and the Redeemed* (Philadelphia, 1957), pp. 53–59.

15 Ben Zvi, *op. cit.*, pp. 64–65.

16 Leon Shapiro "Russian Jewry After Stalin," in Aronson *et al.*, eds., *Russian Jewry 1917-1967* (New York, 1969), p. 446.

17 Schifra Strizower, *Exotic Jewish Communities* (London and New York, 1962), p. 53; Tartakower, *op cit.* I, 172.

18 Jacob Sapir Halevi, *Even Sapir* (Mainz, 1874), II, 31; as quoted by Tartakower, *op.cit.*, I, 208. According to Israel Joseph Benjamin (Benjamin II), they observed "the most essential precepts of Jewish religion," and had "manuscripts of the Law," which, however, they were unable to read (*Eight Years in Asia and Africa* [Hanover, 1859], p. 144).

19 Strizower, *op. cit.*, pp. 67–69.

20 *Ibid.*, p. 59.

21 *Ibid.*, pp. 59–60, 67.

22 *Ibid.*, p. 86.

23 Marcus Nathan Adler, ed., *The Itinerary of Benjamin of Tudela* (London, 1907), Hebrew text, p. 59.

24 David G. Mandelbaum, "The Jewish Way of Life in Cochin," *Jewish Social Studies* (1939), p. 425, and literature there, footnote 2.

25 *Ibid.*, pp. 430, 433.

26 *Ibid.*, p. 443.

27 Benjamin II, *op. cit.*, p. 150.

28 Mandelbaum, *op. cit.*, pp. 448, 450, 451.

29 *The New York Times*, January 12, 1964, p. 13.

30 Ida G. Cowen, "400-Year-Old Synagogue in Cochin," *Hadassah Magazine* (December 1968), p. 39.

31 Cf. A. Z. Aescoli, *Sepher HaFalashim* (Jerusalem, 1943), pp. 1–3; Wolf Leslau, *Falasha Anthology* (New Haven, 1951), p. ix.

32 By Professor Simon D. Messing.

33 Leslau, *op. cit.*, p. xii.

34 *Ibid.*, p. xiii.

35 See footnote 23.

36 A. Z. Aescoli, "Y'hude Habbash ba-Sifrut ha'Ivrit," *Zion*, I (1936), 316–36, 410–35.

37 Leslau, *op. cit.*, pp. xxxviiiff.

38 *Ibid.*, pp. xxf., xxxviff.

39 *Ibid.*

The interested reader will find further information on the subjects covered in this book in the literature quoted in the notes. In particular, or, in addition, he may find it rewarding to consult the works enumerated below.

There are several fine one-volume histories of the Jewish people. Some of them are listed here in order of their publication dates:

Solomon Grayzel, *A History of the Jews,* Philadelphia: The Jewish Publication Society of America, 1947 (Eighteenth Impression, 1967).

Rufus Learsi, *Israel: A History of the Jewish People,* New York: World Publishing Company, 1949.

Cecil Roth, *A History of the Jews,* New York: Schocken Books (paperback), 1961.

Abram Leon Sachar, *A History of the Jews,* fifth edition, New York: Alfred A. Knopf, 1965.

Abba Eban, *My People: The Story of the Jews,* New York: Behrman House, Inc., and Random House, 1968.

Jewish history *plus* Jewish culture and religion are most adequately treated in a two-volume collection of studies by forty prominent scholars entitled:

The Jews: Their History, Culture and Religion, edited by Louis Finkelstein, 3rd edition, Philadelphia: The Jewish Publication Society of America, 1960, 2 vols.

The basic concepts of Jewish religion are discussed in Abraham A. Neuman, "Judaism," in Edward J. Jurji (ed.), *The Great Religions of the Modern World,* Princeton University Press, 1947, pp. 224–83; and Arthur Hertzberg, *Judaism,* New York: G. Braziller, 1962.

For a penetrating historical analysis of the meaning of Exile (Galut) see Yitzhak Fritz Baer, *Galut,* New York: Schocken Books (paperback), 1947.

The best, although by now largely outdated, books in English on the sociology and demography of the Jews are:

Arthur Ruppin, *The Jews in the Modern World,* London: Macmillan and Co., 1934.

449

Arthur Ruppin, *The Jewish Fate and Future,* London: Macmillan and Co., Ltd., 1940.

The sociology of the Jews receives much attention also in the four volumes of *The Jewish People: Past and Present,* edited by a distinguished board of editors, and published by Jewish Encyclopedic Handbooks, New York, 1946-55.

For the participation of the Jews in Western culture consult Dagobert D. Runes (ed.), *The Hebrew Impact on Western Civilization,* New York:Philosophical Library, 1951; and Tina Levitan, *The Laureates: Jewish Winners of the Nobel Prize,* New York: Twayne Publishers, 1960.

For the differences and interrelationships between Judaism and Christianity see Abba Hillel Silver, *Where Judaism Differed,* New York: Macmillan, 1957; and Ben Zion Bokser, *Judaism and the Christian Predicament,* New York: Knopf, 1967.

The largely Sephardi development of Jewish mysticism is treated in Gershom G. Scholem, *Major Trends in Jewish Mysticism,* New York: Schocken Books (paperback), 1961.

The vicissitudes of the Jews under Islam in North Africa are discussed in André Chouraqui, *Between East and West,* Philadelphia: Jewish Publication Society of America, 1968.

For the status of the Jews in the United States consult: Marshall Sklare, *The Jews: Social Patterns of An American Group,* Glencoe, Illinois: The Free Press, 1958; and C. Bezalel Sherman, *The Jew Within American Society,* Detroit: Wayne University Press, 1961.

For the problems of the "ingathering of the exiles" in Israel see Raphael Patai, *Israel Between East and West,* 2nd edition, Westport, Conn.: Greenwood Publishing Corporation, 1970.

463

302
PAT
9034

PATAI, RAPHAEL

AUTHOR

TENTS OF JACOB

TITLE

DATE DUE

1166–1171	Benjamin of Tudela's travels in the Diaspora
12th century	First references to the Jews of Ethiopia
1194–1270	Nahmanides
1275–1286	Moses de Leon (d. 1305) writes the *Zohar* in Castile, Spain
1290	Expulsion of the Jews from England
ca. 1270–1340	Jacob ben Asher, third codifier of Jewish law
14th century	The age of terror for West and Central European Jewry. The Jews are several times expelled from France and invited back again. They are expelled from German towns and then invited to return.
	Intensification of Jewish migration to Eastern Europe
15th century	The Spanish Inquisition burns Jews on the stake
1492	Expulsion of the Jews from Spain. The Sephardim begin to settle in Turkey, Greece, North Africa, Italy, Holland. Several Jews are among the crew of Columbus on his first voyage to America
1525	David Reubeni, the pseudo-Messiah from Arabia, appears in Italy
1540	The Jews are expelled from Naples
1569	The Jews are banished from the Papal States
16th century	The Safed Kabbalists
1488–1575	Rabbi Joseph Karo, mystic, fourth and last codifier of Jewish law (the *Shulhan 'Arukh*)
1520–1572	Rabbi Moses Isserles of Cracow, annotator of the *Shulhan 'Arukh*
1548	First Jews settle in America (in Brazil)
16th–18th centuries	The East European Talmudic academies (Yeshivot). The *Kahal* and the Jewish regional councils in Poland
1648–1658	The Chmielnicki massacres in Poland